THE LATER CECILS

A  BOOK

Also by Kenneth Rose

SUPERIOR PERSON:
Lord Curzon and His Circle

THE
LATER CECILS

Kenneth Rose

HARPER & ROW, PUBLISHERS
New York Evanston San Francisco London

FIRST U.S. EDITION

ISBN: 0-06-013599-9

LIBRARY OF CONGRESS CATALOG CARD NUMBER: 75-6355

75 76 77 78 79 10 9 8 7 6 5 4 3 2 1

Contents

Illustrations

All illustrations were supplied by or are reproduced with the kind permission of the Marquess of Salisbury with the exception of the following: Nos 3, 11, 18 the *Radio Times Hulton Picture Library*; no. 12 the Dowager Lady Hardinge of Penshurst; nos 21, 22 the Dowager Lady Manners; nos 23, 24 Mr John Grigg.

For Matthew and Anne Ridley

The Later Cecils

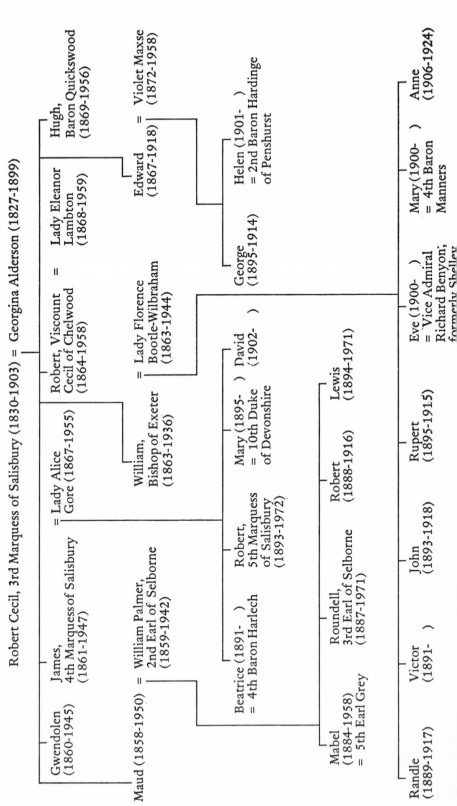

Prologue

By ancient custom, the family of a deceased Knight of the Garter is required to return his insignia to the hand of the Sovereign. On the death of the fourth Marquess of Salisbury in 1947, his elder son, himself a recently installed Knight of the Order, dutifully assembled his father's gold collar and George, his star and his lesser George. But the garter itself, of dark blue velvet embroidered with gold, could not be found. So, at the prompting of Buckingham Palace, the new Lord Salisbury had every corner of Hatfield House searched for the missing object. And no fewer than three garters came to light.

'I like the Garter,' a cynical prime minister once observed, 'There is no damned merit in it.' Yet any family which, through four centuries, has maintained a scarcely unbroken attachment to the senior order of chivalry must have some claim to statecraft. William Cecil, Lord Burghley, was installed a Knight of the Garter in 1572, the year Queen Elizabeth made him her Lord Treasurer. Both his sons, Thomas, Earl of Exeter, and Robert, Earl of Salisbury, received her blue riband. Since then, only three holders of the Salisbury title have been denied it: three wayward, troubled Earls, one of whom died before he was thirty and another before he was forty. In any other family the Exeter line, too, would be thought to have done outstandingly well, although acquiring no more than four garters to the eight of their cadet cousins.

Honours, it is true, sometimes conceal a want of political power or console for its loss. That has not been the experience of the Cecils. No other English family has bred the first Minister of the Crown three times in as many centuries: four if we include Arthur Balfour, whose mother was a Cecil. The first, Burghley, ensured that his son Robert should succeed him as the most indispensable of Queen Elizabeth's subjects.

Nine generations later, after long years as Queen Victoria's Prime Minister, another Robert Cecil passed on the highest office of all to a nephew. Nor have the Cecils found their political progress much impeded by the growth of parliamentary democracy. A Lord Salisbury has sat in almost every Conservative Cabinet from Derby to Macmillan, and the present Marquess is the sixth in succession to have served an apprenticeship in the House of Commons before inheriting the title.

This book largely concerns a single generation of the family: the five sons and two daughters of the third Marquess of Salisbury. (A third daughter, born in 1867, survived for only a few months.) The first of the Prime Minister's children was born in 1858, the last died exactly a century later. Each inherited an historic name, a lively mind, a modest private income and a Christian conscience. They put these attributes to good use. James became, even in middle age, a Conservative elder statesman, William a bishop, Robert the architect and champion of the League of Nations, Edward the guardian of Egypt's finances, Hugh a parliamentarian and Provost of Eton, Maud the dutiful but assertive wife of a proconsul, Gwendolen her father's biographer. Four of the five brothers sat in the House of Lords; so eventually might a fifth had he not died when barely fifty.

In worldly terms they achieved important places and much honour. Only power eluded them. Promise was not matched by performance or character by accomplishment. They could confute but not convince; and although their failures were never commonplace, their successes were often ephemeral. Theirs was the silver age of the House of Cecil.

I

Family History

Four centuries after the Cecils had emerged from the mists and mountains of Wales, Lloyd George claimed them as fellow countrymen. 'He assured me that I was a Welshman,' Lord Robert Cecil wrote in his diary at the Paris Peace Conference of 1919, 'and that the original name of my family was Seisyllt, which he wrote down on a bit of the menu.'

Cecils pronounce it Siss-ill: others please themselves. In an ode on the relief of Mafeking, Alfred Austin ingratiatingly coupled the name of Lord Edward Cecil, son of the Prime Minister who had appointed him Poet Laureate, with that of General Baden-Powell himself:

> Sound for them martial lay!
> Crown them with battle-bay,
> Both those who died, and they
>   'Gainst death could wrestle:
>
> Powell of endless fame
> All, all with equal fame,
> And, of the storied name,
>   Gallant young Cecil!

The compliment failed to please. 'Alfred Austin made *Cecil* rhyme with *wrestle*,' one member of the hero's family wrote to another. 'Pah!'

David Cecil, the founder of the line, was unlikely to have concerned himself with such niceties. A soldier from the Welsh border said to have fought for Henry VII at Bosworth Field, he became a Yeoman of the Guard, settled at Stamford, in Lincolnshire, and sat in Parliament for the borough. His son Richard acquired a comfortable cluster of minor court offices and a share of secularized abbey lands. His grandson William (1520–98), created Lord Burghley, soared to fame as the most powerful and trusted of all Queen Elizabeth's servants. 'Sir Spirit', she

3

called him, declaring that no prince in Europe had such a counsellor; it was the most coveted accolade in her gift. Burghley followed the fashion of his age by claiming a longer and more romantic pedigree than the known facts of his ancestry permitted. But it could add nothing to a reputation that rested entirely on strength of character and a Sovereign's favour. For forty years their partnership epitomized the history of England.

Students of heredity may discern in Burghley many of those traits which, three centuries later, forged a similar bond between another Cecil and another queen. The two statesmen shared an intellectual curiosity and a respect for learning; a distaste for gossip and intrigue; a Christian conscience that did not exclude the pursuit of national interests; a toughness of political fibre tempered by paternalism; a Victorian prudence punctuated by flashes of Renaissance genius; insight buttressed by industry.

By nature a man of peace, Burghley displayed a Churchillian resolve in preparing for war. He encouraged industrial enterprise, not least in the manufacture of cannon, gunpowder and other armaments. He forbade the eating of meat on three days in each week to prosper the fishing fleets on which the country depended for her defence by sea. Far-sighted even in the dismal science of economics, he proclaimed a doctrine that falls on twentieth-century ears with unpalatable monotony: 'Nothing robbeth the realm of England but when more merchandise is brought into the realm than is carried forth. The remedy thereof is by all politics to abridge the use of such foreign commodities as be not necessary for us.' Surviving rebellion at home and invasion from Spain, as watchful in peace as in war, he laid the foundation of the modern English State.

Each of Burghley's two wives bore him a son. The elder, Thomas Cecil (1542–1623), cared nothing for statecraft. After a high-spirited youth he married, settled down to the life of a countryman and was created Earl of Exeter. His inheritance included Burghley, the palace of honey-coloured stone built by his father to support the dignity of a new-found peerage; set in a wooded park near Stamford, it has for centuries remained the seat of the senior branch of the family.

Lord Burghley's younger son Robert (1563–1612) stayed close to his father. Under his tutelage he found himself knighted, a member of the Privy Council and acting Secretary of State before he was thirty; within a very few years of old Burghley's death in 1598 he too was the most powerful subject in England. He served the Queen with diligence, enduring in silence that wearisome badinage which sovereigns sometimes mistake for humour. 'My little man', 'my pigmy', 'my elf' were the royal witticisms evoked by his lack of inches and rounded back.

'Though I may not find fault with the name she gave me,' he wrote later, 'yet seem I only not to mislike it because she gives it.'

But not even Elizabeth would live for ever, and Robert Cecil, by now installed as Secretary of State, determined that the interests of the nation – and his own – must be preserved after her death. 'Be sure to keep some great man thy friend,' his father had warned him. 'Otherwise, in this ambitious age, thou shalt remain like a hop without a pole, live in obscurity, and be made a football for every insulting companion to spurn at.' High policy demanded that the Queen's successor to the throne of England should be King James vi of Scotland, son of the unfortunate Mary Queen of Scots; personal advantage dictated that he should be in Cecil's debt.

Unknown to the ageing Elizabeth, the Secretary of State embarked on a correspondence that struck a delicate balance between his present and his future loyalties. He assured King James: 'When that day (so grievous to us) shall happen, which is the tribute of all mortal creatures, your ship shall be steered into the right harbour, without cross of wave or tide that shall be able to turn over a cock-boat.' So it turned out. On the death of the Queen in 1603, King James ascended the throne of England with scarcely a hostile murmur.

The union of the two kingdoms, however, proved an oppressive legacy. Although Cecil ensured that the crown of England should pass without dispute from Elizabeth to James, he saddled his country with the Stuart dynasty, the most stiff-necked and spendthrift in her history. The true glory of Cecil's supremacy was to pursue the middle way in religion, to embrace and protect that moderate Anglicanism which ultimately survived Civil War, Commonwealth and Restoration.

' 'Tis a great task to prove one's honesty and yet not spoil one's fortune,' Cecil wrote to a friend in the first weeks of the new reign. Within two years he had been created Baron Cecil of Essendon, Viscount Cranborne and Earl of Salisbury. As Lord Treasurer and Secretary of State he directed both home and foreign policy; as Master of the Court of Wards he laid hands on wealth enough to live more like a sovereign than a subject. There was no end to his greed, rapacious even by the standards of the day. From the King he received many gifts of crown land and the right to farm out customs duty on satins and silks. His private enterprises included the acceptance of gratuities from King Philip of Spain and a host of lesser suitors. During the last two years of his life, Salisbury's annual income from all sources rose to at least £25,000, or little less than £500,000 when translated into the purchasing power of the mid-twentieth century.

His expenditure was correspondingly enormous. In addition to the usual household accounts of a man of rank, vast sums drained away on entertainment, on clothes, on works of art, on music, on doctors (always a cherished Cecilian luxury). Above all, he spent several fortunes on dreams of brick and stone. At one moment he was simultaneously building Salisbury House, in the Strand; a fashionable London market called the New Exchange; and two country houses, Cranborne in Dorset and Hatfield in Hertfordshire. The last of these was his crowning achievement.

From his father, Robert had inherited another house in Hertfordshire called Theobalds. 'Begun by me with a mean measure,' Burghley wrote of the original manor, 'but increased by occasion of Her Majesty's often coming.' By the time he had extended it to his satisfaction, Theobalds was the largest building in England except for the Palace of Westminster and Hampton Court. Visitors marvelled at the towered mansion enclosing two great courts; at the fantasy of its painted walls; at an ingenious moated garden with fountains and mazes and marble likenesses of the twelve Caesars. King James stopped there on his progress south to take possession of his new kingdom, and a contemporary chronicler thought his host a fortunate man. 'To speak of Sir Robert's cost to entertain His Majesty were but to imitate geographers that set a little round o for a mighty province.' The King took a fancy to the house, even more to its deer parks, came again, dropped a heavy hint or two. In 1607 the recently created Earl of Salisbury formally surrendered Theobalds to his Sovereign in exchange for a scattered parcel of royal estates that included Hatfield, less than twenty miles to the north of London.*

Bishops Hatfield, as it used to be called, had been laid out by Cardinal Morton a century before and subsequently annexed to the crown by Henry VIII. Two future Queens of England, Mary and Elizabeth, were detained there during the dynastic troubles of their youth; and it was while sitting under an oak in the park that Elizabeth had learned of her accession to the throne. Salisbury cared little for such links with the past. To console himself for the loss of Theobalds he would build as no Cecil had built before; and with characteristic self-confidence he determined to be his own architect. The timbered hall where the Queen had conferred with his own father at her first Council would do well enough for stables; the rest of the episcopal palace encroached on the site of the new house, and down it came.

Completed in 1612 at a cost of nearly £40,000, the equivalent perhaps of £800,000 today, Hatfield has since resisted the whims of both fashion and utility. Its shape remains the traditional E with which loyal Elizabethans saluted their Sovereign. Seen from the north, east or west, the

---

* Neglected by King Charles I, Theobalds fell into disrepair during the Civil War and was demolished. It had stood for not quite a century.

austerity of red brick wall and turret is relieved only by a generous proportion of mullioned window. But from the south, the two projecting
wings enclose a stone façade and open colonnade that give promise of
a gentler way of life; perhaps the touch of Inigo Jones himself may be
detected here. Algernon Cecil, a twentieth-century descendant of the
inspired amateur who built Hatfield, has fancifully described the house
as an epitome of the Queen's reign: the stern perpendicular lines of the
north front contrasting with the delicate horizontal tracery of the south,
just as Elizabeth herself passed from the rigours of plot and invasion
to the sunlit serenity of her last years.

Salisbury's craftsmen similarly enriched the inherited medieval con-
cepts of great hall and long gallery with arabesques of carved wood
and plaster, with the cunning more of the Italian Renaissance than of
Tudor England. Circular staircases of stone gave way to broad flights
of oak, their balusters as ingeniously contrived as any rood-screen.
And the royal patrons of so much beauty were commemorated again
and again by brush and chisel: Queen Elizabeth in portraits attributed
to Nicholas Hilliard and Isaac Oliver (not to mention an elaborate
genealogical tree tracing her descent from Adam), King James by a
life-size statue that dominates and gives his name to the principal
drawing-room.

Between 1607 and 1612 Salisbury stole what hours he could from
Councils and State papers to supervise the building of Hatfield House.
He conferred with the clerks of the works, he watched the red walls
creep higher and higher, he paced the empty rooms, he ordered mulberry
trees and sycamores and vines. Then, by a stroke of fate that most novel-
ists would reject as excessively melodramatic, he died before he could
spend a single night under its roof. He was in his forty-ninth year, not
much loved or even regretted.

Since the death of the first Earl of Salisbury in 1612, Hatfield has passed
in unbroken succession from father to son or to grandson. His political
talent, however, descended less rhythmically. 'For more than a century
and a half', Lady Gwendolen Cecil wrote of her forbears, 'the general
mediocrity of intelligence which the family displayed was only varied by
instances of quite exceptional stupidity.' Mr Harold Macmillan, a connection of the Cecils by marriage, softened his reproach with a literary
allusion. 'They did nothing,' he once told the present writer. 'They were
like characters in Proust.'

The verdict of history on William, the second Earl (1591–1668), is
unanimously severe. Clarendon said of him: 'He was a man of no words,
except in hunting and hawking, in which he only knew how to behave
himself.' Pepys called him 'My simple Lord Salisbury'. And Gardiner,

7

picking up the scent two centuries later, declared him to be 'notoriously incompetent to fulfil the duties of any office calling for the exercise of the most ordinary abilities'.

Yet there is evidence enough to refute such disparagement. For all his supposed foolishness, he was chosen by Charles I to treat with the Scots and by Parliament to treat with the King; by Cromwell to act as a Counsellor of State and to sit in more than one Commonwealth Parliament. This veteran Roundhead – though never a regicide – also displayed a touch of Cecilian astuteness in making his peace with Charles II at the Restoration and in having his grandson appointed a Page of Honour at the King's Coronation.

In his domestic life, too, the second Earl of Salisbury maintained much of the family fortune intact, despite the dislocation of the Civil War. He brought back works of art from his travels, commissioned a magni-ficent tomb for his father and was the friend of Sir Henry Wotton. Pepys visited Hatfield in the summer of 1661, full of praise for 'the house, the chappel with brave pictures, and, above all, the gardens, such as I never saw in all my life; nor so good flowers, nor so great gooseburys, as big as nutmegs'. That does not sound like the establishment of a simpleton.

The second Earl's son Charles (1619–60) did not live to inherit the title, which passed to a grandson, James (1646–83). The third Earl served in the flagship *Royal Charles* against the Dutch and sat briefly in the Commons. But he incurred mild disgrace by his association with the Rye House plot to prevent James, Duke of York, from succeeding to the throne. His antipathy to the future James II persisted. When in 1679 the Duke of York proposed to spend a night at Hatfield on his way north from London, the royal party found the house insultingly unlit, unheated, unprovisioned and uninhabited.

Nor was the third Earl able to halt a decline in the family fortunes caused as much by virility as by extravagance. His grandfather had eight sons and five daughters, his father seven sons and four daughters, he himself five sons and five daughters. The Grand Tour for the boys, dowries for the girls and jointures for the widows all took their toll. With an excess of affection, the third Earl also made generous bequests to his children which the estate could hardly bear. He nevertheless found the money to have himself painted by Kneller, just as his grandfather had been painted by Lely. It was a family virtue. All the Earls of Salisbury and most of their wives sat for their portraits, and never have twenty years gone by without the hanging of a new canvas.

James, the fourth Earl (1666–94), although barely twenty-eight when he died, achieved much fame, all of it undesirable. He depressed the Cecil finances further by gambling away £40,000 and spending almost

£10,000 a year on a disposable income of only £4,000. To pay his debts he was obliged to sell Salisbury House in London. Politically, too, he made a muddle of his life. In contrast to his father, he welcomed the accession of James II; but with inspired miscalculation he declared himself a Papist only two or three months before the Roman Catholic monarch was obliged to flee the kingdom. A gossip of the day described Salisbury's discomfiture: 'When he heard that the Prince [of Orange] was comeing and landed, and how he was received, he lamented sadly, and curst and damn'd all about him, crying, "O God! O God! O God! I turn'd too soon. I turn'd too soon." ' He was arrested for high treason, imprisoned in the Tower but later released. Macaulay, at his most bombastic, surmised moral as well as intellectual and physical weakness: 'His figure was so bloated by sensual indulgence as to be almost incapable of moving, and this sluggish body was the abode of an equally sluggish mind.' Wissing's portrait of Salisbury, painted in 1687, does not, however, depict a man of abnormal obesity.

Even as an Oxford undergraduate, James, the fifth Earl (1691–1728), was observed to be absorbed in matters of dress and ceremonial. He bore St Edward's Staff at the Coronation of George I, but made no other dent on history. Nor did his son, yet another James (1713–80), add any particular lustre to the Earldom he held for more than half a century. His temper soured by beatings he had received from his mother and at Westminster School, he turned his back on not only the duties but also the way of life expected of him. He startled the fashionable world first by marrying his steward's niece, then by abandoning both her and Hatfield in favour of a mistress with whom he lived at Quickswood, a smaller house in Hertfordshire that has since been demolished. His only other known recreation was driving the London coach, a pastime that ensured satirical commemoration by both Hogarth and Pope. Yet even the sixth Earl sometimes recalled his debt to family pride. Although he sold all that he could lay hands on, he did not fail to have his portrait painted, wearing Coronation robes.

Horace Walpole, outraged by the disrepair into which Hatfield had fallen during the prolonged absence of the sixth Earl, welcomed the succession of his son with enthusiasm: 'As the ashes of the Cecils are re-kindling, perhaps a Phoenix may arise.' Two more generations were to pass before a Cecil occupied the highest political office of all for the third time in English history. Meanwhile James, seventh Earl of Salisbury (1748–1823), was a distinct improvement on his immediate forbears. He was Lord-Lieutenant of Hertfordshire, a colonel of Militia, Treasurer and Lord Chamberlain of the Household, a Privy Counsellor, a Fellow of the Royal Society. He put his parliamentary influence at the disposal of Pitt, on whose recommendation he was created a Marquess in 1789 and a Knight of the Garter four years later. A man of elegant taste, he brought in James Wyatt to restore part of the fabric of Hatfield, collected Sèvres, had himself painted by Romney and his wife by Reynolds.

It is to her energy and ambition that the first Marquess owed much of his worldly success. She was Lady Emily Hill (1750–1835), the strikingly beautiful daughter of an Anglo-Irish peer, Lord Downshire. Her relish for the elaborate pleasures of the age amused and sometimes shocked her contemporaries. Creevey, who knew her affectionately as 'Old Sally', hailed her in 1822 as 'the head and ornament and patroness of the *beau monde* of London for the last forty years'. But there was a no less practical side to her nature. She ran an experimental farm and organized charitable relief. 'I have never heard anything like the manner of living at Hatfield,' a neighbour wrote, 'Five hundred poor fed every Tuesday and Friday.' Widowed at seventy-three, she was far from spent. She continued to hunt her own pack of hounds for another decade, tied into the saddle. When too blind to see the fences, she had herself led by a groom who at the critical moment would shout: 'Damn you, my lady, jump!' On the eve of her eightieth year she went on the river with Eton boys one Fourth of June; rarely missed a ball; played a sharp game of whist for crown points until the long gallery at Hatfield lay ankle deep in cards; and on hearing laughter and horseplay from the men after dinner, exclaimed: 'What a row they are making, I wish I was there.' Not even an occasional visit to church daunted her high spirits. In 1834, the year before her death, she heard a sermon on the Fall. The preacher described how Adam, excusing himself, had cried out: 'Lord, the woman tempted me.' At which Lady Salisbury, who appeared not to have heard of the incident before, jumped up in her seat, saying: 'Shabby fellow indeed!'

She seemed indestructible. After once tumbling downstairs in old age, she merely applied to her swollen leg a lotion used for horses, and went about her business as if nothing had happened. But on a November evening in 1835, as she sat alone at Hatfield writing invitations to a *conversazione*, she must have knocked over a candle or allowed its flame to ignite part of her elaborate toilette. Her apartments were in the west wing, remote from those of her son and his family, and the fire was not noticed until it was too late to be checked. In *Oliver Twist* Dickens describes it through the eyes of Bill Sikes:

> There were half-dressed figures tearing to and fro, some endeavouring to drag the frightened horses from the stables, others driving the cattle from the yard and out-houses, and others coming laden from

the burning pile, amidst a shower of falling sparks and the tumbling down of red-hot beams. The apertures, where doors and windows stood an hour ago, disclosed a mass of raging fire; walls rocked and crumbled into the burning well; the molten lead and iron poured down, white hot, upon the ground.

Nothing was found of the Dowager Lady Salisbury except the remains of her jewels. Although they were in pawn to pay for her extravagances, she had borrowed them back for a few days to wear at a party.

'Ld. Salisbury is dead, which makes a vacant blue ribbon,' was Mrs Arbuthnot's heartless epitaph on the first Marquess. His only son James (1791–1868), who succeeded to the title in 1823, evoked a similar indifference from his political contemporaries. His achievements, like those of his father, look impressive at first sight: the Privy Council, the Garter, office in two Tory governments. But the greater prizes eluded him. Perhaps he would have been happier in the Army, a vocation denied him as an only son, and one for which command of the Hertfordshire Militia could be no more than a pale substitute. He was disappointed, even resentful, when the Duke of Wellington, acting briefly as Prime Minister until the return of Peel from Italy, offered him only the decorative appointment of Master of the Horse in the administration of 1834. At the age of fifty he told the Duke, whose younger brother Lord Cowley had married one of Salisbury's sisters: 'The object I have sighed after all my life, from the time when I asked you to take me as attaché to Vienna, to the present, has been employment.' Not until 1852 did he become a Cabinet Minister in Derby's short-lived government, and then only in the sinecure office of Lord Privy Seal. After an interval of six years he also served for some months in the hardly more exacting place of Lord President of the Council.

Some believed that he lacked not so much opportunity as talent. On a visit to Lord Exeter at Burghley, Charles Greville wrote contemptuously: 'Very miserable representatives of Old Burghleigh, the two insignificant looking Marquesses, who are his lineal descendants, and who display no more of his brains than they do of his beard.'

It was in his domestic life that Salisbury made himself memorable. He married a woman endowed not only with a lively and penetrating mind but also with considerable property. He cared for Hatfield as fondly as the founder of his line. And he sired a future Prime Minister.

The match was thought a shade daring for 1821. Frances Gascoyne, as one of her grandchildren wrote, 'came of a stock which was largely, though not exclusively, derived from the citizen class'. Born in 1802, she was the only child of Bamber Gascoyne, son of a Member of Parliament for Liverpool and grandson of a Lord Mayor of London. 'They say he has married her for her money,' the irrepressible Harriet Arbuthnot noted in her journal. Miss Gascoyne's wealth, consisting of valuable estates in Lancashire and Essex, was certainly not unwelcome to her husband. In gratitude he added her family name to his own; it remains Gascoyne-Cecil to this day, although the prefix is rarely used except in formal documents.

Princess Lieven, staying at Hatfield in the early years of the marriage, dipped her pen in vinegar when writing to her reputed lover, Prince Metternich:

> We are a large party – there are diplomats, Ministers, pretty women, jealous husbands, perfumed dandies, long dark corridors, chapels, towers, bats in the bed curtains – everything you need for a romance, or, at any rate, for an affair. The owner of the place has the largest house, the largest chin, and the smallest stature you could possibly imagine. His wife has plenty of money, big languishing eyes, and big teeth. She is lucky enough to fancy she is beautiful, and unlucky enough not to be. She is not without intelligence, but entirely without charm.

Such feline jottings should not be taken seriously. It is true that Lawrence's portrait of Frances Salisbury shows a woman richer in character than in beauty; and that her virtues shone more in the home than in society. But she was accomplished enough to win the fervent friendship of Wellington without incurring a whisper of reproach, least of all from her husband. She became one of the only two women to whom the Duke gave his entire confidence, the other being Mrs Arbuthnot. The most coveted guest in England stayed at Hatfield again and again, asking only that he should not be required to meet the Dukes of Cumberland and Gloucester, one shady, the other fatiguing. Even this condition he waived when, with the Duchess of Gloucester, he agreed to be a godparent to his hosts' infant son Robert, the future Prime Minister. The death of Lady Salisbury from dropsy in 1839 – she was not yet forty – left him stunned with misery and loneliness.

The second Marquess, crushed by the loss of his wife, struggled to bring up a brood of children before remarrying a few years later. In the meantime he turned increasingly to the solace of the land and its responsibilities. The construction of roads, schools and cottages, the relief of the poor, the protection of agriculture; these proved among the most rewarding occupations of his life. A competent, stubborn man, he declined to leave the rebuilding of the gutted west wing of Hatfield in the hands of professional architects. Like the first Earl, he had an eye for pleasing proportion, and the resulting harmony between the new wing and the old shows him to have been as inspired an amateur. Another slice of the Gascoyne fortune was laid out on restoring the original fabric from foundations to roof, a task begun only just in time to save it from probable collapse. The interior of the house, too, he entirely renovated with a scholarly taste acquired during visits to the great museums of Europe. Richer men have lived longer and done less.

The Prime Minister:
Robert, third Marquess of Salisbury
1830-1903

Robert, second son of the second Marquess of Salisbury. Known as Lord Robert Cecil until the death of his elder brother in 1865, and as Viscount Cranborne from 1865 to 1868, when he succeeded his father as third Marquess of Salisbury.

Born 3 February 1830. Educated at Eton and Christ Church, Oxford. Fellow of All Souls College 1853. Chancellor of Oxford University 1869–1903. Fellow of the Royal Society 1869.

Conservative MP for Stamford 1853–68. Secretary of State for India 1866–7 and 1874–8. Special Ambassador to Conference of Constantinople 1876–7. Secretary of State for Foreign Affairs 1878–80. Ambassador to the Congress of Berlin 1878. Secretary of State for Foreign Affairs from June 1885 to February 1886, January 1887 to August 1892, and June 1895 to November 1900. Prime Minister from June 1885 to January 1886, July 1886 to August 1892 and June 1895 to July 1902.

Privy Counsellor 1866. Knight of the Garter 1878. Lord Warden of the Cinque Ports 1896–1903.

Married 11 July 1857, Georgina, daughter of Sir Edward Alderson, Baron of the Exchequer. She died 20 November 1899.

Lord and Lady Salisbury had five sons and three daughters, one of whom died in infancy: James (1861–1947) who bore the courtesy title of Viscount Cranborne until succeeding his father as fourth Marquess of Salisbury in 1903 and was known as Jim or Jem; William (1863–1936), known as Fish; Robert (1864–1958), created Viscount Cecil of Chelwood 1923 and known as Bob; Edward (1867–1918), known as Nigs; Hugh (1869–1956), created Baron Quickswood 1941 and known as Linky or Linkey; Maud (1858–1950), married to second Earl of

Selborne; Gwendolen (1860–1945), known as Tim or TT or Titi; and Fanny (1866–7).
    Lord Salisbury died 22 August 1903.

Robert, third Marquess of Salisbury, spent a dejected and lonely youth. His mother died before he was ten and his father lacked the imagination to modify a traditional education too demanding for a boy of nervous temperament. He was denied the cheerful companionship of nursery and schoolroom that might have softened the austerity of a nineteenth-century upbringing. For although he had three brothers and two sisters, one brother died in infancy and all were separated from him by a gap of at least four years. The eldest, James, who bore the courtesy title of Viscount Cranborne, was in any case the victim of an affliction that impaired both hearing and sight and required him to lead a restricted life. At one time considered unlikely to survive into manhood, Cranborne lived to be forty-three, with every expectation of succeeding to the family honours and estates; that at least was a responsibility that did not haunt his diffident younger brother.

'An existence among Devils,' was how Lord Robert Cecil (the style he bore as the younger son of a marquess) described his first school, a local establishment which he began to attend when only six. Later he passed some happier months in Devon with the Rev. Henry Lyte, author of the hymns 'Abide with Me' and 'Praise, my Soul, the King of Heaven'. Lyte, descended from his namesake, the sixteenth-century botanist, encouraged his pupil to take exercise by studying plants and rocks, thus arousing in him a lifelong interest in scientific research.

Eton, where he spent his boyhood between the ages of ten and fifteen, cast him down once more into misery. He was spared the ultimate horrors of Long Chamber, in which the grandiosely named King's Scholars lived like beasts and survival was accepted by an insurance company as sufficient evidence of an exceptionally robust physique. But even in the comparative haven of an oppidan boys' house presided over by the Rev. W. G. Cookesley,* he suffered prolonged and vicious bullying. Perhaps he exaggarated his tribulations when pleading with his father to remove him. Yet in later life, often summoned to Windsor by Queen Victoria as a Minister of the Crown, he only once crossed the river to revisit the scene of his schooldays; the depression it induced determined him never to repeat the experience. He was unhappy at

---

* Mr Cookesley had a taste for literary society. It was as a guest under his roof that Disraeli wrote the Eton pages of *Coningsby*, that novel of political idealism which Macaulay called 'Young England, by old Jewry'. He later included Algernon Swinburne among his pupils. As the future poet arrived late for school with unbrushed red hair, trailing shoelaces and an avalanche of books slipping from his arm, his tutor would exclaim : 'Here comes the rising sun.'

Eton, but not morose. Nearly sixty years after those dismal days, his contemporary Lord Dufferin was moved to send a farewell letter of affection from his deathbed. The former Viceroy of India wrote to the Prime Minister: 'I don't think you ever knew how much I liked you from the time you were a thin, frail, little lower boy at Cookesley's, even then writing, as my tutor used to say, such clever essays.'

Withdrawn from Eton by his own fervent wish when only fifteen, Robert Cecil studied for the next two years with a tutor at Hatfield. It was an interlude that steadied his nerves, repaired his confidence and enabled him to go up to Oxford at the beginning of 1848. Christ Church was not the ideal college for so retiring a temperament. He had little in common with his high-spirited contemporaries, men more at ease in the preposterous check tweeds of a John Leech drawing than in the gold-tasselled academic dress which the University thought proper for those of noble birth. Shunning their cards and wine, their terriers and tobacco, their stables and steeplechases, Robert found a few congenial acquaintances among the less fashionable members of the college. In serious-minded discussion he laid the foundations of the two creeds that were to sustain him – and later his children – through life: a pious attachment to the Tractarian wing of the Church of England and a high but unromantic Toryism.

Yet he was no namby-pamby. Nearly twenty years before, a band of undergraduate rowdies, provoked by the priggishness of the young William Ewart Gladstone, had one night burst into his rooms at Christ Church and genially knocked him about. The next day the future Prime Minister recorded his thankfulness to God for having mortified his pride and enabled him to exercise the duty of forgiveness. That was not the way of Robert Cecil. When a later generation of revellers planned a similar outrage, Cecil and his friends got wind of it, prepared an ambush and put the bullies to flight. It was an achievement as therapeutically valuable as his election to be an officer of that political nursery, the Oxford Union. Fitful ill-health, however, prevented his completing the course for a degree. On the insistent advice of his young doctor, Henry Acland, later Regius Professor of Medicine, he embarked on a sea voyage to South Africa, Australia and New Zealand that was to be prolonged for nearly two years. But he did not leave Oxford unrewarded. The University which has never allowed social rank to impede academic advancement quaintly sped Lord Robert Cecil on his way with an honorary Fourth Class in Mathematics.

He returned from the Antipodes in the spring of 1853, much restored in health but with bleak prospects of either employment or independence. 'For gentlemen without money,' he wrote, 'there are very few openings of usefulness.' As long as his brother Cranborne lived, even in seclusion, he could expect to share none of the indulgence tradition-ally shown to an eldest son and heir. In any case, his father had re-married in 1847 and was busy raising another brood of children that had to be fed, clothed, educated and dowered.* In turn Robert con-sidered and rejected the careers open to a man of his upbringing and talents with no private income. Although attracted by Parliament, he could not hope for a seat in the Commons without the support of a rich patron. An unreliable physique and doubts about his ability to influence others led him to reject both Holy Orders and the Bar. Soldiering, he confessed, was detestable beyond measure, nor did Victorian England yet accept commerce as a respectable enough calling for the scion of a noble house†

Modest means remained his lot for the next ten years and more. But within a few months of his disembarking at Plymouth in May 1853 there was a sudden shift in his fortunes. In August his distant cousin, the Marquess of Exeter, unexpectedly invited him to seek election to the House of Commons as Conservative Member for Stamford. So strong was Exeter's influence in that small borough, much of which he owned, that for the next fifteen years his kinsman was returned un-opposed to each successive Parliament. Since Members of the nine-teenth-century House of Commons received no salary, Lord Salisbury glumly agreed to pay Robert's election expenses and to settle on him the interest of the £10,000 which he would one day inherit from his mother's estate. To this he added a personal allowance of £100 a year. It was thus on an annual income of only £400 that Lord Robert Cecil took his seat at Westminster for the first time.

Fate smiled on him yet again that year. In November he was elected to a Fellowship at All Souls' College, Oxford. Founded in 1438 by Arch-bishop Chichele to commemorate King Henry v, it enjoined its Fellows to serve God in Church and State. Four centuries later the house of piety had come to resemble a London club, or at best a learned society, its members drawn largely from the descendants of Chichele's brothers. Of the 113 elected between 1815 and 1857, no fewer than seventy-eight possessed the qualification of Founder's Kin; thirty of them were the sons of peers.‡ Although there was an annual competitive examination – in 1853 Robert Cecil sat with sixteen other candidates – it demanded

* His second wife was Lady Mary Sackville-West (1824–1900), second daughter of the fifth Earl De La Warr. She bore Lord Salisbury three sons and two daughters, and after his death was married to the fifteenth Earl of Derby (1826–93), successively Secre-tary of State for India, for Foreign Affairs and for the Colonies.

† By 1896, however, no fewer than 167 peers were directors of companies.

‡ Robert Cecil had inherited his Chichele blood through Catherine Howard, youngest daughter of the first Earl of Suffolk and wife of the second Earl of Salisbury.

no more than a familiarity with classical languages and the ability to write an English essay. A few Fellows of All Souls were scholars; most were in Holy Orders or in Parliament, at the Bar or in the public service, spending perhaps a day or two each week in Oxford. They were men of the world, well-informed and convivial, sharing the same aristocratic background and tastes. Comfortable rooms, one of the finest libraries in Europe and a variable stipend of about £100 a year compensated them for an enforced celibacy. They were also spared that most distracting of Oxford duties, an obligation to teach: with the exception of a handful of Bible Clerks, the college has never opened its doors to undergraduates.

In both his parliamentary and academic elections of 1853, Robert Cecil was more than usually fortunate. Almost simultaneously with his departure from the House of Commons on inheriting his father's peerage fourteen years later the borough of Stamford was disfranchized by the Reform Act of 1867; and within five years of his admission to All Souls, the college statutes were revised to eliminate the privileged preferment of Founder's Kin.

But the third unforeseen happiness of the year that followed his return from the Antipodes was the most memorable of all. He met his future wife.

Georgina Alderson was the eldest daughter of Sir Edward Alderson, one of the Barons of the Court of Exchequer. At Cambridge he had been Senior Wrangler and Chancellor's Medallist, thus securing the highest honours in both mathematics and classics open to any undergraduate. He had made a particular mark at the Bar by his cross-examination of George Stephenson before the Manchester and Liverpool Railway Committee and in 1830 was raised to the Bench in the Court of Common Pleas. By the standards of his age he was a kindly and sensitive judge. 'I wish I could believe that the punishment of death could safely be dispensed with,' he wrote in 1834. But he did press for capital punishment to be waived in certain forms of murder which have since become manslaughter, such as duelling, infanticide, killing under severe provocation and by gross negligence. In a case of machinery-smashing, brought under the Riot Act, he once acquitted the prisoner on the ground that the words 'God Save the King' had been omitted from the proclamation by the magistrate. Alderson explained: 'The Act is so very severe a law that one requires a very minute observance of all its provisions.' Yet he was no enemy of an ordered world. The most famous of his trials concerned the fraudulent substitution of a four-year-old horse for the three-year-old Running Rein in the Derby of 1844. It drew from him an expression of disgust at 'noblemen and gentlemen associating and betting with men of low rank and infinitely below them in society'.

In his own home he instructed his children with a sympathetic touch. This letter to a schoolboy son has well stood the test of time:

I have sent you to Eton that you may be taught your duties as an English young gentleman. The first duty of such a person is to be a good and religious Christian, the next is to be a good scholar, and the third is to be accomplished in all manly exercises and games, such as rowing, swimming, jumping, cricket, and the like. Most boys I fear begin at the wrong end, and take the last first; and what is still worse, never arrive at either of the other two at all. I hope, however, better things of you: and to hear first that you are a good, truthful, honest boy, and then that you are one of the hardest workers in your class, and after that, I confess I shall be by no means sorry to hear that you can show the idle boys than an industrious one can be a good cricketer, and jump as wide a ditch, or clear as high a hedge as any of them.

Lady Alderson cherished an identical scale of values. The daughter of a Devon parson, she was connected by family ties to such intellectual dynasties as the Wedgwoods and the Darwins. Thus Georgina Alderson was from her earliest years brought up with both a reverence for Christian belief and a respect for things of the mind. Yet neither excluded a vigorous appetite for the pleasures of youth or a sympathy for those unable to share her enthusiasms. She was as happy at a theological lecture as at a ball; as much at home teaching in a ragged school as dining with a bench of judges; as lively with her pen as with her tongue. Looking back over a long life, she would one day boast that she had yet to meet the person capable of boring her. Such was the girl with whom Robert Cecil fell in love in his twenty-fifth year. After a long courtship he proposed to her in the summer of 1856 and was accepted.

Measured by the minute social gradations of the Victorian Age, Georgina may not have been the ideal match for a son, even a younger son, of the Marquess of Salisbury. The Aldersons, Yorkshire Unitarians who had settled in Norfolk, belonged to the professional rather than to the landed classes; so apparently did Lady Alderson's family, the Drewes; not until long after her death did a genealogically-minded kinsman discover that the Drewes, no less than the Cecils, were descended from the first Lord Burghley.* It is true that Lord Robert's mother, the Miss

* William Cecil, created Baron Burghley; Thomas Cecil, created Earl of Exeter; Edward Cecil, created Viscount Wimbledon; Albania Cecil, who married Sir Christopher Wray; Theodosia Wray, who married Rowland Langharne; Anne Langharne, who married

Gascoyne whom his father had married thirty-five years before, was encumbered by far closer links with 'trade' than any Alderson or any Drewe. That earlier embarrassment, however, had yielded to the treatment of 3 per cent Consols. The Gascoynes had inherited fortune after fortune; the Aldersons lived on what they earned.

Lord Salisbury was horrified by the proposed alliance. The father of ten children, he had neither the wish nor the means to add to the £400 a year which he already allowed his second son; and he begged Robert to ponder the financial hardship and social isolation to which so impecunious a marriage would expose him. In the autumn of 1856 the impatient suitor reluctantly agreed to put his love to the test by neither seeing nor corresponding with Georgina for six months. But in the letter accepting his father's proposal he could not resist a barbed retort: 'The persons who will cut me because I marry Miss Alderson are precisely the persons of whose society I am so anxious to be quit.' May 1857 found him still resolved to marry: preferably with his father's blessing, but no less determined should it be withheld. The ceremony took place quietly in London a few weeks later under the shadow of a family estrangement. On the eve of his wedding, Robert received two letters. One was from his father, regretting in frigidly polite phrases that he would be unable to attend. The other, even more wounding, was from his elder brother Cranborne: 'Many thanks for your kind letter and for the invitation which it contains. I must decline to assist at your marriage on the 11th of next July as I most fully concur with my Lord in disapproving the step you are about to take.'

Half a century later, as Robert's daughter Gwendolen was searching through family letters while writing his biography, she described the atmosphere in which he had begun married life. 'During the time I am reading, he is the family offender, never alluded to except in terms of virtuous and superior condemnation. . . . The poor old father is more bitter than the sons, but not so intolerably complacent.' Robert and Georgina settled down in unfashionable Bloomsbury, undaunted by the social perils forecast for them. They were amused rather than abashed by a would-be friend who asked where they lived so that she might call on them; when told it was in Fitzroy Square, she replied with regret, but firmly, that she never left cards north of Oxford Street.

An annual income of £400, however, supplemented only by the £100 a year which Georgina brought to the marriage, was hardly enough to keep an active parliamentarian, much less a wife and

David Allen; John Allen; John Bartlett Allen; Caroline Allen, who married the Rev. Edward Drewe; Georgina Drewe, who married Edward Alderson; Georgina Alderson, who married Lord Robert Cecil, later third Marquess of Salisbury.

children.* Robert's horizons grew brighter in February 1858 when a Conservative government led by the fourteenth Earl of Derby replaced the Liberal administration of Lord Palmerston. Among the new Cabinet Ministers was Lord Salisbury, who had by now become reconciled to Robert and Georgina. But any influence which he could exert to have his son appointed an Under-Secretary with a salary was more than balanced by the scorn with which the Member for Stamford criticized the party leadership. Robert remained therefore on the back benches, too rebellious to be rewarded, not dangerous enough to be bought off. Several times during the sixteen months that the government remained in power, poverty prompted him to beg the Prime Minister for a permanent paid post either at home or in the colonies. At one moment he had hopes of becoming a Commissioner of Inland Revenue, at another a Clerk of the Privy Council; neither came his way. And on being offered the Governorship of Moreton Bay (as Queensland was then called) he had to refuse on discovering that his expenses would outweigh his salary. He was well aware that the acceptance of any such appointment under the crown would oblige him to resign his seat in the House of Commons: but it was not a prospect from which he flinched. So near to turning his back on politics was the man who later held the office of Prime Minister for almost fourteen years at the zenith of British power. He was saved from the danger of parliamentary extinction by the fall of Derby's government in June 1859. For the next six years, patronage was in the hands of the Liberals, who had no intention of wasting it on any Tory.

During his early search for a career, Robert Cecil confessed to his father: 'It may, perhaps it will, end in my doing nothing in particular and trying to eke out my means by writing for newspapers.' So it came to pass. The first piece of journalism that can be attributed to him with certainty was published in December 1856. It appeared in the *Saturday Review*, a weekly periodical owned by Alexander Beresford-Hope, his brother-in-law and a fellow Conservative MP. Until he achieved financial independence on inheriting his father's estates twelve years later, Robert contributed anonymously but industriously to that and other papers such as the short-lived *Bentley's Quarterly Review* and John Murray's *Quarterly Review*, the leading Tory journal of the day. At times he was turning out several thousand words a week on a broad variety of topics, particularly politics, and saw his income swell by a useful £300 a year.

Writing, he admitted, was a hateful occupation. But his sustained denunciation of Benjamin Disraeli, the Conservative leader in the

* The statutes of All Souls College required Lord Robert Cecil to relinquish his Fellowship and stipend on marriage.

House of Commons, did not lack relish. There was a foundation of reason in his invective. He despised Disraeli for seeking political power at any price, for stooping to combine with the Radicals in order to displace the Whigs. Tactically, it was a policy that might succeed: indeed, that did succeed in 1858, although for only sixteen months. But for Lord Robert, a Tory administration that poisoned its principles with an infusion of demagogy was not fit to hold office. That Disraeli should have attempted to outbid the Whigs by bringing in his own measure of parliamentary reform, however mild, was an unforgivable affront. Cecil believed democracy to be a dangerous and irrational creed by which 'two day-labourers shall outvote Baron Rothschild'. And the spectacle of a parliamentary candidate submitting himself to popular election was in itself profoundly degrading:

> The days and weeks of screwed-up smiles and laboured courtesy, the mock geniality, the hearty shake of the filthy hand, the chuckling reply that must be made to the coarse joke, the loathsome, choking compliment that must be paid to the grimy wife and sluttish daughter, the indispensable flattery of the vilest religious prejudices, the wholesale deglutition of hypocritical pledges . . .

Those bitter words might have carried more conviction had their author ever undergone the ordeal he purported to describe. In truth, such was Lord Exeter's hold over the borough of Stamford, his cousin Robert had invariably been returned without a contest.

It was perhaps permissible for a Conservative MP to denigrate the workings of democracy in a high-minded defence of property and education. But he could not fail to arouse resentment when he publicly pilloried his own party for its acceptance of Disraeli as a leader: 'It went into the market and bought such articles of the kind as were for sale – mostly damaged goods of unprepossessing appearance, which other buyers had rejected and whose subsequent wear has hardly made good their original cost.'

Cecil pursued Disraeli through the pages of *Bentley's Quarterly Review*, sometimes by implication, at other times by name, always with venom. It was after such an outburst in July 1858 ('There is no escape on earth for man from taxes, toothache or the statesmanship of Mr Disraeli') that an embarrassed Lord Salisbury, a member of the same Cabinet as Disraeli, threatened to stop paying his son's parliamentary expenses. The culprit defended himself with what his daughter has described as a touch of demure malice.

> I write for money [he told his father]. Varying concurring circumstances have left me no other means of gaining money on which I

have any ground for relying except writing. . . . I am bound of course to write no opinion that I do not hold, but what I do write I must write in the style that is most likely to attract, and therefore to sell.

Accepting his son's explanation, which would not have seemed out of place on the lips of a Northcliffe or a Beaverbrook sixty years later, Salisbury continued to subsidize his political career, and even added handsomely to his personal allowance. Well-paid directorships of companies began to come Robert's way, too, culminating in the chairmanship of the Great Eastern Railway. But in 1866 he had to call on his father for an advance of over £5,000 to settle immediate liabilities caused by the failure of Overend, Gurney & Co., the banking house in which he had invested. Salisbury generously complied, for by then Cranborne was dead and Robert had succeeded to the privileged status of an heir. Two years later Salisbury himself died. At the age of thirty-eight, Robert found himself third Marquess of Salisbury and master of Hatfield. The days of hardship were over.

When Robert Cecil defended the asperity of his attacks on Disraeli by pleading the need to create a journalistic sensation, he was telling the truth. But it was not the whole truth. He wrote violently, sometimes hysterically, because that was the way he thought. 'Beneath the taut membrane of rational discourse', a commentator on his political beliefs has observed, 'lies a tense and agitated mind.' All his life he was subject to what he called 'nerve storms'. Precipitated by worry or exhaustion, they would be accompanied by both a depression of the spirits and profound bodily lassitude. The student of psychology may trace them to a lonely, motherless, burdensome childhood; the geneticist to an hereditary infirmity. Three hundred years before, the first Earl of Salisbury had fallen into such prolonged dejection on the death of his first wife that an aunt had warned him against becoming 'a surly, sharp, sour plum, no better than in truth a very melancholy mole and a *miseranthropos* hateful to God and man'. As revealed in his descendant, it was an affliction that induced inward doubts and fears, concealed rather than overcome by an aggressive style.

Robert himself later confessed that in the House of Commons he had been an Ishmaelite: his hand against every man and every man's hand against him. Sustained disloyalty to his leader was punctuated by attacks on the opposition that his fellow Conservatives found no less embarrassing. He once provoked a storm by branding some legalistic manoeuvre of Gladstone's as 'more worthy of an attorney than a statesman'. When called upon to withdraw his wounding words, he delivered a long and elaborate apology – to the attorneys he had unwittingly maligned. In print, too, his polemics would detract from the force of his argument. He is unlikely to have won many converts to the Confederate cause in the American Civil War by comparing the Unionists to Ghengis Khan and Tamerlane. Although such turmoil of the spirit subsided with age, as late as 1874 Disraeli referred to his former tormentor, by now a Cabinet colleague, as 'a great master of gibes and flouts and jeers'.

Had Robert Cecil not been the victim of an interrupted, fragmentary education, he might have achieved a more disciplined mind earlier in life. It is true that during his five troubled years at Eton and in the period subsequently spent with a private tutor he had acquired much knowledge. He was well grounded in the language, literature and history of Greece and Rome, of France and Germany, to a lesser degree of modern Italy. He had roamed widely over English letters and made a special study of Church history. He dabbled in the sciences and did not despise social statistics. Yet something was lacking. William Johnson, the translator of *Heraclitus*, who began teaching at Eton in the year Robert was withdrawn, believed that the value of a public-school education lay less in acquiring knowledge than in making mental efforts under criticism:

> You go to a great school, not for knowledge so much as for arts and habits; for the habit of attention, for the art of expression, for the art of assuming at a moment's notice a new intellectual posture, for the art of entering quickly into another person's thoughts, for the habit of submitting to censure and refutation, for the art of indicating assent or dissent in graduated terms.

Those were not the qualities for which Robert Cecil was known during the years he divided his labours between the House of Commons and journalism.

In time he mastered his febrile temperament, creating a gulf of identity between the young Cecil and the older Salisbury; between the excitable, solitary, back-bencher and the sedate, self-sufficient Prime Minister. The transformation was less complete that it seemed. A French tutor whom he engaged for his children one summer noted '*la petite pointe de malice qui se montre dans les yeux et aux coins de sa bouche*'. Shyness persisted, too, so that he would consult his Cabinet colleagues only with reluctance. But in place of the savage language that had once clouded his intellectual brilliance, he now displayed no more than an ironic banter.

One chord of his mind remained untouched by the conviction that human problems yield to deliberation and analysis. The intellect that so critically explored all other phenomena humbly accepted the Christian mystery without qualification or doubt. When he sometimes heard it urged against the truth of some Christian doctrine that it was morally unsatisfactory or rationally incomprehensible, his only comment would be: 'As if *that* had anything to do with it.' Nor did he see his deliberate abstention from sceptical inquiry as conflicting with his reverence for personal liberty. If Christian belief imposed limits upon the will of the individual, it was for him only in the sense of that collect in the Prayer Book which equates 'service' with 'perfect freedom'.

Christianity permeated his political life, sometimes in a way that later generations have found bizarre. In 1858 he voted against a Conservative Bill relieving Jews from taking the Christian oath on being elected to Parliament, a measure ensuring that for the first time they could sit at Westminster. Supporters of the reform pleaded with Cecil to withdraw his opposition, on the ground that the taking of the oath excluded only the sincere Jew. He replied that it was pre-eminently the sincere Jew whom he dreaded. In proportion to his sincerity, Cecil urged, a Jew would be hostile to all that in a religious sense a Christian body swore to uphold. For Robert Cecil, Christianity could know no neutrality. Yet it was no less a deep, calm, lifelong attachment which, together with his marriage, brought him the only real happiness he knew.

3

Childhood at Hatfield

To be born of an ancient line or reared in a palace was no protection against the rigours of a Victorian childhood. Churchill at Blenheim, Curzon at Kedleston, the future King Edward VII at Windsor: each endured an upbringing which would have shocked many a family of artisans. The crushing poverty of the slums sometimes consigned even infants to slave in the mines and factories of nineteenth--century England; but their parents lacked neither pride nor heart and would no more willingly have condemned their young to be beaten, bullied and starved at a Dotheboys Hall than their old to die in the workhouse.

Haunted by memories of his own dismal schooling, the new Marquess of Salisbury spared his children the excesses of an aristocratic education. He decided that each of his sons should remain at Hatfield at least until the age of twelve, then leave home for Eton supposedly prepared to withstand the moral and physical pressures of a public school. Lord and Lady Salisbury also dared to break the tyranny of the green baize door, the convention that forbade a parent to interfere with the routine of nursery and schoolroom. They refused to confine family life to that evening half hour when, scrubbed and subdued, the children of the rich made a ritual appearance in the drawing-room. Resident governesses and tutors were of course engaged to teach mathematics, history, geography, French, Latin, even some Greek; but the minds and characters of the little Cecils remained the well-guarded preserve of their mother and father.

Although so sensitive to noise that he could work only behind locked double doors, Salisbury was exceptionally fond of children. Seated on a fur rug, he would allow himself to be dragged by his small sons up and down the great gallery at Hatfield. A generation later, weighing eighteen stone and bearing the burden of both Prime Minister and Foreign

Secretary, he obligingly joined his grandchildren in a race down the same magnificent room.

Even more, he cared to exercise their wits, to stimulate them into challenging some conventional fallacy or discerning the flaw in a political slogan. One subject alone he excluded from debate: the Christian life was to be lived, not disputed. Indeed, it was the foundation on which all else rested. Whether in London or in the country, the family invariably began the day with prayers, at first in the modest house on the borders of Surrey and Hampshire made possible by the rewards of journalism, and after 1868 in the private chapel at Hatfield. With characteristic energy, Lady Salisbury herself undertook the religious education of the children. She read to them from improving works, guided them through a daily passage from the Bible and eventually helped to prepare them for confirmation at the age of twelve. She was careful to avoid any touch of mawkishness or emotionalism. Belief was to the soul as bread to the body: an absolute necessity and in no way dependent on feeling. To miss Holy Communion was to starve, and whenever the family was away from home, the first duty on arriving at a new place was to discover a suitable service for the following Sunday. At the Congress of Berlin in 1878, Salisbury made a return journey of over two hundred miles to Dresden one weekend in order to worship in the nearest Anglican church. After the boys had gone to Eton, some difficulty arose about their weekly Communion. It was Lady Salisbury who, armed with her husband's sanction of instant withdrawal, swept down and in a matter of hours solved the problem to their joint satisfaction. Yet she took a broad view of how the rest of Sunday should be spent and shared her father's distaste for 'the mischievous tendency to over-dogmatise in theology'. Particularly for the young, she laid down, the day was to be one of repose and refreshment.

When they grew up, the seven Cecil children experienced their full measure of human ills: grief and disappointment, sickness of body and of heart. An acuteness of sensibility, moreover, sometimes made their sufferings seem to them more intense than those of others. But even from the depths, not one of them ever reacted against the faith on which he had been nourished or lost that sense of purpose which is the mainspring of a Christian life.

Paradoxically, Salisbury felt himself precluded both by temperament and conviction from playing any direct role in his children's religious instruction or from providing facile answers to those conundrums which delight young and lively minds. Secure in his own faith, he shied away from any attempt to justify divine intervention in human affairs. On one occasion, with what his daughter described almost as defiance, he said: 'God is all-powerful, and God is all-loving – and the world is what

it is! How are you going to explain *that*?' Again, he asserted that acceptance of the divinity of Christ did not necessarily exclude a rejection of
the Christian ethic. A too rigorous interpretation of right and wrong,
he argued, was ill-suited to the varying circumstances of human life.
Two such idiosyncratic doctrines, however irrelevant to his fundamental belief, did not make for theological ease in the family circle.

When that great philanthropist Lord Shaftesbury happened to meet
two of the Cecil boys towards the end of his life, he spoke with
admiration of their father, urging them to treasure carefully all his
letters of moral and religious counsel. It was with embarrassment that
they had to confess to never having received a line from him which
could bear that description. Nor were Salisbury's children ever encouraged to share their intimate beliefs with him:

> There was a violent family argument at dinner to-day [one of his
> sons wrote] roughly on the question whether it was right or not to
> regard disease and death as part of God's gifts and blessings – curious
> discussion which necessarily had to be carried on in veiled language.
> My father would not take any part in it and eventually stopped it.

Even the outworks of religion, such as liturgical practices, could be
dangerous if not forbidden territory. Lady Salisbury describes such a
debate:

> We still have almost daily great family arguments on ritualism.
> Linky in his usual character of Grand Inquisitor, Jem trying to agree
> with every one but finding it impossible owing to his unfortunate
> love of truth, Bob laying down the law in a legal manner, Fish un-
> reasonable to the last extent and paradoxical to madness, His Lordship
> humble and silent.*

On every other subject, Salisbury encouraged the children to have
their say, addressing them from their earliest years as intellectual
equals with opinions as much to be respected as his own. 'My father
always treats me as if I were an ambassador,' one of them remarked,
'and I do like it.' They themselves could be undiplomatically robust in
their language. A young girl on a visit to Hatfield from France astounded
the household by calling a dignified governess a goose to her face. The
culprit, much embarrassed, pleaded that she thought it was a term of
affectionate regard, so often had she heard the word applied to the head
of the family by his offspring.

Lady Salisbury, however, demurred at her husband's unbridled belief
in *laissez-faire* on hearing from him how a schoolboy son, left in his
care at Hatfield, had passed the time: 'Having tried all the weapons in

* See 'Family Names and Nicknames', page 322.

the gun-cupboard in succession – some in the riding-school and some, he tells me, in his own room – and having failed to blow his fingers off, he has been driven to reading Sydney Smith's *Essays* and studying Hogarth's pictures.' The alarmed mother commented: 'He may be able to govern the country, but he is quite unfit to be left in charge of his children.'

The episode illustrates Salisbury's conviction that even an adolescent should have a free run of the library shelves, not excluding the vast collection of French novels which jostled history, theology and the classics. But he qualified his licence by insisting that whatever the chosen book, it must be read with concentration and not with that half-attention which he believed to be the bane of a public-school education.

In contrast to the whirling words of his own youth, he also insisted that argument should be conducted with an exactness of phrase and hence of thought. His daughter Gwendolen has described the unnerving finality of his Socratic manner:

> He's not an encouraging person to talk metaphysics with. . . . You've not got to your sixth word before he asks you to define its meaning and when you manfully plunge into your definition he insists upon your again defining every metaphysical or abstract term which you unwarily made use of with the precision of a proposition of Euclid; and after you have floundered hopelessly for about ten minutes, he calmly informs you that he's not surprised at it, as you've been trying to put into human language what either has no real existence or is beyond the grasp of human reason or imagination.

It needed more than Salisbury's playful dialectic to deter his children from talking almost round the clock. Lady Salisbury, always the enemy of joyless routine, was the principal conspirator in flouting their school-room timetable. She did not usually appear at breakfast until mid-morning, having first dealt with the day's correspondence; but once installed, she turned that most lugubrious of meals into a feast of table talk. Newspapers and letters were read aloud, political developments dissected, plans made. A member of the family wrote of her conversation:

> So continuous was it and indeed so brilliant that we used to be caught like flies in the web of it, and twelve o'clock or later came and somehow it would still be going on. If one wanted to leave, the only way was slowly to approach the door still listening and bolt through when one got near enough, but one always did it with regret.

29

A discussion that had begun in the morning might resume at dinner, continue in the drawing-room, prolong itself up the stairs, gather renewed strength at each bedroom door and cease only with the approach of dawn. Nothing could stop the flow except the house catching fire, which it did from time to time, although never as disastrously as in 1835. The cause was the primitive system of electric light which Salisbury installed at Hatfield in 1881, one of the first two houses in England to have it. The need for fuses was not yet recognized and occasionally an overloaded wire ignited the panelling. The family were well trained to deal with the emergency and would hurl cushions at the fire until it was extinct.

Salisbury's practical interest in science caused other interruptions to the rhythm of domestic routine. Once he almost died from chlorine poisoning. On another occasion there was a loud report and he staggered out of his private laboratory streaming with blood and observing with some satisfaction that he knew the exact cause of the explosion: experimenting with sodium in an insufficiently dried retort. He introduced an early model of the telephone, its wires running loose across the floor. From every corner of the house startled visitors would hear the voice of their host testing the intrument with a reiterated: 'Hey diddle diddle, the cat and the fiddle, the cow jumped over the moon.' In 1886, the year Salisbury received Cabinet office for the first time as Secretary of State for India, the Royal Society recognized his inquiring spirit by electing him a Fellow.

One guest who delighted in the vagaries of Hatfield life was the Rev. C. L. Dodgson, the lecturer in mathematics at Oxford better known as Lewis Carroll. When Salisbury was installed in the honorific office of Chancellor of the University in 1870, Dodgson wrote to ask whether he might take photographs of the Cecil children to add to his considerable collection of that genre. Permission was granted. 'I fancy *Wonderland* had a great deal to do with my gracious reception,' he noted. The new Chancellor's interest in a fellow amateur photographer must also have helped. A few weeks later Dodgson was entertaining the children with wire puzzles and verse riddles, and in the following year he made the first of several visits to Hatfield. 'The family are really delightful,' he wrote, 'Perfectly at their own ease, and kindness itself, they make all their guests feel at their ease also.' Like so many academics, he buzzed with strong opinions on public affairs and did not hesitate to press them on his host. His suggestions were sensible and sometimes ingenious: a chain of lookout posts for observing the outbreak of fires in cities, a change in the constitution to enable ministers to address either House of Parliament, a visit to Dublin by the Queen to help heal Irish discontent.

But it was as the creator of Alice that Dodgson endeared himself to the Hatfield household, in spite of preferring to think of himself as the family friend and counsellor. 'I declined to undertake my usual role of story-teller in the morning,' he wrote in his journal on New Year's Eve, 1875, 'and so (I hope) broke the rule of being always expected to do it.' He nevertheless continued to read aloud extracts from works still in manuscript, such as *Sylvie and Bruno*. While writing that insipid romance, he seems to have drawn occasional touches of inspiration from his patrician surroundings. Here, in an exchange between the Lord Chancellor and the Earl (supposedly modelled on Salisbury), he exactly caught the deflating logic of his host:

'This portentous movement has already assumed the dimensions of a Revolution.'

'And what are the dimensions of a Revolution?' The voice was genial and mellow.

Such sophisticated humour enchanted the young less than he cared to believe. Among the childhood friends of the Cecils was one of Queen Victoria's grand-daughters. 'A sweet little girl,' Dodgson noted, 'though with rather unruly spirits.' She too had reservations about their relationship. With a sharpness of recollection undimmed by her ninety years, Princess Alice, Countess of Athlone, still likes to recall his kindness to her at Hatfield. 'But he was always making grown-up jokes to us,' she adds, 'and we thought him awfully silly.'

In quite another way. Dodgson tried to fill an unexpected gap in the children's education. Both Lord and Lady Salisbury, although voracious readers, were blind to the arts, indifferent even to the architecture, pictures and furniture at Hatfield which could have brought so much additional pleasure into their everyday lives. Salisbury, it is true, made certain improvements to the private chapel: but that was a duty more sacerdotal than aesthetic. His appreciation of pictures was distorted by a hatred of pretentiousness that led him to glory in the name of Philistine. When asked to define the word, he would reply: 'One who is assailed by the jaw-bone of an ass.' He had an occasional ear for melody, but it did not extend to the compositions of 'a fellow called Brahms'. And his wife, fearing the appeal of such pleasures to sensuous human appetites, would speak with sorrow of Arthur Balfour's 'unfortunate love of music'. In their choice of furniture, utility and convenience were the only standards. Heirlooms of exquisite workmanship and historic importance stood side by side with crude office fittings. The only discernible difference between Salisbury's sitting-room and his dressing-room was that a pair of brushes lay on a bookcase in the dressing-room. Thus it never occurred to the younger members of the household that they should not play rowdy games of billiard fives in a room lined with seventeenth-century panelling, or ride iron-wheeled tricycles down the marble floor of the armoury or use Charles I's cradle for charades.

In such unpromising soil the Rev. Charles Dodgson attempted to sow the seeds of understanding. He took the children to hear Ellen Terry as Portia in *The Merchant of Venice*; he escorted them on meticulous tours of the pictures in the Royal Academy; he talked and sketched and prepared notes. But his cultural mission made little impression on Hatfield, and it was left to a later generation of Cecils to seek pleasure as much in beauty as in ideas.

The Cecil children grew up in an aura of politics, imbibing from both their parents a resistant Toryism that even in the 1870s was beginning to look a shade old-fashioned. They learnt that power was wielded most wisely when it rested in the hands of educated men of property; that aristocracy was the protector of personal liberties, democracy their enemy; that public opinion, an artificial concept manufactured by 'the journalists, the literary men, the professors, the advanced thinkers of the day', should play no role in the determination of policy; that the duty of the Conservative Party was to oppose any precipitate extension of the franchise and to mistrust 'the arithmetical race of politicians who believe in the inalienable right of eight beggars to govern seven Rothschilds and, what is more, to tax them'; that a political party was a mechanism rather than an institution, worthy of respect only as long as it honoured its principles. Better a lost election, Salisbury argued, than a victory won by the compromise of Conservative beliefs; better a Conservative opposition strong enough to prevent a Liberal government from passing radical measures than a Conservative government whose survival depended on abandoning its heritage. It was a creed that combined the instinct of self-preservation with a genuine belief in what Salisbury called the 'superior fitness' of the landed classes to govern.

Throughout a long political life, Salisbury consistently refused to allow either promise of office or fear of unpopularity to drive him into opportunism. In 1866, his early journalistic insolence forgiven, he received a seat in the Cabinet. Within eight months he had resigned in protest against the introduction by his leaders, Derby and Disraeli, of a parliamentary Reform Bill more sweeping than an unsuccessful Liberal measure of the year before. To many Conservatives his attitude seemed unpalatably astringent. They resented his lofty indifference to both the pursuit and the retention of political power, his disdain for the tactics of party warfare, his rejection of office as the ultimate goal of statecraft. Disraeli might exult on becoming Prime Minister for the first time: 'I have climbed to the top of the greasy pole.' It was not an occupation that appealed to the third Marquess of Salisbury. On two of the three occasions when he himself was prevailed upon to form an administration, he tried to decline the Queen's commission. And in January 1886, at the end of his first brief and troubled premiership, one of his sons could think of no more gratifying gesture than a telegram which read: 'I hear turned out. Many congratulations.' Not until he became Prime Minister for the third time in 1895, buttressed by a strong majority and faced by a weak opposition, did he begin to relish power.

Salisbury's exacting standards have since been revered within the family from generation to generation. 'The Cecils', Mark Rutherford used to say, 'are deaf to the howling of the mob.' They have never feared to embrace unpopular causes or to dissent from unprincipled acts. Hugh Cecil called for the humane treatment of conscientious objectors during the First World War; William fought to improve conditions in the casual wards used by tramps; Maud incurred the disapproval of King George V by her early adherence to the suffragette movement. Bob twice resigned high office: in 1918 as a protest against the disestablishment of the Church in Wales, and nine years later because Conservative colleagues did not share his trust in the League of Nations as an instrument of peace. Salisbury's grandson and namesake, who later became the fifth Marquess, also resigned office on two occasions, once in support of Anthony Eden during the years of appeasement that preceded the Second World War, and again in 1957 over the conduct of negotiations that eventually led to Cypriot independence. Applauded by idealists for their honourable self-sacrifice, they have not escaped the reproof of realists for shirking those painful compromises without which government can become impossible. The hair-trigger conscience wins little admiration round the Cabinet table.

Lady Salisbury upheld her husband's principles with gusts of prejudice. Again and again she breached the tradition that the asperities of party politics should be abandoned at the drawing-room door; even the heir to the throne was once made to feel the chill of her contempt because of some supposed default. Gladstone, however, in spite of occupying pride of place in her gallery of demonology, was occasionally invited to Hatfield and more than once came to tea with her in London. 'The GOM stayed an hour,' Gwendolen wrote to Bob, 'skipping about the room like a man of 25, more than affectionate and full of stories of Sir R. Peel, Lord Melbourne, etc., keeping chiefly to the days of his own high Toryism.' Canon Liddon, of St Paul's, a family friend for many years, has described another such occasion:

> When I got to Arlington Street* I found the GOM and Mrs Gladstone encamped in Lady Salisbury's boudoir. . . . Tea and muffins and conversation for more than an hour on every subject. The GOM complained of Lady S.'s Radicalism, and she of his Conservatism. Among the subjects were Scottish Disestablishment, Deceased Wife's Sister, Sir W. Harcourt, 'Lux Mundi', the Welsh language, the history of the Welsh Church, the qualifications of Welsh Bishops, etc.

The Cecils were less respectful to Mr Gladstone behind his back. GOM, they held, stood not for Grand Old Man, but for God's Only Mistake. And during party games one Christmas, a visiting Lyttelton chose Gladstone's nose as the object to be guessed. 'Should I pay a shilling to see it?' asked an Alderson aunt, and was promptly declared a loser. Lady Salisbury's animosity seems almost to scorch the paper on which she dashes down a furious commentary on the Irish Home Rule crisis of 1886:

> The old Parliamentary *leg* has surpassed his usual infamy. He is now hoping to keep his place by offering to give up the Bill if they will pass the 2nd reading. This you will perceive is as foolish as it is wicked. Ireland would be kept in her present state of anarchy and misery for another year that the Queen of England may have the *honour* of still calling Mr G. her Prime Minister.

Salisbury had mistrusted the demagogue in Gladstone since their stormy scene in the Commons of 1861. Yet a double bond of sympathy gradually drew him closer to the Liberal leader than to any other political antagonist: a shared reverence for the Church of England and a common dislike of Disraeli. In contrast to his wife's implacable scorn, Salisbury would in later years employ no sharper weapon against him than a gentle irony. It sufficed. During a debate on Home Rule in the Upper House, a Liberal peer proclaimed: 'If the English people came with Mr Gladstone at their head and knocked at the door of your Lordships' House, your Lordships would have to give way.' 'Or even,' Salisbury was heard to murmur in a polite voice, 'if they came alone.' It became something of a Cecil family joke that the man they dubbed the Arch-Fiend could scarcely conceal his admiration for Salisbury and had been known to regale a restive Liberal Cabinet with his virtues. 'Gladstone thinks

---

* No. 20 Arlington Street had been in the family since the eighteenth century. The Prime Minister had it pulled down and on its site built a much larger house suitable for official entertaining. At the end of the First World War his eldest son sold it to Lord Michelham and bought No. 21 Arlington Street next door. That too he sold after the Second World War. It has since been demolished.

him "*the* most remarkable man he ever met" and is a perfect bore about him,' Nigs reported. Lady Salisbury was not mollified. 'We hope to succeed in smashing the old lunatic,' she wrote.

A single letter of hers sufficed to despatch a pair of lesser sinners:

> The career of the two Rs – Rosebery and Randolph – brings out very strikingly the weakness inherent on total absence of what is commonly called principle in both. No ship can live in any sea without *some* steering power. Randolph seems to me, however, much the best of the two, as he has heart, and love for his mother and friends. The other is, as far as I can judge, entirely inhuman.

She could never forgive Lord Randolph Churchill for having caused her husband some inconvenience (though ultimately much relief) by resigning as Chancellor of the Exchequer in 1886; that the culprit's own mother, the Duchess of Marlborough, happened to be a guest at Hatfield at the time aggravated his offence. He maintained that his action was prompted by differences with his colleagues on matters of high policy, particularly the defence estimates. Lady Salisbury knew better. It was a resignation, she believed, that he had expected an alarmed Prime Minister instantly to refuse: a manoeuvre inspired not by Cecilian principle but by a Churchillian will to prevail. His bluff was called, his political career snuffed out in a moment. Lady Salisbury allowed no touch of pity to temper her rage. A few weeks later, the Duchess of Marlborough, writing to her on some business connected with the Queen's approaching jubilee, was astonished to have her letter returned in an envelope addressed in Lady Salisbury's hand. In January 1895 she relented:

> We hear the most ghastly accounts of poor Randolph's deathbed [she told a niece]. He never speaks except to ask every evening 'When can we start for Monte Carlo?' The doctor says 'Perhaps tomorrow', and then he says no more till the next day when it is repeated. And he can bear no light at all.

The same letter included a more characteristic sentiment: 'I have been reading Rosebery's speech. How poor, how violent and how dishonest.' Gladstone's successor as Liberal leader could do no right. Even the defeat of his Derby winner Ladas by the 50–1 outsider Throstle in the St Leger Stakes of 1894 evoked a crow of triumph from Lady Salisbury: 'Are not you glad Ladas has not won the Leger? I am delighted. I have read the whole account of the race with the greatest interest – and wish I had put some money on Throstle.' Alas for the daughter of the judge who half a century before had startled society by his strictures on the corrupting tendency of the Turf.

There was a classic simplicity about her loyalties. All who opposed her husband were her enemies; all who supported him were her friends – unless she deemed their support to be tepid or belated. Thus the eighth Duke of Devonshire, having abandoned Gladstone over Irish Home Rule, incurred her censure for the slowness with which he agreed to serve in a Conservative administration. 'I am disgusted with the Duke of Devonshire's vacillating and injurious course in the Lords,' she wrote. 'The truth is the Duke belongs to the well-known and too common class of English politicians, the Hamlets.' That he had as selflessly as Salisbury three times declined the Premiership counted for nothing with her.

Fortunately for the children of Lord and Lady Salisbury, the one politician whom they might have been expected to exclude altogether from the family circle eventually became a welcome guest under their roof. As an outlandish young dandy, Disraeli had graced the parties of the first Marchioness, Old Sally, and in middle life was often entertained by his Cabinet colleague, the second Marquess. 'At Hatfield', he wrote in 1855, 'we dined every day in a baronial hall in the midst of a real old English park at the time of Queen Elizabeth, interminable avenues of lime and chestnut and oceans of fern, six feet high; golden yew trees and glancing deer.' Even while the young Lord Robert Cecil MP was raking his parliamentary leader with journalistic broadsides, Disraeli accepted his hostility with teasing good humour. Staying with the second Marquess at Hatfield when the attacks on him in the *Quarterly Review* were at their most furious, Dizzy suddenly came face to face with the rebellious son of the house who had arrived home unexpectedly. 'Ah, Robert, Robert, how glad I am to see you,' Disraeli exclaimed, enfolding him in an embrace.

That set the pattern of their relationship for more than a decade: magnanimity matched only by churlishness. On becoming Prime Minister for the first time in 1868, Disraeli at once invited the new Lord Salisbury to rejoin the Conservative government from which he had resigned in the previous year on the issue of parliamentary reform. Salisbury sent an offensive message that he had the greatest respect for every member of the administration except one: but that he did not think his honour safe in the hands of that one. Six years later, when at last he did consent to sit once more in Cabinet with Disraeli, as Secretary of State for India, he told his wife: 'The prospect of having to serve with this man again is like a nightmare.'

The two statesmen were never to achieve the easy intimacy between colleagues which lubricated so much of Victorian political life. But as mistrust melted, particularly after Salisbury's appointment as Foreign Secretary in 1878, they worked together with cordiality and mutual respect. The Earl of Beaconsfield, as Disraeli had become in 1876, took a renewed delight in the beauty of Hatfield, one of the few great country houses where he could relax without being bored by small talk or stifled by a rigid regime. He wrote to the Queen in April 1878:

All the Cecil family seem wonderfully clever but natural. There are two daughters, Ladies Maud and Gwendolen (20 and 18). Lord Beaconsfield has rarely met more intelligent and agreeable women, for they are quite women though in the wild grace of extreme youth.

Soon they were invited to join the select group of women friends on whom he bestowed the Order of the Bee – a punning reference to his new title. Others to receive its insignia, a bee-shaped brooch, included the Queen's youngest daughter, Princess Beatrice, and Dizzy's two old confidantes, Lady Bradford and Lady Chesterfield. 'The daughters of the house keep everyone alive,' he told Lady Bradford in the autumn of 1878, 'always on horseback, and in scrapes, or playing lawn tennis even in twilight. The evening passes in chorus singing – all the airs of *Pinafore*. It's a distraction both for Salisbury and myself from many cares.'

The statesman was never too busy to send the girls long letters of mingled instruction and badinage. Here is one from Hughenden dated 27 August 1879:

Dear Gwendolen,

Amid solitude and storms – unbroken solitude and unceasing storms – it delights me to hear from my dear friends, and to be remembered by those one is so often thinking of. . . .

As dearest Maud and you have a weakness for princes, I will give you a trait or two of some of your prime favourites – the Prince of Sweden and Norway (Fortinbras) and the Prince of Baden – at Taymouth.

Sweden went out with the shooting party but unarmed, in each pocket a bottle of medicine! Baden was more warlike; he furnished himself with six cartridges *pour tout potage* but never used one of them, 'not understanding the management of English guns!' You can imagine the significant effect of such little incidents in a Highland house of mighty sport!

Ask Mme. Harcourt, with my kind remembrances, who is M. Valbert, a new writer in *Revue des Deux Mondes*? It is such a finished pen that it is difficult to believe it is a new one. He only appeared this year, with an article on Bismarckian finance, which was a masterpiece, and there have been occasionally some others.

By the bye, I told dearest Maud to read in *Revue des Deux Mondes* the memoirs of Mme. de Remusat, grandmother of the present

Remusat, and who was first lady to Consuless, afterwards Empress, Josephine. Did she? And what did she think of them? She ought to tell me.

My pens, my paper, all but my ink, which is mouldy, are so damp that I fear you will hardly make out this graceless scrawl.

Give my love to your Mama, and your dear sister, and believe me ever,

Yours affectionately,
Beaconsfield.

Three weeks later he wrote again:

Dearest Gwendolen,

Your letter was put into my hands as I was going to Aylesbury on a disagreeable mission, and when I looked very much like the Knight of the Doleful Countenance when he went forth after some mischances on a new expedition; but, I hope, it brought a smile to my face as, I assure you, it brought courage to my heart. One likes to be remembered by those who are dear to us at a critical moment.

The Times is in a great rage that I did not make a polished manifesto instead of discoursing on rent and rates, and has paid me off by giving me a speech which I never made in the form of two columns of incoherent nonsense; but even incoherent nonsense would be better than heedless declarations of unwise policy.

Your letter was most interesting, and gave me some picture of your life, which indeed ought to be a happy one; bathing in the sea and breakfasting in forests; in my mind the two most beautiful objects in the world. After all, there is no scenery like sylvan scenery; it has the most enduring charm; mountains and lakes may give more momentary rapture, but they weary like courts and festivals. No wonder the pagans worshipped trees; for my part I love trees more than pictures. Your description of French forests is very just, and applies very much to continental forests. The Black Forest, for example, is monotonous. One does not expect to see Garth and Wamba there; they require green glades and groups of oaks and spreading beeches. By the bye, the foliage this year in England is rich beyond memory. It almost reconciles me to getting no rents, for I suppose we owe it to the ceaseless showers.

I cannot send you any domestic gossip, and I dare say you and your sister, and Mama too, have such an organized correspondence that you know everything that is taking place under every roof, that one cares to know about.

I live here in complete solitude, but it suits me, and I am wonderfully well. But I have got some guests coming to me on Tuesday,

1, 2 Hatfield House, in Hertfordshire, built by Robert Cecil, first Earl of Salisbury, between 1607 and 1612. He died in the year of its completion without having spent a single night under its roof. After three and a half centuries it remains the principal family home.

The north front is austerely medieval. Seen from the south, two projecting wings enclose a stone façade and open colonnade that give promise of a gentler way of life.

3 Robert, third Marquess of Salisbury, for fourteen years Prime Minister. He was an indulgent parent who talked to his small children as if they were ambassadors and, seated on a fur rug, would allow them to drag him up and down the great gallery at Hatfield.

4 Georgina Alderson, wife of the third Marquess of Salisbury, in 1888. She was a loving but possessive mother who, as her children grew up and married, still required them to spend several months of each year at Hatfield. She preferred sea-bathing to the stiff formality of official entertainment and court life.

5 The Rev. Charles Dodgson, better known as Lewis Carroll, took this photograph of Lord and Lady Salisbury's four eldest children in 1870 or 1871. They later recalled that he had required them to hold the pose for what seemed like hours. *From left to right:* James, later fourth Marquess of Salisbury; Maud, later Countess of Selborne; William; and Gwendolen.

6 Nasr-ed-Din, Shah of Persia, visits Hatfield in 1889. *From left to right:* The Prince of Wales, later King Edward VII; Lady Salisbury; Lord Salisbury; the Shah; a Persian minister; the Princess of Wales, later Queen Alexandra; a Persian courtier.

The Shah proved an unsatisfactory guest. He expressed his wonder that Lord Salisbury did not take a new wife; and when the philanthropist Baroness Burdett-Coutts was presented to him, he peered into her face and exclaimed: '*Quelle horreur!*'

7 Châlet Cecil, on the cliffs at Puys, near Dieppe, which Lord Salisbury bought as a holiday retreat soon after the end of the Franco-Prussian War in 1870. Although it was run on supposedly economical lines to wean the children from the luxury of Hatfield, the household bills for a single week came to £84.

among them Sir Evelyn Wood, VC, KCB! I sometimes think, after so prolonged an isolation, I shall hardly be able properly to deport myself or even speak our native tongue.

I am no great admirer of amateur art under any circumstances, altho' Lady Theodora Guest, née Grosvenor, has presented me with a very pretty drawing of the Grand Canal, which is very Venetian and diaphanous. But of all amateur art I dislike most that which has destroyed art – photography. Mind your fingers! You soon will be going about like Lady Macbeth, 'Out ———— spot!' 'All the perfumes of Arabia' – you know the rest.

Give my love to those I love, and believe me

Ever yours,
Beaconsfield.

Staying at Hatfield, he would say little but liked to walk up and down the gallery with one or other of the girls, limping slightly from rheumatism. Such words as he did utter were memorable. One day when the talk was of political murders he turned his thoughts bizarrely to William Henry Waddington, the somewhat pedestrian French Foreign Minister of English descent and education. 'I hope they won't kill Waddington,' he sighed. 'That would make assassination ridiculous.'* And he bade Gwendolen, already a dedicated student of politics, never to forget that the rarest and most essential of all qualities to be found in a stateman was courage.

Beaconsfield's most dramatic visit to Hatfield took place in the spring of 1880, the year before he died. At the last minute Salisbury was ordered to Biarritz with his wife to convalesce from a severe feverish chill. The invalid nevertheless begged Beaconsfield not to cancel the visit but to make do with the hospitality of the Cecil children. Knowing the fastidiousness of the old Prime Minister's tastes, Salisbury also left orders that he, but he alone, should be served with the much esteemed Château Margaux 1870. 'I feel awkward,' the guest or honour told Lady Bradford, 'but forget my embarrassment in the exquisite flavour.' He needed all the solace at his command during those April days. For as the results of the general election began to reach Hatfield it became apparent that his last government had suffered a smashing defeat. 'This is an incident in your life,' he told his young hosts. 'It is the end of mine.'

'We score in conversation as a family,' one of Salisbury's sons used to boast. 'We are terribly ignorant and idle but we have a great deal of skill in the use of our minds. We have been trained to know what we

* Disraeli's antipathy to Waddington was persistent and possibly unjust. He told Queen Victoria: 'Mr Waddington looks like an *épicier* and I think his looks do not bely his mind and general intelligence.'

mean and not to be satisfied with a phrase.' Here is an example of the themes and variations with which they entertained themselves.

> The family are greatly excited about the infant murderers at Liverpool [Lady Salisbury writes to an absent son] and a tremendous argument is going on as to what is to be done with them. Tim and Nelly think they are not much worse than other boys. Jem says he hopes they won't put them in prison. Bob says it is all the fault of the Roman Catholics (why, I cannot imagine). I am for hanging their parents. Linky has a general view of five years penal servitude for all concerned. All agree in beginning with a flogging – which lends one touch of harmony to the argument. The head of the family inclines for painless extinction.

Those who lacked the stamina of the Cecils found their perpetual debates, often on the most trivial of topics, both a bore and a strain. Eleanor Cecil, the wife of the second son, Bob, wrote in exasperation: 'Chiffon women are dull and tiresome but they don't try to knock one down over a difference in the weather! I sometimes feel as if I must scream if some argument is gone on with for one more minute.' And after a household muddle had come to light: 'How like Hatfield! They think they know everything and have got their heads in the sand all the time. That comes of talking all day long, instead of looking and listening.' Even her husband, who had a lawyer's relish for controversy, agreed with her. He wrote of a younger brother: 'Linky, who has been sitting up all night a great deal lately, tried to explain to his mother and sisters that they were (so far as they differed from him) ignorant and perverse or both. Such a waste of tissue!'

Driven to bed only by exhaustion, the Cecil children could be roused only by hunger. The Latin motto of their heraldic arms, *'Sero sed serio'* or 'Late but in earnest,' was an injunction which they found no difficulty in obeying. Resisting the example of the first Lord Burghley, who at Cambridge had had himself called by the college bellringer at four o'clock each morning, the family breakfasted late. Sometimes the table was already being laid for lunch as the last of them appeared. Not even the eldest son, James, who grew up into a statesman of precise and orderly habits, was immune from sloth. 'We started at 7 a.m.,' Lady Salisbury wrote to her husband during a summer holiday in France, 'and Jim was one of the party !!!!!!!! I don't expect you to believe this but it is true.'

> It really was a demoralizing house [Eleanor recalled half a century later]. I naturally wake early – and at home I used to get up well before breakfast and read or draw in that time – (I have sketched a January sunrise outdoors with the colours freezing on the palate!)

Hatfield cured all that nonsense! I was too weak minded to stand against the current – and took to more and more late morning hours – also the late dinners almost compelled them. Dinner generally well after 8.30 and quite often lasting till nearly 10 o'clock. I fancy her Ladyship being considerably deaf in those latter years liked having people sitting close by and was in no hurry to break up. It was no doubt very bad for all our digestions – one went on nibbling things just to fill up the time – and went to bed very tired and woke up the same.

'Eat and dawdle, dawdle and eat,' was how the wife of a visiting ambassador described their daily routine. Eleanor left a trenchant account of its effect on nerves and stomach:

> Hatfield life was not easy or healthy [she told Gilbert Murray], too much strain and incessant talk and argument and appalling hours for meals and far too much food of rich and not too safe quality. . . . Wartime starvation would have halved their doctors' bills. They were forever talking about their digestion and taking their temperatures.

Unlike many great Victorian ladies, Lady Salisbury had acquired a thorough knowledge of household management. She wrote at a time when the newspapers were full of a railway murder: 'How foolish the police are to be hunting all the chemists' shops for the home of the pestle. Don't they know that in every large kitchen much heavier pestles are used than in chemists' shops!' But in spite of her daily instructions to the chef, what eventually appeared in the dining-room was less wholesome than it looked and often served in worn or cracked china. Standards of cleanliness, ventilation and refrigeration were far from exacting in the mansions of nineteenth-century England and not always detected as the cause of the bilious attacks and infectious fevers that regularly laid low their inhabitants. Salisbury himself may have added to the headaches that afflicted his family by insisting on a minimum room temperature of 60 degrees Fahrenheit. A relic of his sickly youth, it prompted his private secretary to make sure that even Balmoral conformed to his whim when, as Prime Minister, he travelled reluctantly to that glacial royal residence on official business.

The other houses which Salisbury either owned or occupied were equally destructive of health. As Prime Minister, it is true, he declined to live at No. 10 Downing Street, the drains of which were notoriously capricious. But his own London house in Arlington Street, overlooking Green Park, was hardly more salubrious. 'It seems to me absolutely without fresh air,' his son Bob wrote, 'the same air I think as was originally put into it when it was built. No wonder Tim looks so unhealthy and Linky is bloodless.'

Soon after the end of the Franco–Prussian war of 1870, Salisbury bought a holiday house on the cliffs at Puys, near Dieppe, where the family spent part of the summer each year for the next quarter of a century. He thought it good for the children to get away from the luxury of Hatfield, but may have exaggerated the simplicity of Chalet Cecil. Although the silver tea service gave way to plebian japanned ware and Dr Coppini, the boys' French tutor, was shocked to see their father waiting on himself at lunch, the weekly household bills came to £84. Nor did a regard for economy come easily to a son of sixteen who from Puys one August wired the newly-appointed Prime Minister: 'Have lost fifty pound note have telegraphed to wherever I think may have lost it have five pounds what shall I do.' But particularly when in office, Salisbury appreciated the bracing climate and privacy of a foreign resort only a few hours from London; he even revived his boyhood interest in botany and wandered among the rocks gathering a collection of seaweeds.

Lady Salisbury's pleasure was marred by the moral imperfections of the French people. 'Dirty, brutal, liars and cheats almost without exception,' she wrote, '*jus de fripons* I call them. Almost all radicals and freethinkers, of course.' And on reading Anatole France's newly-published Dreyfusard novel, *L'Anneau d'améthyste*, she wished there could be a bowdlerized edition for England, 'as it is so tiresome to wade through filth to get so wonderful a picture of France at this moment'. She was especially irritated by the bright 'Good morning' with which Coppini, in his hopelessly Gallic way, announced his presence each day, a greeting to which her husband alone responded. She put up with such inconveniences, however, as long as she could enjoy her favourite pastime of bathing:

> It is blowing a fierce gale [she reported one summer]. It is very cold and the noise is tremendous. We have lighted the *calorifière* and are going to bar the windows. All the bells have stopped. . . . I console myself by stepping lightly into the sea, hand in hand with Auguste, the *baigneur*.

Yet somehow the children, and in time their young wives, seemed to find neither health nor spirits amid the stiff Channel breezes. It was not only the physical discomfort of windows that did not fit, doors too large for small rooms and a stove that sent a nasty smell through the house. Two daughters-in-law summoned to Puys each fell victim to the *malaise* which had affected a third, Eleanor Cecil, at Hatfield. 'I have had to battle with several attacks of Puys temper and I am quite aware I get very odious,' wrote one. 'I know I hated it,' wrote the other. 'House very crowded, and what with liver and crossness, it got on my nerves and I was often on the point of tears for no reason whatsoever.'

Perhaps Lady Salisbury, for all her virtues, was an unwitting cause of tension. It is doubtful whether the man to whom she had been married in 1857 would ever have shed his shyness and acquired the temperament necessary for high political office without the confidence she inspired in him. The wife of her eldest son, in spite of what she had endured at Puys, wrote in extreme old age:

> The older I grow the more remarkable I think her; and the more one realises the part she played, and enabled him to play in life, by her unhesitating acceptance of all responsibilities and putting the importance of his work before everything . . . a great woman, the greatest one, I think, that I have known in my life.

Dedication to her husband, however, could bear oppressively on others. Because Salisbury liked his family to be perpetually about him, even after they had embarked on their own careers, the unmarried children continued to live permanently at Hatfield; and after marriage, the sons were expected to bring their brides into residence there for several months each year and to accompany their parents for part of each summer holiday in France. Even during the crowded London season from May to July they were obliged to dine at Arlington Street as often as required. One evening the eldest of Salisbury's sons and his wife, having arranged a rare visit to the opera, dutifully cancelled their plans on hearing that Lord and Lady Salisbury would otherwise be alone: they sat down fourteen to dinner. In retrospect the demands of the parents were not resented. 'I can hardly bear to go to Arlington Street,' Eleanor Cecil wrote after Lady Salisbury's death in 1899, 'where I never went for anyone but her – and she the one redeeming bright spot in that gloomy house. However close they sit, it always seems to me as if there were an empty chair.' Another daughter-in-law described Georgina Salisbury as 'a rushing mighty wind in the house'. Such a phenomenon can be stimulating but it does not make for peace of mind.

At Hatfield an abundance of bedrooms and sitting-rooms permitted both repose and retreat, even when the whole family gathered under the same roof; at Puys life could hardly fail to be restless and restrictive. Not until 1895 did Salisbury sell the Chalet Cecil. In the meantime, having rejected several villas near Florence which he thought too reminiscent of St John's Wood, he bought some land above Beaulieu, a few miles from Monte Carlo, and on it built a spacious and comfortable house. Both climate and view enchanted him, and La Bastide, as the property was called, brought much happiness to his last years. On days when the park at Hatfield was shrouded in clinging mist he would wish himself by the Mediterranean and wonder that such an emotion as patriotism could exist.

The acquisition of La Bastide did not end the worry and disappointment of holiday houses. On taking office in 1895 for the third time as Prime Minister and Foreign Secretary, Salisbury felt that the South of France was too remote from London in time of crisis. By chance his old Eton friend Lord Dufferin wished to resign his sinecure office of Lord Warden of the Cinque Ports as he could no longer afford the £700 a year which it cost to maintain the official residence, Walmer Castle. Untroubled by financial cares, Salisbury thought that a house overlooking the English Channel near Dover, yet only two hours from London by train would provide just such a haven as he needed. He therefore sought the Queen's permission to succeed Dufferin and prepared to put the castle in order.

It was a daunting experience. Little had been renovated since Britain's greatest soldier died there in 1852.

> 'I think I shall hate it [Lady Salisbury wrote]. Tinsel picturesqueness and false sentiment about the old Duke of Wellington! I have no sympathy with either and shall lock up the relics and use the room. The Queen says it is the most uncomfortable house she ever was in, and I have no doubt she is right.

Although she found the sea bathing even more invigorating than at Puys, her opinion of Walmer came to coincide exactly with that of her Sovereign. Again and again she complained of its mephitic drains. 'I never think those very old places wholesome,' her daughter Gwendolen added, 'families of microbes of ancient descent still flourishing in the homes of their medieval ancestors.' The family nevertheless continued to use the house until Lady Salisbury had a slight stroke there in the summer of 1899, dying at Hatfield later that year.*

For all but the last two years of her life, Lady Salisbury was a woman of inexhaustible energy and robust health. She therefore found it particularly provoking that neither her husband nor her children should ever be quite free from minor ailments. Here is Linky, aged fifteen, writing to Bob, five years his senior, from the French Riviera:

* The next occupant of Walmer was Lord Curzon of Kedleston, who accepted the office of Lord Warden on Salisbury's death in 1903. His experience was even unhappier. In September 1904, on leave from India between his two terms as Viceroy, he accompanied his wife there for a holiday. She almost immediately fell gravely ill, just survived a desperate struggle and, her health shattered, died less than two years later in London. Curzon blamed Walmer – 'that charnel house, unfit for human habitation' – and resigned as Lord Warden in November 1904. Sir Winston Churchill never used the residence during his twenty-five years as Lord Warden; but his successor Sir Robert Menzies, the former Prime Minister of Australia, likes the castle well enough to spend the summer months there as often as he can.

The family on a pleasure trip is quite the comicest sight yet seen. My father has got a cold, so has Jem (this last also suffers if the sun is too hot). I had a cold and now my stomach is irremediably out. Nigs is also more or less ill. Tim is sleepy and is scarcely thawed after the cold weather which as you know characterizes the littoral of the Mediterranean from the marble palaces of Genoa to the palm trees of Marseilles, except perhaps the southern-facing bays of Mentone or the Mammon-ridden slopes of Monte Carlo (Good, I think a Macaulay or Carlylese style about it, eh?) My mother's energy, strange to say, is unquenched and unquenchable.

Lady Salisbury's attitude to illness was devoted sympathy for two days, expectations of recovery the third, and indignation if the sufferer was not up and about on the fourth. Her children, by contrast, free from the rough and ready treatment of school doctors and matrons, were hauntingly preoccupied with their symptoms. 'My feverish attack was quite interesting,' Tim writes from Rome, 'very slight, never reaching more than 100½ . . .' Linky revels in an epidemic of influenza: 'Quinine flows in torrents. We take another teaspoonful for auld lang syne. Some of us are *six*-grain men.' Maud describes Hatfield as 'more or less of a hospital for the last few days'. And Cousin Arthur, having in the past year succeeded his Uncle Robert as Prime Minister, is not too busy to write from 10 Downing Street: 'Try spraying your nose freely with Dr Dobell's Solution. It is antiseptic and innocuous.'

Not all the young Cecils were as thoughtful as Balfour when affliction struck.

Jem, too [Bob wrote scornfully of his eldest brother one winter], has very nearly got a sore throat or rather, to be quite accurate, has a feeling which might develop into a soreness on one side of his throat. He is, I am glad to say, taking great care. It is hoped he may be well enough to be moved in the middle of the day tomorrow as far as Hatfield.

Yet it was Bob who displayed the most sustained hypochondria of any. 'I'm sure I am going to have a bad illness,' he would complain, 'for I feel so well.' With brisk North Country common sense his wife made affectionate fun of his failing. She once announced: 'Bob has had a terrible night. He got no more than eight hours' sleep.' He tried to cure himself of this morbid strain, but without success. A graze to a finger, a tiny cold in the left nostril, a restless stomach: each was recorded at comforting length. He lived to be ninety-four. Of his six brothers and sisters, all martyrs to thermometer and medicine-chest, one other survived into her nineties and three were octogenarians.

45

'And this is Nigs,' Lady Salisbury would say, 'the stupidest and cleanest of my sons.' A visitor later observed that in any other family the boy would have been thought very clever and rather dirty. It was an impression that the young Cecils often made on strangers. Here is the testimony of Lady Frances Balfour, meeting Nigs and Linky for the first time as she accompanied Lady Salisbury from Hatfield to London:

> At the last minute, two boys tumbled into the carriage, bareheaded, dressed in blue suits with red sashes. Both were completely covered from head to heel in earth, both were talking at the top of their voices. No one was listening, their mother cast an eye on them and said 'I suppose you have been down a rabbit hole.'

It was not that their parents disregarded the virtues of hygiene; by the end of the century they had installed no fewer than twelve bathrooms at Hatfield, an unusual profusion by Victorian standards. But in their scale of values, cleanliness ranked nowhere near godliness. Lady Salisbury herself was always scrupulous in her person. Collar, cuffs and petticoats, all changed daily, glowed with freshness; and on being asked the secret of a complexion that refused to fade with the years, she would reply: 'Yellow soap and lots of cold water.' Yet she cared nothing for the glass of fashion. The diarist Augustus Hare, invited to a garden-party at Hatfield, was shocked at her welcoming the royal family dressed in a large, rough, straw bonnet. During another grand entertainment, as she made her curtsey to the Prince of Wales, her gorgeous toilette was seen to be completed by grey woollen stockings and outdoor shoes. That master of haberdashery the future King Edward VII was once rude enough to say: 'Lady Salisbury, I believe I have seen that gown before.' She replied briskly: 'Yes, Sir, and you will see it very often again.'

Her husband combined an aristocratic indifference to his appearance – 'slovenly and sloppetty', a Cabinet colleague called it – with a forgetfulness that went back to Eton days. 'His hat is generally reported as missing once in every forty-eight hours,' his tutor used to wail. Mature years brought no improvement. At Monte Carlo in 1886 he was refused admittance to the casino because of his shabby suit. And at the end of his life, having forgotten to take his skull-cap to church one Sunday and finding it draughty, he sensibly pulled off a grey woollen glove and balanced it on top of his head for the rest of the service. His sartorial whims naturally incurred the humourless disapproval of the Prince of Wales. As Prime Minister, Lady Salisbury wrote, her husband once went to the Palace 'in a judicious mixture of two uniforms and nearly caused the death of the Heir to the Crown from consternation'. Salisbury's apology to the Prince for having put on the wrong sort of trousers was masterly: 'It was a dark morning and I am afraid that my mind must have been occupied by some subject of less importance.'

The young Cecils, their childhood untidiness rarely noticed and never rebuked, grew up to share their parents' dislike for finery. Gwendolen, having left behind a coat when staying with a married sister, wrote to explain how it could be identified: 'It looks like a man's till you put it on and see its shape, light brown with a velvet collar and a pervading shabbiness.' Nigs, Financial Adviser to the Egyptian Government, would return from an audience of the Khedive, the black skirts of his regulation frock coat emerging from beneath a short covert coat. (It was in such array that he once reproved his colleague, Ronald Storrs, for the supposed solecism of wearing a blue shirt with a brown suit. The offender bowed low and said: 'I stand rebuked by the best-dressed man in Egypt.') Some French visitors to the recently elected House of Commons in 1906 were disappointed by the unrevolutionary appearance of the Parliamentary Labour Party until Bob Cecil strode in to take his seat on the Conservative benches. '*Ah*,' they exclaimed with relief, '*voilà enfin le vrai ouvrier!*' And an obituarist of his brother William, the bishop, wrote affectionately that 'there were often some grains of earth lurking in the crannies of his picturesque, disordered garments'.

Such negligence reflected the contempt for luxury which Lord and Lady Salisbury instilled in their children. Hatfield was a palace; but the austerity of Salisbury's dressing-room was matched by that of his wife's bedroom which throughout her life never contained a sofa. The food was rich and plentiful, as it had to be in a house where entertainment was a political obligation; but it was little regarded and hardly ever discussed. One of the few references to the subject in family letters is a disparaging comment by Bob on the French cooking at his parents' house in Arlington Street: 'I can never even guess what the entrées mean on paper – and I hate them all. Stupid little game tartlets and truffles. Bah! Give me good Roast and Boiled – but chiefly Roast.' A visitor to Hatfield recalls how Jim, helping himself to *sole caprice*, chanced to take only some slices of banana. 'Strange fish,' he murmured incuriously and went on munching. His sister Gwendolen showed even less interest in food. 'You never know what she will do with it,' a hostess complained, 'eat it, or play spillikins, or make a mud pie – or simply leave it.' Most of them, it is true, strenuously opposed the prohibition movement; but that sprang less from a love of alcohol than from a horror of any intrusion upon personal liberty. The minutes of the Oxford Canning Club record that as an undergraduate the future Bishop of Exeter declared amid approving cheers that 'he had never felt any inclination to get drunk, but if he was told not to do so, he would not answer for the result'. It remained a lifelong Cecilian creed.

From their earliest years the children were taught that wealth was a trust; that it was wrong to squander money on their own pleasure or convenience; that, in addition to whatever public or social service was demanded by their position in life, at least one-seventh of their income must be given to charity. Well into old age they would scarcely ever travel first-class by railway, even on long journeys. 'A night of conflict in the train with a Frenchwoman on the perennial window question,' Gwendolen told her sister, 'ending in my sleeping in the corridor.' As the wife of a promising barrister in his mid-twenties, Nelly never went to a dressmaker and seldom bought a hat. When the briefs began to pour in six years later, she was concerned to note that only £513 had been given to charity during 1896. 'Bad,' she wrote, 'not near enough – only a little over the legal amount.' In her household accounts for that year the corresponding figure under 'amusements' is £115, of which £43 had been spent on buying bicycles. All the young Cecils enjoyed holidays on wheels, which at least relieved them for a week or two from the tensions of Puys. Their mother disapproved. 'Insane', was her bleak comment.

There was one comfort which the family never lacked: an abundance of domestic servants. Nigs, aged fifteen, sent this telegram to his father from Eton in mid-December 1882: 'Shall come late in afternoon of Thursday send Smith down to pack my things as usual please.' William, or Fish as he was known, had an establishment of six in the modest house he occupied as Rector of Hatfield. And although Bob and Nelly wondered in the early days of their marriage whether £20 a year was not too much to pay a cook, their wages bill for a London house in 1896 was £264. As by then a manservant earned about £50, a cook £30 and a housemaid £20, their staff must have numbered at least half a dozen.

Yet they could be a troublesome lot. Maud, aged eighteen, complained shyly to an aunt that 'the menservants will sit all day just outside the W., which is a great trial to my modesty'. Linky worried about an incestuous gardener who had married successively a mother and daughter in order to enjoy their income. And years later Gwendolen describes a clash of temperament in the spinster house she occupied in the park at Hatfield:

> I am sorry to say that my new maid . . . is already at loggerheads with the parlourmaid. I have denounced them collectively and separately and they are now indulging in the luxuries of sleepless nights, trembling in the knees and silent tears. They haunt the house with swollen eyelids and martyred expression of countenance, and I long to break both their heads with the poker.

A post-war generation that has learnt, sometimes unwillingly, to clean and cook and carry for itself may feel tempted to look back upon the Victorian way of life with impatience, indignation or scorn. Conditions of servitude could be appalling, particularly in the pinched establishments of the struggling middle classes. But those who took service in huge country houses like Hatfield could expect regular advancement; and at every stage of their ascent through the hierarchy, from pantry boy to butler or from kitchen maid to housekeeper, they found themselves in a society more secure and convivial than any they had known in crowded cottage or industrial slum.

The Cecils were aware that a dependence on the labours of others could be morally enervating.

Its danger [Alice Salisbury, the Prime Minister's daughter-in-law, wrote in an unpublished memoir towards the end of her life] lay in the sheltered conditions, outside so many of the sorrows and anxieties of the common lot and therefore easily degenerating into selfish ease if not held up by a sense of responsibility and public duty. But when the question of 'Who is my neighbour?' was answered with practical knowledge and help, the sense of personal obligation and relation between a man and those who toiled on his estate was a beautiful thing and blessed them both. The days of the old forms of help are past; with the better conditions and the provision of social services by the State they are not needed. But the feelings of friendship and interdependence and sympathy which lay at the root of them belong to the foundations of English life and can survive under all circumstances and changes if the spirit that animated them remains a living thing.

The theme will be examined and developed in later chapters. Here we may pause only to note the warmth and abundance of Hatfield hospitality, particularly on such ritual occasions as the annual tenants' dinner held in the marble hall. Lord Salisbury, his Garter riband and star more carefully adjusted than for any royal levée or drawing-room, would in the course of the evening make a speech that itself became an institution. Without discernible shyness he would touch as easily on farming as on politics, the whole discourse permeated by a note of intimacy, not to mention a pungent smell of roast beef and beer and human beings. Paternalism had yet to become a term of reproach.

Family celebrations embraced landowner and labourer alike. Here is young George Curzon at Hatfield in 1882, a guest for the coming-of-age of the eldest son and heir:

Everything was done in princely style; hundreds of tenants, kids and paupers were fed from day to day. Jim was receiving incessant

49

deputations and presents and making innumerable modest and appropriate speeches. Every night there was a sphere; 150 swells coming down in a special from London for the principal one. There were athletic sports . . . fireworks and every variety of entertainment. Beer flowed like water. . . . The pen of a Disraeli might fittingly have been employed to immortalise the week.

Such events did not always run as smoothly when held on remoter parts of the Cecil domain. The final phase of Jim's coming-of-age celebrations took place at Cranborne, the village in the West Country from which he took his courtesy title. The family arrived there at the end of October to find that a parsimonious agent had provided only a single round of beef to feed 170 Dorset farmers, and a very thin tent in which to eat it. Nor had he remembered to order lamps. Lady Salisbury swept into action. Imperiously taking it on herself to occupy the school, she gave the children a week's holiday, moved in tables, loaded them with an abundance of food and drink, and even had the shops in the market town of Salisbury opened up on a Sunday so that she could buy enough lamps. The dinner was followed by a ball that included a jolly dance called the stamp-on-your-feet. It might have taken its name from Lady Salisbury herself.

The Cecils made no secret of preferring their own company to anybody else's and on all but intimate family occasions regarded the demands of entertainment as a burden. For Lord Salisbury, all public appearances were a penance. He loathed being recognized and even more being complimented. When an ardent admirer pressed him into signing a photograph of himself, he reacted by writing his name across the face. Travelling by train to Scotland in 1884 to deliver an important speech, he found a large crowd awaiting him at Carlisle. He refused so much as to put his head out of the window, but retreated to the farthest corner of the carriage where he sat with a ghastly grin, touching his shabby old wideawake hat. In the following year, again going north to receive the Queen's commission to form a new government, he concealed himself in a third-class carriage to avoid the attentions of journalists and others. Even in the security of Hatfield he once so resented being asked to show himself and to say a few words to a group of Conservative voters from his eldest son's constituency that he fled to London: returning to his home that evening he ran into them at Hatfield Station and was very cross.

Neither as landowner nor statesman, however, could he entirely escape the obligations of entertaining neighbours and political followers. At least every other year there was a grand ball at Hatfield for the County, with two bands and a member of the royal family. They were staid affairs, with few guests under the age of forty. One old lady arrived bearing her mother's apologies at having had to miss her first Hatfield ball for fifty years. Salisbury bore it all stoically. 'The courtesy with which he greeted his guests was unfailing,' wrote Gwendolen, 'though rendered a trifle impersonal by his constant incapacity to identify them.' Quite early in the evening he would slip away to his study. He found even less pleasure in the evening receptions which Lady Salisbury felt it her duty to give in London during the parliamentary session: the family called them 'packs'. When a niece inquired of the Prime Minister whether she should present herself at Arlington Street that evening, he replied: 'Yes, if you enjoy the vexation of the Conservative Party tramping on your toes.' He resented all casual intrusion. An ingenious footman at the London house once tried to anticipate his master's wishes by turning away a caller with the explanation that his Lordship received only Dukes and Cabinet ministers. As the visitor happened to be both, this bold invention proved fruitless.

Salisbury's Cabinet colleagues, aware of the shyness and short-sightedness that made social gatherings a penance for him, were sparing with their invitations. But when an over-zealous private secretary of Balfour's once demanded his presence as guest of honour at a dinner for Conservative supporters, the Prime Minister's conscience stirred. He astounded his embarrassed host not only by accepting but also by asking for a list of the other guests together with their biographical details. All to whom he spoke were enchanted by his affability and knowledge of their particular interests. Just before the party broke up, he beckoned to the private secretary : 'I think I have done them all. But there is someone I have not identified who, you said, made mustard.' The elusive manufacturer was found and led up to receive the patriarchal blessing.

As Foreign Secretary and later Prime Minister, with a huge country house barely twenty miles from London, Salisbury was often called upon to entertain State visitors. 'This summer is remarkable for an incessant plague of rain and Royalties,' he wrote to his eldest son on 13 July 1879. 'They say the former is to cease this week. The latter, I am sorry to say, will not be over before the thirtieth.' Even when he was out of office, invaders continued to outrage his privacy. 'The facility of locomotion,' he complained in a letter to Lord Lytton twelve years later, 'adds to the sorrows of human life in the shape of German Emperors and Princes of Naples. It is a great comfort to me to think that M. Carnot [the then President of the French Republic] has not got an heir apparent.' The entertainment of the Kaiser had to be planned on a characteristically grandiose scale. He, his wife and a vast suite occupied the east wing; the Prince and Princess of Wales were lodged in the west wing, their two daughters squeezed into a single room. The younger members of the Cecil family gave up their beds and were boarded out in houses on the estate. Sixty sat down to dine. As a token of gratitude the German Emperor later sent his hosts a full-length portrait of himself wearing the uniform of a British admiral.

The visit of Nasr-ed-Din, Shah of Persia, left few fragrant memories at Hatfield. To ensure the comfort of the Shah's entourage, the bedrooms on two floors of the house were filled with improvised oriental furniture. Lady Salisbury's thoughtfulness went unappreciated; her guests insisted on passing the night curled up in ascending tiers on the staircase leading to their Sovereign's door. Here is Augustus Hare's account of the Shah's endearing mannerisms:

> He is a true Eastern potentate in his consideration for himself and himself only: is most unconcernedly late whenever he chooses: utterly ignores every one he does not want to speak to: amuses himself with monkeyish and often dirty tricks: sacrifices a cock to the rising sun, and wipes his wet hands on the coat-tails of the gentleman next to him without compunction. He expressed his wonder that Lord Salisbury did not take a new wife, though he gave Lady Salisbury a magnificent jewelled order. He knows no English and very few words of French, but when the Baroness Coutts, as the great benefactress of her country, was presented to him by the Prince of Wales, he looked in her face and exclaimed, 'Quelle horreur!'

Not even La Bastide, the family retreat on the French Riviera, was secure from the sudden descent of princes and princelings. An inundation of these inconsiderate beings in the spring of 1897 provoked Salisbury into coining a variation of the joke he had made about them nearly twenty years before. 'All well here,' he wrote to Linky. 'The mosquitoes have not come yet: the Royalties have, but they only buzz by day.' King of the Belgians, Duchess of Albany, Princess of Bulgaria, Duke of Cambridge: the gilded line seemed interminable. Interest quickened at the prospect of the Prince of Montenegro who failed however to live up to Lady Salisbury's illusions: 'We all expected a grand brigand sort of man, but he was mild and looked like an elderly butler out of place.' That was the tone of amused detachment in which the Cecils usually referred to royal families and their foibles. Here is Jim Cranborne, the most gentle and chivalrous of all the children, describing an expedition to see an Alpine glacier with the well-nourished Duchess of Teck, mother of Queen Mary: 'Of course, qua Royalty, she goes first, and where she can go we may safely follow: neither is there any danger because no crevasse is large enough to swallow her up.'

Queen Victoria alone won their genuine respect, not to say reverence.

During his long years as Prime Minister, Salisbury was occasionally exasperated by the meticulous exercise of the royal prerogative that added considerably to his labours. His conduct of business, however, was governed by the advice of Burghley to his son Robert three centuries before: always to give the Queen his best counsel, as was his duty, but never to try to prevail over her own better judgement, so great were her knowledge of men and her experience of affairs. The regard was mutual. Whenever Queen Victoria spent a few weeks of spring sunshine at Cimiez, as was her habit towards the end of her life, she would invariably drive over to La Bastide for tea, often without warning. There would be a frenzied changing of clothes, tidying of the drawing-room and cutting of bread and butter: but none of the annoyance that greeted the irruption of the lesser royals. 'It is easy to see that she is very fond of him,' a spectator of one such tea party noted. 'Indeed I never saw two people get on better, their polished manners and deference to and esteem for each other were a delightful sight and one not readily to be forgotten.' The children shared their parents' high regard for the Queen and cherished it for years to come. On one of her last public appearances in London, Bob, by now a well-established barrister in his mid-thirties, leapt to the top of some railings to demonstrate his loyalty: 'I waved my hat violently and cheered till emotion stopped me. . . . Railings very high and rather spiky. But the patriot scorns his boots.'

The Cecils extended no such indulgence to her eldest son, the Prince of Wales, who in 1901 succeeded to the throne as King Edward VII. Almost alone of the great country houses of England, Hatfield was barred to him except on official occasions such as the visit of the German Emperor. Certainly there could be no question of his bringing his current paramour, with all the careful selection of fellow guests and tactful allocation of bedrooms that such excursions demanded. When he invited himself to lunch at La Bastide in April 1896, he infuriated the family by staying on until almost evening. 'Imagine going twenty-four hours' journey to get *that* in the end,' was Nelly's scathing comment. They thought him trivial of mind and deficient in morals, but recognized that his mother must bear some of the blame by denying him any work of responsibility. Bob passed on a conundrum he had heard from Lord Cowper: 'Why is the Queen like the weather? Because she reigns and reigns and reigns and never gives the poor son any chance.' In the opinion of the Cecils, the long eclipse proved fatal, and they could never take the King quite seriously. In 1905 he invited Jim, by now fourth Marquess of Salisbury and a member of Arthur Balfour's Cabinet, to accompany him on board the Royal Yacht *Victoria and Albert* for a Mediterranean cruise:

The King [Jim wrote to his brother-in-law, Lord Selborne] with all the little peculiarities about ribands and tailoring which we know, seems to have an intelligence which was stunted by these things early in life and might have flourished but for that. He evidently loves to play a part in politics and plays it rather well, although he seems to have the exaggeration of inexperienced youth.

King Edward was then in his sixty-fourth year, Jim twenty years his junior.

Together with many advantages, the Prime Minister burdened his sons with one handicap. By having them educated at Hatfield until they were twelve or thirteen, Salisbury protected them from the homesickness and cruelty of his own childhood. He nevertheless decided that they should then be sent away to Eton, in spite of the unhappy memories that haunted him to the end of his life. The boys could hardly have been worse prepared for the discipline, athleticism and narrow curriculum of a Victorian public school. Brought up as men, they found themselves for the first time in a world whose values were largely adolescent if not puerile. A nineteenth-century Eton master was not being altogether ironical when he called his memoirs *Seventy Years among Savages*. In such a society of totem and taboo, even the virtues of the Cecils became embarrassments. They had been taught always to tell the truth and to look without desire on material things. They were well read and lively minded and argumentative. They knew more of political and diplomatic manoeuvre than most men of mature years and said so. They believed in personal liberty.

To these suspicious attributes they added more positive faults. In the Cecil household, a cousin noted, ideas of what was important and what was not differed a great deal from those of most other families, and the children could be as noisy, as dirty and as objectionable as nature had made them without fear of rebuke. Nor did they allow either their days or their nights to be governed by the tyranny of the clock. Years later, as they were beginning to make their mark in life, someone made a complimentary remark about them to old Bishop Claughton of St Albans, who had watched them grow up. 'Yes,' he replied grimly, 'it is surprising that Salisbury's sons have turned out so well.'

By the standards of Hatfield, Eton could not fail to be more disagreeable in every way. Even the friendship of other boys, which many would have welcomed, was for them no improvement on that of their brothers. They were simply not interested in extending their social horizons. The French tutor in the holidays at Puys had been almost ignored by his charges. '*Je me trouvais un animal fort intéressant à étudier,*' he wrote, '*et j'étais presque froissé de cette profonde indifférence.*'

Yet another circumstance that set them apart from their contemporaries was an inherited lack of enthusiasm for almost all athletic pursuits. They were of course taught to ride but soon switched their allegiance to the less capricious bicycle (although Jim in his youth and Linky in middle age enjoyed a day's foxhunting). Their father, however, cared nothing for the traditional pursuits of a country gentleman and once confessed that it had taken him years to know the difference between a horse and a cow. He dutifully preserved pheasants for the entertainment of his Hertfordshire neighbours, but unlike most great landowners had no sporting estates in Scotland. When Queen Victoria asked him to stay at Balmoral, her private secretary complained that 'he positively refused to admire the prospect or the deer'. As his weight increased, his only outdoor exercise was to ride a tricycle along specially constructed asphalt paths in the park at Hatfield; a footman would accompany him to push the machine uphill, leaping on to the back axle for the descent. Eventually he could do little more than play an occasional game of billiards (when he so far forgot himself on missing a shot as to exclaim 'Bulgaria!') or walk solemnly up and down the rooms at Hatfield, his hand resting on the head of his huge dog Pharaoh. Unlike Lady Salisbury, who amused the Court by 'larking off to the Derby', he shunned horse-racing and once complained at the postponement of important political negotiations 'because Devonshire is obliged to go to Newmarket to ascertain whether one quadruped can run a little faster than another'. That again was the Cecil children's loss; for however much frowned on by the Eton authorities, stable gossip has always been a passport to conviviality. Most serious of all the gaps in a Hatfield education, the boys were not taught to play football and cricket, an almost essential qualification for public-school prestige.

The Cecils never forgot their years at Eton: but their memories lacked any trace of that sentimental happiness with which so many contemporaries recalled the past. They could not claim to have been ill-used. As each left Hatfield for the first time, he was told: 'If you should ever be in danger of a flogging, take the train home immediately.' At no time did they need to invoke parental protection. But they suffered in other, more obscure ways. Their letters from the damp Thames valley dwell mournfully on heavy colds and twinges of rheumatism, on scarlet fever and fatigue. Even when the *malaise* lifted, they found the companionship uninspiring, the routine oppressive, the teaching tedious and futile. They were taught hardly any English literature or history (although Bob did manage to emulate his father's interest in chemistry by poisoning himself with chlorine); and in spite of a largely classical curriculum, they left Eton quite unable to read the easiest Latin or Greek authors for pleasure.

I should not grudge all the time I spent on classics [one of them wrote], if in learning, or rather not learning, them I had learnt how to work; but that is just what we were not taught. At best we were taught how to cram but never how to extract knowledge and pack it neatly away in the mind for future reference.

Only one of the Prime Minister's children retained enough confidence in Eton to send his own sons there: Jim, the least unconventional of the family. About 1911 his brother Bob drove down to see the school and its latest generation of little victims, his first visit since he had himself been a boy there thirty years before. 'I found where my name was cut in the panelling of Upper School,' he told his wife, 'and thought it all very pretty and that the schoolrooms would never be passed by any Board of Education and ate a very unwholesome tea.' That was perhaps the least dyspeptic of his comments. 'Anything is better than Eton,' he replied when told that another nephew was destined for a rival estab-lishment, Winchester College. The disparagement continued even into old age. 'They seem now to have a system by which the house master directs some of the boys to beat the others,' he reported to his wife in 1934. 'Schoolmasters are very German and always wrong.' He found a sympathetic audience in his two sisters. Gwendolen declared herself unable to decide whether schoolmastering or money-making had the more narrowing influence. Maud, married to Lord Selborne, British High Commissioner in South Africa, tried in vain to have one of her sons educated there but was obliged to send him back to England. 'If his foolish father could only shake off antiquated superstitions,' she wrote, 'and believe that salvation is possible even to people who haven't been to public schools.'

Linky alone allowed criticism of Eton to stray beyond the pages of family letters. In 1929, as one of the leading Churchmen of his day, Lord Hugh Cecil, MP, publicly denounced Eton's Erastian approach to the teaching of Christianity. 'Worship', he claimed, 'becomes going to school chapel and confirmation an event in school life.' The Head Master,* having offered a convincing defence of his methods of instruc-tion, added: 'I still think it curiously cheap to single out your own school as a typical example of futile religion.' The dispute, inflamed by accu-sations of bad faith, might well have left a permanent gulf between Linky and Eton but for an ironic twist of fate seventeen years later. Since the school is a royal foundation, it fell to the Prime Minister of

* He was Dr Cyril Alington (1872–1955), later Dean of Durham and the father of Lady Douglas-Home.

the day to nominate a successor to Montague Rhodes James as Provost of Eton. The office resembles that of dean of a cathedral and is concerned with the religious rather than with the academic life of the school. Stanley Baldwin, most fervent of Harrovians, chose Hugh Cecil.

How the new Provost interpreted his duties will be told in a later chapter. But those who doubted whether a loyal heart lay concealed behind his querulous manner soon had their fears dispelled. He petitioned the Archbishop of Canterbury with a request that the founder of Eton, King Henry VI, should after five centuries of neglect receive official veneration from the Church of England.

4

James, fourth Marquess of
Salisbury
1861-1947

James, eldest son of third Marquess of Salisbury. Bore the courtesy title of Viscount Cranborne until succeeding his father as fourth Marquess of Salisbury in 1903. Known to his family and friends as Jim or Jem.

Born 23 October 1861. Educated at Eton and University College, Oxford. Conservative MP for Darwen 1885–92 and for Rochester 1893–1903. Under-Secretary of State for Foreign Affairs 1900–03. Lord Privy Seal 1903–5. President of the Board of Trade 1905. Lord President of the Council 1922–4. Chancellor of the Duchy of Lancaster 1922–3. Lord Privy Seal 1924–9. Leader of the Conservatives in the House of Lords 1925–31. Privy Counsellor 1903. Knight of the Garter 1917. Served in South African War and in the First World War.

Married 17 May 1887 Lady Alice Gore, second daughter of the fifth Earl of Arran. She died 5 February 1955.

Lord and Lady Salisbury had four children. Robert (1893–1972), known as Bobbety, bore the courtesy title of Viscount Cranborne, a style he retained even after being summoned to the House of Lords in 1941 as Baron Cecil of Essendon, one of his father's lesser titles. He succeeded his father as fifth Marquess of Salisbury in 1947. Conservative MP, 1929–41. Held high office in several governments. Knight of the Garter 1946. David (1902–) was Goldsmiths' Professor of English Literature, Oxford University 1948–69 and appointed a Companion of Honour 1949. Beatrice (1891–) married 1913 fourth Baron Harlech. Mary (1895–) married 1917 tenth Duke of Devonshire.

Lord Salisbury died 4 April 1947.

The career of James, fourth Marquess of Salisbury, appears at first sight to be of paralysing predictability. Eton and Oxford; the local Militia; a serene marriage; the House of Commons at twenty-four, followed by long years of ungrudging service as his father's political aide-de-camp and administrator of the family estates; junior office necessarily delayed until his fortieth year, but a Cabinet post following close on its heels; succession to a seat in the House of Lords; an impregnable reputation for all that is honourable in public life and a willing acceptance of innumerable national and local duties that others might have rejected for their drudgery; an almost prescriptive right to be included in any Conservative Cabinet, but an exercise of it only when Conservative policy matched Cecilian standards of morality. His name, as Louis Napoleon once said of his own, was a policy in itself.

Yet beneath that placid surface ran unexpected currents: contrasts and paradoxes that reveal a character no less complicated than those of his fanciful brothers. The smallest and frailest of the five, he suffered throughout life from physical and nervous ailments that prostrated him for weeks at a time; but they did nothing to diminish a love of soldiering that brought him the command of a battalion in the South African War and of a division in the First World War. Regarded and sometimes revered as the epitome of orthodox Conservatism, he diverged sharply from the party leadership on several crucial issues. Thus he opposed the acceptance under pressure of the Parliament Bill of 1911 emasculating the House of Lords; the measure of 1935 that speeded India along the road to self-government; the appeasement of Nazi Germany. Mild and almost elaborately courteous among family and friends, he was fearless in his choice of political antagonists and could astound national idols, whether Lloyd George in 1917 or Winston Churchill in 1940, with the asperity of his reproving pen.

Even in his search for spiritual perfection, a shy and hesitant pilgrimage, there were startling anomalies. When in 1935 Linky wrote a pamphlet entitled *The Communion Service As It Might Be*, he sent two copies to his sister-in-law, Alice Salisbury, with a covering letter:

> Here is a gift for you and Jem – one each. But I don't at all want Jem to read it. With his sensitive sense of reverence, the discussion of the mysteries of religion which I delight in is to him deeply distressing. So I only give him a copy as a mark of affection, *not* for reading.

Yet in the very same year Salisbury allowed himself to be persuaded into commending (though never joining) the Oxford Group, whose methods of strident self-advertisement were distasteful to him. It was one facet of the single consistent theme which dominated his thought: that there were no wholly material solutions to political problems. 'The vices of the poor, the selfishness of the rich, the hardness of the middle class are moral questions,' he wrote, 'and must be combatted by moral weapons.' In his public life it inspired him not only to defend the doctrines of the Church of England that he had known since childhood; but also, more naïvely, to accept the good faith of any organization that proclaimed a religious purpose. In his private life it took the form of an unselfconscious dedication to the service of God and of his fellow men, a claim that may appear pretentious but for the convincing evidence on which it rests.

The Cecil brothers, who rarely neglected an opportunity of drawing attention to each other's faults of character, showed only tenderness towards the eldest. 'My father said this morning', Bob told his wife in 1897, 'that it required heroism on Jem's part not to mind being overshadowed by Linkey. I don't think Jem gives it a thought. He is a wonderful man.' Twenty years later, another brother, Nigs, writes of him:

> I wish I was as good as he is. He just gives off goodness, he radiates it and he never knows it. He makes one better by just being there. . . . And yet he is never goody-goody and no one laughs more than he does or sees less evil in the world. He will be astonished when he finds he has been preaching all his life, just as some preachers will be when they find they have only been making a noise.

Another quarter of a century and Sir Edward Marsh records: 'Lord Salisbury arrived last night – he has great charm – golden – good – merely to say how-d'you-do to him was a warm pleasure – there is such benignity in his eyes.'

A profound consideration for others governed Salisbury's life. As an Eton boy he would write home with concern to report that a younger brother had a slight twinge of rheumatism after getting wet. His own younger son, Lord David Cecil, recalls how his father took him aside at Hatfield soon after he had completed his final examinations at Oxford and said: 'All these bills have come for you. I didn't want to worry you at such a time, so I settled them. But you should not forget that some of these Oxford shops depend on their bills being paid promptly.' The conflicting demands of truth and tact were not always so neatly resolved. Having been summoned to see the portrait of his wife and younger son by James Shannon, he gazed at it in despairing silence, wondering how he could avoid hurting the artist's feelings. 'I think', he observed at last, 'that is a picture one might get to like very much in time.'

Only those closest to Salisbury were aware of the deplorable health which haunted him throughout a busy life or could estimate the effort of will needed to overcome the handicap. 'Jem followed an almost unbroken precedent by spending Christmas Day in bed with flue,' one of his sisters wrote to another in January 1927. Hardly a year passed without a calendar of pains and fevers, not all of which evoked sympathy. 'Jem thinks he *may* have a cold. *We* all think he's very well,' was the reaction of his sister-in-law Nelly, who suggested he ought to be out more in the fresh air. Such light-hearted accusations of hypochondria would have been amusing enough in their way but for the repeated references to nerve storms and fits of depression which darken the family correspondence. Perhaps they were hereditary or the result of a fall which at the age of seven had left Jim unconscious for three weeks. Sir William Jenner, the most fashionable physician of the Victorian Age, called in to examine the ailing young man in 1883, told him to take more exercise and to amuse himself as much as he could. ('Not a bad prescription as times go!' his mother added.) Two years later Jenner again diagnosed mental exhaustion, and packed him off to Gibraltar. But when the black cloud descended on him, not even foreign travel could raise his spirits. Gwendolen accompanied her brother to Italy on such a journey: 'His fixed gloom of martyrdom was only relieved for one brief moment when we collided with a motor car on the road between Sorrento and Amalfi and were nearly killed – which temporarily cheered him.' Yet he persisted in trailing on doctors' orders from one dismal resort to another, knowing that it would bring no relief. 'Alice, Linky and I vainly urge the rights of the private conscience against medical infallibility,' Gwendolen told her sister. 'What an Ultramontane he would have been if he'd been born a Roman!'

Stoical by nature, Salisbury hardly ever spoke of his fitful bouts of melancholy. But in a letter to his brother Bob about the death of friends, he allowed these few poignant words of self-pity to escape him: 'They are not the saddest thing, however, and are at any rate the cause of a more unselfish sorrow than these festering feelings of failure and discouragement and passing time and the days that are no more.'

It is a sentiment which posterity does not readily associate with Major-General the Marquess of Salisbury, KG.

From their earliest years the Prime Minister's children were reared on a diet of politics. They listened to the perpetual talk of governing men, helped to entertain statesmen and sovereigns, became accustomed to a relentless flow of red despatch-boxes, were as familiar with the parliamentary manoeuvres of Irish Home Rule as with the strategy of Marathon. Jim's experience of high policy was not confined to Hatfield. When barely fifteen he accompanied his parents to Constantinople for an international conference on the Eastern Question, that intractable problem of a decaying Turkish Empire and a covetous Russia. Disraeli, now Lord Beaconsfield, had asked his Secretary of State for India to represent the interests of Great Britain, a mission the reluctant Salisbury rightly associated with 'seasickness, much French and failure'. His wife shared his disenchantment with Constantinople:

> The Turks still refuse everything and are as unreasonable as possible. I really think they *wish* for war, and are mad enough to think they can beat the Russians! You can have no idea of the wickedness and barbarism of this place. I often sit at the window looking over Stamboul and wonder the earth does not open and swallow it up!

Nor did the Sultan succeed in mollifying her by the award of the third class of the Order of Chastity. Jim, however, enjoyed the change from Eton, although a weak digestion rebelled at 'kebab like tough mutton chops and cadaff, a very beastly sweet composition which tasted of hair-oil'. On Christmas Day 1876 he wrote to his brother Bob in England: 'The crew of the Antelope, which is the *stationnaire* here, came up last night to sing Christmas carols which was very nice of them but Papa grunted and said he thought he should have got out of the sentiment of Christmas out here. Wasn't it beastly of him?' The letter continues in Lord Salisbury's hand:

> After leaving this letter kicking about the drawing room for four days, Jim has left it to me to finish. It's all very well for him, who sleeps like a dormouse, to admire Christmas visits: but in a city where the dogs outnumber the human beings and howl all night, and the watchmen to show their zeal thump the pavement with iron-headed sticks in the interval under one's window, it is rather trying to have a solitary hour's rest in the night disturbed by a lot of hoarse cabin boys trying to sing Rule Britannia each with a set of variations of his own.

With characteristic brio, the Special Ambassador went on to instruct Bob, who had recently celebrated his twelfth birthday, in the realities of international diplomacy:

> I have seen the Sultan again. He is a wretched, feeble creature, who told me he dared not grant what we demanded because he was in danger of his life. He is frightened by the divinity students (Softas) who, whenever the Ministers wish to influence him, are sent howling through the streets. They are very picturesque but not in the least dangerous. They say the Russian Ambassador is very anxious for peace – and is bribing the Ministers here. I hope it is true. It is a great thing to get other people to do the dirty work – if dirty work

has to be done. We certainly can't do it. In the first place we haven't the money – in the second place we don't know how to set about it.

It was as Secretary of State for Foreign Affairs that Lord Salisbury accompanied Beaconsfield to the Congress of Berlin eighteen months later. Again he included his eldest son in the party. The negotiations that postponed the utter disintegration of Turkish rule in Europe for a generation were not the only lessons in diplomacy to be learnt in Berlin that summer. 'B. and I had to go to see [the Empress] Augusta today – in evening dress!' Salisbury wrote to his wife. 'She was very foolish and B.'s compliments were a thing to hear!' With the sophistication of the veteran traveller, Jim was afterwards able to write of Berlin to his friend Curzon: 'A tiresome place in my opinion and not in it with Paris and Vienna. Only one fine street and that not much.'

Cranborne, as he was known outside the family, resumed a more conventional education at Oxford. His father, recalling the rowdiness of Christ Church which had caused him such distress thirty years before, wondered whether he should not send his sons to a more austere foundation. At Christ Church, it was true, the Rev. Charles Dodgson would be only too pleased to watch over the moral welfare of the young Cecils. But the Dean, Dr Liddell, had three unmarried daughters, younger sisters of the Alice immortalized by 'Lewis Carroll', for whom Mrs Liddell was in search of husbands. The college also housed a young tutor in ancient history called Reginald Macan, suspected of radical opinions and rationalist beliefs. Salisbury therefore entered his eldest son at University College, an institution apparently free from aristocratic dissipation, matrimonial enticements and religious doubt.

Within a year or two, however Macan decided to marry; and Christ Church, taking advantage of the statute which required a don to submit to re-election on abandoning celibacy, refused to renew his appointment. University College, happening in 1884 to need a new tutor, indulgently appointed Macan to fill the vacancy. In time he was elected Master of his adopted college, presiding over its affairs with devotion and publishing an authoritative edition of Herodotus. There is no evidence that he ever deflected from Christian orthodoxy either young Lord Cranborne or the three brothers who followed him to University College.* Cranborne worked diligently during his years at Oxford, taking a Third Class in Mathematical Moderations and a Second Class in Modern History.

* In 1928 Jim wrote to his brother Bob: 'The Master of University wants to have a picture of us four brothers in one appalling group for the College.' Bob replied: 'I will consent to the picture, without however much enthusiasm.' The artist was F. H. Shepherd and the painting, reproduced between pages 262–3, hangs in the college. There is a replica at Hatfield.

Even as an undergraduate he could not escape political drudgery. On receiving an invitation to speak at the opening of a Junior Carlton Club in Liverpool, he sought his father's advice. Salisbury replied that although 'it's a bore from beginning to end', there were considerable arguments in favour of acceptance:

Power is more and more leaving Parliament and going to the platform: and in the next generation platform speaking will be an essential accomplishment to any one who wishes to give effect to his own political opinions: especially if those opinions happen to be on the unpopular side. It is – to my mind – a peculiarly difficult and unattractive form of public speaking: and therefore the earlier you can begin to practise it the better. Moreover the Lancashire people will aways be important: and a good position among them will be useful to you.

It was in fact in the heart of industrial Lancashire that a few years later Cranborne began his parliamentary career. Disqualified by youth, not to mention inexperience, from taking part in the general election of 1880, he had to wait until 1885 for the next contest; he was then twenty-four, and as the eldest son of the Prime Minister (who had recently taken office after the defeat in the Commons of Gladstone's second ministry) could easily have been accommodated with a safe seat. Instead his father insisted that he should fight the Darwen constituency, which before the new Redistribution Act had formed part of a Liberal territory. Until the election began, he lived for months in the house of the local Conservative chairman, night after night addressing meetings of cotton workers in every corner of the constituency. Party headquarters in London were resigned to a victory for the Liberal candidate, Mr J. G. Potter, who had strong Lancashire connections. But in a contest decided only after a recount, Cranborne triumphed by five votes in a poll of nearly twelve thousand. Hatfield awaited the result with anxiety and when it came was serenaded by a band playing 'See the Conquering Hero'. The only doubtful note was struck by the Prime Minister's younger brother, Lord Eustace Cecil, who thirty years before had with the rest of the family refused to attend the wedding of the new MP's parents. 'Many congratulations on Jem's success,' he telegraphed, 'though majority disappointing.'

Within a year there was another general election, precipitated by the defeat of Gladstone's short-lived third administration on the issue of Home Rule for Ireland. This time Cranborne extended his majority to a comfortable seven hundred. In 1892, however, the Roman Catholic voters of Lancashire, alienated by the determination of the Tories to keep Ireland within the United Kingdom, ensured his defeat. 'You have fully paid your duty to your party in fighting a very difficult seat three times and holding it for seven years,' Salisbury wrote to his son. But, he added, 'you are not physically strong enough or morally insentive enough for a renewal of your Darwen candidature.' So Cranborne successfully sought election at Rochester, a faithful Conservative constituency within easy reach of London, and represented the borough from 1893 until his father's death ten years later.

In the Commons he never quite lost a nervous manner that robbed his speeches of vigour. That perceptive journalist Sir Henry Lucy wrote of him in 1890:

> Lord Cranborne is in many respects the very reverse of his father. He has nothing of the massive, black-bearded visage of the Premier, being on the contrary slight in figure and boyish-looking in the face, making only the mildest attempt at cultivating a moustache, and that up to the present time not a full success. Although he has been in the House for some years, he still is affected by Parliamentary fright. . . . Addressing the House this evening his nervousness was almost painful to the onlookers. . . . He loses all command of his voice and sometimes leads to outbursts of laughter by declaiming a truism or a commonplace in tragic tones.

Outside the Chamber itself he cut a bolder figure. Salisbury, who after migrating to the House of Lords in 1868 never once revisited the Commons as a spectator, relied on his eldest son for confidential reports on the state of business and on the personal standing of party men. Cranborne showed remarkable prescience by writing to his father on 2 December 1886 urging that the Conservatives should help George Goschen to find a seat in Parliament. Narrowly defeated at Edinburgh a few months before, Goschen was prominent among those former followers of Gladstone who could no longer accept their leader's insistence on Home Rule for Ireland. Cranborne saw the value of such a man as a Conservative ally, not least because of the practical knowledge of finance he had acquired as a banker. Before the month was out, Lord Randolph Churchill had resigned as Chancellor of the Exchequer and by early in the New Year Goschen had been persuaded to succeed him – although it was not until February that he managed to have himself re-elected to the Commons. It has sometimes been disputed whether Churchill ever uttered the words attributed to him: 'All great men make mistakes. Napoleon forgot Blücher, I forgot Goschen.' Cranborne's foresight in the matter is beyond doubt.

Cranborne grew up as heir to estates of more than twenty thousand acres that brought in a gross annual income of over £33,000. Most of the land was at Hatfield and elsewhere in Hertfordshire; but there were also farms in Dorset and much valuable housing property in Liverpool, the inheritance of Miss Gascoyne. 'I do not believe that rich people have more responsibilities than poor people,' Lord Salisbury once wrote. 'This doctrine would make responsibility to depend on the effect of your acts, not on the intention.' Both he and Lady Salisbury nevertheless paid minute attention to the needs of their tenants, personally supervising an ambitious programme of cottage demolition and reconstruction; and when the demands of high office left the Prime Minister and his wife little time for parochial duties, their children assumed the burden. It was Cranborne, for example, who while still at Oxford resolved the conflicting demands of philanthropy and game preservation. According to custom, the poor of Hatfield were invited each year to pick up sticks in the park for firewood. One April, however, somebody suspected that they might also be picking up pheasants' eggs, or at least squashing them underfoot. Cranborne thereupon submitted to his father, in a letter as solemn as any Cabinet paper, two possible solutions: either wood-gathering should be confined to trees along the avenues until the end of the laying season, or estate workers should make piles of sticks from which the poor could help themselves. The ultimate decision has not been preserved for posterity.

There was hardly a day when Cranborne did not use his daily ride to visit a farm or cottage. On inheriting his father's estates in 1903 he was prompted by curiosity and conscience to make a thorough survey of all he owned. The state of the Liverpool property disturbed him. For generations it had been managed impersonally from London, but the falling-in of ground-leases spurred him to a radical change of policy. Rejecting the advice of lawyers, who wanted him to sell the dilapidated houses for the substantial sums offered by speculators, he decided on wholesale reconstruction. Ultimately it cost him £40,000, without any increase in rents. Impressed by the methods of Octavia Hill, he also arranged that the property should in future be managed locally and with sympathetic understanding of his tenants' problems. At Cranborne, too, he undertook an elaborate scheme of rebuilding, replacing the tumbledown clay-walled cottages with substantial brick bungalows in the design of which his sister Gwendolen had a hand. A few Dorset men still yearned for their traditional two-storey houses. 'We are like the birds,' they complained, 'we like to go aloft to roost.'

The innumerable cottages built or renovated under Cranborne's direction are memorials more to his heart than to his taste; sanitation and comfort at the most economical price precluded much variety of material or elegance of style. At Hatfield, however, he planned every detail of the restoration of the Old Palace to its original grandeur and took care that such necessary additions as new stables harmonized with their historic surroundings. He personally carved out of wood the delicate models that served as patterns for lamps and locks and door handles. He paid a debt to the past by constructing a muniment room to contain, among other treasures, the 'casket letters' written by Mary Queen of Scots to her lover, Bothwell. Hatfield House itself had to wait another generation before his son, the fifth Marquess, gave it a beauty unknown since the seventeenth century. But Cranborne did at least banish the careless philistinism of his upbringing. There was even music in the drawing-room.

Not for the first time in the history of the House of Cecil, the heir made an ideally happy marriage. His wife was Lady Alice Gore, a tall dark-haired daughter of the fifth Earl of Arran, an Irish landowner of no great fortune. Having caught Cranborne's eye during the London season of 1886, she was invited to Hatfield for the winter ball afterwards remembered as the occasion on which Lord Salisbury received Randolph Churchill's resignation. They were married in the following May, a few weeks before her twentieth birthday.

For sixty years she played just such a role as had fallen to Georgina Alderson a generation earlier. Without Alice's understanding, encouragement and unobtrusive deference to his wishes, Cranborne might never have overcome an innate shyness that was intensified by the eminence of his father and the brilliance of his brothers. She knew how to comfort him during moods of black despair at his own imagined sinfulness and to bear with an autocratic temper that in the home occasionally displaced his usual sweetness of nature. For the first twenty-five years of his life the only women he had known well were a mother and two elder sisters of strong, not to say dominating, character. Now he found both solace and self-confidence in the warm femininity of an attentive wife.

Alice's early years of marriage were not always easy. At Hatfield, where she and her husband were required to live under the benevolent but watchful sway of old Lady Salisbury, the family gazed in disbelief on a wife who at first knew nothing of politics and burst into tears at the terrors of an election campaign. She responded more readily to the tradition of philanthropy which matched her own Evangelical upbringing. But such was her tenderness of heart that, having been appointed a Justice of the Peace, she sat only once in court: she could not bear to see human beings in captivity, much less to pass judgement on them.

In middle life she was as diligent as her mother-in-law, though less oppressively matriarchal, in preserving and repairing family ties. Her children have never ceased to speak of her with a love that remained unclouded by a single unhappy memory. She was an assiduous letter writer, remembered as much for the ordeal of decipherment she innocently imposed on her correspondents as for her sparkling commentaries. Her brother-in-law Nigs, whom she kept well supplied with home news during his years in Cairo, found it best to throw her letters on the floor, then to walk round and round them until her hieroglyphic hand had given up its secrets one by one. They were not always discursive. When Arthur Balfour lost his seat in the general election of 1906, she compressed her message of commiseration into three words: 'D--n. D--n. D--n.'

'She had a laugh like champagne,' a sister-in-law said of her, 'and a power of enjoyment which was only exceeded by her unselfishness in sharing everything good with others.' The great-grand-daughter of Lady Palmerston, she inherited that instinctive appreciation of stylish, civilized society which had illuminated the drawing-rooms of her Whig forbears. Lady Salisbury endured formal entertaining as a necessary burden: Alice relished it as a graceful exercise in friendship. Few other hostesses could have induced two of her guests at Hatfield, an Archbishop and a Prime Minister, to assume the characters of Charles I and Charles II and talk to each other until the rest of the company guessed their roles. 'Your Majesty', said Cosmo Lang, 'led a very lax life.' 'At least, Your Majesty,' replied Stanley Baldwin, 'I never lost my head.' Her good nature and lively intelligence brought her many confidences. Kitchener used her as his secret channel of communication with Arthur Balfour when locked in battle with the Viceroy of India, George Curzon; and Curzon for his part sought her opinion on a young Member of Parliament called Sir Oswald Mosley who wanted to marry his youngest daughter. Yet she never attempted to be a political *grande dame* or to exercise her influence without the knowledge and consent of her husband.

Alice Salisbury's cheerful spirit survived the tribulations of war, widowhood and extreme old age. She endured as much anxiety and apprehension as any woman, but learned to mask her feelings so that those of her family should be spared. Even when her elder son left for the Western Front in 1915 she was thus able to write with apparent humour: 'He went off with such a collection of equipment – pistols, periscopes, field glasses, etc. – and then filled up the chinks with the Oxford Book of English Poetry, the Path to Rome and three books on Christian Science.'

During the Second World War, Hatfield became a hospital and the Salisburys retreated to a few rooms. 'Our great solace', she wrote during the Battle of Britain in 1940, 'are the charming infant airmen who come in and out with injuries of all sorts and who redress one's view of human nature.'

The social historian may also note that, throughout the food shortages of the war years, the chatelaine of that splendid house kept her brother-in-law Linky supplied with plebeian rabbits from the estate so that as Provost of Eton he could continue to entertain the boys to meals; and that in return for such favours he would mildly break the law by sending her some of his personal clothing coupons. 'You will be glad to hear', she assured that dedicated bachelor, 'that I now possess four pairs of stockings and a silk petticoat which otherwise I should not have been able to get.' But housemaids, she noted, had become as rare as great auks' eggs.

Hers was a resilient generation without self-pity. When nearly eighty she went one day to a London hotel to see her exact contemporary, Millicent, Duchess of Sutherland, whose entertainments had been memorable even by Edwardian standards. 'She gave me China tea out of a tin box and cake from a paper bag purchased in a shop at the back of the Savoy in exactly the same atmosphere as in Stafford House, and laughed with the same gurgling enjoyment as in those days.' After her husband's death in 1947, Alice Salisbury contentedly spent the very last years of her life in a small house in a London square. 'I have actually got a garden in the back yard the size of a cat's run; indeed, a rat's run would be more correct. It is a vulgar garden composed of scarlet geraniums and yellow pansies.' Her interest in the present remained as brisk as ever; but a sense of history inspired her to write down for private circulation her memories of childhood, of Hatfield as she had first known it and of her husband. 'They were very happy days,' she reflected, 'with their sense of security both in material life and thought. I do feel so sorry for the young ones for their want of it.'

Like his grandfather, the second Marquess, Cranborne delighted in soldiering; and like him, he discovered that to be an eldest son was in itself a profession that precluded a career in the Regular Army. He found consolation in peacetime service with those reserve forces which have always played as much a part in social life as in national defence.* While still an Oxford undergraduate he joined the Hertfordshire Yeomanry, then transferred to the 4th Bedfordshire Regiment, the county Militia battalion. He took immense pains to master every detail of the military craft and turned the volunteer spirit into something more by recruiting a cadre of non-commissioned officers from the

* He also took to foxhunting, what Mr Jorrocks called 'the image of war without its guilt and only five and twenty per cent of the danger'. But the sport frightened his wife and soon after marriage he abandoned it.

Brigade of Guards. The annual month of training he spent with his men under canvas was perhaps the happiest of the year. The fresh air and physical exertion forced him to forget those perplexities and scuples which clouded both his spiritual and his political life, and sent him back to Westminster with renewed confidence. 'We go to the manoeuvres tomorrow,' he wrote to his father one August, 'so my address will be Northern Army, Wilton Camp, Salisbury. There's glory for you. It is going to be all arranged and very little reality about it. We are going to be defeated.'

Within a year or two, fate obliged him with the real thing: in February 1900 he found himself sailing for South Africa to fight the Boers. 'My cold is much better,' he declared just before embarkation, 'but the fuss and worry of starting are beyond words. I have done everything which one is supposed to do under these circumstances. I have got myself a complete suit of khaki and have made my will.' As it turned out, neither was strictly necessary. The battalion which he commanded was required only to guard lines of communication, although in April he had hopes of taking part in the relief of Mafeking, where his brother Nigs was a senior officer of the besieged garrison. Five months later, 'there was a very little desultory fighting which we viewed from a respectful distance. . . . Every now and then a few hundred men went out and skirmished with the enemy whilst we sat on a hill and looked at half a dozen Boers about three miles off on another hill.' For his services Cranborne was mentioned in despatches and appointed a Companion of the Bath: generous recognition, presumably a tribute as much to long years of training as to the conduct of the 4th Bedfordshires in the field. Another distinction was to have won the regard of the most prickly of his subordinate officers, Montagu Norman, the future Governor of the Bank of England.

That autumn he was unexpectedly recalled to London. His father, now in his seventy-first year and shaken by the death of Lady Salisbury, decided to ease his burden by shedding the office of Foreign Secretary which he had held jointly with that of Prime Minister since 1895. The vacancy was filled by Lord Lansdowne, who agreed that Cranborne should be appointed his Parliamentary Under-Secretary, responsible for Foreign Office business in the House of Commons. Linky was unimpressed by his brother's promotion. An Under-Secretary, he later told Winston Churchill, was 'only a stipendiary echo'.

Although Cranborne had been obliged to wait until he was nearly forty for his first ministerial post, Salisbury could hardly have chosen a more inconvenient moment at which to advance his son. When the full list of changes became known, even loyal Conservatives showed embarrassment or resentment at the number of the Prime Minister's close kinsmen holding high office. One of his nephews, Arthur Balfour, continued as First Lord of the Treasury* and Leader of the House of Commons; another, Gerald Balfour, was promoted to be President of the Board of Trade with a seat in the Cabinet; his son-in-law, Lord Selborne, also entered the Cabinet for the first time on taking over the Admiralty; and Cranborne arrived at the Foreign Office.

In the House of Lords, Rosebery congratulated the Prime Minister 'on being the head of a family with the most remarkable genius for administration that has ever been known'. In the Commons a disgruntled Conservative, George Bartley, initiated a debate on the composition of the new government. He called it 'the Hotel Cecil, Unlimited', after the establishment containing eight hundred rooms recently opened on the site of the first Earl of Salisbury's London house and still associated with the conviction for fraud of its original financial backer, unhappily named Jabez Balfour.

Amid suspicion and ill-will, Cranborne's performance at the despatch-box attracted unusual attention. He was soon in trouble. The Queen had thought him 'very agreeable and clever' when he dined at Windsor. But during his fifteen years on the back benches of the Commons, devoting himself to contentious themes such as the virtues of Church of England schools and the perils of Irish Home Rule, he had never needed to employ the precise yet cautious language of diplomacy. It so happened that after only a few weeks in office, he was asked by a Liberal MP from the floor of the House to elucidate a subtle point of policy. Instead of delivering a conventionally bland reply, he stiffly invoked 'an understanding that the Under-Secretary shall not answer supplementary questions'. Such a practice certainly existed; it would have been unreasonable, even dangerous, to expect the mere mouth-piece of the Foreign Secretary to speak impromptu on delicate topics of international relations. But no previous Parliamentary Under-Secretary had ever been artless enough to say so, and thus to give constitutional weight to what was merely a sensible custom. The Opposition, affecting to believe that Cranborne's gaffe endangered freedom of debate, made the most of the matter and tried to adjourn the House. He committed another indiscretion when the Opposition suggested that Great Britain should not have delayed so long in seeking an alliance with Japan. 'It is not for us to ask for treaties,' he declaimed in the language of Palmerston. 'We grant them.'

* Since 1902, when Balfour succeeded his uncle as Prime Minister, the office of First Lord of the Treasury has been held only by the Prime Minister. Nominally the supreme head of the Treasury, in practice he leaves its administration in the hands of the Chancellor of the Exchequer.

'His first official session has been rather trying for Jim,' Salisbury admitted, 'but he is picking up again.' Others delivered sterner verdicts. Lord George Hamilton, a member of the Cabinet who had received his first ministerial office from Disraeli nearly thirty years before, wrote that 'there will always be a danger of his blurting out by incautious phraseology the very ideas he was told to conceal'. Curzon, from the eminence of the Viceroyalty of India, deplored Cranborne's 'halting obscurities'. Even the faithful Schomberg McDonnell, Salisbury's private secretary, joined the critical chorus: 'Dear old Jim has not been a success at the Foreign Office: this I really believe is due as much to ill-health as anything: and I quite anticipate that on this account he will not be able to hold office much longer.'

When, however, Salisbury retired as Prime Minister in the summer of 1902, Arthur Balfour not only retained his cousin in the reconstructed ministry, but in the following year, shortly after Cranborne had succeeded to his father's title and a seat in the House of Lords, brought him into the Cabinet as Lord Privy Seal. It was a promotion, Curzon wrote, 'that fairly made me jump with surprise'. Other members of the party could scarcely conceal their jealousy. Yet the appointment proved successful. Cranborne (or Salisbury, as he will now be called) was by temperament more fitted to explain and defend government policies amid the calm and courtesy of the Upper House than in the raucous arena of the Commons. 'The Lords are gentlemen,' a contemporary of Salisbury's observed on being asked to steer an incomprehensible measure through the Upper House. 'They will not expect me to understand the Bill.' And as his new office carried no departmental duties, he was able to bring his deliberative mind to bear on a range of problems, including the intricate Licensing Bill of 1904.

That shrewd and not always charitable observer Edmund Gosse, Librarian of the House of Lords from 1904 to 1914, wrote in his diary:

> In the whole weary business of manoeuvring the Licensing Bill through this House, Lord Salisbury has shown himself quite surprisingly skilful. In debate he is firm, swift and yet considerate. He is struggling throughout against ill health, for he has never got over his heavy attack of influenza in the spring, and his pinched white face is pathetic. Yet he never betrays irritability.

Balfour valued his cousin's stabilizing presence in Cabinet, particularly during the prolonged crisis of Tariff Reform. The perennial conflict between Protection and Free Trade had in 1902 once more become an acute political issue. As Colonial Secretary, Joseph Chamberlain hoped to stimulate the commerce of British possessions overseas by a system of imperial preference, or the imposition of duties on all foreign imports except those from the Empire. His proposal, mild in itself, split the Conservatives no less dramatically than his abandonment of Gladstone over Home Rule had split the Liberal party and carried his orchid and eyeglass across the floor of the House of Commons. By upbringing and conviction the Cecils leaned towards Free Trade. But Salisbury believed that Conservatism stood for more important causes than the niceties of fiscal argument; rather than divide the Tory ranks and risk losing the next election to a party of radicals and nonconformists, he would reluctantly accept a moderate tariff on foreign imports. Two of his brothers, Linky and Bob, thought otherwise and were among the most vociferous of the Unionist Free Traders; the humiliations they endured for their cause and the deterioration of their relations with Balfour form part of their story in later chapters. Here it is relevant only to notice the healing touch which Salisbury tried to bring to the dispute; his promotion to be President of the Board of Trade for the last few months of Balfour's wilting government; the fulfilment of his prophecy that internal dissension would ensure a sweeping Liberal victory at the general election in January 1906; and the sorrowful contempt which he developed for his cousin Arthur's vacillation, evasiveness and want of principle. Looking back in later years on Balfour's conduct, he borrowed a metaphor from the hunting field: 'As a leader, if I may say so, he has never ridden over a country, and the besetting sin of always looking for the gate has, I am afraid, done a great deal to debase English public life.' From a cousin who had loved Balfour as a brother, that was indeed a stern verdict.

Twenty-four hours after the resignation of Arthur Balfour's government in December 1905, Henry and Margot Asquith arrived at Hatfield for a three-day visit which neither host nor guest saw reason to cancel. It was thus from a Tory stronghold that Asquith twice motored to London to take part in the business of Cabinet-making with the new Liberal Prime Minister, Sir Henry Campbell-Bannerman, returning to Hatfield on the final evening as Chancellor of the Exchequer. Salisbury would have seen nothing incongruous in the episode; party warfare, he believed, had no place in private life. Throughout the political battles of the next eight years he played an increasingly assertive part in thwarting an elaborate programme of Liberal legislation. Yet he allowed no touch either of passion or of personal reproach to colour his speeches. F. E. Smith, Earl of Birkenhead, perhaps underestimated the influence of sobriety on the Upper House when he complained that 'the material is sometimes a little thin and its presentation a little acrid'. And Curzon, whose *Modern Parliamentary Eloquence* was published in 1913, paid tribute to the oratory of both the third Marquess and of Lord Hugh Cecil but thought Salisbury himself unworthy of mention.

Even had the art of rhetoric accorded with Salisbury's temperament, the power to persuade would have been a wasted talent in a House of Lords so dominated by the Conservatives and their allies. There were 355 Conservative peers in 1906 and 124 Liberal Unionists on whose support they could depend: that made 479, compared with only 88 Liberals of the true Gladstonian faith. The new House of Commons by contrast contained 377 Liberals buttressed by 83 Irish Nationalists and 53 Labour Members: a combined strength of 513, ill-balanced by a mere 132 Conservatives and 25 Liberal Unionists.

That the constitution permitted an hereditary House of Lords composed largely of landowners to amend or even to veto the legislation of an elected House of Commons was undisputed. Yet in an age of expanding parliamentary democracy it was a power that had to be exercised with caution. On several occasions, such as the extension of the franchise in 1832 and again in 1867, the Upper House (although not Lord Robert Cecil, MP) had acted with restraint and allowed the expressed will of the people to prevail. In 1893, however, the Lords had thrown out Gladstone's second Home Rule Bill by 419 votes to 41, the radicalism of the measure having driven a high proportion of Liberal peers permanently into the arms of the Conservatives. From that moment the relationship between the two chambers grew increasingly sensitive. Now, at the beginning of 1906, a Liberal administration commanding one of the biggest majorities in the history of the modern House of Commons found itself threatened by an unusually large and implacably hostile Conservative majority in the Lords. The fears of Campbell-Bannerman and his colleagues were hardly allayed by an election speech from Arthur Balfour claiming that 'the great Unionist party should still control, whether in power or whether in Opposition, the destinies of this great Empire'.

The legislative programme of the new government might almost have been devised to affront the Cecils. The Education Bill of 1906 reflected intense non-conformist resentment at the financing of religious instruction in Church of England and other denominational schools out of local rates, a system the Liberals now proposed to abolish. The Conservatives were equally determined to prevent an abrupt reversal of their own Act of 1902. Salisbury, for whom education without religion was no education at all, played his part in killing the new measure in the House of Lords, not by outright rejection but by returning it to the Commons so amended as positively to strengthen the role of denominational schools. The government had no course but to abandon the Bill.

Salisbury and his brothers considered the Licensing Bill of 1908, which the Liberals wished to substitute for Balfour's measure of 1904, as hardly less offensive. It sought not only to limit the number of public houses in any one district in proportion to the population, but also to punish the brewers for their innate wickedness by imposing a niggardly scale of compensation. Although the Cecils accepted the need for some control of the liquor trade, they regarded the harsh treatment of dispossessed licence-holders as an affront to the rights of private property. Intemperance never found a prominent place in their calendar of sins. As a Fellow of Hertford College, Oxford, Lord Hugh was once required to sit in judgement on an undergraduate found paralytically drunk in the middle of the day. Alone of his colleagues he refused to recommend expulsion. 'I see no difference', he said, 'between eating too much and spending a sleepless night and drinking too much and feeling a little giddy.' In any case, his brother Salisbury argued, the number of public houses was irrelevant to the incidence of drunkenness: he did not feel any more inclined to sleepiness at Hatfield, with its innumerable bedrooms, than at a seaside villa where there were a dozen.*

This time the Conservatives in the Lords rejected the government's Licensing Bill outright, provoking intense anger among the Liberals. But it was not until 1909, the year after Asquith had succeeded Campbell-Bannerman as Prime Minister, that the constitutional conflict between the two Houses of Parliament moved towards a crisis. The Budget introduced in April by the Chancellor of the Exchequer, Lloyd George, although primarily designed to finance old-age pensions and other welfare services, heartened his Radical followers by imposing a range of new taxes on the rich. In addition to a supertax of 2½ per cent on the amount by which all incomes of £5,000 or more exceeded £3,000, there were four separate taxes on land: on future unearned increment of land values, on undeveloped land, on the realization of leases and on mineral rights. The ownership of property had long been a target for Radical invective. In the last year of old Lord Salisbury's life, Lloyd George publicly alleged that three peers – Derby, Sefton and Salisbury – between them drew £345,000 a year from Liverpool rents without contributing a penny to the rates of the city. Salisbury's share was certainly the smallest of the three; and whatever neglect of the housing there may have been in the Prime Minister's day was later remedied by his son. The Budget proposals were far from punitive:

---

* The actor and writer Robert Speaight wrote sixty years later: 'It was rather difficult at Hatfield not to live next door to a public house. . . . The third Marquis of Salisbury had believed there to be safety in numbers; and I am bound to admit that in all the twenty-one years I lived there I never saw a drunken man in Hatfield.'

It will cost Jem an extra £3,000 a year [Gwendolen wrote to her sister in May 1909] but, as he observes, he is very rich and I don't think it need make any catastrophical change in his life. But of course in one way or another he must spend that much less and other people must suffer.

In both Houses of Parliament the Finance Bill embodying the Budget resolutions was opposed clause by clause and line by line. Not until the beginning of November, after no fewer than 554 divisions and several all-night sessions, did the Commons complete all its stages. It was so much vain toil. When the measure came before the Lords at the end of the month it was rejected in its entirety by 350 votes to 75. In refusing to pass a money Bill for the first time since the seventeenth century, they could argue that the Liberals had provoked the breach of constitutional usage by including in the Finance Bill an extraneous measure for the compulsory registration of land. As Salisbury pointed out in his speech on 24 November, such a practice would enable a government to reverse any previous legislation by merely inserting a clause to that effect in a Finance Bill: Great Britain would thus be reduced to single-chamber rule.

Since there can be no government without money, the rejection of the Budget precipitated an immediate general election fought not only on the issue of whether the Commons should retain absolute control over national finance but also on the broader theme of how far the Lords could be permitted to amend or veto any other measure passed by the Commons. Both major parties, as is their custom, claimed to be acting on behalf of the people; one appealed to the authority of the ballot box, reflected in the huge parliamentary majority of 1906, the other to the role of an Upper House in curbing democratic tyranny. 'We do not pretend to an absolute veto on legislation,' Salisbury told the Liberals. 'No, all we do is to say, "If you insist upon this legislation of which we cannot approve, the country shall decide between us." '

The decision of the country in January 1910, however, gave complete satisfaction to neither party. The Conservatives could congratulate themselves on having won back over a hundred seats in the Commons. Yet the Liberals retained, with the support of Labour and Irish Nationalist MPs, a majority large enough to persuade the peers that it was now their duty to pass the previously rejected Finance Bill. Asquith did not at once press his advantage by putting forward a measure that would permanently prevent a repetition of the Budget crisis, and it was in answer to a question about the government's intentions that he made the Delphic response: 'We had better wait and see.' Both he and his Cabinet realized that legislation to curb the Lords' power of veto would itself need the assent of the Upper House; that if the Lords declined to surrender, the government would have to ask the King to create enough new Liberal peers to swamp the Conservative majority; that the King might regard such a wholesale creation as an abuse of the royal prerogative; and that there would be little enthusiasm in the country for a constitutional revolution so reminiscent of a Gilbert and Sullivan light opera.

Lloyd George has got you into a nice mess [Hugh Cecil wrote to Mrs Asquith in February 1910]: nothing left for you but to try and create 500 peers and perish miserably attacking the King. That's what comes of making an irresponsible demagogue Chancellor of the Exchequer.

Asquith could not easily draw back. There was pressure not only from the Radicals but also from the Irish Nationalists who saw the Lords' veto as the only obstacle that stood in their way to achieving Home Rule. In the spring of 1910 the government drafted a Parliament Bill with three main provisions. The Lords could neither amend nor reject a money Bill, the definition of such a measure to be decided by the Speaker of the House of Commons; other legislation could be delayed for no more than two years and one month; and, as a check on a too-dictatorial Commons, the maximum length of a parliament was to be reduced from seven years to five.

When you land here on May 4th you ought to find us on the very edge of a crisis [Gwendolen Cecil wrote to her sister], the King putting up iron shutters and designing the costume in which he is to fly from an infuriated people (it would be an immense consolation to him) or else settling the precedence of the 500 peers.

But within a few days Edward VII was dead and political conflict suspended out of deference to the new King, George V. It resumed six months later after negotiations between the party leaders had failed to find a compromise solution. In an attempt to obtain a clear mandate for his proposals, Asquith called another general election in December; but a country that had grown weary of the dispute voted almost exactly as it had done eleven months before. Throughout 1911 the Conservatives in both Houses fought the passage of the Parliament Bill by every tactical weapon they possessed. In the Commons, Hugh Cecil reinforced an astute command of procedure with an unscrupulous use of disorder. In the Lords his eldest brother relied upon the voice of reason and an authority that was already beginning to carry weight beyond the parliamentary arena. While Hugh was shouting down the Prime Minister, Salisbury was pleading that on certain issues of profound importance – he had Irish Home Rule in mind – a House of Commons no longer restrained by a House of Lords should be obliged to test public opinion by means of a referendum.*

Neither mode of Cecilian conduct deflected Asquith. In July he let it be known that, if the Lords insisted on their amendments, he would advise the King to create enough Liberal peers to ensure that the Bill passed in its original form. Indeed he went further, disclosing that as long ago as November 1910 the King had consented to such a course. That the Prime Minister had extracted a secret promise from a reluctant and inexperienced monarch even before the general election of December 1910 added bitterness to the controversy. As Balfour observed: 'A sovereign may be asked to *act*; it is no part of his duty to *promise*.' The revelation of the royal pledge also put an end to Salisbury's speculative but utterly impracticable hopes that George v might be persuaded to disregard Asquith's demands and to seek a less exacting Prime Minister.

The prospect of a huge new creation of Liberal peers gathered from the hedgerows of politics convinced many Conservatives that further resistance to the Parliament Bill would be, as Balfour put it, 'essentially theatrical'; and that they should therefore abstain from voting against the government when the measure reached its final stages in the House of Lords. Salisbury disagreed. Whatever humiliating consequences might await monarchy and nation, he was not prepared to abandon his principles. He feared the excesses of what would be virtually single-chamber government; he argued that the Liberals had no mandate to curb the powers of the Lords, since their majority in the Commons came almost exclusively from the Irish Members (yet he did not explain why the vote of an Irish Member who was denied Home Rule should count for less than the vote of an English or Scots Member). He forecast that a grotesquely inflated Upper House would soon have to be reduced in size together, he hoped, with some restoration of its former authority. Meanwhile he combined with other inflexibles such as his brother-in-law Selborne and the former Lord Chancellor Halsbury, now in his eighty-eighth year, to throw out Asquith's obnoxious measure.

For a man of shy temperament, Salisbury showed unusual asperity. Suspecting that members of the House of Lords who held court appointments might vote for the government in an attempt to save the King from the distasteful duty of creating peers, he wrote to the private secretary at the Palace, warning him that such conduct would call in question the neutrality of the King. He also sharply reminded the Archbishop of Canterbury, Dr Davidson, that if the prelates in the House of Lords voted for the Parliament Bill, they would alienate just those

---

* It is recorded that the effect of Salisbury's speech on this occasion was 'rather marred by the passing of an aeroplane'.

members of the Conservative party on whom the Church of England relied for political support. (In the event, both archbishops and eleven other bishops supported the government; only two bishops went into the Conservative lobby.) On the eve of the final debate in the Lords he encouraged his fellow 'die-hards' and 'ditchers' with a supper party in Arlington Street. The following night, however, one of the hottest ever recorded in London, his speech failed to inspire. He allowed himself an uncharacteristically scornful reference to Davidson: 'I hoped that we should have been spared an appeal to courage, but the Most Reverend Prelate could not avoid it.' He uttered a petulant but obscure threat: 'If it comes to creating peers, two can play at that game.' And he urged his supporters to 'vote as we believe, be the consequences what they may'.

Until the count was taken, none knew how it would go. Hugh Cecil predicted a small majority in favour of rejection; but he had reckoned without the prudence of so many Conservative peers. Although his brother's faction mustered over a hundred, three times that number abstained; even more disappointing, thirty-seven Conservative peers and thirteen prelates voted in the Liberal lobby rather than endure an inundation of new creations. The government had carried its Parliament Bill by 131 votes to 114.

'Politics are beastly,' Salisbury wrote a few weeks later while recuperating in Scotland from the strain of the constitutional crisis. The Parliament Act and the circumstances in which his party had been browbeaten into accepting it continued to torment him to the end of his days. It was not that the measure itself made any momentous impact on British politics. No government has since needed to employ the clause protecting money Bills (although, ironically, the Finance Bill of 1909 would not have enjoyed its immunity). And during Salisbury's lifetime the statute was only twice invoked to pass legislation rejected by the Lords: once to ensure the disestablishment of the Welsh Church, and again to secure Home Rule for Ireland. He foresaw, however, that a government might before long come to power with a programme far more revolutionary than that of Campbell-Bannerman, Asquith or Lloyd George. What scant defence could an emasculated House of Lords then offer the country? In theory, of course, the next Conservative administration to take office was at liberty to pass a simple Bill restoring to the peers the prerogatives they had lost in 1911. But such an opportunity, delayed by seven years of coalition government, did not come until 1922; and by then the nation was immersed in urgent problems of reconstruction and reform. In any case, an almost wholly hereditary Second Chamber found few allies in the restless mood of the 1920s.

A traditionalist by temperament, Salisbury grew less inflexible with the years. 'I am all for a quiet life,' he sighed at a moment of political tension, 'though I recognize the necessity for new departures and spirited policies occasionally – with reluctance.' He acknowledged that, if the House of Lords was to regain some or all of its lost powers, it would have to possess public confidence; and that public confidence was to be won only by some modification of its hereditary foundation. He found a solution to the problem in the Parliament Act itself or rather in its preamble which expressed a resolve without the force of law:

> Whereas it is intended to substitute for the House of Lords as it at present exists a Second Chamber constituted on a popular instead of hereditary basis, but such a substitution cannot immediately be brought into operation: And whereas provision will require to be made by Parliament in a measure effecting such substitution for limiting and defining the powers of the new Second Chamber . . .

Asquith, admitting that reform of the composition of the House of Lords 'brooked no delay', had in 1912 attempted to honour the terms of the preamble by appointing a Cabinet committee to consider it. But neither they nor similar bodies that met over the years could reach a conclusion agreeable to all parties. Nor did successive governments exert themselves to re-open old wounds as long as the settlement of 1911 seemed to be working without undue friction. Salisbury had no such inhibitions. He cherished the hereditary principle: it would have been remarkable if a tenth earl and fourth marquess had not. But the authority of an assembly of peers, he believed, rested less on inheritance than on its freedom from democratic pressures. 'The independence of this House', he had told the Lords in 1910, 'does not depend so much upon its hereditary characteristics as upon the fact that your Lordships, once appointed, are irremovable. We are in the same position, for example, as the judges.' Like his father, who in 1888 had supported an ultimately abortive measure to create fifty life peers, he was prepared to complement but not to abolish the hereditary element.

In 1932 an unofficial committee of members of both Houses of Parliament sitting under his chairmanship produced its recommendations. The size of the Lords, which had by then grown to over 750, was to be reduced to about 320. The new House would consist of 150 hereditary peers elected from among themselves, 150 'outside' peers elected by county and other local councils, and a handful of bishops and judges. Both categories of peer would sit for twelve years, a third part retiring at four-yearly intervals. Women would not be excluded. And to ensure an adequate representation of Labour, the income of every member which fell short of £600 was to be made up to that sum. The powers of the new House of Lords were to be correspondingly increased. Money Bills remained outside the jurisdiction of the peers, but a joint committee of both Houses would relieve the Speaker of the Commons of deciding what was or was not a money Bill. Finally, and most important of all, once a measure other than a money Bill had been vetoed by the Lords, it could not be submitted again by the Commons until after a general election.

Salisbury, who had served in every Conservative Cabinet of the 1920s but had not sought office in the 'National' government of 1931, embodied his proposals in a Bill which in 1934 received the approval of the Lords by 171 votes to 82. It proved a fruitless victory. The Leader of the House, Lord Hailsham,* announced that the government would provide no facilities for its discussion in the Commons. The decision was understandable; he and his colleagues had troubles enough in economic and foreign affairs without provoking a renewed constitutional conflict. Encouraged by Conservative support in the country if not in Downing Street, Salisbury more than once returned to the theme until it was eclipsed in public interest by the approaching shadow of the Second World War. His dream of a compact and forceful Second Chamber, always elusive, became remote after the sweeping socialist victory of 1945. The Labour party would always look on a strong House of Lords as a potential threat to the swift social reform of its electoral programme; a cowed and unwieldy House of Lords, by contrast, was the next best thing to no House of Lords at all. Not long after Salisbury's death in 1947, the Attlee government cut the veto of the Upper House to a single year.

The Parliament Bill of 1911 that gave Salisbury a cause almost cost him a friend. Three days after the final dramatic vote in the House of Lords, Gwendolen Cecil wrote to her sister: 'Jem's struggle for a charitable judgement of George Curzon's proceedings is more than his nervous system is equal to, and I'm quite longing to find an adequate defence for that worthy.'

Curzon was far from ashamed of his conduct in helping to pass a Liberal measure or, as he put it, preserving the constitution from ridicule. In a private memorandum he condemned Salisbury's diehards for a policy that was 'unstatesmanlike, ill-considered, unpatriotic and unwise'. He described with relish how for a fortnight a committee of fellow moderates had met daily in his house, personally canvassed all doubtful peers and ultimately ensured enough Conservative abstentions

---

* Douglas Hogg, first Viscount Hailsham (1872–1950), Lord Chancellor 1928–9 and 1935–8, Secretary of State for War and Leader of the House of Lords 1931–5, and father of Quintin Hogg, Lord Hailsham of St Marylebone (1907–   ), Lord Chancellor, 1970–4.

to safeguard the Bill. He had received, he admitted, any number of abusive letters and a great deal of personal vituperation. Doubtless he found solace in a succession of effusive notes from Margot Asquith and a staider letter of congratulation from the King's private secretary. 'What a relief that all is well!' Lord Stamfordham wrote that very night. 'The King is quite another man and, if I may say so, is deeply grateful to you for the very valuable service which you have rendered to save the situation.' But the episode marked the end of anything approaching intimacy in Curzon's relations with Salisbury; for the future, there would rarely be more than a fitful cordiality between Conservative colleagues.

Their friendship had begun at Oxford thirty years before, in the spirited political talk of the Canning Club. 'Lord Cranborne', the minutes for 1881 record, 'pointed out the danger to be feared from the enfranchisement of an uneducated class constituting so vast a majority that they would swamp all other interests.' The undergraduate Curzon was even then the more cautious of the two. 'On the theory of Conservatism as based upon class government,' he warned, 'it was advisable to keep silence.' Later that year he stayed at Hatfield for Cranborne's twenty-first birthday and in 1885, as a young Fellow of All Souls with parliamentary aspirations, joined the Prime Minister's family circle in the role of an assistant private secretary. He and Cranborne were elected to the House of Commons with a few months of each other, met constantly in the same enclosed world and occasionally corresponded. Each maintained closer friendships; but in an age that hesitated before exchanging Christian names they were invariably 'my dear Jim' and 'my dear George'. Curzon's private comments on Cranborne's ill success as Under-Secretary for Foreign Affairs, an office he himself had previously filled with brazen confidence, were uncomfortably patronizing; but he could hardly fail to recognize merit in a friend whose father had promoted him from the back benches after only five years in the Commons and sent him out to govern India before he was forty.

The first rift came in the summer of 1904, when Curzon returned to England on leave between the first and second terms of his Viceroyalty. Earlier that year he had accepted the sinecure office of Lord Warden of the Cinque Ports left vacant by Lord Salisbury's death in 1903. Its supposed attraction was the official residence, Walmer Castle, with its sea air and view of the English Channel.* Unlike most former occupants who had used it only for occasional weekends, he proposed to spend long periods there after his final return from India; the family house, Kedleston, in Derbyshire, was several hours' journey from London, and in any case was still occupied by his father.

* See above, page 44.

82

It was the custom that each incoming Lord Warden bought his predecessor's furniture at a valuation. Curzon was reluctant to do so. He intended to refurnish the castle in the elaborate style to which he was accustomed and had no use for the worn pieces of a seaside villa. As he wrote soon after arriving there on a visit of inspection, many of the carpets were swarming with maggots and he was obliged to live on bare boards impregnated with carbolic. Who then should bear the loss of the discarded furnishings, the new Lord Warden or the heir of the old? They agreed to abide by the decision of an arbiter. It pleased neither of them. Salisbury was astonished that Curzon had not been required to buy the furniture introduced by his father, but only those pieces which old Lord Salisbury had taken over from Dufferin in 1896. Curzon complained of the amount of unwanted trash thrust upon him and accused Salisbury's solicitor of acting in a 'malicious, malignant, vindictive and revengeful manner'. On receiving Curzon's cheque for £1,500, the amount of the final, reduced valuation, Salisbury allowed himself the mild comment that 'it has been more bother than the settlement of the French *Entente Cordiale*'. Curzon reacted with a dozen ample pages of reproof and wounded pride that Salisbury should now indulge in unjustified sarcasm at his expense. The whole episode, he added, had caused him 'an infinitude of trouble that had gone far to embitter my brief holiday in England'.

In Curzon's defence it must be said that his nerves were frayed by overwork and the chronic pain of a weak spine, by anxiety about his wife's health and a succession of frustrating quarrels with the Balfour government on Indian policy. Yet even when allowances have been made, it is Salisbury who emerges from the encounter with cool temper and financial generosity.

Later that year Curzon sailed for Bombay to resume a prolonged and bitter battle with the Commander-in-Chief, Lord Kitchener, on the future of military administration in India. Each appealed to the Cabinet at home which ultimately decided against Curzon, thus provoking his resignation in the summer of 1905. What the humiliated Viceroy did not know was that Kitchener had been using Alice Salisbury as a secret channel of communication with the government of which her husband was a member and cousin Arthur the head. By every mail the Commander-in-Chief sent her sheet upon sheet of disparaging comment on Curzon, with the request that it should be made known to the Cabinet. She complied, not out of malice towards Curzon but out of friendship for Kitchener. Following the custom of the Victorian Age, Kitchener had several years before made it his business to further a promising professional career by securing influential political ties. From the moment he took the Prime Minister's fourth son, Lord Edward Cecil, on to his staff for the Sudan campaign of 1896, he was assured of a sympathetic hearing at Hatfield. The letters which he wrote so assiduously to Alice Salisbury for the eyes of the Cabinet did not determine his quarrel with an unsuspecting Curzon; but they helped. He also sent an enormously long apologia to Linky, with the quaint demand that it should be read aloud in the House of Commons during a forthcoming debate on Indian Army administration. By the time it reached London, however, the Member for Greenwich had lost his seat in the general election of 1906.

The entire Cecil family accepted Kitchener's version of the dispute. 'The accounts . . . of Curzon's attitude to the Home Government show him really to be hardly sane,' Gwendolen wrote. 'It is the Walmer furniture translated into politics.' Her sister Maud, hearing that Curzon might be in search of a seat in the Commons,* spitefully observed: 'Having held the semi-divine position of Viceroy of India, he is not quite sure whether he can, without loss of dignity, seek the suffrages of the great unwashed.' Even Salisbury, a stranger to vindictiveness, was moved to exclaim: 'How I dislike brilliant men – I mean for practical life. Just look at George Curzon!'

The menace of an aggressive Germany was never far from Salisbury's thoughts. As an undergraduate who had not long before accompanied his father to the Congress of Berlin, he noted how 'none of its inhabitants can forget that they belong to the first military power in Europe'. In 1901, when there were proposals for an Anglo-German defensive alliance, the Parliamentary Under-Secretary at the Foreign Office emphasized the antipathy that existed between the two countries, particularly on the German side. He wrote to the Foreign Secretary, Lord Lansdowne: 'The feeling is bitter, is deeply rooted and is increasing. It is not in the least likely to be altered by an alliance for many years to come, and if its origin is commercial not even then.' Such an awareness of international realities quickened his interest in the problems of defence and renewed a lifelong enthusiasm for part-time soldiering.

Lord Esher, the confidant of King Edward VII and chairman of the War Office Reconstruction Committee, went down to Hatfield one summer afternoon in 1908 and was moved by what he saw:

It is a real glimpse of another world, and breath of another atmosphere. Salisbury had camped his Militia Battalion under the

* On going out to India in 1898, Curzon had asked for an Irish, not a United Kingdom, peerage, so that he would not be debarred from re-entering the Commons on his return. But he chose the House of Lords after all, successfully seeking election as a representative Irish peer in 1908. Not until 1911 was he created a United Kingdom peer.

trees of the Park, about 400 yards away from the house. Our great country may be on the down-grade, but so long as we have men of his stamp, so simple and strenuous and so aloof from all the temptations which beset men of his class, giving every ounce of his energy which a not very strong frame permits to the service of the country, it is not possible that we can sink very low as a nation. There he was, under the shadow of his perfect Elizabethan place, under trees which may have shadowed *her* before she was Queen, drilling and training seven or eight hundred fine young Englishmen, quite as stalwart as any who fought for the Tudors.

Salisbury took a less romantic view of his military duties. 'I am just back from manoeuvres, where I was on a general's staff,' he wrote to a brother two years later. 'I came to the conclusion that it must be very difficult to be a general and not quite easy to be on his staff.' By the outbreak of the First World War in 1914, the former Cabinet Minister aged fifty-two was still commanding the regiment he had taken to South Africa nearly fifteen years before. But within a few months, Kitchener, by now Secretary of State for War, asked him to take over and prepare for battle a division of the Territorial Army. 'They have promoted me far beyond my military capacity,' declared the newly-gazetted major-general.

Sometimes I think it shows how hard up they are and sometimes that it is merely a job – a sort of rather respectable job to recognize the Militia or the patriotism of the landed aristocracy or the claims or susceptibilities of political opponents. Perhaps a little friendship may enter into it.

With only a tiny staff and hardly any officers from the Regular Army, Salisbury moulded his fifteen thousand civilians into a fighting formation. 'Jem is dreadfully like a general,' wrote his wife, 'except that he does not yet swear, but he will do that next, I feel convinced! But he really has been very efficient, and K. was quite amiable over the Division when he came down to review it.' By the end of 1915 his task was done. He passionately wished he could have remained in command of his men when they took the field against the Germans in the following year, but he recognized that training and command were two very different functions of the military mind.

In quite another way, Salisbury added a footnote to the history of the war. He gave permission for the park at Hatfield to be used for the secret trials of His Majesty's Land Ship Centipede, otherwise the first tank. Those who gathered there on 2 February 1916 and drove over an obstacle course of parapets and ditches included Kitchener, Lloyd

George and Balfour. The last of these, however, was persuaded by his colleagues to disembark before the machine attempted to cross a trench more than three yards wide. As his long frame was being eased feet first through the narrow sponson door, he was heard to remark that there was surely some more artistic method of leaving a tank. In 1919 Winston Churchill, Secretary of State for War, wrote to Salisbury, offering him one of the original machines 'as a memento of the days when we were allowed to make free with the privacy of your grounds'. For half a century it remained at Hatfield, a tourist attraction equalled only by the mournful remains of the oak tree under which Queen Elizabeth I had been sitting when she learned of her accession. In 1969 it was removed to the Royal Armoured Corps Tank Museum at Bovington.

Release from military duties turned Salisbury's thoughts once more to politics. Even after the widening of the Liberal administration in May 1915 to include such prominent Conservatives as Balfour, Curzon and Bonar Law, he shared the growing belief that the coalition lacked both initiative and unity of purpose, and that there could be no victory as long as Asquith remained Prime Minister. He hoped for a complete reconstruction of the ministry and the establishment of a small, powerful War Cabinet under the genial but admittedly irresolute Lord Derby. It was not until December 1916 that Asquith could be dislodged, when his successor proved to be a man far removed in temperament from Derby. Salisbury greeted the change with caution:

> I did not contemplate Lloyd George as the heaven-sent saviour of the Empire but as a *pis-aller*. . . . It may turn out that L.G. is a paragon, but we have made a leap in the dark. All we know was that *he* had got steam and that Squiff was unable to come to the prompt decisions which are absolutely the difference between disaster and no disaster.

The new Prime Minister invited Salisbury to become Leader of the House of Lords; but as the offer was accompanied by neither a seat in the War Cabinet nor a department of State, he pleaded an unwillingness to defend government measures on which he had not been consulted. He remained busy enough, however, as Chairman of the Conscientious Objectors' Board. To strike a balance between the conflicting pressures of conscription and conscience was a demanding task for a man of his mental scruples; in the more perplexing cases he delivered his verdict only after a private talk with the appellant in the prison cell. In 1917 he also accepted a place on the short-lived Reconstruction Committee dealing with topics such as housing and insurance. Before a meeting one afternoon, Beatrice Webb told Arnold Bennett, Salisbury withdrew from his fellow members and prayed aloud by the mantelpiece. She also recorded in her diary that he 'takes himself seriously as a great personage' and 'talks incessantly'. As all his other contemporaries found him modest and unargumentative, Mrs Webb's evidence cannot be accepted as conclusive.

Salisbury felt a growing sense of relief at having declined to serve in the new coalition. He harboured no resentment at Lloyd George's pre-war denigration of the landowning aristocracy, distasteful though he had found it; in the housing of his tenants, in the relief of their poverty, sickness and old age, he set himself standards at least as high as those of the welfare state. What increasingly repelled him was Lloyd George's seemingly reckless indifference to moral principles in both personal and political affairs. Through Salisbury's disdainful gaze, the Prime Minister who ultimately won the war remained the Chancellor of the Exchequer who in 1912 had furtively dabbled in Marconi shares.

He ignored whatever rumours reached him about Lloyd George's private life. But the supposed sale of honours was a topic on which he felt compelled to act. In March 1917 he wrote a deceptively courteous letter to the Prime Minister on behalf of himself and forty other Privy Counsellors. 'You occupy at the present time an exceptional position,' Salisbury told him, 'and we approach you in order to urge the supreme importance of keeping our public life pure and free from reproach.' For many years, he conceded, it had been the practice for political parties to reward their supporters with such honours as peerages, baronetcies, knighthoods and membership of the Privy Council. Now, however, such distinctions were being given in return for no services other than large contributions to party funds. Salisbury disclaimed any attempt to embarrass the government, but hoped that the Prime Minister would accept three recommendations:

1. That when any honour or dignity is conferred upon a British subject other than a member of the Royal Family, or the members of the naval, military, or permanent civil service under the Crown, a definite statement of the reasons for which it has been recommended to the Crown shall accompany the notification of the grant.

2. That a declaration be made by the Prime Minister in recommending any person to the favour of the Sovereign for any such honour or dignity, that he has satisfied himself that no payment or expectation of payment is directly or indirectly associated with the grant or promise of such an honour or dignity.

3. That an audit of party funds should be enforced which would prevent the abuses to which we have referred.

Not everyone may appreciate Salisbury's sense of timing or scale of priorities. Lloyd George, who had been Prime Minister for barely three months and was preparing for a spring offensive on the Western Front, certainly did not. He sent no reply. Salisbury waited several weeks, then wrote again. He gracefully acknowledged that 'the very heavy burden of responsibility which rests upon you at the present time has made it difficult for you to deal with this important letter with as much promptness as you would have desired'. But with almost imperceptible menace he added that there would shortly be a meeting of the forty-one signatories, before whom he would like to lay the Prime Minister's rejoinder. This time he was summoned to the presence.

Lloyd George accepted Salisbury's first proposition; on the second, he drew a reasonable distinction between payment for an honour and the recognition of past, unconditional donations to charitable or other public objects; he rejected the third on several grounds, among them that it would require legislation. He also told Salisbury that he had no objection to a debate in the House of Lords, and received an assurance that 'no attack would be made on the present government and that nothing indecorous would be said'. Salisbury kept his promise. The only startling speech was Curzon's audacious defence of the government:

> People are rather apt, supposing they see in the newspapers that an honour has been conferred upon some person unknown to themselves, to imagine that the honour has been bought. To be unknown to the public is not necessarily to be corrupt. . . .
>
> Just as the soldier gives his valour or courage or genius; just as the artist gives his talents; just as the captain of industry gives his energy or enterprise; just as the man of science gives his inventions to the service of the State, so the wealthy man gives, and in my view is entirely justified in giving, his wealth, which is very often his only asset, for the benefit of the country.

Salisbury and his friends remained unconvinced by such fancy, as well they might. The torrent of honours continued. A year later, twenty-five of the reformers resumed their campaign in a letter to *The Times*. They confused the issue, however, by simultaneously objecting to the proliferation of the Order of the British Empire, a distinction newly established to reward thousands of those who had rendered valuable but inconspicuous wartime service.

> Their indignation [a correspondent wrote] would have impressed me more deeply if I had been ignorant of the fact that every one of

the twenty-five had inherited a title or accepted one cheerfully in his own person. . . . Not one of them is less than a Privy Councillor, while Grand Crosses have been pretty liberally scattered among them.

Not until the Honours List of June 1922 appeared, awarding peerages to three businessmen of dubious reputation, was Salisbury able to rouse public opinion. In one of the most effective speeches of his career, he traced a 'rake's progress' along the road to honour: public services, public services and donations, public services and large donations, donations and public services, donations. Lloyd George was obliged to appoint a Royal Commission of inquiry. Its report, published in December 1922 and subsequently enacted, included the recommendation that a committee of three Privy Counsellors should scrutinize the names of all those submitted for honours and advise the Prime Minister on their probity.

By then Lloyd George had fallen from power, and in that too Salisbury played a part. He had never trusted the Prime Minister or cared for the continuation of a Liberal–Conservative coalition beyond the end of the war. More offended by its opportunist style of government than by its policies, he determined that the cause of true Conservatism should be saved from contamination. In June 1921 he wrote to the *Morning Post* calling upon members of his party to dissociate themselves from an administration in which they no longer retained full confidence. For a man who disliked public controversy it was a bold act that put a strain on his nervous system. 'I have been suffering badly from a conviction of inadequacy and futility,' he told his sister Gwendolen three days later. 'I am afraid I am not of the stuff of which political gladiators are made. However, your approval is a real solace. . . . I feel so dreadfully lonely.' He feared that the fall of the Lloyd George coalition might be followed not by a Conservative renaissance but by a Labour victory. With his two brothers in the Commons, both of whom had by now moved to the Opposition benches, he discussed other combinations of parties and personalities. The only two possible leaders at that moment seemed to be Grey and Birkenhead. 'Either a high-principled Liberal', he noted gloomily, 'or a low-principled Conservative.'

For the present, the coalition survived. But a year later he caught the disillusioned mood of the country in a vigorously worded manifesto:

The time has come when the British people should be fully informed of the sources of the evils which cause the grave peril and chaos in Ireland, the vacillation and errors in dealing with our great dependencies; unemployment on an unprecedented scale, languishing industries, an overgrown bureaucracy, and an overwhelming burden of taxation. The immediate need and the remedy is a rally of the deep-seated Conservative feeling in the country.

Unanimously elected 'Leader of the Conservative and Unionist Movement' in July 1922, he launched a spirited campaign against the Lloyd George coalition with the aid of a fighting-fund of £22,000 raised by the *Morning Post*. He was not alone in seeking to dislodge Lloyd George; but his call matched the growing discontent of others and his reputation ensured a receptive audience. On 19 October 1922, Conservative Members of Parliament in both Houses voted at the Carlton Club to withdraw from the coalition.

The general election that followed the dissolution of the coalition returned a wholly Conservative government to power for the first time since 1905. The more prominent members of the party, Balfour, Birkenhead and Chamberlain, refused to desert Lloyd George and with him prepared for a period in the political wilderness. Bonar Law, however, who agreed to abandon Lloyd George at the eleventh hour, was able to form a more competent administration than historians have sometimes allowed. When Birkenhead sourly observed that it consisted of 'second-class intellects', Lord Robert Cecil replied that England preferred to be governed by second-class intellects than by second-class characters.

Salisbury became Lord President of the Council, an office with few departmental duties that is often reserved for an elder statesman. He found many colleagues but few friends round the Cabinet table. An exception was the Foreign Secretary, George Curzon, who as Lloyd George's ship foundered had leapt nimbly aboard the sturdier vessel of Bonar Law. It had taken Salisbury some time to forget if not to forgive his defection at the time of the Parliament Bill. In 1916, when Curzon joined Lloyd George's War Cabinet, Salisbury wrote to Lord Milner:

> I dare say you know Curzon nearly as well as I do, but I have known him intimately all my life. He is a great friend. That is a bad beginning to a criticism, but in these days one must speak the truth. He is, I need not say, very able, very vigorous and very industrious with a great experience of administration, but he is rough and he is very often wrong.

Soon after the war, however, Curzon made an imaginative gesture that recognized Salisbury's place in national life. As acting Foreign Secretary, he had to find a new British Ambassador to the United States and narrowed his choice to two: Lord Crewe, the much-respected

Liberal statesman, and Salisbury. Curzon laid the problem before Lord Reading:

> Salisbury is the stronger, more virile and abler man, the better speaker, the more living thing. Lady S. is incomparable both as wife and hostess. Their name is proud and historic.
>
> Two fears only do I at all entertain. 1. that he might be thought or might even be too Conservative and not enough of a democrat (tho' indeed Lord S. has always been greatly interested in working-class problems), 2. that being a strong anti-Home Ruler he might not please that section of the American public.

Neither candidate was tempted, although Crewe did accept the Paris Embassy from Curzon three years later. Salisbury replied that he appreciated the importance of the Washington appointment but felt his place to be in the House of Lords. He added humbly: 'As I look at what I have written, I am overwhelmed by the pompous egotism which it seems to exhibit and if you smile at reading it, I should not have any right to be astonished.'

Perhaps he regretted that he was not on the other side of the Atlantic when in October 1922 he found himself deputy-Leader of the House of Lords as well as Lord President of the Council in the new government. For the Leader of the House was Curzon, who did not spare even Salisbury the imperious admonitions that so easily escaped him in those years. When after a few months Salisbury politely suggested proposals for a better conduct of business in Curzon's frequent absence as Foreign Secretary, he was told: 'I am not disposed to accept them, because they assume an abdication on my part of the main functions of leadership, which I had certainly never contemplated and for which I see no present necessity,' and so on for page after page. In vain Salisbury replied: 'If you will be the General and me the Colonel the thing can be done.' Curzon wanted to be both.

A less magnanimous man than Salisbury might have allowed that unpleasant episode to colour his judgement when, a few weeks later, Curzon suffered a crisis in his fortunes more acute than any since his departure from India in 1905. In May 1923, after only seven months as Prime Minister, Bonar Law was stricken by cancer and obliged to resign. The choice of his successor lay between the experienced but domineering Lord Curzon and the callow but placid Mr Stanley Baldwin. Many accounts have been published of the almost unanimous advice tendered to King George V by leading members of the Conservative party: that whatever the balance of personal qualities between the two contestants, a Prime Minister in the House of Lords would be unacceptable to a strong Labour opposition. Salisbury differed from his colleagues. He was having a holiday with his family in Devon when the King's private secretary suddenly summoned him to London. The last passenger train had already left, so he travelled up in the guard's van of a milk train, clad in the frock coat and tall hat that he invariably wore on official business until his death in 1947.

He told Stamfordham that although there were strong arguments in favour of a Prime Minister in the Commons, the claims of Curzon could not be disregarded. The Foreign Secretary had, after all, presided over the Cabinet during Bonar Law's absence. Stamfordham noted that Salisbury 'thought Curzon's faults were improving'; believed him to be 'the only acceptable Prime Minister'; said 'he would strongly recommend his being sent for'. Salisbury's counsel, however, was outweighed by that of Balfour and others; the prize went to Baldwin.

It would be pleasant to record that Curzon in his disappointment at least drew comfort from the quixotic gesture of his old but sometimes ill-used friend. But no such sentiment relieved the misery of his rejection. Six months later, as the Baldwin ministry fumbled towards a disastrous general election, Curzon wrote to his wife: 'All this is the result of the step taken by the King in May last. I wonder what Salisbury, Derby and co. who turned me down think now.' He died in 1925 without ever having known what a friend he had. Salisbury would have been the last man to tell him.

Except for the ten months of the first Labour government in 1924, Salisbury held office continuously from the fall of the Lloyd George coalition in 1922 to the second Labour victory of 1929. They were busy but increasingly bleak years. A succession of illustriously named offices – Lord President of the Council, Chancellor of the Duchy of Lancaster, Lord Privy Seal – gave him a voice in Cabinet and, on Curzon's death, the Leadership of the House of Lords. Yet never again after his months as President of the Board of Trade in 1905 was he entrusted with an important government department, and a minister without portfolio rarely leaves an imprint on events. As chairman of a sub-committee of the Committee of Imperial Defence, however, he was responsible in 1923 for the establishment of a permanent Chiefs of Staff committee. The heads of the Royal Navy, the Army and the Royal Air Force were in future required not only to advise their respective ministers on purely service matters, but also to offer collective advice to the government on broader questions of national defence. Less than twenty years later, Salisbury's far-sighted proposal armed Churchill with an indispensable instrument of war. It also earned its author the regard of Maurice Hankey, Secretary to both the Cabinet and the Committee of

Imperial Defence, and the most exacting as well as the most powerful public servant of his generation.

So rewarding an episode in Salisbury's ministerial life was exceptional. At the root of his restlessness lay a mistrust of Baldwin and a confirmation of the doubts which had led him to prefer Curzon as Prime Minister. 'Our leader, he wrote to Gwendolen at the end of 1923, 'is an excellent man, I believe, but a child wholly inexperienced in the technique of his position.' His lifelong sympathy with Free Trade was outraged by Baldwin's determination to fight a general election on a platform of Protection after only a few months in office, a decision taken without consulting a single government official on the consequences of such a policy. Salisbury's warning that it would be 'a profound mistake' was justified by the electoral tide which in December 1923 swept the Conservatives from power.

Personal factors also diminished his respect for Baldwin. He suspected that the Prime Minister was scheming to drop him and other traditional Conservatives from the government to make room for those prodigal sons who had remained faithful to the Lloyd George coalition, Austen Chamberlain and Birkenhead. Neither was a man for whom Salisbury would willingly sacrifice his political life. 'Chamberlain', he told Stamfordham, 'is identified in the public mind, not unreasonably, with the abandonment of principle and the disintegration of Conservatism.' As for Birkenhead's rehabilitation, he left Baldwin in no doubt that 'all this fatted calf business was a mistake'. The two errant Tories were obliged to remain in the wilderness until Baldwin formed his second administration after the Labour interregnum of 1924.

During his troubled relationship with Baldwin, Salisbury drew comfort from the presence in Cabinet of his brother Bob, who had been brought into the government as minister responsible for League of Nations affairs. 'I see his eyes glinting with suppressed mirth as examples of human individuality reveal themselves. I confess in my case sometimes it leads to an emotion of quite a different kind.' Salisbury was able to do his brother honour in every sense when in November 1923 indifferent health and fears that he might not be able to hold his parliamentary seat prompted Bob to retire from the Commons. At Lord Robert's own request, Baldwin agreed to prolong his political career by sending him to the House of Lords, but as a Baron, the lowest rank in the peerage. Only after Salisbury had personally intervened with the King was his brother created a Viscount, a dignity usually reserved for those who had held senior office far longer than the new peer.

Salisbury had less success in persuading Baldwin to introduce a measure that would simultaneously reduce the size and strengthen the powers of the House of Lords. But at least he had the satisfaction of sharing the scarlet benches of the unreformed chamber with two younger brothers, the recently ennobled Viscount Cecil of Chelwood and the Bishop of Exter; and with two brothers-in-law, the Earls of Selborne and Arran. He would later be joined by yet another brother, Hugh, Lord Quickswood; by two sons-in-law, the Duke of Devonshire and Lord Harlech; and even by his own elder son, exceptionally called to the Upper House during his own lifetime.

Baldwin's failure to invigorate the House of Lords was not the only dereliction that increasingly separated him from the traditionalist wing of his party. Salisbury endorsed his leader's concern for the poor, the sick and the defenceless. But the man who made do with cold Sunday supper at Hatfield so that his servants could go to church rebelled at Baldwin's payment of a subsidy to the coal industry as the price of settling the miners' strike of 1925. The practice, he believed, came uncomfortably close to nationalization and could in turn lead to state intervention in other industries. After years of doubt and disenchantment, he resigned from the leadership of his party in the House of Lords in June 1931 'for reasons of health', and never again sought office. The real cause of his going was contained in a private letter to Baldwin. 'Alas,' he wrote, 'you and I do not belong to the same school of Conservatism.'

Release from the restraints of office enabled Salisbury not only to introduce his own ill-fated Bill of 1934 for the reform of the House of Lords but also to challenge the Conservative hierarchy again in the following year by opposing the Government of India Bill. It was a mark of his deep feeling that on both occasions he flouted the unwritten procedure of the Upper House by making a speech on the first reading of the Bill. From the government front bench, Lord Halifax sorrowfully observed that since 1846 there had been only five occasions, including that day, on which a first reading had not been allowed to pass in silence; and that Salisbury had been responsible for two of them.

With much reluctance, Salisbury had earlier been persuaded to become a member of the joint-committee of both Houses of Parliament on whose report the Bill was based. The examination of 120 witnesses did nothing to alter his initial view that India was utterly unprepared, perhaps inherently unfitted, for democratic government; that the granting of dominion status could lead to the betrayal of helpless minorities for whose welfare Great Britain was responsible; that the proposed concessions to popular feeling would break the pledges given to successive generations of Indian princes. Against the combined strength of the Labour and Liberal parties supported by a large majority of Conservatives, Salisbury and his fellow critics could not hope to destroy the Bill. But they were persistent enough to retard its progress, to focus attention on its alleged dangers and so to depreciate its worth in Indian eyes. 'Seldom,' wrote Halifax in viceregal reproof, 'can a small minority have been able to affect more powerfully and, as I am bound to think, more unfortunately, the fate of a great constitutional enterprise.'

Salisbury remained impenitent. His ally Winston Churchill, deploying a formidable armoury of invective against the measure, called it 'a gigantic quilt of jumbled crochet work, a monstrous monument of shame built by pigmies'. Such florid language was not to Salisbury's taste; but he shared the sentiment.

Religion brought Salisbury no repose: only a tormented search for spiritual perfection. His ordeal was hidden from all but his immediate family. In Parliament and the Church Assembly he seemed to embody the Christian conscience with a serene authority that more artful orators could not emulate. But in his heart he brooded on the world-wide failure of conventional Christianity to repel the advance of materialism; and even the devoutness of his daily life was no protection against a sense of personal sin that would overwhelm him with melancholy.

In his seventy-sixth year he discovered the Oxford Group; or rather, such was the practice of that socially sensitive movement, the Oxford Group discovered him. The connection between Dr Frank Buchman's venture and the ancient University from which it took its name was more tenuous than his apologists cared to admit. Yet it was at a three-day conference under the austere roof of Lady Margaret Hall, the first women's college to be established in Oxford, that Dr Buchman himself initiated Salisbury into the creed of the Group.* To its ethical foundations of honesty, purity, unselfishness and love, it brought the techniques of 'sharing' and 'guidance'. The first was the confession of sins, either privately or within the semi-privacy of a house party, as the members called their gatherings; the second was a direct communication with the Almighty, especially during a period set aside each morning for the purpose.

Exuberance of religious practice was remote from Salisbury's experience and repugnant to his fastidiousness. Even in the seclusion of the home he recoiled from any expression of inner belief; a public exposition of his spiritual struggles was beyond all possibility. The Oxford Group held no personal message for him. Yet both his curiosity and his sympathy were stirred by a movement able to inspire many

* Two years earlier, the Oxford Group had tried to secure the presence of Lord Hugh Cecil, one of the Members of Parliament for the University, at a similar house party. His attitude was altogether more suspicious than that of his eldest brother. In declining the invitation he suggested with a touch of mischief that Lady Astor would be a more worthy guest than himself.

thousands of young people with apparently Christian ideals. In spite of the pressure which the Oxford Group put on him to declare himself a member, he was never in danger of abandoning his own conservative pattern of religious devotion and thought. But until his death in 1947 he remained an active though occasionally embarrassed patron, of more service to the Oxford Group than the Oxford Group was to him.

During those dozen years Salisbury never doubted the sincerity of the movement's aims, however crude he may have found its methods. It is nevertheless surprising that he should not have questioned the character of a religious leader who, he noted after their first meeting, 'is on the closest terms with Himmler in Germany'. Salisbury was well aware of the Nazi menace. In February 1936 he opened a debate in the House of Lords on national defence and in July accompanied Winston Churchill on a deputation of Privy Counsellors that begged the Prime Minister, once more Stanley Baldwin, to face the realities of rearmament. Yet such was his regard for the Oxford Group that between the two events he sent out invitations for a 'house party' to be held at Hatfield in October. His trust survived even Buchman's much-publicized statement to an American newspaper in August: 'I thank heaven for a man like Adolf Hitler who built a front line of defence against the anti-Christ of Communism.' Six weeks later the founder of the Oxford Group was welcomed by Salisbury to perhaps the most bizarre gathering in the history of Hatfield.

The host himself attended to every detail of the two-day meeting. 'I do not know that much is gained by multiplying the number of those who are representing your people,' he wrote hopefully to the Rev Cuthbert Bardsley,* then a member of the Oxford Group inner circle. Buchman nevertheless turned up with a task force of nearly a dozen dedicated disciples. They included Loudon Hamilton, in whose rooms at Christ Church, Oxford, the movement first took shape; Kenaston Twitchell, another early member; the Rev. John Roots, son of the Bishop of Hankow; Sir Philip Dundas, a Scottish baronet; and Roger Faure, a French Protestant.

To meet the team of proselytisers, Salisbury invited a score of his friends, most of them prominent in public life. Among them were Lord Sankey, Lord Chancellor in the last Labour government and a leading Welsh Churchman; two Conservatives of ministerial rank, Sir John (later Lord) Davidson and Lord Eustace Percy; a trio of Indian proconsuls, Halifax, Lytton and Goschen; Sir John (later Lord) Cadman, a

---

* Bardsley, born in 1907 and educated at Eton and New College, Oxford, was ordained in 1932. He became Provost of Southwark Cathedral in 1944, Suffragan Bishop of Croydon in 1947 and Bishop of Coventry in 1956.

dominating figure in the oil industry; a scattering of members of parliament; and any Cecils who cared to come.

Salisbury's own record of the conference glows with enthusiasm:

There was abundant testimony by the Group speakers as to the results in their own lives which had been effected by the Group teaching – the peace, happiness and vigour which had followed. Similarly, in describing their experience of others who had been brought under the influence of the Group, they showed how friction in domestic life, unrest between employer and employed, and violent antagonism in politics had been softened or swept away. Lastly, the impression left upon the audience at the conference was that great numbers of people in country after country are waiting, almost panting, for a lead in things spiritual as the only hope to enable society to stand up against the moral and social degeneration of the time.

Lord Robert Cecil, too, congratulated the Group on having 'invested the old, simple Christ gospel with a new vividness particularly effective with people who have lost or never knew it'. But at the final session he was disturbed by Buchman's apparent readiness to condone the conduct of the Hitler regime:

I rather warmly protested [Bob told his wife] and he explained that he was far from approving such things as the persecution of the Jews. However, Dundas, a rather dour Scotch laird, seemed to say something of the kind and the Frenchman when pressed privately said that he thought that the Croix de Feu were the only hope of France.

Salisbury was a less perceptive judge of character than his brother, and his own reservations about the Oxford Group crystallized more slowly. He accepted that to some it offered a road to salvation; but not that it was the only road. He saw the value of asking for and receiving guidance; but did not believe that it was necessarily to be had on demand or a substitute for personal responsibility. He recognized the obligation of a Christian to share those spiritual experiences which could help others; but not so to treat all spiritual experiences, much less to make them public property. A memorandum he wrote on the Oxford Group in 1937 ended with these words: 'An undue and insecurely founded optimism involves considerable danger. There must be a reaction sooner or later, perilous to the individual who experiences it and, it may be, disastrous to the fellowship and teaching held to be responsible for it.'

As a young man, Salisbury once consulted his father on whether he should accept an invitation to join a certain committee. The Prime

Minister advised him to do so only if he were able to attend constantly to its business. Otherwise, he warned, 'you are perpetually furnishing hallmark to plate whose fineness you have no means of knowing'. Half a century later, still guided by that prudent principle, Salisbury declined to join a movement whose aims he admired but whose methods he could neither commend nor control. His detachment did not prevent him from publicly praising the Oxford Group in general terms as often as its adherents required. At Birmingham in 1937 he told a mass meeting:

> There have been no doubt criticisms of certain methods of this great movement, and these criticisms may or may not be justified. I have here no concern with minor details, but I will say with confidence that the spirit which is behind the effort of the Oxford Group in this meeting or elsewhere is not justly open to criticism.

The ambiguity of that fatal first sentence was never forgiven him. At the time he received no hint of reproach from the Group; even a half-committed Marquess of Salisbury was more useful than none at all. But two years later, after another supposed failing, a young collaborator of Buchman delivered this rebuke to the erring Salisbury, an elder statesman old enough to be his grandfather:

> A few men if they really cared and had had the courage could have saved the Group and Buchman long since from silly, stupid and unwarranted misconceptions of the work. You yourself were in a position to step forward and rid the country of this misconception. Your last week-end at Hatfield was spent on the level of people who wanted Germany to be changed, but who were not willing to change themselves. Sometimes it was almost trivial. And then when you had the opportunity of giving an answer to Germany at Birmingham, you failed.
>
> Let me illustrate. I happened to be with Buchman in Germany near Munich at that time. Advance reports were so enthusiastic that we dashed to an air-port sixty miles away to get a copy of *The Times* with someone who was prepared to take it forthwith and see that it reached the man a great many people want to reach. But alas, when you so clearly disassociated yourself from the Group, it was so inadequate that we were even unable to show it to the person concerned. . . .

Yet the mood of the Buchmanites could swing easily from snarling resentment to an equally embarrassing *bonhomie*. The reproof of February 1939 was followed on Salisbury's seventy-eighth birthday a few months later by a congratulatory ode that concluded:

So sing his birthday praise with joyous whoop
Who serves so well God, King and Oxford Group.

The members of the Group had every reason to flatter Salisbury. From the moment he declared himself willing to endorse their aims if not their methods, they used their influential adherent in a variety of ways. During the constitutional crisis that preceded the abdication of King Edward VIII in 1936 they asked him to try to have one of their number received at court. 'If the King and Ken Twitchell could somehow be brought together,' they told him, 'such a meeting might, under God, have incalculable results for the nation and the world.' The instructions were followed by an addendum. Dr Buchman himself would assume Mr Twitchell's role, having been 'called in consultation in similar situations by Queen Olga and Queen Sophie of Greece only a few years ago'. Salisbury passed on the request to the royal household, but the reply was presumably discouraging: King Edward abandoned his throne without the persuasive talents of the Oxford Group having been put to the test.

A few months later, at Bardsley's prompting, Salisbury wrote to the Archbishop of Canterbury, Dr Lang, begging him to secure an official invitation for representatives of the Oxford Group at the Coronation of the new monarch in Westminster Abbey. Again the quest failed. But Salisbury did succeed in engaging Lord Athlone, Queen Mary's brother, to broadcast a tribute to the Oxford Group specially prepared for him at Buchman's headquarters. Athlone was also urged to extract a message from his nephew, King George VI, to be quoted in his talk. The King, however, declined to become involved, and instructed his private secretary to tell Salisbury why. First, he explained, because of the acute controversy which by now surrounded the Group; and secondly, because he feared the use to which the leaders of the movement would put any such message.

Salisbury's services to the Oxford Group were not always so exalted. He paid for the distribution of its propaganda. He sparred on its behalf with *The Times* and the BBC about allegedly distorted or meagre reports of its activities. He collected the names of fellow peers and politicians prepared to testify to its worth. He asked Anthony Eden to receive Ken Twitchell and Lord Halifax to receive John Roots. He was active in helping the Oxford Group to have itself registered by the Board of Trade under that precise name so that gifts or bequests made to it under such a style would not be ruled legally invalid. Its assumption of the word 'Oxford', which had long irritated its opponents and even its uncommitted well-wishers like Archbishop Lang, could not be challenged. But A. P. Herbert, one of the Members of Parliament for Oxford

University, tried to rob it of advertising value by insisting that the movement should be obliged to add the word 'Limited' to its name. Herbert's campaign failed to move the government, and the name Oxford Group was allowed to be registered without the humiliating suffix.*

Touched by Salisbury's helpful interest in so many aspects of the Group's work, Buchman sought ways of showing his gratitude. On hearing one year that the Cecils were embarking on a Mediterranean cruise, he proposed asking the Greek royal family to receive the travellers in Athens. Salisbury reacted to the offer with supine courtesy: 'I think on the whole, if you will allow me, I will not take advantage of your kind offer. We will go quietly upon our trip.'

In the spring of 1939 a shadow fell across their cordiality. At Buchman's request, Salisbury began to arrange another house party at Hatfield, 'to consider practical steps for promoting Moral Re-armament in this country'. All went well at first. The Archbishop of Canterbury readily agreed to take part, and at five o'clock one morning the thought came to Buchman: 'God had a Plan for the Hatfield week-end and we need to find that Plan. Guidance will give us that Plan.' Then disappointment set in. Buchman was particularly anxious for Baldwin to emerge from retirement, 'that he might be the authoritative voice to bring about the spiritual rebirth of the Empire'. But the wily old man was not to be caught. He replied to Salisbury's invitation: 'We are thinking of going south for a short spell. . . . The offer of the best bedroom nearly broke me down.' Other eminent men also sent their regrets, by now aware of how adroitly the Oxford Group flourished the names of aristocratic or political associates for publicity purposes. The guest list dwindled into mediocrity.

As if at a word of command, Buchman's henchmen turned spitefully on Salisbury. One young mentor told him: 'You failed the nation at Birmingham. You will fail again, and then misinterpret the motives of the people who tried to help. But if you fail this time you will only have yourself to blame, for you have been amply warned.' The letter concluded on a lofty note: 'Tomorrow I am going up with a few others to spend the whole evening with the Preston North End Football Team. They, with their more simple philosophy of life, may be the people who are going morally to rearm England.' Another member of Buchman's inner circle, also in Holy Orders, rebuked Salisbury for his failure to seek guidance during preparations for the second Hatfield house party; how very different, he pointed out, from the organizers of a similar Group gathering at Eastbourne who had won a warm commendation from the press attaché of the German Embassy. Salisbury replied to

* The practical value of the victory was short-lived, as the Oxford Group began increasingly to call itself Moral Re-Armament.

these impertinences with Christian meekness: 'I think it is in the highest degree likely that the spirit in which I approached the invitations was very inadequate, and if it be so I am full of remorse.' A prolonged bout of influenza was a valid enough excuse for him to abandon all further efforts to salvage the house party.

Salisbury shrugged off the episode without resentment. However severely he was accustomed to censure his own conduct, he judged the failings of others with limitless indulgence. Less easy to explain is the regard of a lifelong and dedicated member of the Church of England for a revivalist movement that scarcely ever recognized the divinity of Christ. As Archbishop Lang wrote to Salisbury: 'With all my gratitude for what the movement has done I cannot but note with some anxiety this absence of the distinctively Christian position.'

Nor was the Archbishop likely to be impressed by Salisbury's account of Oxford Group successes solemnly claimed at a conference in Bournemouth during the first months of the war. It would be difficult to find a parable of more inspired irrelevancy for the England of 1940:

> In Papua the hearts of wild tribesmen have been touched. 'God is our chief,' they say, and when their pagan neighbours attack them they no longer fight; they cover their eyes with their hands and there is a pause, and the war-painted warriors fade away.

The man of faith was prepared to accept the testimony of primitive peoples; but the former major-general would lend no support to a hardly less fantastic scheme prepared by the Oxford Group during the early months of the Second World War. It envisaged a huge and officially recognized network of Moral Re-Armament officers spread throughout the British Army, each to wear uniform and to receive travelling allowances and rations. The most Salisbury felt able to recommend to the author of the scheme was that unofficial Moral Re-Armament leaders should be allowed to operate in military units with the knowledge and consent of commanding officers.

In 1941, his eightieth year, Salisbury rendered a last courageous service to the Oxford Group. He tried to persuade Ernest Bevin, the Minister of Labour and National Service, to exempt twenty-nine of their full-time workers from being called up into the Armed Forces; with the support of Lang, he asked that they should instead be classified as ministers of religion or at least as lay evangelists. Bevin would agree to do no more than defer the calling-up of a handful of them, all over the age of thirty, for a few months. Dissatisfied by the decision, Salisbury renewed his plea in the House of Lords. The mood of the country, already resistant to privileged demands, was further stiffened by the shrillness of the Group's campaign at a time of national danger.

Salisbury received the stinging reply that of the seven million people covered by the National Service Act, only the eleven members of the Oxford Group seeking exemption had thought fit to press for it through parliamentary debate. It was a harsh blow for an elder statesman of acknowledged integrity who was also chairman of the influential Watching Committee of back-bench parliamentarians determined upon a vigorous prosecution of the war.

That was not the end of Salisbury's romance with the Oxford Group. But for the remaining half dozen years of his life his mind and energies were directed increasingly towards a reunion of Christian forces in which the Group would play no independent role. At a meeting to discuss the project with the Archbishop of Canterbury and other Anglican leaders at Lambeth Palace in March 1947 he exhausted his last reserves of strength, dying at his house in London a few days later.

It is one of the paradoxes of Salisbury's later life that the man who seemed so perplexed in his spiritual pilgrimage, so pliant in the hands of the Oxford Group, displayed only clarity of thought and robustness of will in all other of his private and public activities. Like many large landowners of advancing years, he prudently transferred the ownership of Hatfield and other family property to his elder son and heir, thus ensuring that Cranborne would avoid having to pay the maximum scale of estate duty at his father's death. Whatever the financial attractions of the operation, it proved to have unexpected personal disadvantages. Cranborne, a Conservative Member of Parliament for Dorset since 1929, was six years later appointed Parliamentary Under-Secretary at the Foreign Office. The triple burden of ministerial duties (including attendance at sessions of the League of Nations in Geneva), a seat at Westminster and the care of a distant constituency left him little time to supervise the estates that now were his and caused him agonies of conscience. Salisbury, by contrast, deprived of the occupation he most enjoyed, 'glowered gloomily bored in the house', as a sister put it.

At the end of 1936 Salisbury and his son therefore came to a new arrangement. They set up an unlimited private company with a nominal capital of £3,100,000 for the purpose of owning and managing the family assets. Salisbury became permanent governing director and chairman of the Gascoyne-Cecil Estates Company, and Cranborne the other managing director. In addition to certain tax benefits, the scheme enabled the father to resume his personal supervision of the estates and the son to concentrate on politics. 'Jem has been to see every farm since Christmas,' Lady Gwendolen wrote from Hatfield in mid-January 1937, 'is now going for the cottages and has altogether taken on a new lease of life and spirits. It is fatal for any of my family not having enough to do.'

As well as assuming other local obligations, from churches and church schools to prisons and remand homes, he attended the House of Lords with unobtrusive regularity. Many of the causes supported by that neat spare figure in the old-fashioned frock coat had been lost a generation or more before. But after his death, peers of all parties paid him a rare compliment; they subscribed to have a bust of him by Benno Elkan placed in the precincts, 'in token of their affection and esteem'.

The most remarkable of the services he rendered his country, and one which he continued to discharge well into his ninth decade, was known to no more than a handful of politicians and civil servants. From 1940 to 1945 he was chairman of an unofficial but influential committee of parliamentarians who undertook a watching role over the conduct of successive wartime governments. The committee had its roots in the opposition of most but not all of its members to the pre-war policies of appeasing the dictators pursued by Baldwin and Neville Chamberlain. The Cecils had long identified themselves with those dissident Conservatives who clamoured for speedier rearmament coupled with a stiffer front against the pretensions of Mussolini and Hitler. Hugh Cecil epitomized the family spirit when writing of the conquest of Ethiopia in 1936: 'The Italian government has killed and is about to take possession. Friendliness to Italy would seem to British opinion morally intolerable; and what is morally intolerable is not politically expedient.' Two years later, when Anthony Eden resigned as Foreign Secretary after a prolonged conflict of views with Chamberlain, his Parliamentary Under-Secretary did not hesitate to accompany him into exile.

> I don't like the Prime Minister's policy [Cranborne wrote]. The impression he gives of truckling to the dictators is, I believe, disastrous. It makes us ridiculous in the eyes of the world. It takes the heart out of our real friends and provides us, at the best, with some very undependable new ones in exchange. It alienates American opinion too, which is of essential importance at the present time. Nor do I think that it lessens the danger of war. But at any rate it must be given a fair trial, and that it is certainly having. In the meantime I am quite happy cultivating roses at Cranborne. The results are both quicker and more satisfying.

There were social undertones to Cecilian contempt for the appeasers. Bob believed that the government would continue to act with timidity as long as it was dominated by commercially-minded, middle-class politicians. The aristocrats, he observed, were 'all for singeing Musso's beard, but S[tanley] B[aldwin], Ramsay [MacDonald], Runciman, Simon and co. and the Chamberlains are terrified if he frowns at them. *Conspuez les Bourgeois* !!' Gwendolen offered a variant on this theme. She thought Halifax, Eden's patrician successor at the Foreign Office, more culpable than Chamberlain himself, since 'a poor old middle-class monster could not be expected to know any better'.

There is no evidence that Salisbury ever shared, much less gave tongue to such wounding sentiments. Yet it was in a like-minded aristocrat, Winston Churchill, that he found his strongest ally in rousing the country from her sloth. Salisbury had never cared for Churchill's flamboyant personality and political fickleness any more than his father had relished those qualities in Lord Randolph. But in their joint call for rearmament they were drawn together by a fierce patriotism, a lifelong love of soldiering and an indifference to personal unpopularity. With the declaration of war on Germany in September 1939, their common cause seemed to have prevailed. Whatever the perils that lay ahead, there could be no further dispute about the claims of defence or the preservations of honour; and, as if to bind the Chamberlain government to its task, Churchill was recalled to office as First Lord of the Admiralty.

Within sight of his eightieth year, Salisbury knew that he no longer had an executive role to play. Yet as the first months of the war slipped by in apparent lassitude, he grew uneasy. The men who had rearmed too little and too late seemed to show a similar want of purpose in their new-found belligerency. In peacetime he had never hesitated to stand up in the House of Lords and remind his party leaders of their duty; in war such a challenge could be interpreted as lending strength to the enemy. So he determined on a more unobtrusive course. A score or so of experienced and independent-minded parliamentarians would meet regularly at his house in Arlington Street to discuss the progress of the war; he, as their chairman, would then convey their conclusions to the government. To avoid the embarrassment of publicity or outside pressures, even the existence of the group was to remain a secret.

The Watching Committee, as it was known, drew its original members equally from Lords and Commons. The peers included Salisbury's brother, Cecil of Chelwood; Hailsham, the former Lord Chancellor; Astor, owner of the Sunday newspaper, the *Observer*; Lloyd, the resolute but headstrong High Commissioner for Egypt whom Salisbury had hastened to vindicate after his enforced resignation in 1927; Trenchard, the Kitchener of the Royal Air Force; and Swinton, who claimed to have been removed from the Air Ministry by Chamberlain in 1938 for showing too much enthusiasm.

From the House of Commons came Duff Cooper, the only member

of the Cabinet who had resigned in protest against the Munich agreement of 1938; Leo Amery,* an apostle of imperialism too uncompromising to be found a place in recent Conservative administrations; Harold Macmillan, a disconcertingly radical Tory; Harold Nicolson, ultimately to find a deeper satisfaction in letters than in politics; Cranborne, and his cousin Wolmer.

The first meeting of the Committee took place on 4 April 1940 and a few days later Salisbury called on the Prime Minister by appointment. Although their conversation, he afterwards wrote, 'was on the most friendly footing throughout', that is not how the record reads. Chamberlain dismissed out of hand the almost unanimous recommendation of the Committee that there should be a smaller War Cabinet composed of ministers without departmental duties. In any case, he added, public opinion would not approve such a change. The brusqueness of the Prime Minister's reply provoked even the mild-mannered Salisbury into retorting that members of his Committee were better judges of public opinion than members of the government.

Nor was Chamberlain any more forthcoming when Salisbury pressed him to relieve Churchill of a burden recently added to that of the Admiralty: the chairmanship of the Military Co-ordination Committee, which, as Churchill himself later complained, brought him 'an exceptional measure of responsibility but no power of effective direction'. Salisbury's account of their talk continues:

> In answer to my question whether he would state what I was entitled to report to the Committee, he would not let me report that he would consider what I had said: all I might say was that he was satisfied with the result of recent changes, though he was always open to give any other suggestions due consideration.

Two days earlier, Norway had been invaded by the Germans. Salisbury, perhaps with less tact than he usually commanded, warned Chamberlain that a British defeat in Norway would have serious consequences. The Prime Minister resented it:

> He replied [Salisbury noted] that the neutrals were greatly in fault; that they did not ask for our help until they were actually attacked. If therefore they suffered in consequence, they would be themselves to blame. . . .
>
> He showed that his conception of international disasters was

---

* His contempt for the Chamberlain government had been reinforced by a conversation with the Air Minister, Kingsley Wood, two days after the outbreak of war. When Amery urged him to set fire to the Black Forest and so aggravate the shortage of timber in Germany, Wood replied that there was no question of bombing either the Black Forest or even the munition works at Essen, which were private property.

limited to whose fault it was, whereas the real question – the only question – is their reaction upon the credit and prestige of this country and the confidence that we inspire elsewhere. Birmingham politics, in fact!

Cranborne shared his father's impatience with a Prime Minister so lacking in vision. Having read Salisbury's memorandum on the conversation with Chamberlain, he replied:

His attitude seems to be dominated by a doctrine something like that of papal infallibility. He can't be wrong – he can't take advice from anyone else. If he has once laid it down that this is the right form of Cabinet to direct the war, it must be the right form. If he has chosen seven men to be members of it, they must be the only men capable of doing the job. If our policy does not produce the results which he expected, that cannot conceivably be his fault – it must be the opposition or the neutrals or someone else who is to blame.

The Committee had reason to feel frustrated by the first encounter of their chairman with the Prime Minister. Nor was its temper improved by a meeting with Lord Halifax on 29 April. In reply to Salisbury's cogent list of government failings, the Foreign Secretary spoke loftily of the disadvantages from which the British Empire must suffer in the initial stages of a defensive war. 'The chairman thanked Lord Halifax,' the minute-book records, 'but said that the Committee was not satisfied.'

Chamberlain's intransigence cost him dear. Within a month of his crusty exchange with Salisbury, a rebellion in the Conservative ranks of the Commons had cut his majority from 240 to 80 and obliged him to make way for Churchill as Prime Minister of an all-party government. Even had the Watching Committee never existed, it is unlikely that Chamberlain's administration could have survived much longer. If, however, he had shown himself more accommodating in his manner towards influential back-benchers, his fall need not have been so humiliating. As it was, those members of the Watching Committee who sat in the Commons hardened their hearts when on 8 May his conduct of the war was put to the vote; eight of the twelve disregarded Salisbury's advice merely to abstain and instead joined more than thirty other Conservative rebels in the opposition lobby.

On the following day the Watching Committee met again and unanimously decided to press for both a change of Prime Minister and an all-party government. Salisbury passed on their views to Halifax the same afternoon. By the evening of 10 May, Chamberlain had resigned (subsequently agreeing to serve his successor as Lord President of the

Council) and Churchill had begun to construct his coalition. It is a mark of Salisbury's shrewdness that, of the men he had chosen for his Watching Committee little more than a month before, no fewer than six MPs and two peers were at once given office in an all-party administration.*

Cranborne was among them, 'Winston gave as a reason that he valued his counsel,' Gwendolen wrote. 'The more probable one I suppose was that he valued his name as a counterweight to the socialists he was inviting in.' Relations between Cranborne and Churchill had not always been harmonious. The Cecils enjoyed telling of the occasion two or three years before when Churchill, at the lowest point of his political fortunes, had been annoyed by the Parliamentary Under-Secretary's loyal defence of government foreign policy: 'You say that because you get £1,500 a year to say it.' Cranborne retorted: 'Well, you'd talk very differently if you had £1,500 a year.'

Salisbury too had never shaken off a mildly distasteful recollection of the volcanic young Churchill at the turn of the century. 'To fly into a fine frenzy over the mustard pot or the sugar tongs', as Schomberg McDonnell said of him, 'is indeed wearisome.' Soon after Churchill's defection to the Liberal party in 1904, Salisbury included in a letter to him the stiff sentence: 'In politics as distinguished from personal matters I have had to do, not with the people who have left us, but with those whom we still retain.' Replying to Churchill's protest, he admitted that a man had a right to change his party, then added: 'And yet in my heart I think it was not your act but your demeanour in so acting which led me to be rude.'

As the country braced itself for a German invasion in the summer of 1940, lingering doubts about Churchill's character were stilled; the prophet had come into his own. Their long acquaintanceship, however, and shared stand on rearmament encouraged the older man to address the new Prime Minister in private with a forceful candour that few others dared to employ. He continued to speak ostensibly on behalf of the Watching Committee. But the members he recruited from the Commons to replace the recently promoted ministers were of lesser calibre; and those from the Lords had mostly had their day. If Salisbury's voice carried conviction in Downing Street and Whitehall between 1940 and 1945, it was by virtue of his own reputation for sagacity.

He found an early opportunity of asserting his right to be taken seriously. Less than a month after the Churchill coalition had assumed office, he sent the Prime Minister two detailed complaints about the way in which cumbersome Treasury control was hampering both the

* In the course of the war, another six of the original members also became ministers.

manufacture of arms in Great Britain and their purchase from the United States. The reply, a complacent document, displeased him. He wrote sharply to Brendan Bracken, Churchill's parliamentary private secretary:

> I have received a letter dated the 25th June signed by the Prime Minister which has greatly surprised me. I say *signed* by him because I am quite sure he is not responsible for its drafting. It is in the style with which I am very familiar, in which a Public Office counters an inconvenient Parliamentary question....

After a point-by-point demolition of the Treasury's defence, he concluded magisterially: 'This peace-time technique for answering inconvenient questions cannot of course continue with such a body as the Watching Committee.'

In a friendly reply the same day, Bracken confided that Salisbury's representations had already prompted some improvement in the old procedure. He added: 'Your Committee's "gingering" activities could not be more useful in times like this. My Master has to champion his Chancellor. But your letters are seen by the Treasury and indignantly digested.'

Herbert Morrison, the chirpy Home Secretary and Minister of Home Security, also received a roasting when attempting to prevaricate on a matter of civil defence:

> There is really no reason in the correspondence between us to beat about the bush as if we were inexperienced Members of Parliament [Salisbury wrote]. You say that your Office worked in the closest harmony with the Ministry of Health. No doubt in one sense that is true: but not in any effective sense.

Soon after the fall of France, he pressed Churchill to remove General Sir Edmund Ironside from the command of the Home Forces on the grounds that he was too old and had not experienced German mechanized warfare. 'No argument that being incompetent as CIGS he might safely be given the command of this country is any good now,' Salisbury wrote. 'The situation is revolutionised.' The Prime Minister replied that 'all discussion on such a subject is likely to spread want of confidence at this dangerous time'. But six days later Ironside was replaced by General Sir Alan Brooke, who had commanded an Army Corps during the retreat to Dunkirk.

The industry and alertness with which the Watching Committee scrutinized the war effort often revealed shortcomings or initiated reforms. Yet many supposed scandals sprang not from human frailty but from inevitable shortages of men and material; and there were times when exhausted ministers could justly resent the scolding they received from warriors in retirement and politicians out of office. After the abortive attack on the West African port of Dakar held by the forces of the Vichy government, Churchill might surely have been spared this letter from Salisbury:

> It seems to be in the direct succession of the futilities in Czecho-slovakia, Poland, Finland and Norway: it indicates an infirmity of purpose which unless it can be expurgated from our procedure may be fatal. If there was in fact a firm resolution not to shed any French blood, it is difficult to see why our ships were there at all, unless it was merely for bluff, which is inexcusable. If it was right to sink two French destroyers it could not have been right to break off the engagement. I suspect the Admiralty were very much to blame. For goodness sake if this be so make the necessary change.

Recognizing the patriotism that inspired his correspondent and the hindsight which so deceptively dispels the fog of battle, Churchill never returned an unkind word. As he laid plans to destroy the enemy in that autumn of 1940, he may even have smiled on reading Salisbury's admonition: 'I hope you will reflect that all doctrines of appeasement defeat their own end.'

Salisbury was not a man to live in the past. Even before the threat of German invasion had receded, he invited a few friends on the Watching Committee to join him in producing a paper on Conservative policy in the post-war world. There was a practical purpose in his idealism. Disturbed by the undiminished vigour of socialist propaganda at a time when his own party was observing a wartime truce, he determined to end what he called 'a one-sided self-denying ordinance'. But as the laboriously drafted document was received without enthusiasm by his colleagues, he withdrew it from the Watching Committee, amended it to accord more closely with his own beliefs and had it published by John Murray as a sixpenny pamphlet.

Although *Post-War Conservative Policy* sold three thousand copies, it sounded no clarion call.* Its austere wartime format does not invite purchase; its text lacks those coruscating polemics which the author's father had brought to the same publisher's imprint eighty years before. In its dozen pages Salisbury commends the virtues of private property and religious education; of peacetime conscription and a reformed House of Lords; of agricultural prosperity and imperial free trade. He exposes the heartlessness of bureaucracy and the economic futility of

---

* It did, however, attract a letter of warm commendation from a young officer in the Royal Air Force called Reginald Maudling. 'I hope,' he wrote, 'at some future time to have an opportunity of standing for Parliament as a Conservative.'

punitive taxation ('It is much easier to destroy wealth than to destroy poverty, but poverty is the enemy, not wealth'). He encourages the organization of labour but also the protection of the individual from unfair political pressures within the unions themselves. He condemns the nationalization of land but not the control of its development, State management of industry but not State intervention.

It is a testament that has worn well with the years.

5

Lord William Cecil
1863–1936

William, second son of third Marquess of Salisbury. Known to his family and close friends as Fish.

Born 9 March 1863. Educated at Eton and University College, Oxford. Ordained 1887. Curate at Great Yarmouth 1887–8. Rector of Hatfield 1888–1916. Bishop of Exeter 1916–36.

Married 16 August 1887 Lady Florence Bootle-Wilbraham (known as Fluffy), daughter of first Earl of Lathom. She died 17 May 1944.

They had four sons, three of whom were killed in action in the First World War, and three daughters.

Lord William died 23 June 1936.

During Lord William Cecil's twenty years as Bishop of Exeter, he was hardly ever known to use the swifter of the two railway routes between the West Country and London; it would have carried him within sight of Eton College and so revived unhappy memories of that distant prospect. The damp Thames valley had given him rheumatism; the other boys in his house had bullied him; his own parents, by encouraging a spirited independence in their children, had left them unprepared for any society less sophisticated than Hatfield. He reacted to the ordeal with a dogged defiance that earned him the reputation of being a queer fish, and it was as Fish rather than William that family and close friends knew him for the rest of his life.

Oxford restored him to a cheerful unruliness. 'I really must decline to answer questions about the expediency of College rules or to argue with you about them,' the senior dean informed him. 'My business is to enforce them when I see them broken.' Such letters often enlivened William's morning mail. After celebrating an unexpectedly successful examination result, he received qualified congratulations from the same stern source: 'Your rejoicings were natural but immoderate. It is just as well for the comfort of sleepy people that you don't pass more frequently.' The junior dean joined the chorus of reproof with quite a long screed beginning: 'I must beg you to co-operate a little more with me in a good cause by bringing your dog less frequently into College. . . .' Even the Metropolitan Board of Works threatened Lord William with prosecution for having ridden a horse across the grass on Hampstead Heath. He left the University in 1885 with Third-Class Honours in Jurisprudence.

The horizons of a nobleman's younger son in the late-nineteenth century were hardly broader than those of his great-grandfather. Unless the family happened to be exceptionally rich, the heir alone was found a seat in the House of Commons. His brothers were directed towards the Army or the Navy, the public service or the learned professions. A scale of propriety governed even that narrow choice. Foot Guards and cavalry scorned regiments of the Line. An embassy was held in more regard than the Foreign Office. Aristocracy condescended to become a barrister but not a solicitor; to seek a rectory or a university Fellowship but scarcely ever a consulting room in Harley Street. As the Victorian Age drew to a close, merchants and company directors increasingly crossed the threshold of acceptability; but finance remained a more respectable occupation than commerce, inheritance preferable to self-help. The Cecils shunned trade in all its forms, not because they despised the drawing-room deficiencies of the 'cotton lords', as the Prime Minister called them, but because as a class the new men were 'pitiless to the poor'.

Lord William shared the family passion for politics. At Puys one summer, noticing a copy of Guizot's life of Sir Robert Peel in the room of the French tutor, Coppini, he burst out: 'I detest Peel. He's a traitor.' The statesman who outraged the landed interest in 1846 by repealing the Corn Laws had then been in his grave for over thirty years. As at least two of William's brothers were determined to enter the House of Commons, he finally narrowed his own choice of career to the Navy or the Church; and having rejected a sailor's life for its 'discipline and salt-pork', he prepared to take Holy Orders. Dr Coppini was shocked: 'This future clergyman who moves in fashionable society, who enjoys hunting and dancing and "will marry a pretty girl" (so his mother tells me) is rather a surprising type to a Parisian who lives not far from Saint-Sulpice.'*

The *bon vivant* himself also had doubts whether he was worthy of

* The Church in Paris where the Comte de Frayssinous (1765–1841) delivered his celebrated addresses on dogmatic theology.

his intended vocation. He therefore put himself to the test by working for several months in the slums of the East End of London. In spite of an innate fastidiousness that shrank from the extreme poverty of Bethnal Green, he emerged with the certainty that he should accept ordination. In 1887 he took up his first appointment as a curate in Great Yarmouth, where he would regularly put to sea with the fishing fleet. Although content to serve in whatever humble station might be found for him, he was spared a long wait for preferment by the death a few months later of the Rev. William Talbot, for the past thirty-four years Rector of Bishops Hatfield, as the parish had continued to be called for centuries. Lord Salisbury, patron of the living, having searched in vain for a suitably vigorous successor, presented his own son to the vacant benefice. Protesting his inexperience, for he was not yet twenty-six, William obeyed his father and was instituted on 31 August 1888. There he remained for the next twenty-eight years.

In the year of his ordination he married Lady Florence Bootle-Wilbraham, a daughter of the Earl of Lathom, Queen Victoria's Lord Chamberlain. They made a striking pair. William was tall and hand-some, bearded but benign; Fluffy, as the family called her, possessed a dreamy beauty and a sweet temper. Unlike other young clerical couples they had few financial cares. William's private income and with the stipend of the Hatfield living together came to more than £2,000 a year. Throughout almost half a century of marriage, however, they lived as simply as any country parson and his wife.

With charactertistic independence they refused to occupy the rectory at Hatfield, agreeably situated at some distance from the town. Instead William asked Lord Salisbury to build him and his wife a modest house in the midst of their five thousand parishioners. The site he chose was in Back Street, an unalluring name since changed to Church Street. But as its walls began to rise he discovered with annoyance that Lady Salisbury had altered the plans, hoping to make the new rectory more a mansion than a parsonage. Only after strong protest did he succeed in reducing its grandiose proportions. He saw nothing in Christian doctrine that required a clergyman to maintain more sumptuous standards of comfort than his flock and some years later illustrated his theme with an engaging anecdote:

> I was talking to one of the old school the other day, and he was explaining to me what kind of a man he should like to succeed him (for he was contemplating resignation). He led me through the well-laid out grounds and showed me the well-appointed hot-houses, the green lawns, the pleasant shrubbery (wilderness, I think, was the term used in Miss Austen's novels), and after we had wandered and

admired all its beauties, he turned to me with an air of one who is secure that his words must convince, and said, 'Must not my successor be a rich man?'

I looked beyond him and saw over a sunlit valley the little village of mud and thatch, and I asked him tentatively if he did not think that his successor should care for the souls of his parishioners.

He waved the question aside as irrelevant by an 'Oh, yes!' and then returned to his point.

Simplicity was the keynote of William Cecil's ministry. He mistrusted all those devices which enterprising clergy sometimes employ to stimulate the reticent: clubs, guilds, missions, entertainments, treats and magazines. They were, he believed, particularly inappropriate for use among his own parishioners, men and women who combined a profound conservatism with an acute sense of what was seemly. Rather would be rely on what he called the two oldest and best tools in the tool-basket, services and visiting.

Shortly before ordination he had received some useful advice from an Alderson uncle with a rural living in Northamptonshire:

> Pray get out of your head the absurd idea that preaching to country folk wants no intellect or theological knowledge. In every country congregation there are people who know more of divinity than the bulk of your Sunday congregation at St Paul's. . . . All Sunday schools teach a good deal and when you first become a parson you will find how much better instructed your congregation is in the Bible than yourself.

It was a lesson the Rector of Hatfield took to heart. A thorough understanding and simple exposition of the Gospels transcended all, although he would sometimes shake his head and say: 'The Bible is a very *awkward* book.' Years later, as Bishop of Exeter, he warned his country clergy to avoid elaborate sermons stuffed with an erudition that only the highly educated could appreciate: 'Forget the squire; let him sleep peacefully. Deal with the soul of the knife-boy behind him, and if you do your work well and the squire should happen to keep awake, why, it will probably do him good.' He gave as much care to the delivery of his sermons as to their content, learning to preach without the distraction of a manuscript. He also delighted in teaching huge rowdy classes of village boys that would instantly fall silent under his gentle touch.

He was pious but never solemn. One Sunday he decided that for a change he would read to his parishioners from the neglected *Homilies of the Church*, published in the sixteenth century:

I first lit on one against excess in apparel [he wrote to his sister-in-law]. It seemed scarcely suitable to enjoin on Stride not to dress in silk or to have his gown faced with fur; so I passed on to the remarks on women's dress. I have forgotten all the bad language but 'carrion flesh' is an expression that I think Fluffy would dislike being applied to her merely because she curled her hair. I gave up this homily when I found a heathen philosopher's opinion quoted with approbation that 'the dress and words of a woman should be scanty'.

The homily on matrimony was scarcely more suitable. There is a most eloquent passage exhorting wives to take their beatings patiently. I then tried the one on fasting and that, though excellent, was largely concerned with the duty of eating fish so that there might be more fishermen to man the navy.

It was the last time he experimented on his flock. As he well recognized: 'To do anything uncommon is to their minds not an eccentricity but a crime.'

The Rector of Hatfield used to have one recurrent nightmare: that he had found a row of cottages in which he knew no one. He believed parish visting to be hardly less important than preaching and would devote many hours each day to the task, even if it dislocated the routine of his own family life. He knew that the best time to visit working men was after they had had their evening meal. 'A doctor does not stop his rounds because the sun has set,' he wrote, 'Why should the spiritual doctor?' In his enthusiasm he would even describe illness as 'a positive boon'. The priest who hastens to an infectious case, he explained, would find 'the look of surliness depart from many a face, and his wayside salute will be returned by the man who used to pass him with a stony stare of indifference'.

He was sometimes fanciful but never patronizing. A genuine understanding, he believed, existed between the aristocrat and the labourer, a mutual trust and respect that flourished best in taciturnity. As Bishop of Exeter he later urged all his clergy to take to heart this lesson in good-mannered communication:

Let me counsel the young cleric to learn the art of silence. It is an art. Silence unrelieved by a single speech would have no more beauty than a night, say, without a star. It is the short enigmatical speech set in great periods of silence that seems most serviceable in affecting our poorer parishioners. Speech should be dark, for the rustic delights in every indirect form of expression. If you ask him how he is, he never answers 'I am well,' or 'I am ill,' but always 'I am middling,' or 'only middling,' or 'pretty middling,' expressions which sound as if they meant the same, but in reality mean things absolutely opposed. He loves dark speeches because he is very distrustful. The middle class outwit the lower quite constantly, and if the lower did not to defend itself by being cautious in their dealings with mankind, they would be even more a prey than they are now to unjust dealings.

The polite small-talk of more sophisticated tea-tables was beyond him, but he perfected a technique of withdrawing his attention while apparently continuing to listen to his hostess with appreciative nods. The deception was not always successful. On one visit he fell into such a trance that Fluffy, having gallantly kept the conversation going, felt obliged to take him away: 'Well,' she explained, 'we must be going now. We only looked in to say how do you do.' Brought to earth for a moment, Fish obediently stretched out his hand, said, 'How do you do?' and followed his wife out of the door, carefully wiping his feet on the mat as he went.

The Rector loved his flock but had no illusions about his mission. He wrote in 1912:

> There is a terrible slackness and torpidity about religion in Hatfield, there is hardly any enthusiasm, the position of most men might be described by saying that they do not mind going to Heaven if it is not too much trouble, but the conception of any idea of suffering for righteousness' sake is absolutely repulsive to them. Alas, what a confession of failure after twenty-four years.

To be both a Cecil and the son of a Prime Minister could have put him at least two laps ahead of his contemporaries in the race for clerical preferment; but it was a contest for which he had few sponsors and no ambition. By temperament he lacked that administrative ability increasingly demanded of those holding high office in the Anglican Church. 'I suppose it is the slight *insanity* of Fish's mind that puts him out of the pale,' Eleanor Cecil wrote, 'an independence of mind bordering on lawlessness.' The caprice of his letters to the newspapers provoked his brother Nigs into hoping that Fish would voluntarily visit some suitable bacteriological establishment in order to be inoculated with paralysis of the right hand. By no stretch of language could he be described as an ecclesiastical statesman.

Nor would he willingly abandon his parish. Although sometimes disappointed by its muted response to his ministry, he knew that Hatfield was his life's work. In any case, he wished to preserve what leisure he could for furthering Christian belief in the Far East.

When therefore in 1908 the first Bishop of Southwark, Edward Talbot, asked him to leave 'all the beautiful things that you have at Hatfield for a slum parish', he declined to move. As in many decisions which confronted him, he was guided by the memory of his father. And Lord Salisbury had spoken contemptuously of the view that souls in London slums were more valuable than those of a country village; that there was necessarily any virtue in exchanging a familiar for an unfamiliar task; or that the success of a mission could be measured by the personal sacrifice of the priest. So the Rector remained at Hatfield, accepting only such minor appointments as Rural Dean of Hertford, honorary Chaplain to King Edward VII and honorary Canon of St Albans Cathedral.

For a woman of sheltered upbringing who confessed that she could find her way about London only by beginning each journey from her father's house in Portland Place, Lady Florence Cecil* displayed unusual stamina in her married life. One Tuesday in the summer of 1905, for example, she took 110 Hatfield mothers on an outing to Woburn Abbey. That evening she went up by train to London, crossed the Channel by night to Dieppe, spent Wednesday in a successful search for a holiday villa, returned to England the same night, arrived back at Hatfield on Thursday morning, filled in the rest of the day with parish visiting, and on Friday bicycled the dozen miles to the cathedral town of St Albans and back.

Twice she accompanied her husband to China, sharing his abortive efforts to establish a Christian university and helping him to write a thoughtful volume entitled *Changing China* that was published in 1910. They found much to shock them there, from slavery and prostitution to floggings and reputed child sacrifices. They were hardly less pained by a notice in the public gardens of Shanghai, a city then largely under European administration. It proclaimed, first, that 'no dogs or bicycles shall be admitted'; secondly, that 'no Chinese shall be admitted except servants in attendance on foreigners'. Another cause for disquiet was the discovery that *La Dame aux Camélias* enjoyed more popularity in China than any other Western work. To convince their Chinese friends that life at Hatfield was far removed from the licence of the Dumas romance, the Cecils presented them with copies of Haldane's *Pathway to Reality* and cousin Arthur Balfour's *Defence of Philosophic Doubt*.

The journey aboard the Trans-Siberian railway was full of incident.

* As the daughter of an Earl she had the choice after marriage of calling herself either Lady Florence Cecil or Lady William Cecil. She adopted the first style. By contrast, Lady Eleanor Lambton, daughter of the Earl of Durham, who in 1889 was married to William's younger brother Bob, chose the more usual style of Lady Robert Cecil.

There were unscheduled stops when the passengers would pass the time picking flowers; the engine ran out of oil, so candles were forced into the axles for lubrication; a lady nihilist was detected and arrested. Yet those oriental adventures seem quite pale beside the Mediterranean holidays on which the Rector and his wife would take their seven children. One of their daughters, Lady Manners, has described Lord William's progress abroad:

> He considered that he should look after the party and do all the paying. At home, the most he would do was to sign cheques. He had been pick-pocketed so often abroad, that he wore a money belt, with little pockets all round. Once he put this on upside down and everything, including our family return ticket, was lost....
>
> He loved the sun and heat, so most of our trips abroad were to the warmer parts of France when we were young, chiefly on bicycles. He always wore yellow glasses, a broad-brimmed hat and a tussore suit. There was always a great deal of speculation as to his nationality. He was generally taken for a Dane. One burning summer, on the Riviera, he decided red was a protection against the ultra-violet rays, so we wore red frocks and the boys red shirts. Garibaldi was still a living memory in that part of the country, so we were more conspicuous than ever.
>
> He was very careful about food and especially water in these out-of-the-way places, and as we stopped for luncheon, at some small open air café in a village, a ritual of purifying the water would be gone through, much to the edification of the assembled crowd, who, anyway, regarded us as a free spectacle. The process was: one tablet pounded up, was put into the water, turning it brown, then, after a wait of some minutes, which seemed ages in our thirsty condition, two more were put in, which cleared it, leaving only an unpleasant chlorinated taste. '*Mon Dieu!*' said the spectators, '*Ces drôles d'Anglais.*'

Home life at St Audrey's could be as jolly as any holiday. Recalling his own youthful unhappiness, William determined that his sons should not be sent away to Eton. Instead they were entered at Westminster School as day-boys, travelling to London by train each morning and returning to Hatfield in the afternoon. That added much liveliness to the family circle. So did the Rector's growing absence of mind. 'No, no, Fish,' Fluffy would have to remind her husband in the middle of evensong, 'the *magnificat*, not the *nunc dimittis*.' She grew restive at his repeated failure to bring back his pyjamas after preaching in distant parts of the country, and the next time he went away made him promise to remember them. On his return home she opened his bag and found to her satisfaction that he had indeed re-packed his pyjamas: also the sheets of the bed in which he had slept the previous night.

It was not only in the small hazards of his daily life that he depended on his wife's watchful eye and serene temperament. He had inherited the family affliction of inexplicable illnesses, often accompanied by exhaustion and depression. In such periods of stress he found his wife's sympathy and support immeasurably consoling. Her own ailments she would shrug off in silence, prompting her sharp-tongued sister-in-law Nelly to observe that Fluffy was the sense and all the Cecils the sensibility.

In grief, however, William showed a Christian resignation that matched her own courage. Three of their four sons were killed in action during the First World War and a daughter died at the age of eighteen. After the last of these blows had fallen, their father wrote:

> Life must be taken as a whole, the sorrows and the joys. The mountain scenery is beautiful because the valleys are deep and the mountains are high. In life we are learning the beauty of God's creation. The valleys are part, an essential part, of its beauty. They are dark, cold miserable: but taken with the mountains they make a glorious whole.

That was his only consolation. He burnt all the letters of condolence he received as they added so much to his suffering.

The outbreak of war in 1914 laid no burden on his conscience. The nearest he ever came to pacifism was in a sermon a few days after the Battle of Omdurman in 1898. 'Fish preached against war except in cases like the Sudan,' his brother Jim wrote to their father, apparently without irony. The Rector saw no inconsistency between Christian belief and a duty to defend the interests of his country. Nor did he hold that forgiveness of one's enemies excluded them from first being defeated. In later years he supported the League of Nations; but a play on the theme of disarmament which he saw performed in a London church aroused in him, his sister Gwendolen reported, 'a state of truculent jingoism which would do credit to Winston Churchill'.

She also noted in 1915 how wartime austerities, such as a compulsory blackout to confuse German aircraft, brought out an authoritarian strain in her brother:

> Fish is enforcing the lighting order with far more vigour than the police, and no one in the parish ever dare allow a thread of light to be seen at the edge of their blinds for fear of the Rector descending on them. He has instituted lantern services, with the church in

complete darkness, and blew up his congregation yesterday for being afraid to come to them. Altogether he is rather enjoying himself.

His precautions were not as absurd as they seemed. In the following year a Zeppelin on a bombing raid was shot down near Hatfield. 'The whole sky down to the horizon covered with a ruddy light,' Gwendolen wrote, 'you could have read a book in the garden.' The Rector joined the villagers in cheering the spectacle: then he recalled that the burning airship was carrying men to their death and for days was stricken with remorse.

After the first of his sons had been killed in action he grew increasingly restless and unhappy at making no direct contribution to ultimate victory; he even wondered whether at fifty-three he should not offer his services as military chaplain. From such perplexities he was rescued by an astonishing letter from the Prime Minister, Mr Asquith. Would he allow his name to be submitted to the King for appointment to the Bishopric of Exeter? Five years earlier his affection for Hatfield and absorption in the work of the China mission would have prompted an instant refusal. In 1916 he could not resist the prospect of new horizons.

His acceptance delighted the family. 'A very pleasant part of the world for his brothers and sisters-in-law to visit him!' Nelly Cecil exclaimed. 'But will he ever button his gaiters?'

Financially, however, there was a catch in it. The stipend of a Bishop of Exeter amounted to a comfortable £4,200 a year. But the new incumbent was specially required to make over one-third of that sum each year towards a retirement pension for his ailing predecessor. As Bishop Archibald Robertson survived until 1931, the Church of England had made no bad bargain on his behalf. William retained enough private means not to feel the pinch, in spite of having lost some of his capital by unwise investments in foreign bonds. He nevertheless decided against using the Bishop's Palace, which had needed eleven servants in Robertson's day, except as an office. His home he made in a much smaller house called Barton Place, just outside the city.

Hensley Henson observed from the splendour of Auckland Castle, his official residence as Bishop of Durham:

> Men value and desire that which is unfamiliar to them. Thus a Cecil, bred up in the ancestral dignity and rich historical associations of Hatfield, desires and enjoys a small house, and the simplicity of a comparatively modest manner of life. A Henson, on the other hand, brought up in a small house, and inured to the discomforts and disadvantages of relatively narrow means, revels in the largeness and dignity of a great historic position.

It was Fish's amiable habit to use a bicycle for the two-mile journey between Barton Place and the Palace. His ingenious mind insisted that it should have straight handle-bars to avoid interlocking with those of other machines, and that it should be painted orange for easy identification. But as often as not he would still fail to recognize his distinctive property. Halfway home one day he realized that the machine – a woman's model, as it happened, painted black – was not his own. So he pedalled back into Exeter, apologized to its anxious owner, lingered for a moment in conversation, raised his hat, remounted the same bicycle and rode away.

Trains had their hazards, too. There is the legendary story of his failing to find his ticket when the inspector asked for it. 'Don't trouble, my Lord,' the official assured him, 'we all know who you are.' The Bishop replied: 'That's all very well, but without a ticket how do I know where I'm supposed to be going?' On the whole he preferred the independence of an open motor car, with frequent wayside stops for talk with shepherds and farmers. He became known throughout the diocese as Love-in-a-Mist.

Life at Barton Place was of shiftless simplicity. The Bishop had a horror of ostentation that extended even to forbidding champagne at a daughter's wedding. He would often urge the rest of the episcopal bench to follow his example. 'As his children use the tablecloth to dry their dog and his food is barbarous', Nelly Cecil wrote, 'it is just as well he has to hide his light under a bushel.' He delighted in an untidy and brightly coloured garden where in an old dressing-gown and wooden sabots he would spend the first hours of the day reading, meditating and feeding the birds. But he was not pleased by his wife's habit of throwing whole crusts of bread out of the dining-room window, when they would at once be gobbled up by the dog. 'I'm afraid the woolly bird got that one,' he used to say. Nothing sounded banal from his lips. 'What doth this fowl?' he exclaimed as a hen jumped on to the table while he was writing a sermon. And when the grateful wartime refugees from Belgium whom he and Fluffy had taken into their house presented their hosts with a silver epergne, his thoughts dwelt more on the cause of their coming to England than on the gift itself. 'Ah, que la guerre est terrible,' he murmured, apparently gazing at its tortured workmanship. Ever afterwards he referred to it as 'la belle asperge'.

His resourceful mind was never idle. He would turn biscuit tins into cupboards and carry his early-morning tea on a tray that had once been a racquet press, an old aluminium soap-box acting as sugar basin. When a member of the household caught pneumonia, he warmed the patient's bed with an electric iron inside a fencing mask. He was fascinated when somebody suggested the installation of central heating in his chilly house and sent for plans. These he improved so that a cosy little radiator nestled under each chair. 'But you will not be able to move the chairs,' a nephew objected, 'it does not sound a comfortable plan.' 'My dear boy,' the Bishop sighed, 'when one is putting in a heating system, comfort must go to the wall.'

Like his father, the Bishop found refreshment in the pursuit of science. He would often choose the themes of his sermons from the pages of the learned periodical *Nature*, giving them interpretations unknown to the Royal Society. In 1931 he was pleased to hear that the wife of the newly appointed Dean of Exeter, Dr W. R. Matthews, held the degree of Bachelor of Science. On their first visit to Barton Place he threw some powder on the fire which burnt up in a bright blue flame. 'Nice colour,' he said. 'Yes,' Mrs Matthews replied, 'copper sulphate.' She had passed the test and proved herself worthy of his intellectual friendship. A few weeks later she was in bed with a cold when the Bishop walked in unannounced, sat down and abruptly began to talk of the nutritive value of shellfish. He had come to the conclusion that shellfish, green salads and vegetables formed the healthiest of diets and he lived on little else. Science, he believed, could avert many dangers. When, however, Fluffy fell down the steep steps of a French railway carriage she can have drawn little comfort from her husband's kindly meant but ill-timed and genetically inaccurate reminder that those descended from apes should use their hands as well as their feet.

During Fish's twenty years in the West Country there was hardly a village where he was not welcomed and loved. He knew their ways, spoke like them, could make them laugh. Walking once in an outdoor procession, choir and clergy outpaced their lame Bishop, who suddenly found he was lost. 'Which way did hounds go?' he asked a knot of spectators. He diverted another congregation by walking majestically up the nave with a large coloured handkerchief hanging from his mouth; he had put it there for a moment while robing in the vestry and instantly forgotten its existence. Parish priests were always fearful of the form his confirmation addresses might take: a dissertation on China, perhaps, or a dying drunkard's thoughts on his deathbed. But however inappropriate his words, they thought it did the children good just to gaze on that benevolent face.

The chiselled intellect of a Hensley Henson scorned William Cecil's imprecision of thought. 'His mind', he wrote, 'is full of half-remembered *mots* and half-digested ideas.' At his best, however, Exeter was no less striking a preacher than Durham, perhaps his superior in expounding simple themes to unsophisticated audiences:

I see people walking about with bits of coloured ribbon and I ask them what they mean. They tell me they wear them as a protest against certain sins such as drunkenness and impurity. But I never meet any one wearing a ribbon to protest against want of charity. And yet it is far worse than any of these bodily sins.

He recognized no limits to Christian charity. Far in advance of his time, he insisted that no greater stigma should attach to the receipt of poor relief than to the receipt of free education. 'In both cases', he wrote, 'the State has been generous, but in the first its generosity encourages virtue in the young; in the second it has acquired the reputation of encouraging vice in the old.' Tramps won a special place in his heart. Having lived for so many years on the Great North Road he had become familiar with their problems and waged a campaign to have the hard boards of their beds in casual-wards replaced by mattresses.

In time of industrial discontent, strikers could always depend on his sympathetic ear. 'They have, after all, a very real grievance,' he wrote of the miners in 1912. 'They are all poor and they believe that the money they are losing is going into someone else's pocket.' He begged his brother Bob to deter the Conservative party from a policy of repression: 'Do persuade all your colleagues to go to the next row of cottages they see and talk it over with the working man.' During later disputes he more than once offered strikers the use of the Palace garden for their meetings and persuaded some of them to attend a service of intercession. A man had only to have the hiss of the world against him for Fish to be found at his side.

The Bishop regarded the clergy of his diocese with the same paternal concern he had shown for the parishioners of Hatfield. Both parsons and ordinands were often invited to stay at Barton Place, a house well endowed with small bedrooms. One shy young guest, embarrassed at being packed off to bed with a sudden heavy cold, never forgot how Lord William himself appeared late at night, bringing him a glass of whisky and hot water. A rigid timetable found no place in his life. Hearing one evening that the vicar of a distant parish was to undergo a serious operation the next day, he at once set out on a mission of encouragement and cheer.

For all his generosity of heart, he demanded absolute obedience on matters of doctrine and liturgy. In the years immediately before his arrival at Exeter, many churches in the diocese had adopted elaborate rituals that did not accord with the Anglican Prayer Book of 1662. He particularly deplored the reservation of consecrated bread and wine: ostensibly a concession to the sick who could not otherwise receive

Holy Communion in their homes, in practice hardly distinguishable from the Roman Catholic adoration of the host. It was to preserve the Church of England from such disturbing reversions that the descendant of the first Robert Cecil made a rare foray into ecclesiastical politics. He was one of only four of the forty-three diocesan bishops in the Church Assembly who voted against the final draft of a revised Prayer Book designed to restore harmony to the Anglican Church. Gwendolen disapproved. She wrote from Hatfield:

> It was foolish of Fish to vote as he did – especially as, unlike the other three, he has no doctrinal difficulty in accepting the book. It was sheer conservatism – hatred of a change from what he is accustomed to. It's the quality which no doubt brings him into touch with the bucolic mind, and made him so successful here and so in sympathy with his present diocese. But I blame myself for not having pressed him more strongly to keep it in check on this occasion – though I don't suppose that it would have been of much use.

That does her brother less than justice. He rejected the revised Prayer Book for reasons of both principle and prudence. He believed it wrong to condone rather than to punish illegal conduct; and he correctly foresaw that the alterations made to the service of Holy Communion would alarm a House of Commons always sensitive to the shadow of Rome. The practical difficulties of enforcing clerical discipline did not dismay him. He proposed that all stipends should be withheld from incumbents who flouted the law. 'Do you wish that those clergy who will not obey shall starve?' William Temple, the future Archbishop of Canterbury, asked him with indignation. 'Yes,' Fish replied.

His brother Hugh, first elected to Parliament in 1895 and one of the most influential laymen in the Church Assembly, took a contrary view. He shared Fish's distaste for such aberrant practices as perpetual reservation, but preferred to make limited concessions which the Anglo-Catholics would respect rather than attempt to quell a growing liturgical anarchy. 'I want revision to end in a clear boundary between what is allowed and what is forbidden,' he wrote. Yet even his considerable command of oratory failed to persuade the House of Commons to sanction the rubrics submitted to Parliament in 1927 and again in 1928. The unworldly Bishop of Exeter had proved a wiser prophet than his omniscient brother.

A determination not to compromise on doctrine also led to a temporary estrangement from Hensley Henson and a refusal to attend his consecration as Bishop of Hereford in 1918. Initially delighted by the preferment of a man who had been his friend for thirty years, he changed his mind on reading some of Henson's theological works. The new bishop's interpretation of the Apostles' Creed, he concluded, was ambiguous if not positively heretical. Henson wrote furiously in his journal:

I am godfather to his daughter and he wrote me quite an affectionate letter when first my appointment was announced. Now he joins the hue and cry. I told the Archbishop that I deeply resented the way in which I had been treated, and I do. My relations with these abstaining bishops will not be exactly easy. . . . They have lent the sanction of their name to the campaign of calumny and insult which has been running its course for the past month. All this it is impossible not to resent, difficult to forgive.

'Fish Cecil came in to make his peace with me,' Henson added on the day after his consecration. 'I was not very placable.'

Breakfasting at Hatfield one morning in 1916, Lord Salisbury is said to have opened his newspaper and exclaimed in alarm: 'This time the Prime Minister really has gone too far.' What had provoked him? Not, it emerged, any further evidence of Mr Asquith's growing incapacity as a wartime leader, but the announcement that the Rector of Hatfield was to be the next Bishop of Exeter.

Almost certainly apocryphal, the story is worthy of those other legends which cling to Fish's memory. Only those who regard promotion to the episcopal bench as an ecclesiastical long-service and good-conduct medal can in retrospect applaud his removal from the devoted care of a parish to the altogether different responsibilities of a diocese. He disliked administration and the interminable talk of committees. His belief in democratic discussion resembled that of Dr Warre, the Victorian Head Master of Eton: everyone should have a vote, and everyone should vote for Dr Warre. He was unmoved by the history of an ancient cathedral and deaf to its music (though he had a deep technical knowledge of organs). While there remained souls to be saved he looked impatiently on members of a cathedral chapter who devoted their energies to theology and scholarship. So he published, but never implemented, a scheme that would dispense with the office of dean, transferring decanal duties to the bishop and his salary to a newly created suffragan; canons were likewise to be driven from their cloisters and obliged to labour throughout the diocese as archdeacons.

Nor did Fish seek that prominent role in national affairs which has often enchanted the bench of bishops. He saw most problems through the eyes of a parish priest; if he had ambitions outside the diocese, they were missionary rather than ecumenical. He was bored by the procedural niceties and legalistic quibbles of Church Assembly and Convocation, and rarely took advantage of his seat in the House of Lords. Like other bishops, however, he would be summoned periodically to Westminster to read prayers to his fellow peers each day for a fortnight. He enjoyed those regular tours of duty: they enabled him to live with his brother at Hatfield and to spend every free moment renewing his links with the parish.

'He genuinely hated being a bishop,' Gwendolen wrote from Hatfield a few days after his death in 1936, 'and looked back to his time here as the happiest of his life. The feeling of the funeral was not so much one of mourning as of triumphant welcoming back.'

6

Lord Robert Cecil,
Viscount Cecil of Chelwood
1864—1958

Robert, third son of third Marquess of Salisbury. Created Viscount Cecil of Chelwood 1923. Known to family and friends as Bob.

Born 14 September 1864. Educated at Eton and University College, Oxford. Called to the Bar, Inner Temple, 1887. Queen's Counsel 1899. Conservative MP for East Marylebone 1906–10 and for Hitchin 1911–23. Under-Secretary of State for Foreign Affairs 1915–18. Minister of Blockade 1916–18. Assistant Secretary of State for Foreign Affairs 1918–19. Lord Privy Seal 1923–4. Chancellor of the Duchy of Lancaster 1924–7. Privy Counsellor 1915. President, League of Nations Union 1923–45. Honorary Life President, United Nations Association 1945–58. Nobel Peace Prize 1937. Companion of Honour 1956.

Married 22 January 1889 Lady Eleanor Lambton (known as Nelly), third daughter of second Earl of Durham. She died 24 April 1959. No children.

Lord Cecil of Chelwood died 24 November 1958.

Even as a child, the architect of the League of Nations was chaffed by his mother for always having 'two grievances and a right'. They grew no less with the years. The inadequacy of the rule of law at Eton led him to take independent but ineffective measures against the bullying of other boys in his house. The Oxford Union, too, resisted his attempts as president to reform its cumbersome constitution. His crusading zeal, Dr Coppini noted at Puys, was matched by *'un esprit très caustique'*. Clearly Lord Robert was destined for the Bar or for the House of Commons, perhaps both. So he determined to read Jurisprudence at

Oxford; and although he could think of several ways in which the syllabus might have been improved, he took a respectable Second Class in his finals. 'There is nothing whatever to discourage you should you think of pursuing the study of the law,' his examiner, the celebrated A. V. Dicey, told him.

Robert did not share Dicey's optimism. His confidence shaken at having missed a First, he wrote despairingly to a friend of his own 'natural mediocrity'. But he had chosen the wrong shoulder to weep on. Cosmo Gordon Lang, the son of a modestly endowed minister of the Scots Kirk, had thrust his way from Glasgow University to the Balliol of Dr Jowett, the presidency of the Oxford Union and a First in History. But only a few days before receiving Robert's cri-du-coeur he had narrowly failed to win the most cherished prize of all, a Fellowship of All Souls. He replied sternly to the Prime Minister's son:

> If like me you had no prospects and little influence combined with a consuming ambition, you might reasonably have fits of the blues: but as you are, be up and stirring – thank God for ample brains, and use them!

For the time being Robert's spirits revived. He served for a few months as one of his father's private secretaries, but the Prime Minister's unwillingness to delegate left him with little to do. He was better employed learning something of the law in practice by acting as a marshal, or private secretary, to assize judges on circuit. One of his masters, he wrote, 'answers to the name of Cave, but more readily to My Lord'. Another absent-mindedly introduced him to a startled dinner party as Lord Randolph Churchill. A third confided that he could stand anything except counsels' speeches: 'Without snuff, I could not get through them.' Back in London he sat as a pupil in the chambers of Swinfen Eady, a busy junior at the Chancery Bar; then, for a fee of 50 guineas, picked up what he could of the Common Law from another future judge, Joseph Walton. But he was spared the cost of buying a set of law books by a thoughtful gift from the library of the retired Lord Chancellor Selborne, whose only son had married Robert's elder sister. Having passed all his examinations, he travelled up to Liverpool assizes, a fully fledged but as yet briefless barrister.

Cosmo Lang, who had begun reading for the Bar a year after Robert, might have followed in his footsteps, perhaps even overtaken him. His election to a Fellowship of All Souls in 1888 erased the bitter memory of his failure two years earlier and gave him both an income and a covetable platform from which to resume his upward progress. But within a few months of that triumph, on the eve of his call to the Bar, he felt himself compulsively drawn towards ordination. Robert, his only confidant, repaid his debt of good counsel by bluntly telling him that he would make a better parson than lawyer; in any case, he added, the pursuit of politics was a far poorer thing than the witness to religion. So Lang took Holy Orders in the Church of England: a vocation that carried the son of the manse, almost effortlessly it seemed, first to York and then to Canterbury. 'It was you', the Archbishop wrote to Lord Cecil of Chelwood more than half a century later, 'who encouraged me to leave the road of law and politics.'

For someone as diffident as Robert, one career at a time was enough. Still only twenty-four, he would persevere with the Bar at least until he had earned enough to enable him to enter the Commons. Meanwhile Westminster whispered no enchantments. Even the Hatfield branch of the Primrose League, the Conservative association recently founded in memory of Disraeli, overwhelmed him with distaste: 'People to be soothed, others to be abused, this man to be poked up, that one to be mollified – the kind of work which makes me doubtful if I could ever endure politics.'

Ten days after that depressing experience there was better news to report. 'I had my first brief today and earned my first guinea at the Bar!' the grandson of Baron Alderson wrote exultantly from Liverpool. 'As I had only to get up and say three sentences I need not have been so ridiculously nervous as I was.'

It was fortunate that Robert Cecil's forensic talents were not more in demand during 1888. For in January, while staying with the Wyndham family at Clouds, in Wiltshire, he fell in love with a fellow guest, Lady Eleanor Lambton. Until their marriage exactly a year later, he had thoughts for little else.

Nelly, as the family called her, was a grand-daughter of 'Radical Jack', the Earl of Durham who drafted two of the most far-reaching State papers of the nineteenth century: the Reform Bill of 1832 and, seven years later, that inspired handbook of colonial policy entitled *Report on the Affairs of British North America*. She inherited his lively mind, his incisive pen and his contempt for the conventions, but neither his hot temper nor his vanity. Robert was enchanted by this slight, dark beauty whose teasing wit provoked one of his rare excursions into verse:

> 'Life is all very pleasant for you,'
>   Said fair Chloe one night at a ball,
> 'You men, you have plenty to do,
>   We poor women have nothing at all.'

129

> I urged her to paint or to play
> > To write or to knit or to sew,
> To visit the poor and to pray,
> > To each and to all she said, 'No'.
>
> At last I exclaimed in despair,
> > 'If you really are anxious to be
> Of some use, and for none of these care,
> > You must marry! Why not marry me?'

Even after their formal engagement in the summer of 1888, the two families gazed warily at each other. In her Christian beliefs Nelly was as stalwart as any Cecil. But her nine brothers, most of whom served in the Army or the Navy, lived by a code of honour that was not always related to Holy Writ. They accounted sins of the flesh to be less soul-destroying than such transgressions as dishonesty, untruthfulness, hypocrisy and self-righteousness. 'Their moral position,' Robert noted, 'is that of an Eton boy.' He also found Lambton Castle a more taciturn household than Hatfield, even when the whole tribe were assembled. They talked little, and then mostly about horses: to embark on religious themes would have been thought an astonishing eccentricity. But Robert had to admit that their reserve was deceptive; when pressed, they revealed a knowledge of literature, painting and music deeper than his own. He also admired their thoughtfuless in trifles and their hatred of fuss.

He remained uneasy, however, about one tenet of the Lambton creed: that to be unnecessarily ill-dressed or unkempt came near to crime. It was a point on which he had every reason to be sensitive, confessing that the only man whose clothes fitted even worse than his own was the Emperor of Japan: his person, it seemed, was so sacred that no tailor dared venture to measure him. There was nothing divine about Robert's own dishevelment, which drew from Cosmo Lang the pained rebuke: 'If you cannot dress like a gentleman, I think you ought at least to try and dress like a Conservative.'

Lord Durham, Nelly's eldest brother and the head of the family, was no less concerned about the finances of his future brother-in-law:

> For years probably you would not have more than £1,400 a year between you [he warned Nelly]. You have some idea of the yearly cost of dressing yourself, but you have to add to that the future cost of travelling and cab-fares. Cecil must have clothes too! Out of the remainder of your income you would have to pay for a house and servants and your food. If he remains at the Bar he cannot expect to make any money for some years. If you have children you will

find it terribly hard to live in comfort or in a style the least approaching that which you have been accustomed to. Until you find yourself deprived of these luxuries you cannot guess how much you will miss them. It is like wearing worsted stockings instead of silk – and is irritating in spite of one's desire to make the sacrifice!

Lady Salisbury, too, always upset at the prospect of losing a son in matrimony, proved difficult. Nelly had already encountered that formidable woman in the previous year, just before the marriage of her friend Alice Gore to Cranborne, and sixty years later wrote a sprightly account of it:

> Alice said, 'Oh, Lady Salisbury, this is Annie and Nelly Lambton.' Lady S. paid not the slightest attention to this: we might have been a pair of footstools. We were amused and I think rather respected her for not pretending to be interested when she wasn't. A year afterwards she *had* to recognize my existence and thought I would be a fast and expensive wife for Bob and would want all sorts of things. Lord Salisbury, said 'No, having had them she is more likely to be ready to do without them.' Clever of him? I never was fast and always terrified of smart women.

Shortly after their engagement, Bob wrote to his fiancée: 'Just at first my mother was a little disturbed at the idea of a new daughter-in-law. but she has *quite* got over it now.' Nelly, however, was never as dutiful as Lady Salisbury would have wished. When that kindly autocrat ordered visiting-cards for her bearing the style 'Lady Eleanor Cecil', Nelly announced that she preferred to be known as Lady Robert Cecil and threw them on the fire. Neither Lady Salisbury nor Lord Durham need ever have worried about Nelly's sense of economy. The young couple managed happily on the £1,000 a year which the Prime Minister settled on each of his married sons, supplemented by a small Lambton endowment and by whatever Bob could earn at the Bar. Like another Lord and Lady Robert Cecil thirty years earlier, they took a modest house north of Oxford Street and lived on a sparse budget. They rarely travelled first-class by train and only after long debates decided to employ a cook at £20 a year. Nelly made most of her own clothes and her husband resigned from White's, never the most frugal of clubs.

In the autumn months that elapsed between engagement and marriage, a bigger danger to the impending match than any spectre of poverty was Bob's lack of self-confidence. Twice a day when separated from his fiancée he would bombard her with long and morbidly introspective letters that ceased only with the wedding. One of them offers an explanation for his *malaise*:

I have lived all my life in a family where, whatever qualities I may have given myself – as you know, I am no miser in *that* respect – I was always forced to admit that some one of my brothers or sisters infinitely surpassed me. I was not as clever as Linkey or as good as Jem or as amusing as Nigs. And I came firmly to the conclusion that I was by nature second-rate. . . . It was therefore almost incredible to me, and is so still, that you should like me better than any one else.

Nelly's response to his professed unworthiness was sympathetic but firm: 'I suppose you have been smoking two cigars half an hour before luncheon: you are as full of humours as a sick schoolgirl.' Bob admitted that he was unusually sensitive: 'Writing to me must be rather like working in softwood with a very sharp tool. The slightest slip may cause quite a deep wound.' Nelly warned him, only half in jest: 'I shan't write to you any more if you pick my letters to pieces like a carrion-crow!' Two months before their marriage, he signed a private declaration:

I solemnly resolve that I will do my utmost never to allow the slightest shadow of distrust of Nelly to grow up in my own mind so that I may avoid among other things distressing her by 'unprofitable' questions.

Robert Cecil.

He placed it in an envelope, on the outside of which he wrote: 'To be opened only if contents are forgotten.'

All this emotional travail Nelly accepted with the utmost poise. For more than seventy years she played a constant role in her husband's fortunes both as a devoted wife and a shrewd counsellor with a political judgement often superior to his own. Her marriage, although childless, was serenely happy. She took a humorous view of life and loved to recall one of the earliest compliments which Bob ever paid her. 'I really think you were the prettiest woman there tonight,' he said on their return from a party. Pause. 'My patience, they *were* an ugly lot.'

During his seventeen years as a barrister, Robert Cecil built up a respectable practice that brought him independence but never affluence. He took whatever work came his way: petty crime, libel, commercial and patent cases, election petitions, arbitration, special inquiries, Coronation claims and Private Bills at the Parliamentary Bar. In 1895 the *Birmingham Gazette* forecast that he would one day be a Tory Lord Chancellor. Few shared that fulsome opinion; but the conscientious young man with the stooping figure (the legacy of a childhood fall down an underground cistern at Puys) could always be depended on to protect the interests of his clients. Here he describes a dilemma at Liverpool when defending a man accused of unlawful killing:

> About an hour before my case came on, the leading counsel on the other side suggested that as he wanted to get away I should advise my client to plead guilty to the charge of manslaughter, and he would then not press the charge of murder. But if I would not do so, he half threatened to press the murder charge – a monstrous thing and putting one in a beastly position.

Cecil stood firm. The prisoner was found not guilty of murder but guilty of manslaughter and received three months' imprisonment, a far lighter sentence than would have been imposed had he initially pleaded guilty to manslaughter.

The family gave him a brief whenever they could. He helped to defend his father against a charge of defamation brought by an Irish Nationalist MP whom the Prime Minister had publicly accused of incitement to murder and outrage. Arthur Balfour, too, retained his cousin to resist a petition improbably accusing him of providing free beer for his Manchester constituents during the general election of 1892.

'It grieves me immensely,' Robert wrote from Liverpool during his first weeks at the Bar, 'to find how utterly unimportant I am outside the tiny circle I live in in London or Hatfield.' That was not entirely true. There were plenty of litigants who assumed that it could do their cause no harm to be represented by the Prime Minister's son. Nor were their cynical hopes always misplaced.

> 'By the help of the most glaring partiality of the judge [Robert wrote of a prisoner accused of wounding with intent to do grievous bodily harm] I succeeded not in obtaining his acquittal but in reducing his offence to a common assault. I am not altogether pleased with the result. . . . It certainly seemed as though Grantham was straining justice to give me a success, and I am afraid others thought so too.

Mr Justice Grantham had every reason for showing gratitude to the Cecil family. A former Tory MP, he had been elevated to the Bench in 1886 for political reasons and his subsequent conduct as a judge did nothing to justify the appointment.

Robert noted a similar episode in 1895, when the habitually disobliging Mr Justice Hawkins suddenly began to show civility to him in court. 'It is just possible that he only realised my name today for the first time. . . . Perhaps he wants a baronetcy when he retires – or to be asked to Hatty next Sunday? One never knows.' Rather more than three years later Lord Salisbury, with some misgivings, had Hawkins created a peer. But that was none of Robert's doing. Indeed, if his father did happen to consult him about judicial appointments, the answer could be uncomfortably candid. Thus when another Conservative MP, Thomas Bucknill, was appointed a judge of the High Court in 1899, Robert wrote:

> I was rather nasty to my poor Papa over Bucknill's appointment. But I don't know what to say if he asks my opinion. I said he was a very fair political appointment but would never be a great judge.... He was rather hurt – and I am altogether dissatisfied with myself.

Perhaps Lord Chancellor Halsbury, who during his seventeen years on the Woolsack made several controversial nominations to the Bench, got wind of Robert's austere disapproval. A few days after the conversation between the Prime Minister and his son, Robert walked into the St Stephen's Club for lunch and finding Halsbury alone, joined him at his table. 'He was not very pleased to see me,' he told Nelly.

Meanwhile his practice grew, but at so sedate a pace that in 1891 he found the leisure to publish, as co-author, a textbook of commercial law. In the same year he transferred from the Northern to the South-Eastern Circuit, a move which brought him a little additional work and enabled him to spend more time at Hatfield. The first time he showed to particular advantage was in a case brought by Alfred Nobel in 1894–5. The inventor of dynamite alleged that the British Government, by its manufacture of cordite, had infringed his patent of an earlier explosive called ballistite. Cecil, retained for the crown as junior counsel to Sir Charles Russell and Sir Richard Webster, showed a mastery of technical detail that ultimately denied Nobel his claim.* Lady Salisbury wrote from La Bastide:

> One line to thank you for your letter and to congratulate you on having led two Attorney-Generals to victory! for of course without your coaching they would have been nowhere! How everything turns to use. Do you remember our finding you out returning to Eton with your pockets full of gun cotton? No doubt the taste for explosives you then showed has borne fruit now!

Substantial briefs, however, continued to elude him, and Salisbury advised his son to abandon the vicissitudes of the law courts for that calm but prosperous backwater, the Parliamentary Bar. In the committee rooms at Westminster its practitioners represented railway companies, local authorities and similar bodies seeking compulsory powers to acquire land or water or to interfere with private interests in other

---

* More than forty years later, in recognition of his devotion to the League of Nations, Cecil received the Nobel Peace Prize. It was one of several which continue to be awarded annually out of the huge fortune left by the Swedish chemist at his death in 1896.

8 The eldest of Lord Salisbury's five sons, photographed by Lewis Carroll in about 1870. Jim was a nervous, sensitive, sweet-natured child, plagued throughout life by indifferent health. He nevertheless achieved distinction both as soldier and statesman, and lived to be eighty-five.

9 Viscount Cranborne, the courtesy title which Jim bore from 1868 until succeeding his father as fourth Marquess of Salisbury in 1903, in the uniform of the Hertfordshire Yeomanry. The portrait was painted by Sir William Blake Richmond in 1882 and presented to Cranborne at his coming-of-age by the Hertfordshire and Essex tenantry.

The annual month of training which he spent under canvas was perhaps the happiest of the year. 'We go to the manoeuvres tomorrow,' he wrote one August 'so my address will be Northern Army, Wilton Camp, Salisbury. There's glory for you.'

10 Viscount Cranborne, by now Conservative MP for Rochester, with his wife Alice and elder daughter Beatrice, in about 1895. Without his wife's understanding, encouragement and unobtrusive deference to his wishes, he might never have overcome an innate shyness intensified by the eminence of his father and the brilliance of his brothers.

11 The fourth Marquess of Salisbury in 1943, aged eighty-two. Three years earlier he had played a notable part in the fall of Neville Chamberlain as Prime Minister; and for the rest of the war Salisbury continued to reprove his successor, Winston Churchill, whenever he thought it for the good of the country.

12 Lord William Cecil as a much-loved Bishop of Exeter, photographed with the celebrated bicycle on which he would ride about the city. He hated ostentation and would urge the rest of the episcopal bench to follow his example. 'As his children use the table-cloth to dry their dog and his food is barbarous,' a sister-in-law wrote, 'it is just as well he has to hide his light under a bushel.'

13 Family group, 1896.
Back row, left to right. Earl of Selborne, Lord Hugh Cecil, Lord William Cecil, Marquess of Salisbury, Lord Edward Cecil.
Middle row. Countess of Selborne, Viscount Cranborne, Marchioness of Salisbury, Lady Robert Cecil, Lord Robert Cecil.
Front row. Viscountess Cranborne, Lady Gwendolen Cecil, Lady Florence Cecil, Lady Edward Cecil.
Foreground. Lord Salisbury's dog, Pharaoh.

ways. Such business was in general monopolized by a small group of barristers who did not appear in other courts and whose legal knowledge was thus too specialized to qualify them for promotion to the judiciary. For Robert that was no deterrent; the ambition of his middle age was a seat not on the Bench but in the House of Commons. But he was certainly tempted by the financial security of the Parliamentary Bar. 'I could probably make £50,000 in five years if my health stood,' he wrote to his wife in 1897, 'and then go into Parliament if that pleased me. On the whole I think I'd better give the other another year or two's chance – though it is beastly slow.'

So he continued to practise mostly in the civil and criminal courts, and two years later felt justified in applying for the silk gown of a Queen's Counsel. He relished variety. One week would find him defending a Shrewsbury town councillor who admitted having bribed 300 of the 360 voters; Cecil pleaded that his client was of exceptional stupidity and so saved him from imprisonment. Next he was resisting on behalf of the Duke of Norfolk the claim of another peer to an ancient Earldom of Norfolk; some of the preliminary research in the case was done for him by a young law pupil called Clement Attlee. And in 1905, his last year at the Bar before election to the House of Commons, he received a fee of no less than £5,000 in an arbitration to determine the value of Singapore docks.

Perhaps his most satisfying forensic triumph took place not in court but at a meeting of the Bar Council in 1899. By a majority of fourteen to eleven, the other members accepted his motion that all prisoners should have the opportunity, if they wished, of being defended by counsel. Four years later his proposed reform was entered on the statute book as the Poor Prisoners' Defence Act.

Robert Cecil's life at the Bar would have been entirely tolerable but for its supposed pleasures. During his early days as a junior counsel in Liverpool he wrote to his future wife:

> I have got to go through a loathsome ordeal this afternoon. A lot of elderly men, all professional barristers, will dine together tonight and when they have sufficiently enfeebled their intellect by wine one of them will get up and make a speech filled with folly and indecency; and another will follow in a similar way. Then all round the table they will begin to accuse one another of imaginary offences against the unwritten circuit law, and each person so accused will be fined and the money applied to purchase wine for the circuit, and this will go on with all sorts of childish ceremony for two mortal hours or more. Pity me, dear Nelly!

Hatfield had not prepared him for such occasions. Of all the Cecils, he least showed that graceful indifference to social distinctions expected as much of the aristocrat as of the Christian. He was repelled, embarrassed and only occasionally amused by what he saw of the middle classes. Since much of his career as barrister, politician and champion of the League of Nations had necessarily to be spent among them, he was obliged to mask his prejudices. But in private correspondence he dwelt again and again on their failings and rarely used the phrase 'middle class' except in a pejorative sense. As a newly-joined member of the Oxford Union in 1883 he told his brother: 'This is about the first letter I ever wrote from here and I think that it'll be the last. People may say what they like, but I hate the lower middle classes and they infest the Union.' Another vignette comes from Norwich assizes ten years later:

'I'm down here with a thoroughly middle class man – not a bad fellow and decidedly intelligent. . . . I don't think I shall stay with the middle classes any more. I don't deny their intelligence, nor even in the case of my Norwich host culture, but they are squalid some how and I'm never at my ease with them. And then they have such uncomfortable furniture.

He found it more congenial to be the guest of a peer with large estates in the Midlands. 'An ass, but a gentleman,' wrote the grandson of the Gascoyne heiress, 'a Tory of the old school, full of a sense of duty. They're all right, unlike these miserable Middle Class employers, with better heads perhaps but no hearts or public consciences.' Nelly Cecil agreed with her husband. 'Do the middle class good to lose their cooks,' she observed during the domestic austerities of the First World War, 'they treat them like dogs when they've got them.'

Astonishingly, even Arthur Balfour could be found wanting in aristocratic demeanour. For although his mother was Lord Salisbury's sister, his paternal grandfather had made a fortune supplying provisions to the Royal Navy during the Napoleonic Wars, and sharp Cecilian eyes sometimes discerned a lingering commercial taint. 'Odd how the middle-class blood will out,' Lady Robert observed to her husband in 1907 after Balfour had terrified his guests by driving them at a speed of forty miles an hour in his dashing new motor car.

Such sensitivity was remarkable, for of all the Cecils none trod a more conventionally middle-class path than Robert and his wife. They kept a modest establishment in London and did not acquire a place of their own in the country until 1900: a small house in Sussex so exposed to wind and rain that they called it Gale Cottage. 'Bob got down here on Friday and is already beginning to be very bored and restive,' Nelly wrote to a god-child one August. 'It is pouring today and he has been practising carpentry on my antique mahogany furniture.' Mostly, however, he spent his leisure reading. He was addicted to Jane Austen, a novelist matched in his estimation only by P. G. Wodehouse; and except for detective stories and an occasional book of devotion he declined to extend his literary boundaries. 'I'm afraid he's a very impenitent barbarian,' Nelly concluded after failing to make him read beyond the second page of Meredith's *Diana of the Crossways*. Her own range was far wider. As a girl she would absorb Carlyle while her maid dressed her hair for a ball, and later became a professional reader of manuscripts for John Murray, the publisher. She also contributed a stern defence of the unpermissive society to the *National Review*. 'Better dead', she wrote ironically, 'than be called respectable, bourgeois, Philistine. The artistic person goes softly all his days in fear of respectability. He fears respectability as a timid boy fears being called a muff, as the middle-aged fear growing old.'

Bob described himself as the least incompetent sportsman of the family. Even in his outdoor pursuits, however, he shared the tastes of the middle classes whom he so despised, preferring tennis and golf to hunting, shooting and stalking. Only in middle age did he acquire an interest in fishing that was never more than tepid. He wrote to Nelly about a parliamentary candidate:

> His wife is pretty but with that curious hardness and want of sympathy which so often goes with hunting in women. . . . I am sure there is something degrading about horses. Whether it is the nasty beasts themselves or the ridiculous positions they are allowed to take I don't know, but anyhow I hate them.

Here he describes a sporting tour in Scotland:

> I have been sentenced by my wife to 14 days' hard in the Highlands. By good conduct I got off two days and shall be out next Monday. The gaolers are civil enough but the discipline is severe. . . . By an admirably humane provision the warders undergo the same and in some cases even more severe treatment than the prisoners. Two of them have today been sent out all day on the shelterless hills. They have to crawl about on their hands and knees as long as another official called a stalker orders them. But they are forbidden to complain and when they come home will have to profess that they have enjoyed themselves. I have got off with a trip on the Loch in a motor boat.

Nelly was made of sterner stuff. From the unaristocratic and windswept resort of Mundesley-on-Sea, in Norfolk, she wrote:

One of the pleasant characteristics of a holiday is that however cold the evenings you have no fire after dinner. Jem sits in a military mackintosh with a thick rug disposed around his legs. Bob lies on the sofa covered with cushions. I sit upright on a hard chair and read Dostoievsky's *Le Crime et le Châtiment*, which seems to have some bearing I cannot exactly explain on our present situation.

Motoring was among the few open-air pastimes which Bob and Nelly enjoyed. They acquired an early steam model of uncertain temperament. But Bob drove more demurely than his Cousin Arthur. When once the engine refused to function except in reverse gear, he completed his journey by steering it slowly backwards for some twenty miles, eventually arriving unperturbed at the great north door of Hatfield. The Lambtons, hippophiles to a man, thought it an unspeakably vulgar pastime.

The commercial values which the rising middle classes brought to Conservatism disturbed Robert Cecil more than their social inadequacies.

> If the Unionist party [he wrote] were free from Tariff Reform and the middle classes – in which I include the Chamberlains, Bonar Law, Milner *et hoc genus omne* – we should get on all right. I don't think the working men are prepared for socialism as yet and they'd prefer the old Tory party to the Nonconformist lot.

So romantic a conception of working-class allegiance was already in eclipse by the early years of the century. Fifty-four members of the Labour Party were elected to the Commons in 1906; only seventeen years later there would be enough of them to form a government under Ramsay MacDonald. But Robert correctly foresaw that the substitution of money for land as the dominant interest within the Conservative Party would leave many traditional Tory causes unprotected. The power of the House of Lords, the Irish Union, the established Welsh Church, the teaching of corporate Christianity in State schools: each, to the indignation and sorrow of the Cecils, was ultimately abandoned by a middle-class Conservative leadership.

Hardly had Arthur Balfour succeeded his uncle as Prime Minister in 1902 than the ranks of the party were divided by the most intractable issue of all. Since the repeal of the Corn Laws in 1846, Great Britain had flourished on Free Trade. But in May 1903 Joseph Chamberlain, Colonial Secretary for the past eight years, announced his conversion to Tariff Reform, resigning from the government four months later in order to rouse the nation. To impose duties on foreign imports, he claimed, would both stimulate home industries and provide revenue for social reform. Those, however, were only incidental benefits. It was part of his imperial mission to strengthen the ties between the mother country and her possessions overseas by offering them economic advantages denied to the rest of the world; and such a system of imperial preference could operate only if tariff barriers were raised against foreign competitors. Both the creed and its apostle repelled the Cecils. Tariff Reform they condemned as commercial selfishness dangerously translated into international affairs; Chamberlain they mistrusted as a Birmingham manufacturer and renegade radical of nonconformist background.

Robert Cecil could not have chosen a worse moment at which to seek a parliamentary seat. The strength of Chamberlain's views within the party ensured that by 1906 only a handful of Unionist Free Traders would remain on the Conservative benches in the Commons; by 1910 they were almost extinct. Some, like Winston Churchill, were driven to cross the floor of the House; others, like Robert's brother Hugh, Member for Greenwich since 1895, were defeated at the general election of 1906 by the intervention of both a Liberal and a Tariff Reform candidate; the remainder either withdrew from the field or prudently changed their beliefs to win official endorsement.

The resentment of the Free Traders during those years of strife was directed as much at Balfour as at Chamberlain and his henchmen. Had the Prime Minister stated how far he was prepared to go in meeting the demands of the Tariff Reformers while simultaneously declaring that the issue should not be treated as a test of party loyalty, he might have held together the two warring wings and mitigated if not prevented the smashing defeat of the 1906 election. As it was, he not only declined to commit himself to any precise position, but equally failed to protect those Free Traders whom the Tariff Reformers accused of apostasy. 'They are the mutineers, the traitors within the camp to his mental view,' Gwendolen Cecil wrote bitterly, 'while Joe is only an over-impulsive, rather wrongheaded but still loyal and dutiful son.'

A glittering armoury of personal qualities set Balfour apart from other governing men: his grace of body and mind, his detachment from greed and ambition, his absorption in music and in speculative philosophy, his moral sensibility, his courage and his courtesy. Yet they were dowered with an intellectual nonchalance, an indifference to the realities of political life that unfitted him for leadership.

Many years later, reminiscing in old age with Stanley Baldwin, he turned to his niece, Blanche Dugdale, and asked: 'Was I a Protectionist or a Free Trader in 1903?' She replied: 'That is what all the country wanted to find out.' Even to the House of Commons he confessed that he had 'no settled convictions' in a conflict of ideas that was already beginning to tear his party to pieces. Gwendolen, as politically alert as any of her brothers, was shocked by his placid indifference. Staying with him in Scotland during the autumn of 1903 she wrote despairingly:

He has not read one of the speeches or looked at a single newspaper. I gave him a short résumé of some of Joe's worst fallacies and extravagances and hope that I genuinely shocked him ('You depress me very much, my dear'). But his only interest in the subject, a slight one, is still in the theoretical arguments which can be waged against a fanatical and irrational Cobdenism, which he tacitly assumes to be the only enemy he has to fight. He doesn't realize yet that the bulk of his party is rushing headlong into an irrational protectionism which he would object to at least as strongly.

Gwendolen had at least prised some response from him. Other members of the family were less fortunate. Robert, about to embark on his own political career, used at this time to add a pathetic postscript to most of his family letters: 'Have written to A.J.B. but as yet have had no reply.' Nigs affected to believe that his cousin's medicinal use of cocaine had produced a moral deterioration. Hugh stung him into a rare display of asperity but little illumination. 'The last two pages of your letter strike me as rather Pecksniffian in point of form,' Balfour wrote from Downing Street, 'but I am quite prepared to set you a much needed example in charity and to accept them as sincere.' Corresponding with Cousin Arthur reminded Nelly of Newman's agonized message to Manning: 'I do not now know whether I am on my head or my heels when I have active relations with you. In spite of my friendly feelings, this is the judgement of my intellect.' She went on to lay bare the ambiguity of his public speeches:

He will continue to be a Free Trader, as he has always been, and he will bring in Protective Tariffs which 'do not divert commerce' nor have 'any of the evil consequences' assumed, and therefore are scientifically consistent with Free Trade, etc., etc., etc. It reminds me of temperance advertisements of non-alcoholic drinks which have the same stimulating effects as wine (and when analysed much the same proportion of alcohol!)

Behind the derision with which they spoke of Balfour's sophistry lay deep distress. 'So much of my father's life', Robert wrote, 'was devoted to restoring to the Conservative party the character that Peel and still more Dizzy had destroyed. And it looks as if his nephew were going to throw away his work.'

．　　　．　　　．　　　．　　　．

Nelly called the London borough of East Marylebone 'a most unattractive constituency ruled by small shopkeepers and big'. Her husband was nevertheless fortunate to become its Member of Parliament at the general election of 1906. Since the beginning of the fiscal controversy he had openly proclaimed himself a Free Trader, being spared the intervention of a rival Tariff Reform candidate only because 'they had too short notice to get a decent one'. The simultaneous defeat at Greenwich of his brother Hugh, far from inducing him to act with caution, renewed his dedication to the cause. One Cecil had fallen in defence of Unionist Free Trade; another was instantly at hand to continue the crusade.

Robert suffered few of the usual disadvantages of a newly elected MP. Since childhood he had relished what Lytton Strachey called the delicious bickerings of political intrigue. Many of the outstanding figures on both sides of the House were family friends and as a member of the Parliamentary Bar he had for several years haunted the corridors of Westminster. Although even the most successful lawyers rarely reproduce the triumphs of the courtroom before a critical audience of fellow MPs, he avoided that forensic pedantry which has cut short more than one promising parliamentary career. Outside the Chamber he allowed neither political passion nor moral disdain to mar an almost too elaborate courtesy.*

The state of the parties in 1906 was also to his advantage. The 157 Conservatives and Liberal Unionists who had survived the Liberal landslide included only a pathetically small handful of Free Traders; as the most articulate of them, the Member for Marylebone was at once able to play a lively role in harassing both the government and the hardly less detestable heretics who preached Tariff Reform from his own benches. For the first few weeks of the new parliament Chamberlain led the party in place of Balfour, who had been defeated at Manchester. 'The more I think of it,' Robert wrote to Linky in January, 'the more impossible it seems to me to allow Joe to lead me even temporarily.' Even the evasiveness and ambiguity of Cousin Arthur was preferable to the relentless hostility with which Chamberlain strove to purge the Unionist party of its Free Traders.

When Balfour did return to the Commons in March as a Member for the City of London, he had apparently learned nothing from the electoral rout which a firmer leadership might have avoided. On his very first afternoon as Leader of the Opposition the House happened to be debating fiscal problems and Balfour happily resumed his spinning of dialectical webs. To a storm of Liberal cheers, Campbell-Bannerman cut

---

* Years later, accosted by a Geneva prostitute while returning to his hotel from the League of Nations, he politely raised his hat and murmured: 'Merci, pas ce soir.'

through the gossamer with a contemptuous: 'Enough of this foolery.' For the first but by no means the last time in his political career Robert Cecil felt unable to support his party and voted with the government in favour of Free Trade. 'His constituents are very angry,' Nelly wrote, 'and are going to excommunicate him at a meeting next week – that is unless he beguiles them with a quotation from Burke on the independence of Members which he intends to read out. I expect they won't care twopence about Burke.' For the time being, however, he survived.

His elder sister Maud Selborne, married to the British High Commissioner for South Africa, sent him some sensible advice in his predicament:

> Don't stir up bad blood in the party against yourself, merely because you disagree with them on this point. My father opposed household suffrage, but when it was carried, he did not think that any reason for severing his connections with the party, and I don't see that Tariff Reform can possibly be considered of more importance than the Reform Bill of 1867. . . .
>
> What I want you to impress upon the somewhat dull mind of the average Conservative elector is, that although you disagree with him about Tariff Reform, you agree with him on other points. The danger is that he should regard you as a Radical in disguise. . . .

Certainly he did nothing to earn that reproach during his denunciation of the new government's Education Bill. A fellow Tory described him as 'a benevolent hawk, if there be such a bird, anxious to swoop upon the Liberal Party to remove it from its evil environment of Radicalism and Nonconformity and secure it body and soul for the Church'. Nor did the Liberals welcome his support even on non-party social questions. In 1907 he organized an informal committee largely composed of Radical MPs to discuss remedies for infant mortality.

> They regard him with profound distrust [Nelly wrote], and think he has some private end to serve – otherwise he couldn't possibly interest himself in any subject directly affecting the 'people', who are of course their own peculiar property. Can any good thing come out of Hatfield? they ask, and are quite confident that it can't.

But the pressure put upon him and his fellow Unionist Free Traders by the increasingly powerful Tariff Reformers remained the dominant political factor. Fearing, correctly as it turned out, that he might not be able to retain his seat at Marylebone as a wholehearted Free Trader, he called for an all-round moderation of views. He himself would accept tariffs at least for retaliatory purposes against foreign protectionist powers; in return, he hoped that Unionist Free Traders would not be opposed in their own constituencies by Tariff Reformers. Discussing the proposed compact with Balfour in March 1908, he added the veiled threat that he and his youngest brother, still in the wilderness, might otherwise join Rosebery in forming a new centre party. Bob sent an account of the talk to Linky:

> I saw A.J.B. yesterday for one solid hour by the clock. He was more than charming and full of personal flattery for myself from which I augured the worst. But to do him justice I think he really would regret my own ostracism. The position he took up was that he wished to keep the Free-Traders, but I gather that wish was not of an uncomfortably ardent character. At any rate he would go no further than this, that if a Free-Trader were adopted as candidate by an Association he would openly discourage any Tariff Reformer from running against him. On the other hand the Central Office would not give assistance by way of speakers or money to such a candidature. This seemed to me even then, and still more on reflection, practically useless. It would be considered by all ardent Tariff Reformers as a covert encouragement rather than the reverse. So that on leaving him I said the result of our conversation appeared to me to be practically negative. This he evidently did not quite like and ultimately offered to consider the original 'terms of peace' that I sent to Walter Long.* He was very much disturbed evidently at the idea of my joining Rosebery and said with great candour that it was open to you and me to destroy the Tory Party, that it was a matter for us to consider whether we really proposed to risk the Church and the Constitution for this 'wretched question'.

Nothing came of Robert's threat to form a new party of the centre. But in the absence of any conciliatory gesture from Balfour, he approached Asquith, who had recently succeeded Campbell-Bannerman as Prime Minister. With extraordinary optimism he asked whether, in constituencies represented by Conservatives, the Liberals would be prepared not to put up their own candidates but to leave the Unionist Free Trader and the Tariff Reformer to fight it out between them. Asquith's answer was mildly sympathetic but of no practical value:

> My own disposition (but I speak only for myself) would be to discourage Liberal opposition to a Unionist Free Trader in constituencies which are what I may call naturally and normally Unionist in general politics. But there again the difficulties of definition are considerable, and one would probably be driven back to the formula

* A prominent member of the Unionist Party who had offered his services as mediator between the two factions.

– so dear to the weaker members of the Judicial Bench – that 'each case must be decided by reference to its own particular circumstances'.

By August 1909 Robert was warning Balfour that he would 'prefer a moderate Liberal government to any other solution'. But the insolence with which Lloyd George had just defended his controversial Budget at Limehouse convinced him that such a haven was chimerical.

> I see no distinction of importance between such a speech and the old revolutionary doctrines of plunder [Robert wrote to Linky]. Unless he means that no property should be recognised unless it is earned, he means nothing. I don't see how I could ever give a vote which would replace such a man in office once we get him out. How cursed politics are!

Rather than accept so unsettling a Liberal government, he would even be prepared to swallow 'a moderate dose of Tariff Reform'.

Until he abandoned his resolute stand on Free Trade, he had to endure nearly two more years of mild political persecution at the hands of his own party. Shortly before the general election of January 1910 the threatened intervention of a Tariff Reform candidate at East Marylebone drove him to seek a seat against more conventional opposition at Blackburn, in Lancashire. He was heavily defeated but retained pleasant memories of the campaign. When Salisbury wrote offering to pay his election expenses, he endorsed his brother's letter with a vernacular, 'Goo' Laad!' Nor, in spite of later differences, did he ever forget the courage and generosity of F. E. Smith, the only Tariff Reformer who dared to speak on his behalf in the constituency. Denied any hope of contesting a safe Conservative seat, Robert was again beaten at the general election of December 1910 when opposing a Liberal in North Cambridgeshire.

'I think pretty soon I must write and tell A.J.B. that I no longer regard him as my leader,' he told his wife during those months of political exile, 'and then I can be quite friendly with him again. At present I don't much like meeting him'. Balfour's advice to the Tory peers not to reject the Parliament Bill of 1911 added to his cousin's despair. 'The sooner A.J.B. goes the better,' Nelly declared. 'He has made mental dishonesty respectable.' Within a few weeks the horizon had brightened. Balfour resigned the leadership of the party, exhausted by eight years of unappreciated prevarication. And Robert won a by-election caused by the death of the Member for Hitchin, in the Cecils' home county of Hertfordshire. Questioned during the campaign about his views on Tariff Reform, he replied that he was in favour of retaliatory duties, if required, in order to induce other countries to reduce their own tariffs; that he supported preferential treatment for trade within the Commonwealth, but not a tax on corn or general protection; and that he would not oppose any fiscal measures approved by the leaders of his party. The prodigal son had returned.

The delicate adjustment he made to his economic beliefs hardly exposes him to a charge of opportunism. Throughout the battle for Tariff Reform he remained an uncompromising Free Trader; only when the issue receded into the background of politics, eclipsed by the controversies of the Parliament Bill and Home Rule for Ireland, did he announce his partial surrender to Protection. Moreover, in undertaking not to vote against any tariff proposals favoured by his party leaders, he rightly suspected that such legislation was no more than a remote possibility. Certainly his own family, who could be stern critics, did not think him guilty of inconsistency. Alice Salisbury wrote to her brother-in-law Nigs soon after Robert's victory at Hitchin:

> I cannot tell you how he has come on during the last six years. I had not heard him speak for a long time. I went to several of his meetings. He has grown mentally quite enormously and not only mentally but I should say morally too, at least he gives you that moral effect that your father used to give; as if he belonged to a different class from the ordinary man, and whether you agreed with him or not, you can no longer disregard him.

His party, too, took him back into favour. In 1913 he was appointed to the select committee of the House of Commons investigating two linked matters: the negotiation of a contract between the government and a Marconi company for the construction of a chain of wireless stations throughout the British Empire, and allegations that certain Liberal ministers, including the Attorney-General, Sir Rufus Isaacs, and the Chancellor of the Exchequer, Lloyd George, had speculated in Marconi shares. In framing its conclusions, the committee divided along party lines. The Liberals exonerated the ministers, the Conservatives did not. It fell to Robert Cecil to draft the minority report on behalf of his party. In spite of his legal training and experience, it appears from the verbatim transcript of evidence that when cross-examining Isaacs he was outwitted again and again. On paper, however, he could be devastatingly incisive, and sixty years later his report carries more conviction than the exculpatory document produced by the Liberal majority:

> We are of opinion that the Attorney-General acted with grave impropriety in making an advantageous purchase of shares in the

Marconi Company of America upon advice and information not then fully available to the public given to him by the managing director of the English Marconi Company [his brother, Mr Godfrey Isaacs], which was in course of obtaining a contract of very great importance – a contract which even when concluded with the Government had to be ratified by the House of Commons. By doing so he placed himself, however unwittingly, in a position in which his private interest, or sense of obligation, might easily have been in conflict with his public duty.

We think that the Chancellor and the then Chief Ministerial Whip, in taking over a portion of the Attorney-General's shares on the same advice and information, are open to the same censure; and we hold this to be also true of the purchase of the shares for the Liberal Party funds by the Chief Whip, so far as such purchase was due to the same advice and information. . . .

Cecil added that the persistence of damaging rumours and suspicions was due to the reticence of the ministers, particularly during an earlier debate in Parliament. Questioned about an alleged purchase of shares in the English Marconi Company, Isaacs had declared: 'Never from the beginning . . . have I had one single transaction with the shares of that company.' He was speaking the truth, but not the whole truth; he omitted to add that he had bought and sold shares of the American Marconi Company. 'We regard that reticence as a grave error of judgement,' Cecil wrote in his report, 'and as wanting in frankness and in respect for the House of Commons.'

In June 1913 a parliamentary debate on the findings of the select committee saved the careers of the impugned ministers by only 346 votes to 268. Within a few months Isaacs, amid much tart comment, was appointed by Asquith to be Lord Chief Justice of England. Thereafter he gave many years of outstanding service to his country as judge, special Ambassador to the United States, Viceroy of India and Foreign Secretary. Lord Reading (as Isaacs became in January 1914) bore no resentment towards the man who had framed so harsh an indictment of his conduct. 'He has always been extraordinarily nice to me,' Robert told his brother, 'in spite of Marconi.'

Nor did Lloyd George show him the slightest ill will. But in 1913 the humiliated Chancellor could not resist defending himself against Conservative aspersions by hinting at financial impropriety on the part of Balfour fourteen years before. The accusation rested on a purchase by Balfour in 1899 of £1,000 of shares in Whitaker Wright's fraudulent London and Globe Finance Corporation, every penny of which was later lost.* Balfour wrote to Robert in October 1913 asking whether he ought to bring an action for defamation against Lloyd George:

> I understand that, without naming me, he indicates that in the matter of the Whitaker Wright prosecution. I put myself in the position where public duty and private interest clashed. This seems to be very childish. . . . I invested, and lost, a small sum of money in the Whittaker Wright smash. But what this private misfortune had to do with my public duty I am utterly unable to understand.

Robert advised his cousin not to pursue the matter which, like so many other political controversies of those years, was soon engulfed by the tide of war.

The loyal and lively comment with which Nelly sustained her husband during his struggle for political survival was no ordinary solace. Since 1897 she had been almost totally deaf. Each of the many specialists she consulted at home and abroad offered a different diagnosis of the condition. 'Nervous, gouty, rheumatic, anaemic! Lord, what a combination!' she wrote. 'And what cures one kills the other.' In the face of repeated failures to discover a cure she showed both courage and common sense: 'Mrs Prothero trod on a dog's toe and he squeaked loudly. Prothero turned to me and said, "Can you hear that?" which I thought a very sensible remark. It's such a bore when people treat deafness as a sort of improper disease not to be mentioned in polite circles.'

Increasingly she centred her life on Sussex rather than on London, bridging Bob's frequent absences at Westminster with a daily exchange of letters. Little escaped those sharp eyes, and she was much in demand as a correspondent. 'I found this gem in the *Observer*: "It is the strangest Easter the country has ever seen, an Easter which has lost almost all its significance except the religious one." '

The days passed pleasantly at Gale. She loved birds and animals, flowers and trees. There too she found the leisure to pursue her literary friendships, never much to her husband's taste. Nelly wrote of one new friend in the spring of 1906: 'She is mad about Greek and looks like a Greek herself, which is very unfair as she is probably going to be a good author as well.' That was Virginia Stephen at the age of twenty-four, not yet married to Leonard Woolf or known to the world of letters except as a shy contributor to *The Times Literary Supplement*. 'What

---

* Balfour's handling of his private fortune was uniformly incompetent. He and his brother Gerald also managed to lose about £250,000 investing in processes for the use of peat as fuel.

a mercy it would be,' she told Nelly, 'if one could write without reading
– and read without writing, but a wretch of a journalist never can
separate the two.' Cast by her fellow members of the Bloomsbury
circle in the role of Egeria, she was too fastidious to share their brazen
self-confidence, too sensitive to imprison herself in their rigid categories of belief. Yet in her relationship with Eleanor Cecil she showed
a novelist's curiosity about the supposed luxury and wickedness of
aristocratic life that was not always free from disapproval. Sometimes
her theme was whimsically goodhumoured: 'It is a wonderful night,
and you I suppose are attending some great ball; wearing a coronet,
dressed all in pale green satin, with ropes of pearls, and diamonds on
your brow.'

In similar teasing vein she wrote to Nelly during the air raids of the
First World War: 'I rejoiced to hear of your following the Zeppelin in
a taxi; such it is to have the blue blood of England in one's veins: my
literary friends hid in cellars, and never walk at night without looking
at the sky.'

Sometimes, however, Nelly detected the influence on Virginia of
Clive Bell, 'a silly little decadent brother-in-law who fills her mind with
poisonous class jealousy – of all silly things in the world – and makes
her believe we despise literary society. Poor things, we never get a
chance of knowing what it is.'

To illustrate the point, she noted a conversation with Virginia about
that high-spirited Victorian hostess Lady Dorothy Nevill.

> Virginia: 'Wasn't Lady Dorothy very improper?'
>
> Nelly (really astonished): 'Improper? Oh no! I *never* heard *that*
> about her.'
>
> Virginia: 'Thought there was some story?'
>
> Nelly (remembering ante-diluvian gossip): 'Oh, well, yes. I believe
> she did have an illegitimate child when she was seventeen.'
>
> Virginia (demurely): 'Rather unusual, isn't it, to have an illegiti-
> mate child at seventeen?'

Nelly later wished she had replied airily, 'Not at all in our class,' but
did not think of it in time. Towards the Bloomsbury circle in general
she bore no ill will. In 1917, at Virginia's request, she wrote to Lord
Salisbury pleading the case of Duncan Grant, the painter, who was
about to appear before the tribunal hearing appeals by conscientious
objectors.

'I don't often read poetry and never remember it,' Nelly used to say,
'but like to have the scent of it round about.' It was in just such a mood
of friendly detachment that she maintained her links with the world of
letters. As an occasional publisher's reader for John Murray she helped

Rose Macaulay to revise her manuscripts, turned down Galsworthy's *The Island Pharisees*, would have no truck with A. C. Benson's 'soft, plausible self-contradictory sentences'.

For William Hale White, the novelist better known by his pseudonym of Mark Rutherford, she reserved an almost filial attachment. In 1909, when he was nearly eighty, she wrote as a stranger to praise his book on Bunyan and was summoned to his cottage in Kent. Already an accomplished lip-reader, she was moved by the instinctive sympathy with which he pierced the barrier of her deafness. Their friendship flourished swiftly. During the remaining few years of his life Nelly relieved his loneliness and pain and depression with thoughtful little attentions: letters, occasional visits, presents of books and flowers and game. Each summer, too, she and Bob would lend him Gale for a week or two so that he could escape the hated noise and dust of the motor car that even in 1910 he recognized as a threat to the civilized life. Nelly's own awareness of the peril was delayed by her husband's child-like delight in those early machines. But twenty years later she protested: 'The roads are too dangerous: looks as if saturation point were reached.' Bob's own recantation was dramatically penitential: in 1929 he became the first President of the Pedestrians' Association.

Robert Cecil was within a few weeks of his fiftieth birthday on the outbreak of war in 1914. Too old to fight, he sought work with the Red Cross and organized a department that attempted to trace soldiers missing in battle. The melancholy of his task was partly relieved by the patriotic euphoria of those early wartime months. In November he dined in France with the Commander-in-Chief of the British Expeditionary Force, Field-Marshal Sir John French, and made a note of their conversation:

> He went on to emphasise that the Germans had been completely beaten in the West and that they knew it. He was also very sanguine about Poland and evidently thought that the Germans would very soon begin to ask for terms of peace which both he and his staff were anxious should be exceedingly moderate, and indeed when I suggested that we ought to have Heligoland I was severly snubbed. Nor would they even hear much about an indemnity. . . .

Armchair optimism rapidly gave way to the realities of the Western Front: a four-year campaign of attrition that claimed, it must have seemed, almost an entire generation. Of old Lord Salisbury's ten grandsons, five were killed in action. Edward Cecil, whose only son was the first to fall, spoke for them all when he wrote: 'It was in a sense an awful family loss but I cannot be quite sorry now. It is a splendid thing to leave life as clean and bright as that. It is a great honour and distinction.'

No such heroism illuminated the political front. The Conservatives affected to be outraged by Asquith's determination to place on the Statute Book during an agreed party truce two measures as contentious as Irish Home Rule and the disestablishment of the Welsh Church. Ignoring the simultaneous legislation that postponed their operation until the end of the war, Cecil advised his parliamentary colleagues to treat the government as they would cardsharpers, 'no longer as gentlemen and no longer fit for the society of gentlemen'. By April 1915 he had lost all faith in the ability of Asquith's administration to wage war. Prime Minister, Chancellor of the Exchequer, First Lord of the Admiralty, Foreign Secretary: each was examined in turn and found wanting:

> It is a serious disadavantage to have a Prime Minister who has no courage and little initiative. Then Lloyd George, who is really doing quite well in domestic affairs, suffers from profound ignorance when he has to face foreign questions. Winston with all his ability and qualities has done very badly. His craving for applause makes him boastful of success and so timid about failures that he conceals all unpalatable news which he can. Moreover his vanity makes him interfere with everything usually in the wrong way. Grey retains his reputation due to his methods and his character rather than to the results of his tenure of the Foreign Office. For after all he has failed in almost all his larger enterprises....

Not even his Sovereign could do right. Cecil was annoyed with the King for sending him a message of disapproval in reply to his call for the suspension of Ascot races; and no less affronted when George V determined to set an example of austerity to his subjects by publicly renouncing alcohol for the duration of the war. 'We have all got to follow suit to our infinite disgust,' he wrote. 'How Asquith and Haldane will manage, I can't think.'

A month later the Prime Minister broadened his government to include members of the Conservative party, and Cecil was offered a choice of junior ministerial posts. He elected to be Parliamentary Under-Secretary at the War Office, then discovered that the outgoing occupant, who happened to be Asquith's brother-in-law, wished to remain there. So instead he became Parliamentary Under-Secretary under Sir Edward Grey at the Foreign Office. It was a chance decision that for the first time turned his mind towards a serious study of international affairs and ultimately inspired him to devote his life to the cause of peace.

Both Grey and his own party leader, Bonar Law, would have liked to see him emerge from the scramble for office in the 1915 Coalition as a member of the Cabinet. To console him for his exclusion he was appointed to the Privy Council, a dignity denied to most junior ministers, even to his eldest brother when Parliamentary Under-Secretary at the Foreign Office fifteen years before. The regard of senior colleagues for his character and abilities had two further results. He was consulted by Grey more as an equal than as a subordinate; and in February 1916, while retaining his junior appointment at the Foreign Office, he received the additional office of Minister of Blockade, with a seat in the Cabinet. His position, according to the Permanent Under-Secretary, 'was almost that of an independent Secretary of State'.

Nelly took a less grandiose view of her husband's duties. 'Bob lives like a warehouse clerk,' she wrote. He laboured to ensure that food and other essential materials did not reach Germany from neutral countries; that her exports should be so crippled as to deter other nations from trading with her; and that commodities such as coal and jute, of which Great Britain had a near monopoly, should be withheld from the re-calcitrant. The task demanded diplomatic as well as commercial skills. Until the United States entered the war in 1917, British claims to board and search all Atlantic shipping provoked deep American resentment. Cecil Spring-Rice, the British Ambassador in Washington, wrote tartly in 1916 to a colleague in the Foreign Office:

> You may remind Lord Robert that there was a time when the Cecil family were regarded with some suspicion by the British democracy, which looked upon them as superior persons who had an inordinate share in the good things of government. They were also suspected of having a low opinion of their fellow countrymen who so delighted to honour them. This is rather the feeling of many Americans towards England.

A year in office convinced Robert Cecil that Asquith was no war leader. 'I have at last found a useful way of occupying my time in Cabinet!' he told Nelly on Downing Street paper. The letter, written literally under Asquith's eye, continues: 'The PM makes an excellent secretary of the Cabinet, a genius at drafting and even at presiding over this distinguished body. Provided you reconcile yourself to the fact that he never proposes anything or, if it is at all disagreeable, drives it through.'

Lord Robert was also dismayed by current chatter about his chief's private life. 'Philandering and bibulousness even in the young', he wrote primly, 'are repellent.' It was nevertheless with reluctance that in December 1916 he transferred his allegiance to Lloyd George. 'To a junior colleague like myself', Cecil wrote of Asquith, 'he was delightful. Considerate, rapid and unshrinkingly loyal under all circumstances.' That could not always be claimed of the new Prime Minister, whose strength as a national leader was in Cecilian eyes flawed by memories of Limehouse and Marconi, and by a growing suspicion of both moral and political recklessness.

In the redistribution of political office, Cecil remained in his subordinate role at the Foreign Office. But during the frequent absences of the new Foreign Secretary, Arthur Balfour, he wielded the full powers of the department, eventually receiving the unusual designation of Assistant Secretary of State. His promotion drew a testimonial from the most exacting of his senior officials. 'I look forward with complete assurance,' Sir Eyre Crowe told him, 'to the day when you will be our Secretary of State and/or (as our business men say) Prime Minister.'

Lloyd George, too, trusted Cecil's judgement and took him on several missions to France. Certainly he proved a more convivial companion than the dour Bonar Law. Here is Lord Robert's account of an interlude at Versailles during Allied talks on an armistice with Germany:

> It was a strange experience: L.G., full of Celtic enthusiasm, describing with much imagination and moderate accuracy the scene as he conceived it in the days of Louis Quatorze; Bonar looking on in gloomy indifference, while I tried to remember fragments of Saint Simon to add a few historical details to L.G.'s picturesque improvisation! At the Petit Trianon Bonar's gloom became intensified, partly owing to the continually falling rain, and at last he said, with profound depression, 'If I had known you were going to do this I would not have come out with you!' So we returned to luncheon and battled all the afternoon with the French and Italians.

Even the generals liked Robert Cecil. 'An honest level-headed fellow,' Field-Marshal Haig wrote in his diary after entertaining him at GHQ. Few other politicians fared as well.

Shocked by the death and destruction of a world war, Cecil sought to devise a way of preventing its recurrence: some universally accepted plan by which no aggrieved nation would resort to arms until all means of conciliation had failed. The problem had taxed the minds of innumerable idealists down the ages, and the memorandum which Cecil circulated to his Cabinet colleagues in the autumn of 1916 did not at first seem any more promising than its forerunners. It developed two themes. If any difference should arise between states, each was to refrain from acts of violence until a conference had met to consider the dispute; and if any state should fail to show restraint, the others were required to enforce her submission by means of commercial and financial sanctions. Like Sir Edward Grey, Cecil believed that the outbreak of war in 1914 might well have been averted had Austria been persuaded to refer her quarrel with Serbia to international negotiation or arbitration.

The memorandum was considered by a committee of jurists and diplomats under the chairmanship of Sir Walter (later Lord) Phillimore; it emerged as the first draft of what later came to be called the Covenant of the League of Nations. The Cabinet accepted it with caution rather than with cordiality. A widespread desire for peace did not extend to approving proposals that might be thought to erode national sovereignty or security. Even before circulating his memorandum in 1916, Cecil had been prevailed upon by Crowe to delete any reference to the need for international disarmament. He wrote to Nelly in August 1918:

> I am in a fuss about the League of Nations. There was a short talk about it at the Cabinet yesterday and I found the atmosphere very chilly. L.G. has never really cared about it and is almost against it now under the influence of Amery, Hankey and co. Not one of them except Barnes and possibly Smuts and A.J.B. really approves. . . . I have always known that the Continental bureaucracy is opposed to us and blood lust is obscuring the American vision. What ought I to do? Without the hope that this war was to establish a better international system, I should be a pacifist.

The Foreign Office had taught Cecil neither the jungle realities of international affairs nor the political limits of altruism. When the Cabinet was drafting its declaration of war aims, Hankey urged him not to insist on a general adherence to the principle of self-determination.

> I pointed out to him [the Cabinet Secretary wrote] that it would logically lead to the self-determination of Gibraltar to Spain, Malta to the Maltese, Cyprus to the Greeks, Egypt to the Egyptians, Aden to the Arabs or Somalis, India to chaos, Hong Kong to the Chinese, South Africa to the Kaffirs, West Indies to the blacks etc. And where would the British Empire be?

To be forty years ahead of his time won Robert Cecil few laurels in the hard-headed England of 1918. Even his knowledge of geography was reputed to be sketchy. In the Foreign Office one day he called for a map of the Austro-Hungarian Empire, then complained to Lewis Namier, of the political intelligence department, that the long straggling territory of Galicia had been wrongly coloured; it should, he explained, be Hungarian, not Austrian. When Namier replied that Galicia happened to be his native land and was indeed in Austria, there was a pause. 'What a funny shape Austria must be,' murmured the minister who for three years had organized the blockade of the Hapsburg monarchy.

Without the more practical skills of a few dedicated allies, Cecil might never have seen the fulfilment of his hopes: a League of Nations complete with council, assembly and permanent secretariat. By a pleasing irony, the most effective of them was the South African leader, Jan Christian Smuts, who had once borne arms against a British Army that included two of Robert's brothers. Now he sat in the War Cabinet by special invitation, an immensely respected and visionary figure. He wrote a pamphlet elaborating Cecil's original conception, commended it to other representatives of the overseas Empire, ultimately saw it embodied in the Treaty of Versailles.

Cecil never relished political office as such, only the use he could make of it to pursue his ideals. 'Some of my friends tell me that I am quite unfitted for political life because I have a resigning habit of mind!' he wrote in 1918. In recent years he had several times threatened to resign for reasons which his colleagues found obscure or inadequate. They included a dispute with Kitchener about the terms on which Great Britain should agree to an exchange of prisoners of war with Germany, and the failure of the Allies to intervene in Siberia. When at last he did insist on resignation, in November 1918, the cause seemed arbitrarily remote from the pressing problems of the hour: the government's determination to reanimate the Bill disestablishing the Welsh Church, a measure suspended in 1914 for the duration of the war. To the Cecils, however, it was as momentous a question as any. On the dissolution of parliament in the following month, Bob nevertheless stood for re-election to the Commons. And in spite of having rejected the certainty of high office in the prolonged Lloyd George Coalition, he at once asked for and received an appointment to the British delegation to the Peace Conference in Paris. He was to help Smuts in negotiating the establishment of a League of Nations, a role which would bring him the authority but not the responsibility of a minister, the means of control but not the subordinate status of an official. Thus do even the unworldly sometimes contrive to eat their cake and have it.

The League of Nations emerged from the Paris Peace Conference of 1919 much as Robert Cecil had envisaged it three years earlier. The commission charged with defining its constitution and powers started from the principles that nations in dispute, whether members of the League or not, must try to settle their differences by every peaceful means before resorting to war; and that any nation which flouted such a procedure should be subjected to trade and financial sanctions, even, if necessary to military force. A complementary declaration in favour of the reduction and limitation of national armaments was, to Cecil's satisfaction, no longer opposed by the British government. In less fanciful mood, the commission recommended the establishment of an international court of justice and of permanent co-operation in the fields of labour and health. As the husband of a fervent but non-militant suffragette, Cecil found particular pleasure in ensuring that women should be eligible for all League appointments.

He regretted that no representatives of ex-enemy powers had been invited to sit on the League commission, and in common with his colleagues assumed a moral obligation to protect their long-term interests; hence the commission's decision to establish League headquarters in aseptic Geneva, untouched by the lingering wartime passions of Paris or Brussels. He also pleaded with Lloyd George to mitigate the severity of some of the territorial and financial settlements which, he feared, the Allies were about to impose on Germany: the cession of Upper Silesia to Poland, the dismemberment of the Saar valley and the exaction of £1,000 million of reparations within two years. 'I cannot help feeling,' he told the Prime Minister, 'that in these negotiations our moral prestige has greatly suffered.' A few days later, after a meeting with Colonel House, the American delegate, he wrote in his diary:

> Found that all our beautiful plans for admitting Germany very early to the League of Nations and for reconsidering all the pin-prick clauses as soon as she was admitted had been, I will not say rejected, but gravely disapproved of by the French and not supported, apparently, by Ll. G. The result is that I am afraid most if not all of it will go.

It grieved Cecil that so few other Allied statesmen at the Peace Conference shared the magnanimity shown by the League commission towards a beaten enemy. He thought the Italians perverse, the French vainglorious, and both extraordinarily greedy. Even President Wilson, whose belief in the League matched his own, was found wanting: 'I do not quite know what it is that repels me: a certain hardness, coupled with vanity and an eye for effect. He supports idealistic causes without being in the least an idealist himself.' As for Lloyd George: 'He certainly is a very poor diplomat – always "scoring", the foolishest exercise in the world if you want to get your own way.' In lighter vein he added: 'There, how good and clever I am, and above all how modest!' Such self-mockery is endearing. Yet his querulousness was unreasonable. He failed to recognize that the Allied Prime Ministers were exposed to the conflicting pressures of treaty obligations and popular opinion, of natural justice and national pride; that even the wisest and most humane of democratic leaders is ultimately the servant of a fickle electorate; that to negotiate with the high-mindedness of a Robert Cecil is not practical politics.

In Cecil's eyes, the League was all; and when, in the middle of the Conference, Lloyd George tried to obtain a reduction in American naval strength by threatening President Wilson with a withdrawal of British support for his cherished Covenant, Cecil begged Balfour to intervene with the Prime Minister: 'I certainly am not prepared to try and carry out a policy which in my judgement is wrong in itself and exceedingly hazardous to a cause in which I passionately believe, and to which I am pledged by every obligation of honour.'

His former Cabinet colleagues had cause to be irritated by such caprice on the part of a man who neither carried the burden of ministerial responsibility to Parliament nor was prepared to accept the subordinate role of an official. 'They look rather askance at me,' Cecil told his wife. 'Austen's bureaucratic soul was much shocked and both Winston and F.E. mentally raised their eyebrows. . . . The P.M. of course prefers an irregular situation – morally, intellectually and administratively.' Whatever annoyance Lloyd George himself may have felt, he treated Cecil with unbroken consideration, even entrusted him with the further task of representing Great Britain on the Supreme Economic Council. As early in the Conference as February 1919 he also pressed Cecil to become British Ambassador in Washington, seeking perhaps the enchantment that distance supposedly lends to the view. Lord Robert, like his eldest brother a few months later, declined the appointment. The Covenant of the League was too fragile a plant to be left in less scrupulous hands than his own.

In any case, he enjoyed peacemaking in Paris. The American financier Bernard Baruch, meeting him there for the first time in 1919, expressed wonder at finding a well-preserved fifty-four and not an elderly sage with a long white beard. Throughout the Conference, Cecil kept a diary in which he noted the foibles of his fellow statesmen as fully as the progress of negotiations. 'One gets to know all these great people in undress, as it were,' Salisbury wrote after reading it, 'many of them a little thin without the padding.' Wilson emerges from its pages 'inclined to think that he is President not only of the US but of the world as well'. Balfour's 'desire to avoid taking a decision has now grown into a passion'. The French delegate Larnaude, with Gallic frivolity, 'was very much grieved with me because I would not adjourn the meeting to enable him to attend a *sauterie* at which his niece was dancing'. Cecil's fears for the future of the League never impaired his appetite for gossip:

> Aubrey Herbert told me that he and a friend of his in Rome had been talking to a certain Pantaleone, a government official, who assured them that he kept 1,500 scoundrels in the pay of the Government to do 'dirty jobs'. 'What kind of jobs?' they asked. 'Well,' replied Pantaleone, 'one of the deputies made a speech the other day which we disapproved of, so I ordered some of my men to seize him in an omnibus or tram and cut his beard off.' The two Englishmen gasped, and asked whether it had been done. 'Yes,' said Pantaleone, 'only the bother of it is, they cut off the wrong man's beard!'

The social historian may also be grateful to read that, on 19 March 1919, Lord Robert Cecil thought it worth recording that the Marquise de Polignac took out a little box at dinner and publicly powdered her nose.

Cecils have rarely been good party men. Even as Prime Minister, Lord Salisbury used to say that if the Conservative party were to abandon the principles for which he supported it, he would walk down the steps of the Carlton Club for the last time without a backward glance or a feeling of regret. It was an attitude which his son Robert found no reason to abandon. The pre-war hierarchy of the Conservative party, led by his own cousin, had failed to save him from relentless persecution at the hands of the Tariff Reformers, a campaign that for a time cost both him and his brother Hugh their parliamentary seats. Ten years later, the persistent suspicion and contempt with which so many Conservatives regarded the League of Nations threatened to destroy what he conceived to be his life's mission. The Coalition which sustained Lloyd George in office after the general election of 1918 consisted overwhelmingly of Conservatives led by Bonar Law. Baldwin is reputed to have described them as 'hard-faced men who looked as if they had done well out of the war'. The influence on events of this fresh infusion of commercialism into the Conservative ranks has sometimes been exaggerated; demands for a harsh peace treaty with Germany came as much from Tory landowners and merchants who had sat in previous parliaments as from the new men. Yet among the 334 Conservatives in the Commons of 1919 there were few who did not share a single stubborn belief: that whatever else might be said for the Treaty of Versailles which they ratified in July 1919, the League of Nations was at best the dream of idealists, at worst a disguised and potentially unpatriotic instrument of pacifism.

For his part, Cecil thought the Coalition leaders unhelpfully aggressive.

He lunched one day during the Peace Conference with Curzon and Churchill: 'I found them exceedingly militarist in their point of view, considering various extensions of British power in Russia and elsewhere. I feel more and more the difficulty of working with that lot, at any rate in foreign affairs.'

A year later he told his wife: 'Ll.G.'s speech was very non-Leaguey, I thought. Till he goes there is, I fear, little or no hope for the League – but I see no way of getting rid of him.' In common with his brothers, he also despised the disreputable style of Lloyd George's government, from the sale of honours to the use of the 'Black and Tans' in Ireland. Where then was he to find a political haven? As early as November 1919 he considered throwing in his lot with Labour, whose views on foreign policy and on co-partnership in industry often coincided with his own; but it is difficult to see how a Cecil could ever have accepted Labour's approach to religious questions or to the rights of private property.

The only other possible allies were those Asquithians, about half the Liberals in the Commons, who had refused to serve under Lloyd George after the change of premiership in 1916; like their leader, many of them paid the penalty of losing their seats at the general election of 1918. Whatever Cecil's doubts about Asquith as a wartime Prime Minister, he admired and respected him, and in 1920 infuriated his fellow Conservatives by openly supporting him against a Coalition candidate at the Paisley by-election. But it was in the less oppressively patrician figure of Edward Grey that he sought a popular leader, begging his old chief at the Foreign Office to put himself at the head of a new party composed of Asquithian Liberals, anti-Coalition Conservatives and temperate supporters of Labour. When Grey declined to act without Asquith's approval, Cecil wrote to Asquith: 'What is wanted is a public declaration from you that in order to secure a Government which could be trusted you would be prepared to take office under Grey.' Asquith's reply was glacially unenthusiastic:

I have no personal bias in the matter. Office as such has no attractions for me, and I have been in the first place long enough to satisfy the most voracious ambition. Nor do I know in the least whether Grey, who is my oldest and most intimate political friend, would desire or assent to such an arrangement as you propose. . . .

I must, therefore, tell you quite frankly that I have abundant evidence from many quarters that any such announcement as you suggest would be received in the party as a whole with bewilderment, and in its most active and militant sections with something like consternation.

That was the end of the matter. Grey, welcoming his reprieve, disappeared to spend the rest of his days among birds and fishing-rods. As Cecil himself came to realize, it was absurd to imagine that a new political party could be built on such insubstantial foundations as 'moderation' and a dislike of Lloyd George. 'I do not believe in Bob Cecil's "moderate" party,' Lord Esher observed. 'There are no such people among effective politicians. "Moderates" are bisexual.' And even Hugh Cecil, most volatile of parliamentarians, felt obliged to warn his brother 'against hatred of L.G. becoming an obsession and unbalancing your mind'. Another Member of Parliament, Sir Oswald Mosley, believed that the Cecils made a profound error in holding themselves aloof from Lloyd George, the only statesman of the day with both the vision and the energy to animate the League of Nations. 'They buttoned up their prim little overcoats against the chill of Lloyd George's methods, while their country and Europe caught pneumonia from the icy blast of the next war.' Mosley's verdict continues:

> Lord Robert in his saintly personality and in the high endeavour of his politics represented probably the last attempt for a long time to make the contemporary world sensible, humane and civilized, a world of well-arranged peace. He was nearly a great man, and he was certainly a good man; possibly as great a man as so good a man can be. There is something in a basic concept of Greek thought, stressed by the neo-Hellenists, that an element of the Dionysian is necessary as counter-point to the Apollonian in the perfect harmony of creative nature. Lord Robert too suffered in some degree from the inhibiting emotions which should never intrude in action. When the emotions were touched, plain sense was liable to fly out of the window. It is always sad to see such minds clouded by feelings irrelevant to great purpose, deflected from practical achievement by the triviality of personal likes and dislikes. It is a common condition in these delicate aristocratic constitutions which cannot easily endure the dual strain of thought and action.

His problem of political allegiance unresolved, Cecil contented himself with leaving his place on the government benches and sitting among the Opposition as an Independent Conservative.

One summer evening in 1921 Robert Cecil heard his brother deliver a sermon in St Paul's Cathedral on England's responsibility for moral leadership. He afterwards wrote to Nelly: 'I have had a great feeling that I have been "called" to preach the League spirit in public affairs and there seems so much in the Bible about that kind of thing. . . . And yet there is the great danger of hypocrisy and self-deception as with Gladstone.'

It was with just such dedication and humility that he embarked on his mission. First, however, he had to overcome a humiliating obstacle to his plans. Widely mistrusted by the Conservatives, not least by the Foreign Secretary, Lord Curzon, he had also irritated Lloyd George by his flirtation with the Asquithian Liberals. The government therefore refused to send him as a British delegate to the first sessions of either the Council or the Assembly of the League. Once more Smuts played a decisive part in Cecil's career by inviting him to become a member of the South African delegation. The appointment caused surprise but only occasional resentment.

Installed at Geneva,* Cecil gazed upon his achievement with some disappointment. The forty-one nations represented did not include the three on whom, little more than twenty years later, world peace would ultimately depend. Germany was still considered too wicked to sit among her civilized conquerors; Russia shunned the League as an institution of capitalist intrigue; the United States Senate had declined to ratify the Treaty of Versailles which embodied the Covenant. The achievements of the League during its early sessions were nevertheless more practical than its detractors had forecast. It attempted, sometimes with success, to settle differences between Finland and Sweden, between Poland and Lithuania, between Yugoslavia and Albania. It set up one commission to supervise the administration of ex-enemy mandated territories and another to consider the reduction of armaments. It co-ordinated measures to curb the 'white-slave' traffic in prostitution, the smuggling of opium and the spread of typhus. It drafted a constitution for the International Court of Justice at The Hague.

As one of the architects of the League, Cecil undertook a lecture tour of the United States in the spring of 1923, extolling the merits of inter-national co-operation. His hosts drove him hard. 'By the time I leave this country,' he confided to his diary, 'I think I shall be actively sick if any-one mentions the League.' The most depressing episode was a visit to the half-paralysed Woodrow Wilson, whose intransigent refusal to accept any amendments to his original concept of the League had unwittingly prevented America from ever becoming a member. 'Remember,' he told Cecil, 'we are on the winning side, and make no concessions.'

Back in London, Cecil found it 'almost heart-breaking' that successive British governments showed only indifference towards the League, in

---

* Rose Macaulay wrote an affectionately disrespectful novel entitled *Mystery at Geneva* (Collins, 1922) about Cecil's early connection with the League of Nations. The protagonist is Lord John Lester, one of the delegates from Central Africa. Balfour appears as Lord Burnley, author of *Scepticism as a Basis for Faith*.

spite of the tributes which they prudently attached to their official declarations of foreign policy. Neither Lloyd George nor Bonar Law, who had become Prime Minister after the Carlton Club revolt of 1922, ever thought it worthwhile to attend a single meeting of the League. Curzon, too, Foreign Secretary in both administrations, held aloof from its deliberations.

Even Balfour, supposedly the most idealistic of Conservatives, made no secret of preferring the traditional methods of diplomacy to the open discussion favoured by the League. When France occupied the Ruhr at the beginning of 1923, he begged Cecil not to make a speech on the subject at Geneva. Cecil refused to accept his cousin's advice, but assured him that he did not intend to make things more difficult. 'My dear Bob,' Balfour replied, 'I am quite sure you do not intend to, but I am equally quite sure that you will.' A few months later Balfour complained of an article written by Cecil for *The Times*, belatedly accusing the British delegates to the Paris Peace Conference of having left President Wilson in the lurch. In protest he resigned as Vice-President of the League of Nations Union: an amorphous body of well-wishers under Cecil's presidency which over the years gave the impression of drawing its active members more from the left than from the right and of seeking peace by pacifism rather than by preparedness. When Bob sought to persuade him to withdraw his resignation, Balfour brusquely agreed to a meeting only on condition that he did not mention the League of Nations. For Nelly Cecil, Cousin Arthur's defection from the League revived all the scorn she had felt during the battle for Tariff Reform. 'He chose Highbury instead of Hatfield,' she wrote to Gwendolen, 'Clemenceau instead of Wilson, Lloyd George instead of Bob . . . a progressive and tragic failure.'

But with the appointment of Baldwin to succeed the ailing Bonar Law only a week after that distressing encounter with Balfour, Cecil's hopes for the League instantly revived. It was not that the new Prime Minister showed any more enthusiasm than his predecessors for its business sessions; indeed, he compounded his negligence that first summer in office by declining to give up a single day of his holiday at Aix-les-Bains, although the spa lay only fifty miles from Geneva. He redeemed himself, however, by boldly inviting Cecil to join the Cabinet as Lord Privy Seal, with special responsibility for League affairs. For a few wild hours Cecil even imagined that he might be about to become Foreign Secretary on the expected resignation of Curzon, deeply affronted at having been passed over for the premiership. But the Marquess, as the political world ironically called him, decided that he was indispensable to the office he had dignified for the past four years, and Cecil had to be content with the lesser post.

It has not been uncommon during the present century for a minister charged with some special task of foreign policy to sit in Cabinet on equal terms with the Secretary of State himself. As wartime Minister of Blockade, Cecil had done just that, establishing a harmonius relationship first with Grey, then with Balfour. Neither of those two statesmen, however, was as jealous of his reputation and pride as Curzon, whose first act on resuming office as Foreign Secretary in the Baldwin administration was to forbid Cecil a room in the Foreign Office. Within days of his appointment, the new Lord Privy Seal wrote ominously to Curzon:

> I cannot conceal from myself that the arrangement you suggested yesterday does not quite come up to that which I had understood was agreed upon. Still in these circumstances it is not so much the form as the spirit in which any arrangement of the kind is carried out that signifies, and I have great confidence that you and I will be able to work together so as to enable me to carry out a League policy such as I am pledged to carry out by much that I have said in the country during the last three years.

Curzon replied bleakly: 'I think that with good will the plan I suggested will work. But I do not wish there to be any misunderstanding about the fundamentals, since the L. of N. business is now under the Foreign Office and I am not prepared to delegate my responsibility to anybody.'

That tart exchange was the prelude to an increasingly irritable correspondence between 'My dear George' and 'My dear Bob'. In some ways it recalled the letters that only a few months before had passed between Curzon and Salisbury about the Leadership of the House of Lords. Bob, however, could be a more stubborn antagonist than his eldest brother. After complaining that the Foreign Office had repeatedly failed to consult him on matters affecting the League, he added:

> You seem to think that I am trying in some way to make myself a kind of rival Foreign Secretary. Do please disabuse yourself of any such idea. . . . I am anxious to co-operate with you as fully as I can, and it was for that reason and that reason only that I desired a room in the Foreign Office, because I felt sure that otherwise your advisers if not you yourself would always view even my most innocent action askance.

The olive branch was brushed aside. 'If I have any suspicions in this case,' Curzon asked rhetorically, 'are they altogether without foundation?' He reminded Cecil that he had always worked amicably with previous ministers responsible for League affairs:

But when their successor first asks for a room in the Foreign Office, and then asks to be chairman of a committee sitting in the Foreign Office, when further he sends round and wants to see Foreign Office files about matters (e.g. China and Tangier) which do not at present, at any rate, touch the League at all, and finally when he addresses the Cabinet without consultation on a Foreign Office matter, the conclusion is not unnatural that . . . he aspires to be a kind of Assistant Secretary of State who is entitled to take the initiative in all matters that do not merely now, but may in the future, touch the sphere of the League.

Cecil failed to mend his ways. 'He is a terrible nuisance to me in the Cabinet,' Curzon told his wife, 'talking interminably and always wrong about Foreign Affairs.' The final explosion occurred after the Lord Privy Seal, on his own initiative and without informing the Foreign Office, had discussed with President Millerand of France ways of improving the strained state of Anglo-French relations. Curzon wrote furiously to Baldwin:

> I am afraid that I cannot continue to be responsible for the conduct of Foreign Affairs if any of my colleagues is at liberty to act in this way; and unless you can assure me that such incidents will not recur, I can have no alternative but to ask, though with the most profound regret, to be relieved.

During the remaining few months of office left to the government, Curzon and Cecil professed to patch up their differences and in September 1923 worked in accord to contain a dangerous situation created by Mussolini. The Italian dictator, outraged at the murder on Greek soil of his country's representatives on an international boundary commission, had bombarded and occupied the island of Corfu. Even Curzon, who during his years at the Foreign Office had virtually ignored the existence of the League, recognized that its peace-keeping provisions had been designed to deal with just such an act of aggression. 'The machinery of the League must be put in motion,' he declared. 'Telegraph to Bob Cecil instructing him to go full steam ahead.' In Geneva a few days later, the Lord Privy Seal accordingly reminded the assembled delegates of their obligations under the Covenant.

Unhappily, that was in effect the limit of intervention by the League. French reluctance to condemn Italy obliged the League to remit the settlement of the problem to a council of ambassadors who first agreed to accept, then rejected, a just solution suggested by Geneva. Had it been implemented, Mussolini would have been obliged to leave Corfu in return for no more than a Greek apology and the promise of an indemnity to be decided by the International Court of Justice. As it was, he felt strong enough to claim immediate and substantial reparations as the price of withdrawal. Curzon, believing no vital British interest to be threatened, gave his assent to the modified plan. Mussolini, as an angry supporter of the League remarked, had triumphed like a drunken driver, not by reason of his own skill but because all sober people had been concerned to get out of his way. The League of Nations had failed its first exacting test and set a dismal precedent that haunted it to the end of its days.

A few weeks later, with practised hand, Cecil drafted a letter of resignation. His principal motive for withdrawing from the government, he explained to Baldwin, was the lack of confidence which the Conservative party showed for the League. But his decision, he added, was reinforced by the Prime Minister's determination to fight an immediate general election in defence of Tariffs. At the last minute Cecil had second thoughts and the letter was never sent. Instead he agreed to remain in the government, but to ask for a peerage. He would thus maintain his links with the League, but be spared both the fatigue of wooing a country constituency and the risk of being unseated for his unorthodox views. Even that decision was not taken without several changes of mind. At last, on Christmas Eve 1923, after Salisbury had intervened with the King to ensure that his brother did not become a mere Baron, Robert was gazetted Viscount Cecil of Chelwood. Across the final letter in the bundle of papers dealing with his peerage he wrote the words: 'Political Deathbed.'

The implication of those despairing words is clear: that without the encumbrance of a peerage he might have achieved even higher office, perhaps the highest of all. What evidence is there to support that illusion? In spite of the Christian principles which ruled his life, he did not despise the prizes of politics. In January 1919, shortly after resigning from the Coalition on the issue of disestablishing the Welsh Church, he wrote to his wife from Paris:

The new Government does not sound very attractive – sour grapes, in fact. I try and school myself to care only for my work, which is deeply interesting and important. But there is no doubt I have a very ambitious nature which besides being wrong is incredibly silly. But it is just like being in a queue. It is useless to tell oneself that one gets nothing by pushing; the impulse to push is there though it may be controlled.

Bad isn't it, and I can't accuse you, as men generally do, of being the cause of it.

As he well knew, however, his political desires were both honourable and altruistic. If they remained only partly fulfilled, it was because his interests centred almost wholly on foreign affairs. His sister Gwendolen said of him in 1922: 'The difference in clearness and confidence of vision when he is talking foreign or home policy is very striking. I believe he would be an admirable Foreign Minister: his home policy would depend very much upon the company in which he ultimately finds himself.' Yet his repeated insistence that the corner-stone of British foreign policy must be resolute support for the League of Nations was not an argument to entice the Conservative voter. His idealism was sometimes respected, more often derided, rarely shared. The intruder at a meeting of the League of Nations Union who declaimed through his megaphone, 'Robert Cecil, you are a bloody traitor,' was both rude and wrong. But he echoed the suspicions of very many Tories who felt that dependence on the whims of any international assembly was both corrosive of national sovereignty and an insult to the millions who had fought, died and suffered for their country during four years of war.

In those circumstances, Cecil was fortunate to find in Baldwin a Conservative Prime Minister bold enough to entrust him with the task he most coveted. It is difficult to imagine what other or more welcome portfolio he might have held had he not, when already in his sixtieth year, accepted a peerage.

Before he could take his seat in the House of Lords, the general election of December 1923 had proved Baldwin's protectionist policy as disastrous as both the Cecil brothers in his Cabinet had forecast. The first Labour government accordingly assumed office in January 1924 and lasted for ten months. Cecil was asked unofficially whether he would consider joining the new administration as Foreign Secretary. In spite of the gulf that had widened between him and his Conservative colleagues, he refused. 'I could not,' he wrote, 'with my family and history, hope to receive the support from Labour which would be necessary in order to carry out such a foreign policy as I desired. The truth is that attachment to a non-party cause is inconsistent with acceptance of party office.' He nevertheless looked with goodwill on the Labour government and saluted MacDonald, who became his own Foreign Secretary, as the first British Prime Minister ever to attend a session of the League of Nations.

The return of the Conservatives to power after the general election of November 1924 brought Cecil an unexpected invitation to rejoin the Cabinet. Curzon, who at last relinquished the Foreign Office in favour of Austen Chamberlain, wrote to his wife:

Baldwin came to lunch here alone. He frankly admitted the inconsistency about Bob Cecil but had been won round by Jim Salisbury and by the idea that the League of Nations people in the country would be offended if he were omitted and Birkenhead included. But there is some, though a faint, hope that he may refuse, since A. Chamberlain, with whom I had a long talk on the subject, has followed me in absolutely refusing him a room in the Foreign Office or allowing him back as a sort of Deputy Secretary of State. I heartily hope he will decline.

In spite of some misgivings, Cecil did, however, accept Baldwin's offer of responsibility for League of Nations affairs together with the Chancellorship of the Duchy of Lancaster, an office that carried a seat in Cabinet yet few departmental duties. Duff Cooper described his first ceremonial appearance at the opening of the new parliament:

The King and Queen sitting on their thrones with their crowns on, the King reading the speech extremely well, the Prince of Wales on a smaller throne in the robes of the Garter, looking most like a fairy prince, his pink face and golden hair rising out of ermine, beautiful as an angel, the Peers looking like chessmen, F.E. looking very fine standing on the left of the throne carrying the sword of office, never moving a muscle – and best of all, saintly Bob Cecil wearing some wonderful robes* and carrying something, standing on the right of the throne and looking incredibly wicked and scheming, like the evil counsellor in the fairy tale, or the bad uncle of a mediaeval king.

From the enchantments of pageantry Cecil fled to the harsh realities of international affairs. 'We had a full Cabinet today,' Baldwin wrote to Curzon in January 1925, 'except for one of two invalids and yourself and of course Bob who is in an opium den at Geneva.' There Cecil was joined by a reluctant Chamberlain, who cannot have found either the atmosphere or his fellow British delegate at all congenial.

We listened to an eloquent speech by Monsieur Paul-Boncour [Cecil wrote] in which he expressed his profound disagreement with British policy. I remember whispering to Sir Austen that the speech made me feel very mean, since I really agreed with every word of it. He made no reply.

* They were not the only robes to grace that angular frame. After his election to succeed Joseph Chamberlain as Chancellor of Birmingham University, Mrs Chamberlain lent him her late husband's academic robes. Thus did the mantle of the Tariff Reformer fall ultimately on Free Trade shoulders. Cecil returned the compliment by nominating Joseph's son Austen for an honorary degree.

Nor could Cecil bring himself to admire the diplomatic skill with which the Foreign Secretary concluded the Treaties of Locarno that autumn. Although they provided for the admission of Germany to the League as well as the settlement of the ancient frontier dispute between France and Germany, Cecil thought them too local in their scope, too redolent of secret bargaining, too independent of Geneva.

By March 1926 he was once more on the brink of resignation, complaining to the Prime Minister that Chamberlain scorned the publicity without which the League could not thrive: 'He appears still to think that what he calls Locarno methods can and should be applied to the Council and Assembly of the League. In this he will undoubtedly have the support of the continental Foreign Offices, who still sit at the feet of Metternich and Bismarck.' When Baldwin soothingly replied that Cecil could do more for the League inside the government than out, he agreed to remain. But eighteen months later, on the breakdown of the Naval Disarmament Conference at Geneva, Cecil again threatened resignation. The Cabinet, he claimed, had gone back on its word by withdrawing agreement to American demands for parity. This time the Prime Minister was less accommodating. Cecil wrote mournfully to Salisbury: 'I formed a distinct impression that he scarcely read and had not appreciated either of the letters I had written to him . . . and that he was on the whole rather glad to be rid of me.' His resignation was accepted without a conventional expression of regret and he never again either held political office or was invited to take part in the counsels of the Conservative party.

He met his fate with good humour. 'It is rather embarrassing,' he told Nelly, to be treated as a hero because I got tired of appointing magistrates in Lancashire and being snubbed by Austen Chamberlain for a very minute salary ! ! !' Perhaps he was fortunate to have stayed the course as long as he did while remaining in fundamental disagreement with his colleagues on the one theme that absorbed his entire interest. Gwendolen believed that a defect of temperament prevented her brother from accepting the inevitable compromises of political life. The abortive disarmament negotiations between Great Britain and the United States that provoked his resignation shows him to have been not only incapable of appreciating the fears of the Cabinet but also astonishingly remote from reality. As the relative power of six-inch and eight-inch guns was argued across the conference table, Cecil proposed that the solution would be for all naval cruisers to carry seven-inch guns.

From Winston Churchill, his most formidable antagonist in Cabinet on the naval question, came some generous words: 'Such a resignation as yours helps to dignify public life and to strengthen the position and repute of politicians generally.' The warmth of the tribute from so unpredictable a source supports Cecil's repeated denials that he was ever willing to dismantle his country's defences in the supposed interests of world peace. His policy was more chimerical: a general reduction of armaments by international agreement. He wrote to Churchill that same summer:

> You believe that future war is practically certain, that the best way of avoiding it is the old prescription of preparedness, and that in any case the first duty of the Government is to collect such armaments as may be necessary to prevent defeat.
>
> I regard a future war on a big scale as certainly fatal to the British Empire whether we win it or lose it, and probably also to European civilisation. I think therefore that the first duty of the Government is to throw their whole strength into the effort to substitute some other method of settling international disputes. ...
>
> Perhaps our differences may be put in this way – you hold the old maxim 'si vis pacem para bellum'. I would rather say: 'si vis pacem para pacem'.

The argument was not always sustained at that lofty level. 'Nothing would suit W.C. better than to be the Mussolini of England,' Nelly told her husband in 1924, 'and once in the saddle we should hear little more of L. of N.' A quarter of a century later, when most Britons still had cause to recall Churchill's bellicosity with gratitude, her prejudice persisted: 'His passion for war and everything to do with it seems the only unchanging thing in his nature – it colours all his language and one supposes his thinking. He probably thinks of his watercolours as assaults upon the landscape.' Bob was gentler in his criticism: 'I dined next Winston last night at Grillions. He was very affectionate and tried to persuade me he was a convinced Leaguer. But he only woke up really when he began to talk about Marlborough and Bolingbroke.' In extreme old age, however, discussing with Gilbert Murray why the League had failed to keep the peace, Cecil admitted that he had misjudged Churchill: 'A great mistake I made was in not working more closely with Winston, who I think was really strongly in favour of the League, subject to his overmastering belief in force as the only effective agent in international affairs.'

If Churchill was unjustly branded as a warmonger, so Cecil bore the unmerited stigma of pacifism (used here in the sense of deliberately offering no resistance to aggression). It was a charge which he resented. He never ceased to preach that in the last resort the League must sanction the use of force; and when his own country had at last been roused to the menace of Nazi Germany he both spoke and voted for rearmament as patriotically as any of his former Tory colleagues. But he did consort with pacifists. After each successive quarrel with the Conservative party he found himself with fewer allies to the right, almost no enemies to the left. And as President of the League of Nations Union, ostensibly a non-party association of those who subscribed to the principles of the Covenant, he became identified in the public eye with its pacifist and radical extremists. 'My powerlessness to guide the Union', he told his sister Maud in 1926, 'is one of the reasons, perhaps the strongest, why I often think of resignation.' He retained his office, however, and ten years later almost to the day received a stern warning from Churchill:

> It seems a mad business to confront these dictators without weapons or military force, and at the same time to try to tame and cow the spirit of our people with peace films, anti-recruiting propaganda and resistance to defence measures. Unless the free and law-respecting nations are prepared to organise, arm and combine, they are going to be smashed up.

Cecil probably agreed with him, but did not feel it was his duty to purge the League of Nations Union of its embarrassing elements. He contented himself with one tiny gesture. Presiding over a public meeting at which the audience sang the *Internationale* instead of the National Anthem, he left the platform in protest.

'It is Bob's serenity that I really enjoy,' one of his sisters wrote at a time of particular tension in League affairs. 'It is like his father's when things went wrong – the result, no doubt, of a fundamental Christianity.' Quite late in life, at the request of a friend, he put down on paper the essence of his faith. An endearing apologia of no more than five paragraphs, it is free from both the sense of unworthiness that oppressed his eldest brother and the spirtual pugnacity that stimulated the youngest:

> Why I believe? Firstly, because I was born into a family of believers. Both my parents were convinced Christians and so were my four brothers and two sisters. I grew up, therefore, regarding Christianity as part of the surrounding circumstances of my life. I started as a Christian.
>
> As I grew up, doubts began to press on me. Nothing profound; just the general sensation that I lived in a world in which I could see and hear and touch and that religion – belief in God and Christianity – was beyond the reach of ordinary senses. Could it be true?
>
> And then it seemed to me that there were other things beyond the

reach of the senses which were nevertheless certainly true. For instance, eternity. Time is clearly endless. There can be no beginning or end of it, since beyond the utmost future or past there must still be time. And the same is true of space, so that when I look up to a starry night I can not doubt that beyond the furthest star, space still extends endlessly. Here, then, are two things – Eternity and Immensity – which are obviously true and essentially incomprehensible. If that be the case with them, why not with religion?

Christianity is not a vague theory. It rests on positive evidence, partly historical and partly moral. Before we accept it as true, it is this evidence which must be examined. Did the events recorded in the New Testament, and especially the Resurrection, actually occur? The historic evidence for them is at least as strong as that for most other historical events. And morally, Christianity does correspond with the highest ideals of human aspiration.

But I will not claim that I am even now one of those fortunate people who never feel a qualm of doubt. I can only say with the father pleading for the life of his child: 'Lord, I believe; help Thou mine unbelief.' It is deeply consoling to me that the avowal was accepted as sufficient proof of faith.

Religion blended naturally into all the other activities of a busy life. While at the Bar he wrote to the Master of the Temple one Ash Wednesday suggesting that mid-week evening services be held in Lent, and consulted Linky on how best to convert a fellow lawyer 'who thinks a two-guinea summons of more interest and importance than the truth of Christianity'. In the period of Anglican agitation which followed the rejection of the Revised Prayer Book in 1928 he also accepted Archbishop Lang's invitation to act as chairman of a commission to inquire into the relations between Church and State.

Like most men who are secure in their beliefs, he could enjoy the humours of religion without embarrassment. The vicar intercepted him as he came out of church one morning: 'Lord Cecil, will you sign this petition?' He inquired to whom it was addressed. The reply delighted him: 'To Almighty God.' He insisted, however, on a measure of austerity in his religious observances. After attending the annual Remembrance Day service as a Cabinet Minister he wrote to Nelly: 'The ceremony at the Cenotaph was very well done and in a way impressive. But it is too mixed – patriotism, religion, loyalty, snobbery, officialdom – to suit me.' Nor did every incumbent in Holy Orders meet his exacting social standards:

> To church at St Michael's where the new cleric preached in a strange vulgar voice with many uncouth gestures like clapping his

hands violently and repeatedly. What I heard of the sermon did not seem remarkable. Rather old-fashioned with a lot about Hell. It seemed very successful for the place was cram full – mainly servant girls to look at – but a good many others.

Cecil's early dislike of what he supposed to be middle-class attributes grew no less sharp with the years. Touring the provinces on behalf of the League of Nations Union, he would entertain Nelly with daily accounts of all he had courteously endured in the cause of international peace and understanding. This comes from Hull in 1927:

You can have Scarboro' as far as I am concerned – a bleak, bitter place. But we had an excellent meeting, quite full and very attentive. I stayed with an M.C.M. [Cecil's prudent abbreviation for Middle Class Monster]. The lady was the daughter of the clergyman at —— and wished to talk to me about Lady Lothian and Lady Brownlow and Lady Pembroke and Lady Talbot, etc. etc. He was better but rather inarticulate. A nice boy in the building trade. I slept in the World's Worst Bed. As a raised map of one of the mountain systems it might have done better. So that like Lady Clare Vere de Vere's friend, I 'lacked repose'. In fact I got quite a lot of sleep. Here I am in a cultured home with central heating and all the latest books, I expect. If you must have the middle classes, I prefer them educated.

He was not, however, prepared to tolerate superciliousness in others. The following year, again in Yorkshire and with Archbishop Lang a fellow guest, he wrote of his host: 'His Grace of York despised him utterly. But I'm not sure that I did not find the middle class chieftain as pleasant as the middle class Archbishop.'

Jews, too, were rarely mentioned in Robert and Nelly Cecil's private correspondence without a phrase of disparagement from which neither Rothschilds nor Sassoons were immune. During the shortage of coal in 1919 Nelly wrote to her husband from Sussex: 'I suppose the golfing Jews get it all – but one must pay to be a Christian.' Life at Gale must indeed have seemed hard when only a few weeks earlier she had been staying at her old family home, Lambton Castle, with 'a coal fire in my bedroom here and butter and cream'. Presumably there were no golfing Jews in County Durham. Such anti-Semitic gibes, however thoughtlessly uttered, do not read agreeably; but they were everywhere more widespread in the years between the wars than later generations care to remember. With the rise of Hitler, Cecil became one of the first Englishmen publicly to condemn the Nazi persecution of the Jews.

Nor was the hauteur of those casual judgements at all characteristic of the Cecils' habitual modesty and benevolence. 'We live in very middle-class professional circles,' Nelly wrote in 1938, 'I feel a fish out of water in the country houses of my relations.' By the standards of the landed aristocracy they were never rich. Much of the £28,000 which Cecil left at his death in 1958 had been earned at the Bar more than half a century before; for the rest they managed well on an inherited private income of about £2,000 a year, sometimes supplemented by a ministerial salary, more often by political journalism. They were never tempted into extravagance. Bob's open distaste for field sports and Tory politics debarred him from those elaborate weekend entertainments that prolonged the spirit of the Edwardian era until the eve of the Second World War; in any case, he was kept busy enough at Westminster and Geneva, or addressing meetings of the League of Nations Union up and down the country.

The daily letters which bridged their separation reflect an intense involvement in home and foreign politics, but little interest in the arts and only the lightest of literary appetites. Both Bob and Nelly shared with Gilbert Murray an affection for the novels of P. G. Wodehouse hardly inferior to the adulation reserved for the League of Nations. 'If we haven't got the whole of his collected works,' Nelly told Murray in 1938, 'it is partly our economy but chiefly the fine taste and imperfect honesty of our guests.' The newly invented crossword puzzle also absorbed much of the Cecils' leisure. 'I behaved very badly this morning,' Bob wrote one summer day in 1929, 'doing the *Daily Telegraph* crossword before I got up! Then I did the *Daily News* at luncheon and the *Evening Standard* after tea – what a disgusting waste of time.' Such verbal agility, as he told Nelly, had unexpected results: 'Driving to the station this morning I thought of a new anti-litter poster: "Pigs!! Keep your litter for the sty!" Conciliatory and persuasive, eh!'

No pastime, however, occupied him more happily than the watch he kept on his own health. 'The Cecils', Winston Churchill once observed, 'are always ill or resigning.' In both vocations Bob gave of his best; two actual and several tentative resignations were well matched by the innumerable minor ailments that punctuate his correspondence. Indigestion, biliousness, loss of voice, insomnia, chill on the liver, eczema, tonsilitis, hay fever, gouty poison, exhaustion after walking home from Grillions Club wearing too heavy a coat: he spared his wife no single symptom of all he endured. 'I spent my time in the train', he once wrote to her, 'partly in reading and partly in considering whether I had got the flue – which appears not to be the case.' The demands of therapeutics occasionally clashed with those of piety. Having given up wine as a Lenten penance one year, he wrote to Nelly from Paris:

I regret to tell you that I am no longer a teetotaller! The fact is I have a cold in the head and yesterday I thought I would try a *petit verre* of brandy on strictly medical grounds. Decided success! So I had another for dinner and again for lunch today: After all as I explain to my conscience – which is rather pedantic – brandy is *not* wine and I only undertook not to drink wine! Then brandy is a recognised medicine! Anyhow there it is and the broad fact remains that my cold is better!

His wife responded with the qualified sympathy deserved by an invalid robust enough to survive into his ninety-fifth year. When as a Queen's Counsel he complained that losing a case in court had caused his health to take yet another turn for the worse, she briskly replied: 'Well it's a fine thing if you are going to have a new disease every time you are beaten. We'll soon get through the medical dictionaries at that rate. For my part I think only of JUSTICE!' She was determined, too, to cure him of the Hatfield *malaise* that had sometimes clouded her own early years of marriage: 'You go to bed much too late. There is plenty of time to gossip in the day time and it's just as easy to go to bed and to get up at the proper time every day if you make a habit of it. Nobody wants to hear you talk so much.'

But mostly the teasing was affectionate. In a glow of devotion, her scarcely veiled allusions to hypochondria would be resisted by the pretence that his afflictions evoked neither pity nor even interest. The game continued cheerfully into old age. When nearly eighty, Bob did in fact suffer a most unpleasant accident, bruising his ribs in a fall from the platform at a public meeting. 'Lots of people asked after them,' he told Nelly after attending a large luncheon a few weeks later, 'but did not seem to care to go into the subject as thoroughly as I wished.'

Less than a year after Cecil's resignation from the Baldwin government, one of the few Tory members of parliament to share his belief in the League of Nations begged the Prime Minister to recall him to office. Cecil, he pleaded, was worth a million votes to the party. Most Conservatives, however, agreed with Lord Birkenhead who, on hearing that Cecil intended to vote against the government, replied genially: 'That makes me quite certain I am right.' Behind the humour lay the tragedy of Cecil's political career. He saw in the League the last hope of preserving world peace; but for all the imprint he made upon his own party he might have been clad in cap and bells.

Labour's attitude towards Cecil was more sympathetic, and when MacDonald took office again in 1929 the new Foreign Secretary, Arthur

Henderson, invited him to resume his duties at Geneva. He was required neither to join the government nor to sit on the Labour benches in the Lords; his role was that of a temporary but much-respected civil servant. Certainly Henderson treated him with more consideration than he had received from any previous Foreign Secretary, even promising him a room in the Foreign Office. The permanent officials, annoyed by his intrusion, maintained that there was none to spare. 'No room in this great building?' Henderson replied. 'Let us go and look.' Eventually Cecil was installed in the large but little-used Cabinet Room, so called because Bob's father had held Cabinet meetings there when both Prime Minister and Foreign Secretary. To complete the filial link, he sat at a desk immediately under Lord Salisbury's portrait. The officials tried to take their revenge by denying him a flow of telegrams and despatches. In that too he ultimately had his way although, as he told Nelly, 'it has been as troublesome as the order of precedence at a mediaeval conference'.

The two years which Cecil spent representing the Labour government at Geneva were uneventful and only mildly rewarding. Administration, cautious talks on disarmament, more fruitful discussions on social problems: the sessions passed pleasantly enough. But London showed little enthusiasm. When he told Lloyd George that he hoped the British Commonwealth would occupy a central position in international affairs, 'like that of the Liberal party in home politics', Lloyd George replied: 'Good God, is it as bad as all that?' Ramsay MacDonald, after a perfunctory visit to Geneva, also disappointed him by taking no further interest in the League. In December 1930 Cecil felt ashamed at having to admit to an inquirer that he had not seen the Prime Minister for the past nine months. But he was touched that year by an unexpected gesture from MacDonald, Baldwin and Lloyd George, who on behalf of their respective parties sponsored a public testimonial in his honour. It took the form of a portrait by Philip de Laszlo. Gwendolen Cecil, although delighted by the unanimous homage of three Prime Ministers, suspected that each was out to capture the League of Nations vote for his party. She was probably right.

In August 1931 the all-party 'National' government formed by MacDonald with the support of only a handful of his Labour colleagues renewed Cecil's appointment as a delegate to the League. Within weeks he was involved in attempting to maintain the Covenant in the face of Japanese aggression against the Chinese province of Manchuria. It was the most severe test the League had endured since Mussolini's occupation of Corfu eight years before, and ultimately could be seen to mark the beginning of its decline into utter impotence. The new Foreign Secretary, Lord Reading, was too engrossed in the home economic crisis to care overmuch about a distant conflict in which his country had no direct interest. Cecil took a broader view of events. Labouring to stiffen the resolve of both his master in London and his colleagues in Geneva, he wrote to Nelly: 'We had a little secret committee here to decide what can be done if the Japs are obstinate. I have just dictated a report pointing out the various means of coercion open to us. They make a formidable total.'

Japan would have been particularly vulnerable to the imposition of economic sanctions. But Sir John Simon, who succeeded Reading as Foreign Secretary in November, either rejected Cecil's repeated suggestions of vigorous action or left him without any instructions at all. Even had the League shown a firm collective front towards the aggressors, it was at its weakest in the Far East, including neither the United States nor Russia among its members. What little chance remained of asserting its authority slipped away during meetings of the League council in Paris. 'Of course these Asiatics are the limit!' Cecil wrote to his wife. 'As soon as one begins to get a little more reasonable, the others become outrageous. . . . And so it goes dragging on! Ugh, the pigs!' The futility of it depressed him intensely. 'I'm all for strong measures,' he declared, 'but not for strong words followed by feeble acts.' It would be difficult to coin a more fitting epitaph on the League of Nations.

After 1932 Cecil never again represented his country as a delegate to Geneva. But as President of the League of Nations Union he continued to press its principles upon successive British governments. The impunity with which Japan was able to wage war against China did not in itself convince Cecil that the peace-keeping machinery of the League was defective: it had simply not been used. He realized that a strong and impatient aggressor would never submit her case to the League except under the threat of economic or military sanctions. Yet the only powers capable of exerting such pressure on a culprit either did not belong to the League or were understandably unwilling to accept distant and costly commitments that might prove electorally unpopular. But supposing he could prove that the Cabinet's reluctance to intervene in the Sino-Japanese dispute had failed to reflect the true wishes of the British people: might that not inspire the government to offer more substantial support to the League in the face of future international aggression?

Thus was conceived that ambitious test of public opinion called the Peace Ballot, begun in the autumn of 1934 and completed in the early summer of 1935. An army of canvassers put six questions to every accessible person aged eighteen or more, and received answers from no fewer than eleven and a half million of them. Most of the questions were tendentious: 'Should Great Britain remain a member of the League of Nations?' and 'Are you in favour of an all-round reduction of armaments by international agreement?' Another one confirmed the belief of Conservative critics that the centre of gravity of the League of Nations Union was well to the left of centre: 'Should the manufacture and sale of armaments for private profit be prohibited by international agreement?' (More than 90 per cent of those polled nevertheless replied: 'Yes.') The two most important questions were as follows:

> Do you consider that, if a nation insists on attacking another, the other nations should combine to compel it to stop by
> (a) Economic and non-military measures?
> (b) If necessary, military measures?

In answer to the first question, the voting was ten million in favour and 600,000 against; on the second question, the figures were 6,784,000 in favour and 2,351,000 against. There was thus a majority of over 85 per cent in support of economic sanctions. No less significantly, a majority of 74 per cent, or nearly three to one, was prepared to endorse the use of force as a last resort.

The publication of these figures coincided with another acute international crisis: the impending invasion of Ethiopia by Italy. Would Baldwin, who had just succeeded MacDonald as Prime Minister, now feel able to promise the League military as well as moral support? At first it seemed that Cecil's hopes were to be realized. The new Foreign Secretary, Sir Samuel Hoare, assured the Assembly in September 1935 that Great Britain believed in collective security and would be second to none in meeting her obligations. When Mussolini refused to call off the invasion of Ethiopia, Italy was formally declared the aggressor and subjected to limited sanctions. Thereafter British foreign policy relapsed into caution, although Hoare's attempt to negotiate a secret settlement that would have dismembered Ethiopia so outraged British public opinion as to cost him his job.

Cecil believed that Hoare's promise to the League had been lightly given on the eve of a general election, readily forgotten after an overwhelming Conservative victory. There may have been truth in the charge. But Cecil's acceptance of the Peace Ballot figures at their face value took no account of either political or economic realities. The canvass had been accompanied by a campaign that reduced the issue to one of peace or war. Disarmament and sanctions meant peace; arms and national security meant war. For nearly seven million voters to declare in a glow of moral fervour that they were ready to wage war on any aggressor named by the League was a gesture that demanded no

immediate sacrifice. In practical terms, however, there were two in-
superable obstacles to such a course. It demanded a heavy expenditure
on arms which none of the political parties was prepared to recommend
to the electorate. Nor could it be pursued without the co-operation of
France, a nation that had no intention of going to war with Italy for
the sake of preserving Ethiopian independence. Gilbert Murray, as
dedicated an advocate of Geneva as Cecil himself, wrote to him in
later years:

> What terribly rotten wood we believers in the League of Nations
> were using for our great edifice. Great Britain not really reliable,
> France utterly the reverse, Germany and Italy both enemies of the
> League, America and Russia absent. Even in England where we really
> had educated public opinion we were crippled by the pacifists. An
> enormous majority for the League, but a majority which crumbled
> badly when it came to military sanctions.

'Gilbert makes me very nervous when he speaks,' Cecil once told his
wife. 'He always seems on the point of giving the whole case away –
and sometimes does.' But Murray was not alone among supporters of
the League in holding that the Peace Ballot had weakened Great Britain's
resolve. In 1941, when Cecil published a volume on the League entitled
The Great Experiment, Salisbury wrote to him: 'I thought and still
think that the Peace Ballot policy was a mistake. The effect was to
hamper rearmament, which was . . . as things had been allowed to
develop, essential.' Cecil defended himself with spirit against his
brother's grave accusation:

> As for the Peace Ballot, there really is no ground for saying that it
> hampered rearmament. The question asked did not suggest unilateral
> disarmament and the effect of it was to produce Hoare's fighting
> speech at Geneva on September 11 from which he and others ran
> away as soon as it had secured an electoral victory. . . . Winston told
> me at the time that he warmly approved the Peace Ballot but that it
> must be accompanied by rearmament, to which I assented. . . . I
> supported by vote and speech all the Government's rearmament
> proposals.

Jim's reply was courteously enigmatic:

> Thank you very much for your most long and interesting letter. I
> am glad to think that such differences between us as emerge from it
> depend rather upon a different recollection of the facts, or perhaps
> I should say the inferences to be drawn from the facts, than upon
> any essential opinion.

It is understandable that Cecil should have been anxious to dissociate himself from the pacifist undertones which many Conservatives read into the Peace Ballot. For in the same year that Mussolini completed his conquest of Ethiopia, Europe became aware of a new and darker menace. 'As for Hitler,' Nelly had written on his appointment as Chancellor of Germany in 1933, 'there is nothing so moderating as office. The worst of it is he looks so awfully stupid.' A few months later the Czech statesman Eduard Benes, lunching with Bob in Geneva, rebutted her on both counts: 'He gave me a long talk about Hitler's foreign policy,' Cecil reported home, 'which is apparently to absorb Austria and Czecho-Slovakia, create an independent Ukraine as a counterpoise to Russia and Poland, suppress the Corridor and generally stamp on Poland.'

So it came to pass. In March 1936, Germany opened her ambitious programme of expansion by reoccupying the demilitarized zone on the left bank of the Rhine. Cecil's immediate reaction was to welcome it as 'tremendous news': for here was an unexpected opportunity for the League to reassert its dwindling authority by proposing economic sanctions against the aggressor. Five days later euphoria gave way to disenchantment:

> I still should have preferred vigorous action to compel Germany to evacuate, but I felt, first, that the country would not support that, and second, that the Cabinet had not the vigour to carry it through. I am still rather unhappy. If the Germans get away with this they will certainly repeat the manoeuvre. . . . Our chance was to give a striking example of collective security with Italy, but neither France nor our Cabinet would do it!

As Hitler's armies gnawed their way across Central Europe with impunity, Cecil found a mournful satisfaction in attributing his country's impotence to the counting-house instincts of the new Prime Minister. He was saddened but not shocked by Neville Chamberlain's open abandonment of the League as an instrument of preserving peace. What did anger him was its replacement by ingratiating approaches to the dictators: 'Such a policy,' Cecil wrote, 'made a strong appeal to the English, particularly, perhaps, to the commercial class. To them the idea of talking things over, if any differences arose, with rival men of business was familiar. It was "common sense".' But personal diplomacy could be effective only if Hitler and Mussolini were as sincere in seeking peace as Chamberlain and Halifax; only if Great Britain was strong and seen to be growing stronger. Neither condition was met during those dismal years of 'appeasement'.

At the Congress of Berlin in 1878 Disraeli had spoken to Bob's father about his more irresolute colleagues: 'They are all middle-class men, and I have always observed through life that middle-class men are afraid of responsibility.' The aphorism was absorbed into the Cecil creed and sixty years later led Bob to believe that aristocrats had a near monopoly of courageous independence. His social categories, however, were too rigid. Halifax, fifth Baronet and third Viscount, proved as pliable a Foreign Secretary as any; and a letter written by Nelly in November 1936 also challenges her husband's sanguine opinion of the patrician class: 'Nearly *all* my relations are diehards and tender to Mussolini (not so much lately) and to the Nazis and idiotic about "Communism", which to them means everything not approved by the Conservative Central Office.' Soon afterwards she began a file of correspondence to which she attached this label: 'An attempt – unsuccessful – to persuade leading Conservatives in Society to show German visitors that political and religious persecution, imprisonment without trial, murder and torture are not social recommendations in this country.'

The Cecils themselves were no less beyond reproach in their zeal for national defence. As for the 'appeasers', they were to be found in an overwhelming majority at every social level and in every political party. Bob was surely remote from reality when he told Nelly in December 1937: 'If only I were twenty years younger how gladly would I join Labour.' He was speaking of the party which until the very brink of war in 1939 continued to vote against both rearmament and conscription.

Throughout the years of deepening gloom, one episode brought the Cecils much cheer. In 1937 Bob received the Nobel Prize for Peace. Among the many congratulations which he received was a grandiloquent document that began:

> The Conquering Lion of the Tribe of Judah,
> Haile Selassie I.,
> Elect of God, Emperor of Ethiopia.
> May this reach the Right Honorable Viscount Cecil of Chelwood.
> Peace be with You. . . .

The letter came, however, not from the Imperial Palace in Addis Ababa but from a suburban house in Bath where the most eminent victim of the League's failure dwelt in unhappy exile.

The outbreak of war with Germany in 1939 was no more than a temporary setback to Cecil's hopes for a civilized and peaceful world; his belief in the powers of human reason and international negotiation remained intact. Winston Churchill, recalled to office as First Lord of the Admiralty but not yet Prime Minister, invited him to lunch early in

1940. 'I proposed that the House of Lords should make a committee to consider Peace Terms,' Bob reported to his wife, 'and was well snubbed.' He fretted at having so little to do. Even at seventy-five, membership of his brother's parliamentary Watching Committee was no substitute for the cause that had absorbed all his energies for the past twenty years. Some of his new-found leisure he spent in querulous correspondence with ministers about the maladministration of their departments. He complained to the Postmaster General about the telephone service, to the Minister of Food about the shortage of fresh herrings in Sussex, to the Minister of Fuel about the meagre ration of coke allocated to so exposed a house as Gale. But neither he nor his wife flinched for an instant when in the summer of 1940 the landing of German troops seemed imminent. Nelly hoped to lay hands on a stock of grenades and to 'have a shot at the invaders'; she had to make do with nothing more lethal than a stirrup-pump. 'It will be fun to use the jet and spray on objects in the garden when we are not on fire,' she wrote cheerfully. In November a bomb dropped by an enemy aircraft did in fact blow out all their windows. It caused little other damage; Gale had been built to withstand such impertinences.

Throughout the long drift to war, Nelly had rejected recurrent Tory pleas that the Nazi and Fascist dictatorships provided necessary bulwarks against Communism. And when in 1941 the German armies marched deep into Russia, her tolerance of Britain's brave but belated ally turned to fervent admiration. 'I am driven mad by my Conservative relations,' she wrote in 1944, 'who keep throwing 20,000 murdered Polish officers at Russia's head – or rather, as they can't get at hers, at mine. I calculate it will be another ten years before the Bolshevik panic subsides.'

At the general election of 1945 Nelly added her vote to a sweeping Labour majority, 'first for foreign affairs and secondly for dealing with financial monopolies and the secret domination of the British Federation of Industries [sic] and their like'. Bob shared her suspicion that selfishness and greed were attributes more of the employer than of the employed. In reply to a worried letter from Salisbury about industrial strikes and absenteeism he wrote:

I don't think the working class have on the whole behaved badly. As far as the hardships and sufferings of war generally are concerned they have been very good. Far more individuals have been rendered homeless than those of other classes and it is a more serious disaster for poor than for rich. The same is probably true of food. As for wages, they seem to me on the whole to have behaved well – certainly better than they did in the last war. The truth is that the wage is not only a means of livelihood to the working man. It is also, unhappily, a flag in the prolonged controversy between capital and labour. He regards it as something essential to his independence which he has gained by prolonged industrial efforts.

An alert but increasingly deaf member of the House of Lords, Cecil took his seat in the new Parliament. He told Nelly:

I looked at the Front Bench Opposition and realised that except for Bobbety and Munster it was occupied by 'Capitalists'. The truth is that under Pitt the Tories had a good chance of establishing a 'friends of the poor' attitude, but allowed themselves to be drawn off by Peel.

Labour's promise of improved industrial relations at home and a more international outlook abroad prompted Cecil to give his guarded support to the new government. He asked to receive the Labour whip, or weekly guide to parliamentary business, on the understanding that he would not be obliged either to speak or to vote on party lines. At first it appeared that his visionary hopes would be fulfilled. Nelly was positively ecstatic. 'I like Attlee *very* much,' she told Gilbert Murray, 'the most Christian-living P.M. in our time? He seems so to me, not excluding Bob's father, though I loved and trusted him completely.' Murray took a cooler view of the new administration: 'When shall we get a really Progressive Party in power? One that will give us Life Peers, Women Peers, Simplified Spelling, Greek in all Secondary Schools, and so on and so on.'

Cecil's expectations were more modest. But five years of Labour rule convinced him that he had made a mistake. Had he not lost his electoral vote on becoming a peer, he wrote soon after the general election of 1950, he would have cast it for the Conservatives. As Labour dragged on for another year with a minute parliamentary majority, Cecil's impatience mounted. 'Here is an industry,' he wrote during a strike of gas workers, 'that for half a century has been free from trouble and is now thoroughly discontented. Nationalization seems to me utterly stupid – the outcome of a few foreign doctrinaires.' No member of the Carlton Club could have put the case for private enterprise more succinctly.

Shortly before the general election of 1951 that finally swept Attlee from power, Cecil sent a message to Lord Woolton, chairman of the Conservative party and the man who more than any epitomized the shopkeeper in Tory politics. At eighty-seven, Cecil explained, speech-making up and down the country was beyond him; but if he could be of any help to the Conservative cause by writing to the newspapers or in any other way, he would be glad to comply.

Cecil's disillusionment with Labour also owed something to the course of its foreign policy in the post-war years. 'The League is dead,' he declared on revisiting Geneva in 1946, 'long live the United Nations.' But his honorary life presidency of the United Nations Association, the successor to the League of Nations Union, brought him little satisfaction. When Nelly first met the Foreign Secretary, Ernest Bevin, she described him as 'looking like a political Pickwick, almost too benevolent to be true'. Her scepticism was justified. Alone among Foreign Secretaries, he declined either to accept honorary office in the UNA or to receive its deputations. 'He refused altogether to see me,' Cecil complained. 'He is the only Minister who has ever done so.' Bevin's suspicions of the UNA were understandable. As even Cecil confessed: 'I am often very much concerned about the way Communists or near-Communists have a voice in our affairs.' The persistently obsequious attitude of some members towards the Soviet Union eventually obliged him at the age of ninety to offer his resignation as honorary president. He was persuaded to remain, but insisted that the prefix 'honorary' be spelt out in full on the association's letter-head. He was also distressed by the appointment of Julian Huxley, whom he described as 'the standard bearer of agnosticism', to be director-general of the United Nations Educational, Scientific and Cultural Organization (UNESCO).

'It is a great nuisance getting so old,' Gilbert Murray wrote in his ninetieth year to Cecil, 'and never knowing whether you haven't said "Jerusalem" when you meant "Paddington".' His near contemporary suffered no such inhibitions (nor, if the truth be told, did Murray himself). Half a century of frustration and disappointment in public affairs had left Cecil untouched by either resentment or despair. His mind remained as clear, calm and reasonable as it had ever been, his spirit still fortified by the Christian message of his childhood at Hatfield. Deafness and frailty alone prevented his regular attendance at the House of Lords, and in excusing himself from the opening of a new parliament in 1955 he hoped that the Queen would not attribute his absence to any want of loyalty.

He gave much thought in old age to the reading of lessons in church. As he told the Bishop of Chichester, Dr G. K. A. Bell:

If they are read in the Authorised Version, although it is a splendid work of genius apart from all religious considerations, it does mean that every now and then the meaning of the original authority has been substantially altered. If, on the other hand, the lessons are read out of the Revised Version, not only does the congregation lose a good deal of the cadences and structure of the Authorised Version but also considerable injury is done to the everyday authority and use of the Bible. . . . Is it better to have an absolutely correct translation and lose the frequency with which the New Testament is quoted directly and indirectly, or is it better to maintain the Authorised Version with such defects as actually exist in it?

Cecil solved the problem by collating the two texts, departing from the majestic and familiar prose of the seventeenth century only where the Victorian version made for clarity of understanding. The Oxford University Press, however, already committed to an entirely new translation of the Bible, politely rejected his manuscript. He was more fortunate in the publication of two autobiographical works, *A Great Experiment* (1941) and *All the Way* (1949), although Gilbert Murray, with the licence of the candid friend, told him that he lacked both the necessary egotism and malice to write successful memoirs.

He was a correspondingly gentle book-reviewer whose notice of a volume of Churchill's war memoirs drew an appreciative response from the author. 'Very nice of Winston to send that telegram. But why did he do it?' Cecil noted suspiciously. 'The review on re-reading is all right and true. But not specially illuminating. He is a curious man.' As the review begins, 'This is a wonderful book by a wonderful man,' Cecil seems to have misjudged Churchill's simple pleasure at the tribute of an old friend.

His own pen was lively to the end. A few weeks after his ninety-first birthday, Nelly found him at work on a memorandum entitled 'The Condition of Europe'. Four months later, in February 1956, the architect of the League of Nations received a letter from Queen Elizabeth II enclosing the insignia of a newly appointed Companion of Honour. (Florence Nightingale had had to wait only until her eighty-eighth year for the Order of Merit.) Cecil was neither elated by the recognition of the crown nor cast down by his long neglect; he had never put an inflated value on himself. 'Here I am 94 years old,' he wrote in a last fragment, 'fairly healthy; with no special talents or vices. But I should like to leave some record of a life without any great achievement or disaster but yet pleasant to myself and tolerably agreeable to others. Is that worth while?'

When Bob's deafness grew almost as impenetrable as Nelly's, they fell into the habit of leaving little notes for each other about the house. 'I'm sorry you thought me sad tonight,' he wrote in one of them. 'I am not sad. Only I do like life – perhaps too much – and so like my mother I sometimes get a wave of sadness at its approaching end. But I do recognise all I owe to you!!' On the seventieth anniversary of their marriage, Nelly greeted her husband with a letter:

My dear,

This is our Wedding Day. You don't know how much I love you – what a joy and comfort you have been from the beginning to the end, and the happy days you have given me *continually*. Bless you!

It was the answer to a prayer he had written in 1888, shortly after she had become his wife: 'God bless you and take care of you, my Nelly! May He mercifully ordain that we may grow aged together.'

Bob died on 24 November 1958, Nelly five months later.

7

Lord Edward Cecil
1867–1918

Edward, fourth son of the third Marquess of Salisbury. Known to his family as Nigs and to his friends as Ned.

Born 12 July 1867. Educated at Eton. Gazetted to the Grenadier Guards 1887. Served Dongola Expeditionary Force 1896, diplomatic mission to Abyssinia 1897, Sudan campaign 1898, South African War 1899–1901. Distinguished Service Order 1898. Retired with rank of colonel 1907. Agent-General of the Sudan Government and Director of Intelligence at Cairo 1903. Under-Secretary of War and subsequently Under-Secretary of Finance to Egyptian Government 1906. Financial Adviser to Egyptian Government 1912–18. KCMG 1913.

Married 18 June 1894 Violet, second daughter of Admiral Frederick Augustus Maxse. Three years after her husband's death she married Alfred, first and last Viscount Milner (1854–1925).

Lord and Lady Edward Cecil had a son, George (1895–1914), killed in action in the First World War, and a daughter Helen (1901–), who married second Baron Hardinge of Penshurst.

Lord Edward died 13 December 1918.

'I write as a younger son always ought to write to his father,' Lord Edward Cecil informed Lord Salisbury at the age of sixteen, 'for money.' He was no less confident in his choice of a career. Cranborne dedicated himself to politics, William to Holy Orders, Bob to the Bar. The fourth brother, born in July 1867, determined to be a soldier. Most fathers would have been proud of such a preference. But Lord Salisbury had never regarded the bearing of arms in peacetime as a rewarding vocation. Replying to a request from his own father in 1855 that he should become Colonel of the Middlesex Militia, he wrote: 'Your proposition gave me stomache-ache. . . . I detest all soldiering beyond measure. As far as taste goes I would sooner be at the treadmill.'

Thirty years later the reluctant warrior had become the indulgent parent. He not only endorsed Edward's wishes without hesitation, but used all the influence he commanded as Prime Minister to launch him on a military career. 'My father has been learning the Army List by heart,' Bob noted, 'and discusses the question at every dinner party he goes to.' One obstacle remained. Edward, or Nigs as the family called him, was physically more robust and in character more cheerfully gregarious than his brothers: just the sort of young man destined to serve his Queen and country. An Eton education, however, had failed to teach him the art of passing examinations, and admission to the Royal Military College at Sandhurst proved beyond him. Fortunately that was not the only avenue to a commission. A candidate could instead have himself appointed an officer in the Militia, or local volunteer force. Later, as a trained amateur soldier, he would effortlessly transfer to a regiment of the Regular Army and find himself on precisely the same footing as those who had passed through Sandhurst. The process required social qualifications but was no more of an intellectual ordeal than joining a club or following a fashionable pack of hounds.

The machinery worked with exceptional smoothness for Lord Edward. Like his eldest brother before him, he received a commission in the Militia battalion of the Bedfordshire Regiment; and the Prime Minister readily extracted a promise from the Duke of Cambridge, Commander-in-Chief of the British Army, that in a year or two a place would be found for his son in the Grenadier Guards. Nigs was meanwhile to spend some months in Germany, learning the language and observing at close quarters the most militarist nation in Europe.

There he acquired that facetious humour with which for the rest of his life he liked to depict the utter absurdity of foreigners. Student duels in Baden reminded him of Lewis Carroll's solemn contest between Tweedledum and Tweedledee; and from Hanover he deplored the customary midday meal, 'eight to nine pounds of solid food, chiefly raw ham, lobster, salt-pork and cabbage in an advanced state of decomposition'. But he was sensible enough to know that Lord Salisbury would appreciate a straightforward account of the intimate family dinner to which Prince Bismarck, the German Chancellor, invited him in February 1886. Nigs began with a description of his host at the age of seventy:

He was tall and straight, his shoulders broad, but no stoop. . . . His face was deeply wrinkled and bagged. His chin was double and the skin hung down. The eyes wide apart and singularly protruding; they looked weak. . . . The expression melancholy, tired and old: but this last only when at rest: when in motion, young.

Even in the privacy of the home, Bismarck wore uniform. At first, he explained, he had hated the habit. Now he found it convenient, as it saved him the trouble of changing whenever he saw the Emperor, perhaps as often as five times a day. He added that he would reverse the custom of the British Army which sometimes obliged officers to wear uniform as a punishment. Bismarck also confessed to his guest that he once used to make expeditions to Flanders in search of fine Burgundy wine, but that now it hurt him to drink anything except Hock and Mosel. Nor did he any longer smoke cigars, having calculated some ten years before that he had consumed over a hundred thousand of them. So he gave them up, 'though at one time, he said smiling, he would not have stopped in the middle of a good cigar to save his family'. Instead he puffed at a porcelain pipe fully three feet long, while sustaining the conversation in German, French and English.

From personal revelations, the Chancellor turned to politics, with his unamiable son Herbert in a supporting role. They discussed why all tailors were radicals in Germany and all shoemakers in England. This led them to an explosion of rage about Charles Bradlaugh, who as an atheist had been prevented from taking his seat for Northampton in the House of Commons:

> Prince Bismarck concurred in Herbert's cursing of Bradlaugh and asked about his means, profession, etc. On Herbert's expressing a wish to hang him, he said that we had no legal rope. Both he and Herbert seemed to advocate coercion strongly, and he concurred in Herbert's view of shooting down the mob in any gathering of nationalists. . . .
>
> Herbert said we told our House of Commons too much on diplomatic questions. Prince Bismarck assented, and Herbert further said that our House of Commons ought to change its name to House of Mob as it no longer represented the Commons of England but the mob.*

---

*Herbert grew no more ingratiating with the years. In 1890, shortly after the Emperor William II had dismissed Bismarck from power, Lord Salisbury returned the hospitality shown to Nigs by inviting Herbert to Hatfield. Lady Salisbury, hearing that he was broken by his father's fall, enlisted the sympathies of the house-party for him. 'But he quenched them by his loud authoritative manner, flinging every sentence from him with defiant self-assertion,' a fellow guest wrote. 'He was especially opinionated about Henry VIII's wives, utterly refusing to allow that Anne of Cleves did not precede Anne Boleyn. He is a colossal man and a great eater, and would always fill two glasses of wine at once, to have one in reserve.'

'Probably the most extraordinary dinner I shall ever have in my life,' Nigs told his father.

The Grenadier Guards, to which he was gazetted in April 1887, offered nothing as memorable to a very junior officer. But he enjoyed the pleasures of London society and all too readily settled down to what his sister called 'the compulsory lounging of regimental life'. In September 1890 he was rescued from mental enervation by a summons from Lord Wolseley, the general commanding the British troops in Ireland, to become one of his aides-de-camp. The Duke of Cambridge pointed out to Wolseley that Cecil had yet to complete four years of duty with his regiment and would not therefore be eligible for an appointment on the staff until the following April. 'People are very critical,' he warned, 'and might for example think as the Prime Minister's son some special favour had been shown in his case, whereas in others it had been refused.' The Commander-in-Chief must nevertheless have agreed to stretch a point, for within a very few weeks Nigs sent this account of Ireland to his father:

> It looks like England in debt. We are in Protestant country now and I believe the cleanest part of Ireland. It is a trifle dirtier than Dieppe harbour. There is no potato disease round here but the fields look to my inexperienced eye terribly weedy and ill farmed. . . . The squalor of the whole country is remarkable. The dirty ragged shoeless hatless children. The vile old hags you see sitting on the doorsteps. The drunken men reeling in the street at any hour of the day or night. The amount of broken windows, the ill-paved worse lighted street. The shabbiness of the houses, the filth of the roads and the awful smells are all things which impress the English mind most unpleasantly.

Suspecting that someone was tampering with his mail, he wrote and heavily underlined at the top of the first sheet: 'If any one opens this letter in the post, I hope he understands that all I personally would do to a Nationalist agitator is to hang him like a dog.'

He disliked his new duties.

> An aide-de-camp [he told Bob] is a cross between a wife, a private secretary and an official *alter ego*. As a wife I accompany the boss everywhere, order dinner, preside at table, look after his comforts and his health. As a private secretary I write some of his letters (he don't trust me much) and interview tiresome people and answer his dinner invitations. As *alter ego* I sign for him, pay for him, am consulted instead of him. I am afraid I am not much good as an aide-de-camp. I never thought I should be. I am too careless, too easily bored,

too rash and too cautious. The type of man who is really good at the game is a man of the old-womanish type.

Except for Wolseley, the only other officers he saw regularly were 'two dry old fossils of colonels, ornaments of the staff in Dublin. I will readily back any two respectable corpses to cause as much laughter as they do in any stated time.'

No such charge could be brought against Garnet Wolseley. Created a peer for his victory over the Egyptian nationalist Arabi Pasha at the battle of Tel-el-Kebir in 1882, he had added the Sudan campaign to his laurels three years later. He was strong but not silent. At Hatfield soon after his return he told Salisbury that he would never forgive Gladstone for personally delaying the despatch of the expedition and so costing General Gordon his life. 'Very talkative, terriby indiscreet and consequently very amusing,' Gwendolen wrote of the visitor. Wolseley's temperament scarcely mellowed with the years. Cecil sent home this description of him in the autumn of 1890:

He is vivacious and witty in his conversation but scarcely ever relates or discusses anything that has not much to do with himself, and the first person singular is the portion of verbs which he most affects. He is poseur to a ridiculous extent and is as full of vanity and as susceptible of flattery as a passée beauty. He is obstinate and brooks no contradiction but if he thinks he is wrong edges round till he gets right. He is given to goody-goody military remarks which are almost warbles of an enlisted Pecksniff. He is very Irish in his wild way of talking and one can often see in him a battle going on between the indiscreet Irish soldier and the self-seeking cautious politician. You can't trust what he says as he does not hesitate to warp facts to suit his argument and seldom if ever states a case fairly. He is a good man I think and religious though it fits in oddly with the rest of the patchwork he would call his character....

That is not the sort of tribute usually paid by an ensign in the Brigade of Guards to his Army commander. But then Edward Cecil had been chosen as much for his pen as for his sword. Wolseley hoped that his aide-de-camp would discreetly keep his name and his virtues before the Prime Minister, although not in quite the tone they ultimately reached Hatfield. It was a role to which all Salisbury's sons had to accustom themselves; the death of a Dean, a Master of Trinity or a Regius Professor instantly filled their postbags with the claims of would-be successors.

In the summer of 1895 Wolseley himself was the supplicant. While

spending his leave in Homburg he heard a rumour that on the impending resignation of the Duke of Cambridge as Commander-in-Chief of
the British Army, General Sir Redvers Buller would be appointed to
fill the vacancy. 'That means, of course, military extinction for me,' he
wrote to Colonel Spencer Childers, a senior member of his staff in
Dublin. 'It is a horrible end to my career to be superseded by one of my
own lieutenants whom I may say I created a General Officer.' Childers
knew where his duty lay. He instantly passed on the gist of his master's
letter to Cecil, who had by then rejoined his regiment in London,
begging him 'to say a word' and 'to let the Prime Minister know
privately . . . how deeply Lord Wolseley feels on the subject'. 'My dear
Cecil' hesitated to trouble his father, who had embarked on his third
premiership only two weeks before. Then another letter arrived from
the faithful Childers. Wolseley had now heard that the new Commander-in-Chief was likely to be not Buller but the Duke of Connaught,
Queen Victoria's third son; accordingly, he would not wish to stand in
his way. But, Childers continued:

> Lord Wolseley is naturally anxious not to find himself (while full
> of energy) without employment; and there is more than one office
> which he would greatly like to be appointed to: they are the Embassy
> at Berlin (which Sir E. Malet is relinquishing) or to succeed Lord Elgin
> in India. With regard to the former Lord Wolseley believes it was
> actually meditated in 1885, and it was understood that the appoint-
> ment of a soldier would be particularly acceptable to the German
> Emperor. With regard to India, it has always been Lord Wolseley's
> consistent view that the growing military expenditure in that country
> will never be properly controlled so long as a non-military Governor-
> General is unable to hold his own against the prepondering influence
> of the Commander-in-Chief backed by the enormous force of military
> opinion in India; and Lord Wolseley believes that it would be in his
> power successfully to resist this pressure and to grapple with the
> military expenditure.

Cecil now sent the entire correspondence to his father, together with
an account of his reply to the first letter Childers had written on
Wolseley's behalf. It does him much credit:

> I answered that such a rumour had been wandering through
> London; that I knew nothing as to the intentions or acts of H.M.
> Government; but that I, in common with my military brethren, re-
> gretted this if it were true – as if Buller and my old chief were in the
> balance, we should know soon enough who was the greater. . . .
> The other letter I enclose, between ourselves it made me roar with

laughter and feel a little sick. Of course there is no answer but I dare not offend Wolseley. You see what a lot of bother I am in. Shall I write back and have anything to do with it? I sometimes wish you were not P.M.

The Viceroyalty had already been promised to George Curzon who, as Wolseley foresaw, proved unable to hold his own against so strong an Indian Commander-in-Chief as Kitchener. But Wolseley's own ambitions appeared likely to be satisfied in August 1895 by the offer of the Berlin Embassy he coveted. In the end he did even better. Buller's near certainty of succeeding the Duke of Cambridge had vanished on the fall of the Liberal administration in June; the Queen was persuaded to withdraw her championship of the Duke of Connaught; and by November Wolseley was Commander-in-Chief, although with much reduced powers. It is not easy to say how much good his vicarious correspondence with the Prime Minister's son did him. It cannot have done him harm.

A few months after his arrival in Ireland, Nigs confessed to his father that he was more than £1,000 in debt. The news shocked Salisbury. His annual gross income amounted to well over £30,000. But it came primarily from land, his rural commitments were heavy and England was suffering from a severe agricultural depression. However precarious the times, Salisbury nevertheless remained a generous father, each of his sons receiving a settlement of £1,000 a year on marriage. In small ways, too, he behaved handsomely. When Bob, as undergraduate president of the Oxford Union, asked him for a donation he replied: 'In the words of Theodore Hook – when he was informed that subscription to the Thirty-Nine Articles was required – how much is it considered proper to give?' On receiving £17 from Nelly in payment of railway and steamer tickets he had bought for her, he sent back both letter and cheque endorsed with the single word, 'stuff'. And each Christmas, so that his unmarried daughter Gwendolen should not, as he put it, 'be cut out by her sisters-in-law', he bought her a fine necklace chosen by himself. That the settlement of his son's debts would have to come out of the provision he was making for Gwendolen's future caused him to address Nigs in unusually stern language:

> The sum is large – and it is a nuisance to pay it. But if it was merely a question of extravagance, I should be satisfied with expressing a hope that you would attend more carefully to the details of your expenditure.
> What makes me say something more is the fact that this large sum has been rolled up, less by extravagance, than by gambling: and

that from the circumstances it is evident that you belong to the class of men who lose their self-restraint when they are at the gaming table. Of the people who game, there are two sorts – the people who are very fond of it, but who are quite cool at the table, and can stop when they please: and the people who, at first at least, are not very fond of it, but who get excited at it, and lose their heads. To these last – and I am afraid you belong to them – the taste for gambling is one of the extremest danger. . . .

'I have paid £1,126 8s. 6d. into your account at Cox's,' Salisbury told Nigs a month later. 'I should avoid all play except of the sort that corresponds to whist with shilling points. . . . Please do not run me into any more large sums.' Lady Salisbury added her own reproach. 'I am sure if you saw his sad worried look when he speaks of it,' she told the culprit, 'you would never touch a card again while you live.'

In the midst of the poverty and discontent which so depressed Edward Cecil during his first months on Wolseley's staff there flourished another Ireland: perhaps it would be more exact to call it a microcosm of England. As the Queen's representative, the Lord Lieutenant reigned and entertained with a viceregal flourish that made the muted regime of Windsor seem positively dowdy. Neither the dynamite bombs of the Fenians nor an almost complete boycott by the landed gentry were allowed to interfere with the ordered progress of levées and drawing-rooms, court balls and state banquets.

One young visitor from England in the early months of 1894 found the Dublin Castle circle decidedly unreal. 'The only one I feel really at home with', Miss Violet Maxse wrote to her mother on 18 February, 'is Lord Edward Cecil. He doesn't go to balls, worse luck, but he's been to call three times and I shall meet him tonight at a dinner the Guards are giving for the Viceroy.' Nine days later: 'He is curiously unlike any Guardsman I have ever seen and we made friends quicker than anything I have ever yet done. I wonder if it will be lasting?' It was. On 13 March she announced briefly:

> My darling Mother,
>   I am going to marry Edward Cecil. We settled this last night.
> Your loving
Violet.

Nigs displayed less confidence. He wrote to Bob:

> I have proposed to and been accepted by Miss Violet Maxse and I want your help in the coming storm. . . . I shall be abused by my family, etc. I don't care a *rap* . . . Do, old boy, do your best for me. I

have not slept for four nights, so I am incoherent but so happy – only I know what a horrid row I am in for.

Bob replied soothingly: 'I'm sure she is charming. As for storms, they don't matter. They're only misguided affection and three of your brothers have been through them without injury.' But Nigs's fears were not misplaced. His mother never cared to lose a son in matrimony: and of all her daughters-in-law, Violet seemed the least likely to win her heart. She was the daughter of Admiral Frederick Maxse, a hero of the Crimean War but also an atheist and radical. As if those were not handicaps enough in Cecilian eyes, the Admiral and his wife had separated while Violet was still a child. Brought up by her father, she attended her first dinner party – at the house of Mr and Mrs Matthew Arnold – when a precocious fourteen. She spent part of her youth in Paris studying painting and the violin. There she acquired a coterie of admirers that included Degas and Rodin, Clemenceau and Dufferin, the British Ambassador. Another close friend was Meredith, who borrowed both Maxse's character and his unsuccessful attempt to enter the House of Commons for his novel, *Beauchamp's Career*. It is hardly surprising that, when this fair-haired, vivacious girl presented herself at Arlington Street for the first time, Lord Salisbury should have told her with menacing geniality: 'Hatfield is Gaza, the capital of Philistia.'

Only one member of the Cecil family gave his entire blessing to the match. 'Your news delights me,' Arthur Balfour told Nigs. 'I can't conceive how you got Miss Maxse to accept you: but I should have thought ill of you if you had not at once proposed to her; for she has all the merits which your lover-like rhetoric attributes to her.' Such approval did nothing to mollify Lady Salisbury, who suspected Violet – wrongly as it happened – of belonging to that self-consciously brilliant set of friends known as the Souls. She wrote to Nelly:

That a girl should be favoured by Arthur B. and Pembroke is much against her and she has been brought up a heathen I hear – I even doubt if she has been baptised! All the rest I like. It will be good for Nigs to have a clever wife and one accustomed to take care of expense and I hope he will convert her. I don't believe in pious Pagans and my only objection (*real*) to the Souls is their heathenry. The world, the flesh and the devil are far too strong to be conquered by anything but the three creeds! 'Art', 'refinement' and 'intellect' are all bosh without them and will never keep you straight. There's a sermon for Holy Week!

On the following day Lady Salisbury wrote disagreeably to another of her confidantes, Lady Frances Balfour: 'No doubt, as Mrs Orme used to say of the housemaids, we shall soon "tone her down".' Salisbury also showed concern at the bleak financial prospects of the young couple. In promising Nigs a settlement of £1,000 a year, he added:

Your pay I believe is about £200: and you know what chances you have of increasing it. If I understand you rightly, the lady has nothing. You must, therefore, consider very carefully whether, for several years at all events, you can be happy, and make your wife happy, on £1,200 a year. . . . For many years of my married life I had much less: and I do not think I was less happy than I have been since I was richer. Several people in our rank of life have had similar experience. But it will require a certain amount of sustained effort and of contempt for the opinion of other people.

To his relief, he discovered a few days later that Violet had £400 a year of her own. Not even a joint annual income of £1,600, however, seemed likely to protect Nigs and Violet from fitful insolvency. Only a few weeks after their marriage in June 1894 another £700 of Nigs's debts came to light.

The ceremony itself, at which Lord William Cecil officiated, brought together the worlds of politics and letters. The register was signed by Salisbury, Balfour, Asquith, Chamberlain and Morley, the Chief Secretary for Ireland: it was as the guest of his private secretary, Colonel Herbert Jekyll, that Violet had first met her future husband in Dublin. Wilfrid Scawen Blunt counted six poets in the church: Alfred Austin, George Meredith, Alfred Lyall, Edward Arnold, Oscar Wilde and himself. At the reception he was amused to find himself 'flattened like a herring' between a tall Dutch clock and Lord Salisbury; during the Irish land troubles of 1887 the Prime Minister had particularly welcomed the imprisonment of Blunt for inciting unrest in Galway. Their honeymoon was spent at Blackmoor, the home of Lord Selborne's family in Hampshire. Unfortunately, Nigs wrote many years later, the cook of that philanthropic household turned out to be 'an aged cinder-sifter or something of that sort who was out of a job. We had to telegraph to the Admiral for cold and potted meats, and I have put down half Violet's nasty tempers to her incautiously eating some pie made by that old harridan. It soured her for life.'

That unpromising start set the pattern for much of their marriage. Limited means coupled with what Nelly called 'their Park Lane ideas' justified Lord Salisbury's fears. Although not obviously extravagant, they were incapable of managing their finances with the same meticulous care of the Prime Minister's other married children. Rarely during those first years were Nigs and Violet entirely free from the irritant of near insolvency.

Nor did Violet ever fit comfortably into her new family circle. 'I hope you will some day give up calling me "Lady Salisbury",' she was reminded eight weeks after her wedding. 'None of my other children do it, and it makes me rather sad. Your very affectionate mother, G. Salisbury.' The Prime Minister suspected his daughter-in-law of indiscretion. After reading some letters written by Nigs during his first foreign campaign in 1896, he warned her: 'If he tells good stories of his superiors – or criticises them – either the superiors in England or in Egypt, keep his observations to yourself as much as you can. These superiors have long arms and are sometimes vindictive.' Three years later Bob told his wife: 'Violet absolutely freezes up my father now. He will not even refer to a religious topic when she is there and only talks generalities about politics.' The Cecils were embarrassed as much by her manner of argument as by the liberalism of her religious and political beliefs. Here once more is Bob, the most critical of her brothers-in-law:

I always like Violet alone. And I nearly always dislike her in society. I think it is the competitive air about her conversation in society which is so tiresome. She treats the whole thing as a kind of game in which it is her business to be more brilliant and to attract more attention than others. . . . And competition as unveiled as Violet's comes perilously near bad taste.

What most separated her in spirit from the Hatfield way of life was her inability to accept the faith of a Christian. During her early years of marriage more than one member of the family tried affectionate persuasion. Linky pleaded that, by already recognizing Christian morality, she could not be far from Christian belief, and lent her his copy of Liddon's *Elements of Religion*. Gwendolen ended a similar appeal: 'Forgive me, Violet, I resolved long ago not to bother you with religion till God Himself should have chosen His own time and spoken to you. . . . But I do love you and want to help.' To both she replied that she would prefer not to discuss religion with them. 'You see,' she said, 'if I answer what you say, it will hurt your feelings and I couldn't bear that.' So they sent her to be instructed by Dr Winnington-Ingram, the future Bishop of London. 'I spent some hours with him,' Violet wrote, 'and I was not asked to go again.'

During the anxious financial discussions that followed Nigs's engagement to be married, Salisbury pressed some sensible advice on his son: 'I wish you would lay to heart that you will get neither a career nor an improvement in your fortune without Staff College: and that you will not get Staff College without some slight effort at study.' In spite of the happy distraction of his first child, born in September 1895 and christened George, Nigs worked hard to pass the entrance examination. But the Staff College at Camberley proved as difficult for him to penetrate as the Royal Military College at Sandhurst. 'Lord Methuen,' Gwendolen wrote consolingly, 'who is in a tearing rage as all the men in his command have failed, made indignant remarks upon the *impropriety* of the mathematical paper – quite a new view of the possibilities of mathematics.'

Salisbury had been naïve to suppose that the military progress of a Prime Minister's son depended only on professional qualifications. For in the spring of 1896 Nigs found himself an aide-de-camp to the Sirdar or Commander-in-Chief of the Egyptian Army. On his first visit to Hatfield a few years before, Herbert Kitchener had startled that nocturnal household by getting up at six in the morning. Nigs, who began the day at 9.30 when he felt energetic, may have wondered whether Kitchener was the sort of general to cultivate. He nevertheless invited him to dine in the officers' guardroom at St James's Palace and, fortified by champagne, asked for an appointment to his staff some day. On the eve of the conquest of the Sudan he was summoned to Cairo. The new aide-de-camp had no illusions:

> My father was Foreign Secretary and Prime Minister, and it was to please him it was done, and for that reason alone. Lord Cromer [Consul-General in Egypt] was not in favour of a forward Sudan policy, and Kitchener was. My father's support was vital to his whole plan and I, by reflected light, became of importance.

Since the withdrawal of Wolseley's expedition in 1885, the Sudan had relapsed into tribal barbarism. The purpose of Kitchener's campaign was to liberate that territory from the Dervish empire, even against the wishes of its inhabitants, and to substitute for the oppression of the Khalifa a paternal rule such as Cromer had imposed on Egypt. The River War, as Winston Churchill called it, opened in 1896 with a cautious advance up the Nile towards Dongola. It ended two years later with the battle of Omdurman, almost a thousand miles south of Cairo as the crow flies: but an infinity, it must have seemed, over a terrain of desert and rock and cataract. The conquest of a country of one million square miles and two million people, Kitchener boasted to Cromer, had been achieved at a cost of little more than £2 a square mile and £1 a head.

Cecil did not at first take to his new master, whom he found inconsiderate and uncouth. That, however, was far outweighed by the opportunity of glory in the field. Battalions of the Brigade of Guards rarely saw foreign service except during a major war, and nearly ten years as a Grenadier had brought Nigs no wound more honourable than a twisted ankle acquired while playing golf with Arthur Balfour in Dublin. On 18 June 1896, the anniversary of Waterloo, he described to Bob his baptism of fire:

We fought the Dervishes the other day. . . . I was not in half such a funk as I expected. I was much more afraid of being afraid. It was very exciting and not a bit brutalizing as one does not at all realize the enemy are men. We, however, were very little exposed or rather fired at, so perhaps I better not talk.

Violet received a longer account of that first engagement at Firket:

The Dervishes did fight wonderfully walking about perfectly quietly under the fire of two brigades in line at 300 yards distance. It takes many volleys to kill or hurt one man, especially as the smoke hung. The Egyptian and Black troops fought equally well and they advanced so regularly that it looked like a Hyde Park field day. Even when charged they kept up their volleys very well and certainly they are even better than was hoped. Of course we outnumbered the enemy heavily, but still we attacked a strongly held position over a plain and without cover and it was a very creditable performance. There was no fuss, no hurry, no hanging back, and I was astounded at their orderliness and handling. No white was hurt except Legge, who got cut in the hand but is doing very well. . . .
  Then we rode home had a bottle of champagne at dinner and tumbled into bed and slept.

During the next few weeks, however, the expeditionary force ran into every sort of misfortune. Cholera claimed the lives of nearly a thousand soldiers and camp followers; sandstorms prostrated an entire brigade; unprecedented floods swept away the arduously constructed railway and choked the boiler of a new locomotive with mud. Even the most powerful of the river gunboats blew up with a loud report as it carried the Sirdar himself upstream. 'I was on board at the time and was seriously annoyed,' Nigs wrote home, 'so very inconsiderate.' After such a succession of delays it was not until late September that Kitchener's army defeated a Dervish horde at Hafir and advanced to capture Dongola.

Each week the Sirdar required his aide-de-camp to send Lord Salisbury an account of the campaign. On reading the draft of one of them, Kitchener told Cecil that the style was too cold; then dictated an example of the purple prose he thought more suitable for a Prime Minister's eyes. Cecil, knowing his father's horror of rhetoric and the astonishment with which he would receive such an effusion from his own son, refused Kitchener's guidance. The only flourish he allowed himself was to end one of his austere despatches to Hatfield with the words: 'Do sit on the War Office heavily.'

As Kitchener consolidated his forces for the next stage of the advance towards Khartoum, he temporarily lost the services of his aide-de-camp. Abyssinia, as Ethiopia was then known, had in March 1896 demonstrated her growing strength by defeating an Italian army of thirty thousand men on her northern frontier. The British government therefore decided to send a diplomatic mission to Addis Ababa, both to ensure Abyssinia's friendly neutrality during Kitchener's campaign against her Sudanese neighbour and to thwart the political and commercial designs of the French in that part of Africa. Rennell Rodd, a member of the Diplomatic Service, was appointed to lead the British mission. Cecil, promoted to captain, commanded a small protective force. Others who rode with them from British Somalia up into the mountain capital of the Emperor Menelik included Reginald Wingate, a future Governor-General of the Sudan; Count Gleichen, a German princeling permitted by his cousin Queen Victoria to serve in the British Army; and Tristram Speedy, who thirty years before had accompanied Lord Napier on a less pacific expedition to Abyssinia.

They were a versatile band. Wingate, director of military intelligence in Cairo, wrote up the official journal and as treasurer had charge of immense quantities of Maria Theresa silver dollars. Gleichen, on the intelligence staff of the War Office, became an authority on camp sites and water supplies. Horace Pinching, the medical officer, noted for his control of infectious disease in Egypt, made a passable crême-de-menthe out of surgical spirit, sugar and peppermint essence. Cecil assembled a collection of beetles and butterflies.

He was also the hero of two dramatic episodes on the march. Large quantities of rope, essential for securing baggage, began to disappear without trace. One day Cecil noticed that a man seeking employment as a mule driver looked oddly stout about the waist. A search revealed four coils of brand-new rope. Thereafter none was issued except in exchange for the frayed remains of the old. His second moment of glory was in retrieving the load of a camel that had stumbled over a precipice. It contained many of the gifts chosen to win the Emperor's goodwill: a set of fine silver plate, a pair of gold-inlaid rifles, a Persian silk carpet, the mounted head and skin of a polar bear, field glasses, the life of Alexander the Great printed in Amharic. 'Other nations', Menelik later told Rennell Rodd, 'have treated me like a baby and given me musical boxes, magic lanterns and mechanical toys. You have given me what is useful and valuable. I have never seen such things before.'

At Harar the mission paid its respects to the governor, Ras Makunnen,

14 Arthur James Balfour, who in 1903 succeeded his uncle, Lord Salisbury, as Prime Minister. The affection of his Cecil cousins was tempered by his irresolution during the Tariff Reform controversy, not to mention the lack of consideration he showed in 1907 by driving his dashing new motor car at a terrifying forty miles an hour. 'Odd how the middle-class blood will out,' a sister-in-law observed. For although Balfour's mother was Lord Salisbury's sister, his paternal grandfather had made a fortune supplying provisions to the Royal Navy.

15 Lady Eleanor Lambton, soon after her marriage to Lord Robert Cecil in 1889. For more than seventy years she played a constant role in her husband's fortunes both as a devoted wife and shrewd counsellor, with a political judgment often superior to his own. She took a humorous view of life and loved to recall one of the earliest compliments Bob ever paid her. 'I really think you were the prettiest woman there tonight,' he said on their return from a party. Pause. 'My patience, they *were* an ugly lot.'

16 Cecils in conclave: drawn by Max Beerbohm in 1913. For more than half a century the three brothers – Bob, Jim and Hugh – formed a united front on the controversial questions of the day. They believed in such waning causes as religious education, Free Trade, a strong House of Lords, the British Empire. But they embarrassed their fellow Tories by embracing a quite separate set of heresies: votes for women, sympathy for conscientious objectors, the League of Nations.

17 Like his brother the Bishop, Lord Robert Cecil had his Radical moments. Here are the two conflicting sides of his character as seen by his friend and fellow Member of Parliament, Sir Mark Sykes, in 1914.

18 Lord Robert Cecil at the Foreign Office during the First World War. His operation of the economic blockade against Germany and Austria touched a sensitive conscience and inspired him to devote the rest of his life to the preservation of peace through the League of Nations.

19 Bob, by now Viscount Cecil of Chelwood, in serene old age. His clothes had been the despair of colleagues and friends ever since the young Cosmo Lang, not yet Archbishop of Canterbury, had pleaded with him: 'If you cannot dress like a gentleman, I think you ought at least to try and dress like a Conservative.'

20 In 1870 Lieutenant Lord Edward Cecil, Grenadier Guards, was appointed to the staff of General Lord Wolseley, Commander-in-Chief in Ireland. 'I am afraid I am not much good as an aide-de-camp', he told his brother Bob. 'I am too careless, too easily bored, too rash and too cautious.' Nor did he much care for Wolseley's character: 'He is as full of vanity and as susceptible of flattery as a passée beauty.'

father of the future Emperor Haile Selassie, then made for Addis Ababa. Perhaps it was not by chance that almost to a man the British stood well over six feet in height; wearing ceremonial dress for their reception by the Emperor, they appeared memorably imposing. But on Rodd alone fell the burden of negotiation. He emerged from the imperial palace after two weeks of bargaining with a treaty that fulfilled nearly all his hopes: permanent diplomatic representation, preferential commercial relations, the settlement of some vexed frontier disputes, an embargo on the supply of arms to the Dervishes. After an exchange of decorations that included the Order of St Michael and St George for Menelik and the Star of Ethiopia for Cecil, the mission began its long trek back to Somalia.

Cecil rejoined Kitchener in time for the resumed advance up the Nile and the crowning triumph of Omdurman. Success and self-confidence had mellowed his chief; there were fewer days of sultry anger or evenings of morose silence. His aide-de-camp saw nothing of the proud conqueror in the man who entered Khartoum quietly and almost alone to search for the place where Gordon had fallen. An old gardener came weeping, afraid that even after fifty years of service he would be sent away. Kitchener spoke to him gently. To the poor, Cecil noted, he was always kind.

The Sirdar showed both gratitude and a sense of theatre by choosing the Prime Minister's son for the honour of carrying his despatches back to England. From Khartoum to Cairo, Nigs took only four days, clinging for five hundred miles to a luggage wagon on the desert railway and breaking the previous record by four hours. He rejoined his regiment at the end of 1898 as a brevet major with the Distinguished Service Order, several mentions in despatches and a chestful of medals.

The past two years, however, had changed his character as well as his prospects. 'On the whole,' his mother wrote to him when he was eighteen, 'I should say you were the most popular and agreeable of the family except perhaps Jem.' As a young officer he was known as a wit at the Beefsteak Club and the Irish scholar John Mahaffy declared he would pawn his boots to dine with him. But behind the *bonhomie* there came to lurk a fierce and contemptuous temper. The private diary which he kept during the Abyssinian venture of 1897 is remarkable for its aspersity. Occasionally his quips are of schoolboy cheekiness: 'We were a long time getting off owing to the donkeys – biped and quadruped.' He labels one brother officer: 'Weak and a bore . . . pig-headed fool.' Another, he writes, 'is fond of a good glass and is a raconteur and plays parlour tricks which make me hot all over and think how ill grey hairs become a jester'. Even when allowance has been made for hardship and exhaustion, for a long separation from wife and child, the diary is of unrelieved misanthropy. Acquaintances continued to find him as elegantly entertaining as ever; those close to him detected an inner melancholy that was no stranger to the Cecil family.

Cecil was not allowed to enjoy London for long. Summoned to the War Office by Lord Wolseley on 3 July 1899, he received orders to sail for South Africa five days later. His task was to help Colonel Robert Baden-Powell in raising two regiments of irregulars for the defence of Bechuanaland and Matabeleland, threatened by the impending war with the Boers. However abrupt his departure from England, he was not required to abandon either his wife or the stately amenities of peacetime travel. A few hours to spare at Southampton passed agreeably in the company of Lord Montagu of Beaulieu, an even earlier pioneer of motoring than Bob Cecil. 'He took us for a drive in the country,' Violet wrote, 'before taking us to our boat, where my maid had unpacked and settled us in.' Nigs described it as 'very nice, but I can't help thinking a trifle dangerous'.

On landing at Cape Town on 25 July, they stayed at Government House with the British High Commissioner, Sir Alfred Milner (who was to become Violet's second husband in 1921). While Baden-Powell went up country to collect recruits and garrison Mafeking, Cecil set about trying to assemble stocks of ammunition, clothing and other stores. He was handicapped by the obstructive attitude of General Sir William Butler, commanding the troops at the Cape, who made no secret of his Boer sympathies. As the Prime Minister's son, however, Cecil was able to raise no less than half a million pounds on his own note of hand and to stock Mafeking with four times the amount of stores the government had thought necessary for its defence. Without his forethought, the town could scarcely have survived one of the most celebrated sieges of modern history.

He would nevertheless rather not have been caught in Mafeking by the outbreak of war in October and obliged to gaze upon his handiwork throughout the entire 217 days of the ordeal. The news of his mother's death in November, chivalrously sent to him by the enemy under a flag of truce, added to his dejection. Now and again he managed to smuggle out a message for Violet, folded into a scrap of paper an inch square:

> We have a chicken-hearted set of Boers against us and barring the shells and sniping don't have a bad time and we are used to those.

> Please don't worry. We are practically invincible.

> All well after our fight this morning.

Except we are bored to death, no hardship. We have started all sorts of factories for every kind of thing. We are even making our own matches and stamps for local use. . . . I was wretchedly seedy for a time, dysentry, fever and mental worry, but now that is behind me.

The cheerful tones in which Nigs reassured his wife were deceptive. He never afterwards cared to talk of his experiences in Mafeking and years later, hearing that Baden-Powell might be coming to live near Great Wigsell, in Sussex, where he and Violet had a country house, he told her: 'I dread anything that reminds me of that ghastly time, I really dread it.' During the siege itself, however, his duties as chief of staff left him little leisure for introspection. His responsibilities even included the organization of all boys aged from nine to fifteen into a drilled and disciplined cadet corps that was the forerunner of the Boy Scout movement; one young hero, riding a bicycle, appeared on the Mafeking postage stamps after the withdrawal of the original issue bearing Baden-Powell's head. Cecil also helped to devise a scheme of food-rationing. Lady Sarah Wilson, Winston Churchill's aunt, was reduced to giving her luncheon guests minced mule and curried locusts.

Violet, with the wives of one or two other officers in the field, was meanwhile invited by Cecil Rhodes to live at Groote Schuur, his estate near Cape Town. From there she ran an energetic campaign to supply the sick and wounded with comforts from home: pyjamas and slippers, sponges and tooth-brushes, none of which the War Office thought necessary for the private soldier of 1900. Gwendolen became her London agent, turning No. 20 Arlington Street into a temporary warehouse. At the best of times, Bob said, living there was like camping out in a government office. Now guests had to climb over bundles of nightshirts and towels to be greeted by the Prime Minister sitting on a soap box and complaining that the house smelt like a grocer's shop.

Horrified by the state of the military hospitals in South Africa, Violet wrote bitterly to her sister-in-law:

I sent all the pillows straight to Bloemfontein where they have got nothing, not even beds – you would have thought that in two months hospitals could have been provided with beds, but the RAMC would think beds most unnecessary and the Red Cross would be surprised at the demand, and there is no civilian criticism at Bloemfontein so you may imagine the state of things.

It took four months nagging to get these hospitals here decent – now they are good – and there is no one to nag up-country . . .

MacCormac [Sir William MacCormac, senior consulting civil surgeon] wants a peerage, so he would rather that people died like flies than venture the mildest criticism. He passed a hospital at Orange River where 400 people were without beds or food and where there were no nurses as 'excellent'.

She appealed to the Prime Minister himself, assuring him that 'far more people have been killed by negligence in our hospitals than by Boer bullets'. Her letter continues:

In spite of the whole country being a dairy farm, the patients never get anything but tinned milk. The nurses are overworked and are getting sick – two died last week. It is enough to make one cry. The only thing these people mind is exposure – is it impossible to convey to them that some account will be asked, not of the way they spend their money but of the medical results?

She contrived a visit to Bloemfontein to see conditions in the hospitals for herself, but was ordered back to Cape Town within twenty-four hours. Soon afterwards Milner received a message from the Queen deploring the presence in South Africa of so many visitors, 'especially ladies, who seem to have no particular call of duty or business'. Violet, suspecting she might have incurred royal disapproval, was much relieved to be assured by Gwendolen that the Queen had only the other day asked tenderly after her. Beauty and high spirits allied to determination and powerful connections could hardly fail to make her conspicuous in Cape Town. Officers on leave from the front flocked to Groote Schuur for her lively talk. Those out in the field entrusted her with little commissions. Jim Cranborne asked for the plays of Shakespeare; the future Lord Derby for ostrich-feather fans in his racing colours of black and white; the Duke of Westminster for gossip and affection. It was the happiest time of her life.

The relief of Mafeking in May 1900 was for Violet and her husband the end not only of a long separation but also of the war itself. He spent a few months as military governor of twenty thousand square miles of the Transvaal, observing with a touch of Abyssinian astringency that his Boer subjects were quite the most finished set of liars he had ever come across. By Christmas, however, he and Violet were back at Hatfield and reunited with little George, who on the night of his father's release had been allowed to light the town bonfire with a red, white and blue taper. Among the congratulations awaiting Nigs was a letter from the Duke of York, later King George V:

I was delighted to hear of your safe arrival yesterday at Hatfield. I welcome you home again after all you have gone through, especially your spendid defence of Mafeking. How pleased and proud your dear mother would have been at your return.

> I think you know that I am a collector of stamps, and I am most anxious to get some or a set of the Mafeking Besieged stamps *without post marks*. I thought perhaps that you might have some at your disposal, or could tell me who I could write to for some. I have got a complete set of them used, but an *unused* set would be a most valuable addition to my collection.

The old Prime Minister also had a characteristic greeting for his son. 'Don't bother about repaying the £1,000,' he wrote. 'I am sensible that you must pay for the luxury of going through an eight-month siege.'

Lord Edward Cecil was barely thirty-three when he returned from South Africa with the brevet rank of lieutenant-colonel. In the rigid hierarchy of the Grenadiers, however, he remained a captain with no particular claim to promotion. The Brigade of Guards has always discouraged an officer from seeking glory outside the regiment and declined to be impressed by any political connection he may flourish. Daunted by the prospect of resuming a barrack-square routine after nearly five years of initiative and adventure, Cecil therefore applied for secondment to the Egyptian Army. Sir Reginald Wingate, Kitchener's successor both as Sirdar and as Governor-General of the Sudan, was glad to welcome back an officer with local experience as well as an old comrade of the Dongola campaign and the mission to Menelik. In March 1901 Cecil received a contract of service binding him to Egypt for the next two years. He remained there for the rest of his working life.

'Wingate has again reported on me as his best staff officer,' he told Bob early in 1903, 'and said things about me which must have kept the Recording Angel scribbling for hours, but that is his lookout.' Nigs renewed another friendship when Kitchener, on his way to take up the appointment of Commander-in-Chief in India, paused to survey his former empire. He wrote to Alice from Khartoum:

> From the moment we started from Cairo K. informally but firmly annexed the Sudan. Before, however, getting here we stopped at Assuan, where he announced to our amazement that he had not sold his Island and proceeded to land on it and lay out the plan of a house. A fierce sun was beating on us but four wretched officers trailed tapes and pegs about and did impossible sums on the backs of envelopes for two hours while K. stood in the middle and saw they did not idle away their time. My present Master and myself went off meanly to see a more or less legendary store yard three miles down river, but the others had quite a busy morning.
>
> Subsequently I ventured to enquire how the general impression,

which was shared by the would-be purchaser, had got about that he had sold his island. 'There are three,' said K., 'and the one I sold is the small one lower down the river.' 'What, the black rock,' I most incautiously said (it is not 30 ft. square and has a solitary thorn bush on it). 'The smaller stony one,' corrected the Great Man. Curiosity overmastering my terror, I asked if the purchaser had understood this. 'Not at first,' said K. indulgently, 'but I explained it. Besides, he has a son in the Hussars.' The subject then dropped.

Since crossing the border we have lived under a merciful despotism. Everyone in turn has had the errors of the last three years clearly but kindly explained to them. . . . 'Ah, Kennedy, I thought I told you to build these houses two stories high.' A hurried explanation. 'Yes, a very great mistake. Quite spoilt, but they can be pulled down later.' Such is the ordinary type of conversation I listen to.

In the autumn of 1903 Cecil's gentler interpretation of Great Britain's imperial role brought him promotion. He was posted from Khartoum to Cairo as Agent-General of the Sudan. 'I am Foreign Affairs, Board of Trade and have a roving commission to advise H.E. on any points,' he announced to his family. 'I have also the Intelligence work and a weird little kingdom of my own called the Sinai Peninsula, chiefly inhabited by vultures, two jackals and a few wandering Arabs.' He showed an increasingly confident touch in handling civil and diplomatic affairs, balanced by a growing impatience with military men. 'There is a pig-headed obstinacy about a soldier which is quite maddening. He won't argue but merely says that he may be stupid and all that but he adheres to his opinion.'

Cecil had hardly taken up his new duties when he found himself the victim of just such inflexibility. The War Office reminded him that he still held a commission in the Grenadier Guards; that he had not yet taken the written examination for promotion from captain to major; and that although he was by now a brigadier-general in the Egyptian Army, failure to pass the test would cost him his brevet and oblige him to revert to the rank of captain in the British Army. Both Cromer and Wingate pleaded with London that Lord Edward were better employed as administrator than brushing up his military history; they could do no more than have his ordeal postponed. In due course he satisfied the War Office examiners, but never needed to resume British rank. For in 1904 Cromer selected him to be Under-Secretary for War in the Egyptian government, promoting him a year later to the even more responsible post of Under-Secretary for Finance. Thereafter the part Cecil played in Egyptian affairs was essentially civilian.

'The Lord is the only really satisfactory public man I know now,' Cecil wrote during his first months as an Under-Secretary. Egypt recognized but one Lord. Evelyn Baring, first Earl of Cromer, became British Agent and Consul-General in 1883, the year after Wolseley's troops had occupied the country to restore order and to uphold the rule of the hereditary Khedive. In that seemingly unobtrusive role he imposed his will on Egypt for almost a quarter of a century. He rescued her from bankruptcy, irrigated her land, restored her economy; he reduced taxation, abolished forced labour, rooted out corruption; he promoted higher standards of justice and public service, of education and health. There was nothing he was not prepared to do for the Egyptians except entrust them with the administration of their own institutions. His creed may be found in a memorandum drawn up on his instruction in 1905 for the enlightenment of newly-joined members of the Anglo-Egyptian service, but not made public at the time lest it should leak into a hostile press:

> When the work of reform first commenced, it was thought that the object in view would be best attained by limiting the number of British officials as far as possible. Their duty was to consist almost entirely in guiding and advising the native officials, in whose hands rested almost the whole of the executive business of administration. . . .
>
> Unfortunately, and to the great regret of the authorities responsible for the gradual extension of British executive interference, this principle has not proved successful. Experience showed that the native official, considered as a class, however gladly he might welcome or intelligently receive the advice and instructions of his English superior, had not yet reached either the stage of intellectual development which would enable him to carry out those instructions with efficiency, or of moral courage enough to face the terrors of unsupported responsibility. . . .

Much less was there a place for representative government in Cromer's grand design. He wrote at the end of his long stewardship:

> The method of Parliamentary institutions is thoroughly uncongenial to Oriental habits of thought. It may be doubted whether, by the adoption of that exotic system, we gain any real insight into native aspirations and opinions. . . . Our primary duty is not to introduce a system which, under the specious cloak of free institutions, will enable a small minority of natives to misgovern their countrymen, but to establish one which will enable the mass of the population to be governed according to the code of Christian morality.

Cromer nevertheless reminded his officials that Egypt neither was, nor ought to become, a British colony:

The one and only object which we should keep in view approaches almost pure altruism – to confer upon a people whose past is one of the most deplorable ever recorded in history, those benefits and privileges which they have never enjoyed at the hands of the numerous alien races who have hitherto held sway over them; and to endeavour to the utmost of our power to train up, by precept and example, generations of Egyptians who in the future may take our place and carry on the tradition of our administration. . . .

It was not enough, Cromer declared, for the paragon to possess only intellect and energy: still not enough to buttress those qualities with worldly knowledge and a rigid sense of justice, with unswerving integrity and an impeccable private life. He must also display kindness of heart, patience and courtesy. 'The Englishman is in Egypt as a guide and friend,' he concluded, 'not as a master.'

Students of Egyptian history have since discerned flaws in that imposing structure of government. They assert that Cromer's paternalism was offensively patronizing; that his concern for the supposedly child-like and voiceless millions of fellahin bred in him a corresponding disrespect for the Khedive, a disparagement of the educated middle class and a contempt for the nationalist; that his prolonged trusteeship of an increasingly restless people masked a determination to keep the route to India in British hands. Except by Wilfrid Scawen Blunt, few such claims were made during the years that the Lord ruled Egypt. Gwendolen Cecil, who with her brother Hugh was a guest at the British Agency in December 1903, wrote of Cromer: 'The moral authority, the way in which he has stamped his individuality on all around him, is absolute. . . . I cannot give you a greater proof than the fact that Linky and I have not yet been late for dinner or lunch.'*

Cromer appreciated the orderly mind of the new Under-Secretary who, like himself, had begun life as a professional soldier. And Cecil enjoyed working for a master who 'always wants everything finished the day after he thinks of it'. His immediate superior, Sir Vincent Corbett, exercised the prerogative of the Financial Adviser in teaching every other ministry its business; and since he delegated many of his duties to the Under-Secretary, Cecil rapidly acquired power as well as an unofficial seat on the Council of Advisers.

* The Lord did not so easily adjust his own routine to the customs of a court. Arriving in London on leave, he asked for an audience with the King. It was granted, for three days later. Cromer told the private secretary at Buckingham Palace that he had hoped to be received that very afternoon in order to catch the night train for a holiday in Scotland. 'He seems to take me for the Khedive,' King Edward VII replied.

I am trying to get these tiresome people to reform their administration and they naturally don't like it [he wrote to Bob in November 1906]. Every one agrees that the other Departments are in sad need of drastic reform but that what their own show requires is to be left alone as it is on the whole being extremely well run, etc. However, by steadily worrying I have really induced a lot of people to think about it, and the Lord is backing me up for all he is worth.

He added with renewed confidence in February 1907:

Finance is a very nice job but it seems to irritate people. If you tell a man he is not a good doctor when by profession he is a lawyer he does not mind; but if you suggest to him that an item is on the wrong side of the sheet he grinds his teeth and resigns. The resigning fever is dying down now that we have made a rule to accept all resignations with enthusiasm.

The resigning fever, as it happened, had not quite died down. Six weeks later Lord Cromer himself resigned.

'Don't speak to me of Egypt,' Cromer told Jim Salisbury in 1910. 'All my twenty-five years undone in two. Yet I have no one but myself to blame, for I recommended Gorst.' Cromer had little cause for self-reproach; by any standard, Sir Eldon Gorst was incomparably well qualified to succeed the Lord in Cairo. He had already shown his aptitude for Egyptian affairs as an enlightened Adviser to the Ministry of the Interior, then as a Financial Adviser of monetary knowledge and diplomatic skill. If he was also fiercely ambitious, hot-tempered and occasionally devious, there remained a considerable balance to his advantage. Nor, it seemed, would he be likely to pursue any except a Cromerian policy. He defined his aim as 'not merely to give Egypt the blessings of good administration but to train the Egyptians to take a gradually increasing share in their own government'. Those were almost the same words that Cromer had authorized in his apologia of 1905. Between the two proconsuls, however, lay a gulf of intent. Gorst favoured a rate of progress that Cromer thought recklessly fast; and whereas Cromer had treated the Khedive and the Egyptian Ministers as constitutional shadows, Gorst determined to take them into his confidence.

'If Gorst succeeds Lord Cromer,' Edward Cecil used to tell a friend in the British Agency, 'I leave Egypt by the first boat.' And when he failed to carry out his threat, he paid the penalty of a deposed court favourite. Almost at once he lost his seat on the Council of Advisers, to which as a mere Under-Secretary he had no absolute claim. Then

Corbett, the Financial Adviser, quarrelled with Gorst and asked to return to the Diplomatic Service. Had the post fallen vacant while Cromer still reigned, it would probably have gone to Cecil. As it was, he wrote:

> Gorst is most anxious I should not succeed Corbett and tried to get him to give me a bad character. He is openly very hostile to me behind my back and has reversed practically everything I have done. . . . I think he wishes to be able to point out that all my work is so bad that he cannot promote me.
>
> Of course the whole policy is now Khedive, and as I followed the Lord's line of anti-Khedival, my position is very difficult. . . . To have one's career practically wrecked because one carried out loyally the policy of the late king is not reasonable.

Nigs sent Violet further details of his disgrace and darkening prospects:

> Gorst alleges (though not to me) that I am ignorant of the country, that my Arabic is very bad and that I am anti-Native and generally inefficient. I am not anti-Native but I believe in speaking the truth and saying that this country must be in leading strings for many years to come and that the best way to teach them government is to govern them well: and this necessitates a fairly strict English control. . . .
>
> The talk in Cairo is that *all* 'Cromer's men' are to go and their places taken by the men trained by Gorst when he was in the Finance.
>
> If I therefore got the offer to go anywhere else, it might be well worth doing it if my prospects were decent. I fear being stranded in my old age with nothing to do and as poor as a church mouse.

Such an offer did appear possible in the spring of 1908. Hugh Cecil wrote to his brother from London:

> Just a line to say that I chanced to meet Winston at dinner and he explained to me at much length and in confidence that impressed by your abilities – 'all of you seem to me like Prime Ministers' – and with the familiarity with high politics which he thinks we all possess and which he believes will enable you to manage tiresome white settlers, he is anxious to make you governor (or whatever it is) of East Africa. Lord Elgin he fancies is not unfavourable but he cannot be certain.

It was followed by a letter from Churchill himself, who as Under-Secretary for the Colonies had recently toured Uganda. But it proved less promising than Hugh had led Nigs to expect. Churchill explained that the appointment was neither vacant nor in his hands, and that he would simply like to know Cecil's wishes before formally recommending his name to the Colonial Secretary, Lord Elgin, at some future date. As it turned out, the Governor of East Africa did not resign until the following year. By then Elgin had retired and Churchill been promoted to the Board of Trade. The appointment went not to Cecil but to another of Cromer's former officials, Sir Percy Girouard.

Cecil therefore continued to carry out the strictly routine duties of an Under-Secretary, initiating nothing in his own department, knowing little of what passed in others. He found Sir Paul Harvey, Corbett's successor as Financial Adviser, 'very trying – a cross between a spoilt child and a woman, with a dash of jealous prima donna sifted in'. That was a sad judgement on a man of civilized tastes who later spent his retirement compiling and editing the Oxford Companion to English Literature. But Cecil's mood was by then one of near despair. 'On the whole,' he told Violet, 'I believe I ought to serve quietly on and wait for better times. Gorst has, however, announced his intention of ending his days in this country, so my sentence is penal servitude for life.'

Cecil would have been justified in using that bitter phrase to describe his marriage. Lady Salisbury, deploring her son's choice of bride in 1894, expressed a confident hope that Hatfield would 'overpower' Miss Maxse. The spell failed to work. Violet retained an impregnable atheism, a combative temperament and a thirst for intellectual society unlikely to be satisfied outside the capitals of Europe. The demands of military service aggravated her restlessness by exposing her to long separations from Nigs. Between the Sudan campaign of 1896 and his departure for the Egyptian Army in 1901, they were hardly ever together except for a few weeks at a time. Inevitably she began to lead a life of her own, and even after Nigs had established himself in Cairo as an Under-Secretary, she refused to make her home there. Once or twice Violet came for a brief visit. But between 1901 and 1917 their only regular contact was confined to the month or two during which he took his annual leave in England.

Nigs accepted the estrangement with scarcely a word of reproach. His wry humour, however, never quite concealed his sorrow. Unable to escape from Cairo one August, he told Salisbury: 'I begin the summer as a man of my own age and gradually get older and older until September when I become senile and pre-historic, querulous and garrulous with at least two grievances of an obscure and uninteresting description which I will relate to every one I can find to listen to me.'

The separation also caused him acute financial worry. From the moment he joined Wingate at a salary of £720 he was burdened by the need to maintain two establishments: a modest bachelor apartment for himself and a small country house in England for Violet and their two children. 'My private affairs seem in such a tangle,' he confessed from Khartoum. Not until 1906 did Gwendolen report that her brother was 'putting by money and will get yearly richer'. Nevertheless, the personal budget of the Under-Secretary for Finance only just balanced:

> I have had much to my regret to refuse a rise of salary as it is quite impossible for me to refuse other people's demands for increases and allow them to give me more myself. I, or rather Violet, wants the money badly and though I was right to refuse I feel very sorry I had to do it. I shall feel still sorrier if V. ever finds out which I hope she won't.

Within a few months Cromer had gone, Gorst ruled in his place and Nigs feared a premature end to his career in Egypt. He wrote to Violet:

> If I were not so poor I should not mind as I could quietly go on till the smash came, but when I think of you and the children and Wig-sell my heart goes into my boots. To be married to a man you don't care for is bad enough, but to an unsuccessful man to boot is poor luck.

Gwendolen Cecil believed all the poor luck to be on her brother's side. She said of Violet: 'I am afraid she has lost the last chance of making the marriage a success. If she had been sympathetic and gone to him now that he is in low water, it might have retrieved much.' Although not prepared to join her husband in Cairo, Violet did try to help him by abusing Gorst to Lady Hardinge, wife of the Permanent Under-Secretary at the Foreign Office.* But that, as Stanley Baldwin observed when Mme Caillaux shot the editor who had disparaged her husband, the French Finance Minister, was 'not the sort of support you want from your wife'.

Most things French appealed to Violet: not least the ease with which an incompatible marriage could be dissolved. Her husband, however, like all Cecils, regarded marriage as a sacrament and its vows as binding. In any case, Edwardian society continued outwardly to respect the proprieties of the previous reign; neither divorce, nor even formal separation, was a seemly solution to marital discord. So Lord and Lady Edward

---

* In 1921 Alexander, son of Lord and Lady Hardinge of Penshurst, married Helen, Lord and Lady Edward Cecil's only daughter. He became Private Secretary to King Edward VIII and King George VI, succeeded to his father's peerage in 1944 and died in 1960.

Cecil remained man and wife, yet going their separate ways. Although Nigs corresponded politely with his wife across two thousand miles, he desperately missed a family life, finding what consolation he could in the company of his colleagues' children. The little daughter of the Legal Adviser in Cairo recalled one such descent from Olympus:

> Building bricks of this epoch invariably came from Germany and included Gothic arches and stained glass windows and a general improving stress upon ecclesiastical architecture, but Ned Cecil rose above this and built a lighthouse with a lighted candle at the top surrounded with stained glass windows, and turned off all the lights and caused us all to be ships in the darkness keeping away from the rocks.

For George and Helen, their father's annual leave at Wigsell was an adventure that illuminated the rest of the year. The house itself was too old, dark and damp for his taste. But with the inventive spirit of a landscape gardener and no outside labour, he made the little hillocky wood at the bottom of the orchard into a place of enchantment: winding paths, a tiny bridge, even a waterfall. In every cranny of stone he would plant his favourite wallflowers. Another retreat from casual visitors was the photographic dark room, a compound of mess and magic which the children found irresistible. His own clothes, too, bore the scars of utter dedication to his art.

Writing regularly to his children from Cairo, he kept alive in them that Christian belief which he found such a solace in time of misfortune. They were often at Hatfield, much to his relief, well insulated from the perils of their mother's atheism. He would also warn them, only half in jest, against her domineering personality:

> You should, if you will take my advice, never argue with one of the Maxse family about the French Revolution or anything else. It is a pure waste of breath. . . . Look what a mess I made of trying to get your mother's papers into order. I foolishly went off and bought for her the most up-to-date filing cabinet on the market. I was at the time head of the Egyptian archives, five or six hundred employees. I had reformed their system from top to toe and been thanked for it. I was the recognized authority on the subject. She was more than kind and nice about it, but would have nothing to do with the system of filing.

Behind the banter he was sick at heart. The double blow of a precarious career and a strained marriage sometimes seemed almost too heavy to be borne. He wrote to Violet in anguish: 'I do like pleasant things so much and pretty people and laughing, and I get so sick of the grind and the black looks. . . . No nerves left, my home broken and nothing to look foward to but dreary old age.'

When Edward Cecil wrote from Cairo in 1909 that 'Winston would make an ideal politician here and be revered for his honesty and steadfastness of purpose', he intended no compliment to the President of the Board of Trade. Like other disciples of Cromer, he believed that Gorst's well-meaning curb on the authority of the British official had merely encouraged the enrichment of the Egyptian pasha at the expense of the fellah. 'I don't think I ever saw anything, even my bank balance, decline so fast as British influence has done here,' Nigs noted. 'It melts while you look at it.' Amid such discontent, shared by some but not all of his colleagues, there flourished an unsettling cynicism. 'You pretend to like people you despise, you affect to admire ideals you don't believe in and you preach confidence in your own government at home which you had abandoned years ago.'

The Ministry of Finance matched his mood. He and his staff occupied what had originally been the harem of a pasha's palace: a string of small, ill-lit rooms as faded and fly-blown as their painted ceilings, dim looking-glasses and furniture of red plush and gilt. It was a seedy yet not inappropriate setting for the business of the day. As the Under-Secretary scrutinized the shady proposals put to him by speculators, both Egyptian and European, he developed a sensitive nose for fraud. One favourite operation invariably opened with a concessionaire's offer of a nominal sum for a large tract of waste land, valueless as long as it had no freshwater irrigation. On it, the purchaser explained, he intended to cultivate an unusual crop which unlike cotton thrived on the salty and impure water already to be found there. Having bought it cheaply, he would put every sort of pressure on his friends in the government to supply him with fresh water, then sell the land to cotton growers for more pounds than he had paid pence. Cecil came to recognize with inward glee the professions of altruism that invariably accompanied such designs: the desire of the concessionaire to increase government revenue, to bring new industries to Egypt and to spare her a dangerous dependence on a single crop.

Even the Khedive and his Prime Minister took an interest in one such scheme to which Gorst and Harvey, the Financial Adviser, inadvertently gave their assent. It is significant that both Cecil and William Hayter, the Legal Adviser, felt they were risking their careers in reporting that the whole project was a swindle. The Agency, however, at once accepted their advice and the plan was cancelled.

Cecil also took a connoisseur's delight in the labyrinthine claims for pensions which it was his duty to examine. He wrote of one optimistic plea:

> As a work of fiction it was admirable, but very complicated to fol-
> low and containing things one does not like to think about on a hot
> day, such as, if a man's service begins according to his story at a date
> when you know he was only two years old, is it likely that he was, as
> stated at that time, the most trusted Inspector of Customs? or can
> one by an effort believe that he was dismissed from the service by a
> series of plots which were carried on by all the high officials of the
> Government, with Lord Cromer's assistance and the countenance of
> all the judges of the Mixed Court? or to say that he stole was a lie,
> for there was nothing to steal, and he replaced it on the next day,
> when the accounts were found correct, but his chief stole largely?

He was constantly resisting attempts by Egyptian dignitaries to strain the rules in favour of their friends. At one meeting of the Council of Ministers, the Prime Minister asked for a grant of £50 out of government funds for a retired official who had exchanged his pension for a lump payment, then spent the lot. Cecil vetoed the proposal. 'What,' the Prime Minister said, 'have you no pity for this poor old man?' Cecil replied: 'Certainly I have. Let us raise the £50 between us out of our own pockets. Here is £5.' As the Under-Secretary had given £5, the ministers, groaning, each had to give £10; as they gave £10, the Prime Minister, almost weeping, it was observed, had to give £20. Cecil wondered whether they would ever forgive him.

When not positively dishonest, Cecil believed, the Egyptians were scatterbrained and incompetent; sometimes amusing in their artfulness, but hardly ever to be trusted with ministerial or other responsibilities except under European control.

> I am just back from a Council of Ministers [he told his daughter],
> where I have been trying to explain elementary finance to them. You
> would have understood in half a second but they just cannot, and my
> only consolation is that I left them all with very bad headaches.

The least stupid, he considered, were the Coptic Christians; in them, however, he recognized no link with the Creed as practised at Hatfield. He wrote of one such colleague:

> The dark colour, woolly hair, wooden expression of countenance,
> and want of personal cleanliness, proclaim him a Copt of the Copts.
> He bears all the marks and possesses the vices and virtues of a race
> that has been oppressed for ages. The patient manner, the mixture of
> servility and dignity of deportment, and the absolute concealment of

his personal wishes and feelings, are all characteristic of his people. The Copts are liars because for years it has been dangerous for them to speak the truth; crooked and cunning because by those qualities alone could they get a living; proud in their contempt of the Moslem, servile in view of his power to oppress them, careless of their personal appearance from ages of concealment of their riches by this means.

If there had to be Egyptian ministers and senior officials, Cecil preferred an exuberant ruffian like the Minister of Public Instruction: 'I have a sneaking affection for him, as he has the rough, rather jolly way of the peasant, which contrasts very favourably with the oily snake-like manner of the town-bred Egyptian, and he has a sense of humour of an elementary kind.'

Lord Edward gave an equally patronizing testimonial to the Minister of Public Works, 'whom I like as much as I like any native, but whose conversation is chiefly composed of intermittent but thoughtful expectorations'. He again wrote disdainfully of Egyptian politicians a few weeks later:

Even the wisdom of their Excellencies has been thrown into the shade by a gentleman who looks after the Khedive's estates and who seriously proposes to drain the marshes along the sea coast by digging deep holes and letting the water run away.

I could not help suggesting that he had better be careful, as if he let out the Mediterranean it might raise grave international troubles. He only said that it was quite safe, as the holes would not be large enough. I fear he will repeat my remark to someone, when I shall be exposed.

The Egyptian Nationalist movement evoked the same goodhumoured nonchalance. Although discouraged from expressing an opinion on internal politics, Cecil enjoyed amusing himself on public occasions by nodding and smiling to the extreme Nationalists as they glared at him from the other side of the room. 'Their friends immediately edge away from them, believing they are spies. I made one man so miserable by my cordiality that he got up on the plea of illness and left. I caught him at the door and thanked him for his services, and he has been, I believe, explaining it away ever since.'

When every allowance has been made for the stiff social attitudes and thoughtless xenophobia of the Edwardian Age, the depressing conclusion remains: that during more than fifteen years of dedication to the welfare of Egypt, Cecil found no single Egyptian worthy of his friendship. 'It is not,' he once wrote, 'as some falsely hold, a corner of the

Empire inhabited by future proconsuls and the grateful people they govern (as if anyone ever did like being governed!), but an enormous and unending *opéra bouffe.*' The *mot* fails to do justice to the material benefits of British rule or to the sense of mission which Cecil shared with his fellow officials. Across half a century, however, their concern appears professional rather than sympathetic; always protective but sometimes condescending and occasionally contemptuous.

He found Cairo as narrowly provincial as the Chatham of *The Pickwick Papers*: an enclosed world of officialdom that thrived on petty rivalries and social convulsions, with a hierarchy every bit as rigid as the structure that supported Dr Slammer and Mrs Colonel Bulder and Ensign Snipe of the 97th Regiment.

> One watches with amusement [Cecil wrote] the standoffish manner of the Inspector of Interior speaking to the young Public Instruction boy, and one knows that presently one will see the latter treat a junior commercial with the same edifying hauteur. . . . It should be a comfort to a junior, if he ever feels aggrieved by the manners of those farther up the ladder, that in the mind of the aggressor the junior is superior to every foreigner or native that ever existed.

Cecil made few lasting friendships among his British colleagues. Working days were often darkened by squabbles and jealousies, leisure hours by a leaden hospitality. 'Please, Lord Edward, don't try to smile at a party again,' a guest once begged him. 'It is really terrible to see your face.' He found it difficult to dispel the loneliness of an unwilling celibacy. Although he admired the wives of his fellow officials for their family devotion and the courage with which they met all the nerve-fraying anxieties of an expatriate life, they lacked the sophistication he craved. Military wives offered high spirits and diplomatic wives elegance; but they rarely remained in Egypt for more than two years before accompanying their husbands to another post.

In contrast to the depressing formality of Cairo, Alexandria revived the pleasures of youth. Its cosmopolitan society, he told Alice Salisbury, was composed of Levantines, Greeks, French and Italians, 'who, without being openly disreputable, are rather on the edge'. He added shyly: 'It is hard for me to remember I am married at times. The result is one gets mixed up with people one had much better not know too well. I feel as if I were not as steady as I could wish.'

Cecil's reputation nevertheless remained free from any taint of scandal. Only once did he shock his colleagues: and that was three years after his death. The fault lay with his widow, who in 1921 published a collection of the humorous sketches he had written years before to entertain the family. *The Leisure of an Egyptian Official*, as the volume was called, carried the customary declaration that no character had been drawn from life. It did not prevent survivors of pre-war Cairo from identifying both themselves and each other in its pages. The author, whom they had known to be short-tempered but never unkind or even discourteous, revealed an unsuspected strain of misanthropy. He had apparently thought most British officials to be snobs or bores, their wives faded in appearance and deficient in intellect. Egyptians were rogues or clowns, Frenchmen excitable and self-important, Germans arrogant and devious, Americans nasal and ponderous, Jews craven and mercenary. Alone of his bizarre circle, he esteemed 'Baron Sodisky', an Austrian diplomat with an adventurous command of English. Describing the rise of a friend from humble birth to high office, the Baron would patiently explain: 'He broomed in the street. He was a street wiper.'

Lord Edward was no less a master of the striking phrase. He wrote of one colleague's wife that her colour had come out in the wash of life. Undertaking a journey with another was like travelling with the Flying Dutchman: 'One moves in a perpetual storm of small unpleasantnesses.' Conversation with their husbands became 'a wearisome iteration of antiquated fallacies.' At least there was novelty in the couple who believed archaeology to be in some way connected with Noah. His pages are rich in aphorism:

> I wonder why all eggs in Egypt taste musty, as if they had been laid by a mummy?
>
> Passengers are regarded as a sort of unsavoury pest with which a ship becomes infested whilst lying in port.
>
> An Englishman will eat anything if it is served hot, there is plenty of it, and he is sure he knows what it is. The fear that a designing foreigner may one day make him unknowingly eat a cat is still present in some form or another in most British minds.
>
> It is curious that all people of a certain social grade sniff when they are out of temper. I wonder if there is any medical reason for this?

In more genial vein, he could invigorate even so hackneyed a theme as the comic retainer. This is how his servant packed his bags for a visit to England:

> I once crossed Europe with half of my only trunk taken up by a typewriting machine, of which no part could be used as clothing. Even the ribbon could scarcely be regarded as a sufficient costume by itself, however cunningly arranged, anywhere but in Central Africa. Though this took place in early days and he undoubtedly knows

better now, he still thinks that I want to play golf *en route*, presumably on the steamer, and that I make my official entry into London on horseback.

Then there is the confusion of the cloakroom at the end of an evening party at the Agency:

> I see a timid youth with two large wide-awakes, one in each hand, bleating vainly for his cap, whilst an irritable tourist has been given three walking-sticks and nothing else, which is certainly insufficient clothing for a cold night. Knowing my way about these affairs, I slip under the counter, go straight to the coal-scuttle, where I am lucky enough to find my hat and coat untouched, and, casting myself into the crowd, I fight my way to the door.

A scene as he leaves his office late for lunch has worn less well with the years:

> [I] jump into the nearest cab, which apparently had been retained for a portly notable, who was waddling thitherward from the door of the Ministry of Interior, giving vent to shrill cries of anger and distress at this high-handed act. I pretend to think these are only greetings; and I courteously acknowledge them whilst the driver starts his horses off at a gallop. When I last see the notable, who has at length recognised me, and who is the proud possessor of a land claim against the Government of a particularly nebulous kind, he has changed his peacock-like screams of rage for a torrent of salutations backed by an obsequious smile.

Cecil might conceivably have played that sort of joke on a fellow Englishman, but never on an Egyptian, notable or otherwise. By 1921, however, there were many readers of his posthumous book only too willing to believe that British officials in Egypt habitually behaved like that. *The Leisure of an Egyptian Official* confirmed its author's reputation as a wit, but added nothing to his stature as a public servant or an apostle of Cromerian imperialism.

Needless to say, Cecil had set out to amuse himself and a few trusted relations with a light-hearted caricature of official life in Cairo; he certainly never intended it to be read as a considered apologia of his stewardship. Most of the pieces were written during his least happy years in Egypt, when he had apparently been passed over for the appointment of Financial Adviser and could expect no further promotion. Nor did he intend them to be read outside the family circle, much less published. The first part of the manuscript was completed in the autumn of 1911 and submitted to the critical eye of Nelly Cecil. 'I am so glad you like it,' he told her. 'It was such a pleasure to write as I have no one I can joke with about people here now, and it was a great relief to be able to put it down.' Nigs added that most of the characters were real, but with changed identities. More of the sketches followed in December, accompanied by a warning: 'I am sending you some more of my silly stuff. It is for family consumption only as I could only live in a cellar under an assumed name if some people saw it. So don't let them copy it however much they pray and beg.' Nelly took his point. 'I now entirely understand your cautionary instructions,' she replied. 'I expect Jem will be scarified and will lock it all up in the muniment room, where it will be discovered centuries hence, side by side with the casket letters.' Ten years later every word was in print, and a new generation failed to detect that the author's family jokes masked an underlying seriousness and a deep devotion to the prosperity of Egypt.

It was insensitive of Violet to publish so inadequate a memorial to her husband, and one that could cause pain in the changed political climate of 1921. But she had, after all, seen little of Nigs and even less of Egypt during his long years in Cairo. What remains puzzling is that Lord Milner, whom she married in February 1921, eight months before the publication of the book, did not dissuade her. He had himself been Egyptian Under-Secretary for Finance from 1890 to 1892. More recently, as Colonial Secretary in the Lloyd George government, he had conducted long negotiations with the Nationalist leaders in Cairo and reported in favour of Egyptian independence. But the Cabinet rejected his recommendation, and in the month of his marriage he retired from political life. Milner of all men could scarcely have doubted that *The Leisure of an Egyptian Official* would be damaging to Cecil's reputation and offensive to Egyptian pride. Yet apparently he did nothing to prevent its publication. Perhaps he was anxious not to inaugurate his marriage by differing from a woman of imperious will who rarely either asked or took advice.

In April 1911 Sir Eldon Gorst telegraphed to London asking permission to return home at once for medical treatment. Three months later he was dead of cancer. The last person outside his family to see him alive was the Khedive of Egypt, who interrupted a holiday in Paris to say goodbye to his friend. Gorst died a disappointed man. Almost from the moment of his arrival in Cairo, events had moved against him. An exceptional flooding of the Nile in 1907 caused widespread damage and a sharp increase in poverty. The representative bodies which he had set up as a step towards Egyptian self-government wilted under threats from the militant Nationalists. In 1910 the assassination of Butros

Pasha, the gifted Copt whom he had recommended to the Khedive as Prime Minister, obliged him to abandon liberal sentiments in favour of coercion. Even the warmth which he injected into his relationship with the nominal ruler of Egypt proved harmful to both. Gorst was accused by his compatriots of having diminished British authority by meddling in local politics, the Khedive condemned by Egyptian extremists for having sold himself into bondage.

Asquith's Cabinet hoped ultimately to allow Egypt her independence. But Sir Edward Grey saw that the immediate need was for an administrator of Cromerian authority. Just such a proconsul happened at that moment to be restlessly unemployed. Kitchener, home from India after seven years as Commander-in-Chief, was disgruntled at having been passed over in 1910 for the Viceroyalty, which went to Hardinge. Egypt, however, offered almost as covetable a field for his ambitions. Gorst died on 10 July 1911. On 24 September Kitchener was received at Cairo railway station wearing the unaccustomed civilian splendour of grey frock coat and black silk hat. Officially he held no higher rank than that of the most recently arrived, and thus the most junior, consul-general. In effect he was undisputed governor of an exceptionally important crown colony.

None welcomed the change of regime more than his former aide-de-camp, Lord Edward Cecil. Kitchener's policy did not exclude limited constitutional concessions to nationalism; but its principal aim was to restore contentment through economic prosperity rather than political discussion. That in turn involved a reversal of Gorst's determination to curb the power of British officials. As in the days of Cromer, fellahin could once more petition supreme authority against the oppression of pasha or moneylender, knowing that their grievances would be heard and remedied. Throughout Egypt the name *Kuchnir* became as potent as the *el-Lurd* of the previous two decades.

Within a few days of Kitchener's arrival, Cecil by chance received a letter from Cromer, who had been asked to find an Englishman willing to reorganize the finances of Siam. Had Gorst still reigned in the Agency, Cecil might have been tempted by the offer. As it was, he replied that his present salary was little less than the £2,000 a year offered by the Siamese government; and that by resigning from the Egyptian service he would lose not only his rights to a pension but also the now immeasurably brighter prospects of succeeding Harvey as Financial Adviser.

Promotion came more swiftly than he expected. Harvey, outraged by the huge sums which Kitchener ordered to be spent on land drainage and reclamation, protested too vigorously. He was instantly asked to resign and by November 1912 Cecil sat in his place. The new Financial

Adviser's rehabilitation was completed by appointment to be a Knight Commander of the Order of St Michael and St George. But he cared nothing for such things, and pleasure at Kitchener's mark of confidence was outweighed by dark thoughts of an investiture at Windsor.

Nigs's family thought it amusing that someone so incompetent in managing his own limited fortune should handle vast amounts of public money with the utmost skill and confidence. In his very first year as Financial Adviser, he was defrauded by a secretary of a substantial sum in his personal account, a loss instantly repaired by the generosity of Jim Salisbury. Simultaneously he controlled a budget of nearly £20 million, interfering at will in departments as varied as railways and the public debt, the Army and irrigation, education and the customs. The most exacting of his duties was pacifying not Egypt but Lord Kitchener. 'To cope with K.,' he told Alice, 'one should not be over twenty-five and in good training.' And a few days later: 'His energy is quite appalling. He starts a new scheme every morning which he wishes finished by 8 a.m. the next day. All the staff and the senior officials go about with an air of hunted rabbits.'

The Khedive, too, who had much resented Kitchener's rough ways as Sirdar, found little mellowing with the years. 'His Highness was so nervous when he was talking to him,' Cecil reported, 'that he did not know what he was saying. I think he had a dim idea K. might have a death warrant signed by Grey in his pocket.' On tour in the provinces, gazing with satisfaction on the rich green crops by which he measured Egyptian progress, Kitchener radiated an endearing *bonhomie*. The social round of Cairo, however, filled him with dread, and would-be hosts had to pay for the privilege. Not even the Adviser to the Interior or the Commander-in-Chief of the British Forces was exempt from what Cecil delicately called his habit of 'annexing' any object that took his fancy: 'Ronny Graham only saved three valuable rings by the devotion of an attaché who hid them under the stairs, and General Maxwell missed small Egyptian antiques the day after K. had dined with him.' The manner in which Kitchener returned hospitality was also memorable. Cecil wrote home in March 1914:

We had an Agency ball the other night. Very original I called it. Only selected members of each family were asked – sometimes the wife, sometimes the husband, often the deceased. I never saw a ball room full of such irritated people, but the crown was the supper which consisted exclusively of some rare and curious old prawns and a particular new brand of champagne at 1s. 3d. the bottle. My, how ill everyone was. I think K. did it to learn them to ask for balls.

The Financial Adviser detected a deeper purpose in another such party given by Kitchener: 'His cook is no mean toxicologist and I fancy is practicing on us against the day when his services will be required for the Khedive.'

The Khedive, as it happened, was disposed of more deftly. When Turkey entered the war against the Allies in October 1914, the Asquith government was tempted to annexe Egypt, over which Turkey continued to claim a shadowy but ineffective suzerainty. Instead, Egypt was declared a British protectorate, a milder course that equally well disposed of Turkish pretensions while giving legal form to a *de facto* British occupation that had already lasted more than thirty years. The Khedive, who could not be trusted to support the Allied cause against Turkey, was deposed and his uncle Hussein Kamel installed in his place with the superior title of Sultan. Nor did Kitchener ever set foot in Egypt again. On leave in England in August 1914, he was at once appointed Secretary of State for War.

Cecil found himself in a position of exceptional independence when he returned to Cairo that autumn. The change of constitution in no way diminished the scope of the British Advisers. It was they, not the Egyptian ministers, who formed what in all but name was the Cabinet; and among them the Financial Adviser acquired a dominant position comparable to that of Prime Minister. As long as a Cromer or a Kitchener brooded possessively over Egypt, even a well-trusted favourite like Cecil felt obliged to tread with care. But for some months after the outbreak of war, the office of High Commissioner (as the Agent and Consul-General was now called) remained vacant. It was filled in 1915 by Sir Henry McMahon. 'He is quite charming,' Cecil wrote, 'and I could never want a nicer chief. He is strong and confident with a great knowledge of administration and a very highly developed sense of humour.' No less important in the Finanical Adviser's eyes, he had spent much of his career in India and lacked first-hand knowledge of Egypt.

Untrammelled by superior authority, Cecil took several bold decisions for which he was afterwards remembered with gratitude. Immediately before the outbreak of the South African war he had foreseen the impending scarcity of military stores and made private purchases for Mafeking amounting to £500,000. Now he repeated the coup, snapping up 250,000 tons of coal from England on his own responsibility. The cost was £1,500,000. Two years later the price had doubled. Cecil several times tried to rejoin the Army and showed an almost childish envy at his eldest brother's promotion to major-general.

When it became obvious even to him that he could not be spared he found consolation in helping equip the expeditionary forces based on Egypt. The role of Financial Adviser, he told his daughter, was 'very like being a Minister in the Middle Ages, with the great advantage that no one cuts off your head'.

Some of his fellow Advisers would gladly have tried when in October 1914 each of them received a peremptory letter from him. It stated that he and the Director-General of Accounts had as a gesture of patriotism temporarily renounced one-third of their salaries, the money to be repaid without interest whenever it suited the Egyptian government. And he invited his colleagues to do the same. The response was disappointing, a furious screed from four of the six Advisers to whom his appeal had been addressed:

> Without giving us any opportunity of discussing with you the momentous step you were about to ask us to take, or inviting the expression of our views concerning it, without offering us any evidence that the gravity of the financial situation was such as to render so great a sacrifice on our part essential, you have elected to confront us with a 'fait accompli', to which publicity has been immediately given in the Press, and which is acclaimed as an heroic initiative. We accordingly find ourselves in the disagreeable dilemma of either following, blindly, in your footsteps, without having any evidence or conviction of the necessity for the course which you have chosen to adopt, and at a personal sacrifice, as we believe, out of all proportion to the benefit likely to be derived from it by the Government; or else of exposing ourselves to criticism, in the newspapers and among the people, as functionaries so lacking in public spirit and self-sacrifice that they refused to abandon any portion of their pay, in spite of the meritorious example set them by the high officials of the Ministry of Finance....

Cecil replied to what he called 'this foolish round-robin' in the same high style of wounded indignation:

> I submit it is to be deplored that at a time like the present, an official who has before him a task of which the difficulty can hardly be exaggerated, and who needs every possible assistance, support, and consideration, should have, apparently, a sort of combination against him by his brother officials: and this without one word of warning or remonstrance....

Tempers flared all too easily as family tragedy was added to the strain of overwork. In the very first month of the war Cecil's only son

George, fighting on the Western Front in his father's regiment, the Grenadier Guards, was reported missing, later discovered to have been killed in action a few days before his nineteenth birthday. 'I am very unhappy about Violet,' Nigs told Alice. 'It is awful for her to believe that she will never see him again and that he is only dust. I pray and hope that she may be helped to see.' He cherished the crucifix given to the boy at baptism by his godfather, Hugh Cecil, and subsequently engraved with a triumphant epitaph: 'Died for his country September 1st 1914 near Villers Cotterets in France having continued Christ's faithful soldier and servant until his life's end.' The memorial which Violet chose for her only son took the form of a new miniature rifle range at his old school, Winchester. Just before Christmas 1915 her friend Rudyard Kipling performed the opening ceremony. He fired the first shot, scored a bull's-eye on the target and was cheered by the assembled boys.*

Deeper issues than a voluntary cut in salary divided Cecil from Ronald Graham, who was the Adviser to the Ministry of the Interior. One represented the benevolent authority of a Cromer or a Kitchener, the other embodied the pliant optimism of a Gorst. Cecil wrote of his colleague's conduct in the early days of the war:

> His one idea was compromise, and the result was a constant struggle which very nearly ended in his giving way to the Egyptians on more than one point and made my position intolerable. . . . Whenever the Ministers started some idea of staving off the evil day by some financial dodge which would inevitably mean ruin later on, he used to sympathise with them, and of course they got more and more difficult to hold.

Their differences sprang as much from training as from temperament. Graham's years in the Diplomatic Service had taught him that compromise was a virtue. Hatfield had encouraged Nigs to define a compromise as 'an agreement between two men to do what both agree is wrong'. In October 1916, resenting the complete accord between High Commissioner and Financial Adviser, Graham wrote a letter of waspish denigration about both to Reginald Wingate, Governor-General of the Sudan for the past seventeen years:

> We all feel that Sir H. McM., however conversant he may be with frontier tribes, is not up to the complicated job here and never will be and at the present moment he is far too much in the hands of

---

* Nearly twenty years later, Violet gave a sixteenth-century painting of the Crucifixion to Hatfield chapel in memory of George and his father.

223

Cecil, whose influence I believe to be dangerous. At any rate, even if Cecil's theories are right, which I doubt, he is regarded by the Sultan with so much dislike and suspicion that it shakes my whole position for it to be imagined that he is directing policy.

The evidence of other British officials refutes that charge against Cecil. McMahon himself congratulated the Financial Adviser on 'the respect and confidence of the Sultan that you enjoy'. Hayter, the Legal Adviser, also wrote of him: 'He treated the Ministers like human beings, not like figure-heads, and they repaid him with very real affection and confidence.' Graham nevertheless won the day. At the end of 1916 he was transferred to London as the Assistant Under-Secretary at the Foreign Office in charge of Egyptian affairs. There he swiftly succeeded in having McMahon recalled from Cairo and Wingate appointed High Commissioner in his place. Had Kitchener not been drowned on his way to Russia a few months before, Cecil might have sought his help in thwarting Graham's design. As it was, he had no stronger card to play than his brother Bob, Minister of Blockade and Parliamentary Under-Secretary at the Foreign Office. Lord Robert's reaction, however, was stiffly departmental: 'It is not a matter on which I can claim to be consulted, since it neither affects the blockade nor the parliamentary position of the Government. Moreover, I am sure you will agree that questions of appointment can only be dealt with properly by the responsible Minister.'

Sir Reginald Wingate's displacement of McMahon heralded the end of Cecil's unusually powerful position in Cairo. The new high Commissioner, in spite of his twenty years of friendship with the Financial Adviser, was determined that he and he alone should represent Great Britain in Egypt. Less than a month after taking up his duties in January 1917 he opened his campaign. In the first of several letters to Lord Hardinge, recently returned from India to resume his former post as Permanent Under-Secretary at the Foreign Office, he reiterated Graham's earlier complaints. Cecil's unsatisfactory relations with the Sultan and the Egyptian ministers, he claimed, were hampering the fulfilment of British policy. Wingate went on to suggest that an unbecoming conflict could be avoided if Cecil were at last allowed to rejoin the Army; but insisted that should he prefer to continue as Financial Adviser, his role must be unmistakeably subordinate to that of the High Commissioner.

Neither prospect pleased Cecil, who was now on leave in England. He had come to realize that a re-employed officer in his fiftieth year could expect nothing more heroic than a staff job far behind the fighting line. Yet to return to Cairo on Wingate's terms would be not only humiliating but also harmful to British interests. 'No one,' he told Salisbury in July, 'is quicker to detect friction than the Oriental.' He added:

> If I had to do with an abler man, or as I was very nearly saying, a less foolish one, I have no doubt I could find a *modus vivendi*. But he has always, as a matter of policy, got rid of any strong man who was near him. This was shown in the Sudan again and again. Further, his vanity, fostered by the almost unique position which he has held, has to be known to be believed. He will stop at practically nothing to get rid of anyone whom he fears may be a competitor....
>
> I am afraid you will think my last grumble is rather a sordid one but, as you know, my ambition has always been to be at the head of Egyptian affairs, as I should have been if Lord Kitchener had lived.

A few days later Cecil resolved the dilemma by accepting a new post as assistant military adviser to the Minister of Munitions in London. Then he changed his mind and by October 1917 was back in Cairo as Financial Adviser. To Wingate's other shortcomings he now added an anxious subservience to Whitehall:

> He is really pitiable. He is afraid of his own shadow.... He fancied today that in a telegram the F.O. had ordered him to do something, whereas they were only consulting him. I assured him this was the case and he kept on saying, 'Well you are responsible, you are responsible, make it clear in the telegram I will do whatever I am told, make it quite clear.' It was the limit. . . . What can you do with a weak frightened man of inferior intellect?

The question was rhetorical. With unsuspected artfulness, Cecil had already struck back at Wingate. He had spent part of his long leave in England secretly attempting to persuade both his brother Bob and his cousin Arthur Balfour, by now Foreign Secretary, to assign the control of Egyptian affairs to a new government department, independent of the Foreign Office. Such a reform, he hoped, would break the hold of Hardinge and Graham over Wingate and restore British policy in Egypt to a Cromerian robustness. Hardinge warned Wingate of the plot:

> You will, I am sure, understand what a difficult position one is in here in connection with your Financial Adviser and his two official relations in this Office. I find that the utmost tact is necessary and I cannot help feeling how unsatisfactory the position is. Between you

and me, there is undoubtedly a great deal of underground intrigue going on, in which your Financial Adviser seems to be a past master, but you may rest assured that Ronald Graham and I are perfectly sound in our views and do our utmost to keep things on straight and proper lines. It is, however, no easy task, and I may mention that recently Edward Cecil has produced a memorandum upon the Administration in Egypt in which he advocates the control being taken away from the Foreign Office and vested in some outside department recruited from Heaven knows where. Ronald Graham and I have written very strong memoranda against the scheme, but I understand that it is going to be brought by the Parliamentary Under-Secretary here before the War Cabinet with the suggestion that it should be submitted to some committee appointed to consider it *ad hoc*. . . . If people would only try to concentrate upon doing their duty and winning the war instead of starting these hare-brain schemes, it would save a lot of time and trouble and probably be more to the advantage of their own interests. . . .

The War Cabinet, however, reacted with concern to Cecil's plea, setting up a small but strong committee to examine the memorandum and to hear evidence. It consisted of Balfour, Curzon and Milner, the last of whom proved the most adroit ally of all. He wrote to Cecil in December 1917:

The Egyptian Administration Committee is not dead but dormant. I am trying to keep it so intentionally. My own conviction, growing ever stronger, is that a very radical change is required in the management of Egyptian, and other related business, at this end. And I know your brother Bob quite agrees with me. But A. J. B., who knows absolutely nothing of the subject, and Curzon, who only knows it very superficially, do not realise the gravity of the thing, and were quite prepared for some very trifling changes at the F.O., which would have been pure eyewash and have delayed any real reform indefinitely. That being the case, as I was in a minority, I thought it much better to hang up a decision than to take a wrong one. Hanging up, as you know, is always easy, so I put in a long memorandum expressive of dissent, and asked for another meeting to discuss it. Of course no-one wanted another meeting, and that gave the thing for the time being its quietus, so there we are.

Eventually Cecil won a modified victory with the establishment not of a separate government office for Egyptian affairs but of a new Middle East department of the Foreign Office. By then, however, he had lost all responsibility for Anglo-Egyptian relations. In the last weeks of

1917 he fell gravely ill with what was belatedly diagnosed as tuberculosis.

During that first feverish bout in Cairo, he lost a pound in weight each day and the doctors despaired of saving him. 'Don't forget to pray for me,' he told his daughter, 'it is such a huge help.' Then he rallied, and by the new year was in a sanatorium at Leysin, in Switzerland. He wrote drolly to Nelly a few days after his arrival:

> I am a little more cheerful than I was. During my voyage everyone has treated me with the lachrymose respect one pays to the dying. The commander of the antiquated ark they called a ship that brought me to Marseilles said it did not matter how one died for one's country, either in the battle or slowly in the bed.
>
> The consul at Marseilles alluded feelingly to my father and touched on what he would have felt about it all. The vice-consul at Geneva said it must be a great comfort for me to look back over a useful life.
>
> Poor old Horace Rumbold sniffed audibly and we had a most affecting leave taking which will render our next meeting if it ever comes off a little flat.

Long hours of sleep and fresh air gradually restored his strength. After more than twenty years of the Nile Valley relieved only by damp English summers, he relished the austere white landscape, the freedom from flies, the stimulating fall in temperature: 'The late Lord Bacon as far as I remember died from incautiously trying to freeze a hen in snow with a view to starting a cold storage company. If he had lived here he could have left the hen on the table in his bedroom and chipped bits off her when he wanted them.'

For a time he wished to read nothing more demanding than 'a very horrid shilling shocker . . . that begins with two murders and a suicide and ends by an explosion and general incendiarism'. He also asked Violet to stop sending him the illustrated society papers, 'all so vulgar and stupid'. As lassitude receded, he took to tapping out long letters to his family on an ancient hired typewriter that somehow, he complained, had never learned to spell. He move easily from reminiscences of his official career to curious symptoms of his illness that he knew would thrill Linky; from a distant prospect of home politics to the parochial dramas of a sanatorium; from the failings of the public-school system to the prevalence of fainting-fits in eighteenth-century France. The postal links between neutral Switzerland and an England still at war were irregular, and he could not understand why for weeks at a time he received no replies. Then the reason emerged. He wrote to Helen in April 1918:

> Your sainted mother has apparently had a long discussion with the censors, the result of which is that I get no letters. It is like going with some people to a restaurant, where they have a terrific battle with everyone from the page boy up to the director-in-chief, and finally indicate their position. The only thing you don't get is anything to eat.

In September Violet was able to travel to Leysin with her daughter for a short visit, where they found Nigs much improved in health. But the reunion turned his own thoughts to an uncertain future. He could hardly hope to resume his duties in Cairo, and the prospect of retiring permanently to an uncongenial house in England filled him with dread. He confided to Alice Salisbury:

> I am also still a good deal worried over Wigsell as I feel sure it will be madness to try to live there and I know what a bother there will be if I don't. I wish the Germans would make a last effort and blow the beastly place up when no one was there. I seriously think that passing my leaves there was a very considerable cause of my final breakdown, it is so lowering and depressing. Like my father, I don't get on in low-lying places. . . . I was an ass to let them buy it. I thought I was being good-natured and unselfish, and I was merely being silly and shirking discussion.

Edward Cecil was to be spared the decision of choosing a future home. Throughout his months in Switzerland he had noted with grim humour the progress of the influenza epidemic that was sweeping Europe. 'I thing Bob should wear a gas mask in the office,' he told Nelly. 'It would give a touch of local colour and is the only really effective remedy. Of course you can have your visitors baked, but they hate it so.' By the autumn a strict quarantine had been imposed on travellers from one Swiss village to another. At the end of September the disease began to spread through the sanatorium. 'I hear it never attacks men over forty-five,' Nigs jested, 'an admirable rule if it is kept to: but I should like an undertaking in writing.' He died on the night of 13 December 1918, aged fifty-one.

Replying to a letter of condolence later that month, his sister Gwendolen wrote:

> I remember the passionate, undisciplined, pleasure-loving boy – very, very dear even in his faults – perhaps counting for all the more because of the heartaches and anxious fears for his future which he

brought. And I contrast it with the man I have known these twenty years – the slave of work, never sparing himself, never seeking or pushing himself, throwing all the force of his vivid temperament and brilliant intellect into the service of others.

He left a gross estate of only £10,059. But the Egyptian government was not entirely forgetful of his widow and daughter. To each it awarded a pension of £141 a year, Helen's annuity being terminable on marriage.

Lord Hugh Cecil
Baron Quickswood
1869–1956

Hugh, fifth son of third Marquess of Salisbury. Created Baron Quicks-
wood 1941. Known to his family and close friends as Linky or Linkey.
Born 14 October 1869. Educated at Eton and University College,
Oxford. Fellow of Hertford College, Oxford, 1891–1936. Conservative
MP for Greenwich 1895–1906 and for Oxford University 1910–37.
Privy Counsellor 1918. Served in the First World War as lieutenant,
Royal Flying Corps. Member of House of Laity, Church Assembly,
1919–45. Provost of Eton 1936–44.
Lord Quickswood died, unmarried, 10 December 1956.

Lord Hugh Cecil's biographer searches in vain for the innocence of
childhood. Almost from the cradle, the youngest of the Prime Minister's
sons bound himself to Anglican principles and Tory creeds. At five he
was reputed to have indicted his nurse as a Socinian, generously conced-
ing that for long he himself had not been quite orthodox. His political
beliefs were no less absolute. Mr Gladstone, a guest at Hatfield in the
early 1870s, was confronted one day by a small boy vehemently rebuk-
ing him for being a bad man. The Liberal leader, who never cared to
let that sort of challenge go by default, put forward an ingenious defence. 'If I were a bad man,' he pleaded, 'your father would not have
asked me here.' Hugh stood his ground. 'My father,' he replied with
deadly precision, 'is coming to kill you in a quarter of an hour.'

By the age of seven he had read all Macaulay's essays and acquired an
historical perspective of his own. In December 1877 he wrote to
Gwendolen expressing satisfaction at the capture of the Turkish town

of Plevna by the Russians. 'I am as joyful as I can be,' he wrote. 'This important event has pretty well cured my cold.' Eight years old, he was already absorbed in two lifelong interests: public affairs and his own uncertain health.

In appearance, too, he seemed hardly to change with the years. His tall, frail figure weighed only seven stone at eighteen and little more at eighty. The face was always pale, bony and ageless, the voice high-pitched and incisive, the eyes alight. His stooping shoulders, his tip-tupping gait, his hands plucking restlessly at his coat: all belonged as much to the Oxford undergraduate as to the Provost of Eton. Family and friends knew him as Linky; his brothers, it was said, saw in him some supposed resemblance to the Missing Link, that hypothetical creature midway between man and ape.

Hugh Cecil believed that controversy, particularly when acrimonious, was one of the privileges of a civilized life. Both intellectually and by temperament he was well-endowed for such a vocation. Hatfield encouraged him to read copiously, though at random; in that vast library he sharpened his mind on whatever came to hand, stored up powder and shot for dining-room debates, delighted more in exposing fallacy than in seeking support for his own impregnable beliefs. As an Eton schoolboy he displayed what Dr Coppini called *'une intelligence prodigieuse'*. At Oxford he took a First Class in History; and although All Souls eluded him, he found compensation in a Fellowship at Hertford College.

The Oxford Union gave him his first public platform. Like all dedicated disputants he did not confine himself to great issues of Church and State, but acquired a mastery of procedure that was obstructive and vexatious and fun. He found a more attentive audience at the Canning Club.

> It is irritating [he told his fellow Tories in 1890] to hear the wrongs of the labourer. Never have wages been higher; never the price of bread so small a part of the workman's daily expenditure. How can he say then that he is badly off? His own improvident marriage is the cause of most of his misery.

An agricultural labourer in 1890 earned a little under fifteen shillings a week. Linky, a lifelong bachelor who lived free at Hatfield until appointed Provost of Eton nearly half a century later, was already enjoying an allowance from his father of £800 a year.

In the last decade of the nineteenth century it was not in itself thought inflammatory for an aristocrat to attribute endemic poverty to the imprudence of the poor. What distinguished Hugh Cecil from other publicists was an ability to express extreme views in the most unacceptable form that could be devised. Thus he would describe marriage with a deceased wife's sister, a union forbidden by canon law but recently allowed by civil law, as 'an act of sexual vice'. And during the Abyssinian crisis of 1935 he confronted Churchill with this unpalatable analysis of his conduct: 'I understand, Winston, that you have become in favour of the League of Nations now that it seems likely to lead to a war.' Churchill was worthy of his steel. 'There is,' he replied, 'a mischievous plausibility in what you say.' Others, less nimble-tongued, were disconcerted by what Cecil himself called 'bowling at their heads'. Kinship was no protection. He once engaged his cousin Algernon Cecil, historian and convert to Roman Catholicism:

> 'Algernon, why have you grown that absurd beard?'
> 'Our Lord grew a beard.'
> 'Our Lord was not a gentleman.'

Linky did not intend his sallies to wound or the weight of his ripostes to crush, and he would be both puzzled and contrite on learning that his pugnacity had caused resentment. There were other touches of Dr Johnson in his character. He relished the dispute no less than the cause, brought his powerful mind to bear as much on trivia as on themes of enduring grandeur; but he had no fine opinion of himself, and those who penetrated his prickly defences found Christian humility and an ultimate sense of failure.

'I hear Linky is quarrelling with his Nonconformist supporters at Greenwich,' Lady Salisbury wrote in 1894. 'That young man's theology is terrible.' It did not prevent his election in the following year as Member of Parliament for the borough; but an obsessive concern with religious questions continued to dominate both his public and his private life. Ambitious for her son's political gifts, his mother had unwisely dissuaded him from taking Holy Orders. Westminster, however, served only to provide him with a more prominent platform than any pulpit. 'I wish he would take up some other subject too,' she sighed on hearing of an impending speech on ritualism, 'but he has no interest in anything else and is becoming narrower and narrower.' Here Bob describes an evening in the family circle at Arlington Street in 1897:

> AJB came to dinner to-night and by some mischance the conversation drifted on to Ecclesiastical politics. Whereupon Linkey denounced Arthur in the most violent way openly accusing him of breach of faith, political incompetence or treachery and threatening immediately to turn him out. At last things reached such a pitch that my father was forced to point out that L.'s business was to

convert and not to denounce and I said that though I agreed with L.'s opinions and with much of what he said, I did not agree with his methods. Thereupon L. became calmer but was still in such a state of excitement as to be unable to take part in subsequent conversation.

Linky was persuaded to send a written apology to his cousin, who with characteristic generosity replied: 'I did not think you at all disagreeable last night; your tiredness must have made you exaggerate in recollection the vehemence of your polemics. . . . I can assure you that *no* frank speaking will ever alter in the smallest degree my affection for you and yours.'

Even in his calmer moments, Linky had few regrets at the intensity with which he spoke on religious subjects. He once admitted how impressed he had been to read that the spiritual revival of the medieval Church could be said to date from the burning of Giordano Bruno: until then, Christians had not cared enough to persecute one another. And he went on to confess that he admired the zeal more than he deplored the cruelty. For Linky, the most insidious enemy of Christianity was not paganism but indifference. With the passion and eloquence of a Cardinal Newman, he would condemn the blurring of identity between revealed Christianity and a vague adherence to the teaching and example of Christ; the apathy that declined to elevate one creed above another; the misplaced fastidiousness that judged it as impertinent to inquire into a man's religion as into his source of income or his marital affairs. 'Many people in England,' he chided, 'think of a Church as a kind of spiritual chemist's shop to which one may send for a bottle of religious grace whenever one happens to want it; they have no sense of belonging to an unseen Kingdom with a loyalty to an unseen King.'

As late as the turn of the century, however, there were still more English children being educated in Anglican and Roman Catholic schools than by the State; and the Member of Parliament for Greenwich was tireless in pressing for State endowment without State control:

> Impartiality between religious bodies [he wrote] is not to be achieved by attempting a compromise based on eliminating the more controversial parts of various religious systems and amalgamating the residuum, but by extending an equal measure of assistance and countenance to all sorts of religious opinion. The problem is to be solved by accepting the parent as the arbiter of his child's faith, and putting the State into the position of the parent's deputy, faithfully carrying out, without bias, the directions that the parent may give, and teaching the child with equal efficiency and zeal whatever religious opinions the parent's chosen denomination may profess.

The Education Act of 1902 which went far towards satisfying his demands incidentally established his reputation as a parliamentary orator. He was not well equipped for the role: the voice was too shrill for sonority, the nervous gestures too distracting. Yet he cast a spell of utter submission over the House. Reverting to the gulf that separates pious agnosticism from true faith, he spoke of those who possess the sensitive conscience of a Christian while unable to accept Christian theology:

> These men, it may be said, erect in the mansions of their hearts a splendid throne-room, in which they place objects revered and beautiful. There are laid the sceptre of righteousness and the swords of justice and mercy. There is the purple robe that speaks of the unity of love and power, and there is the throne that teaches the supreme moral governance of the world. And that room is decorated by all that is most beautiful in art and literature. It is gemmed by all the jewels of imagination and knowledge. Yet, that noble chamber, with all its beauty, its glorious regalia, its solitary throne, is still an empty room.

George Curzon, himself a majestic master of words, sent congratulations from Viceregal Lodge, Simla, and later found a place for the passage in his *Modern Parliamentary Eloquence*. He wrote that it combined 'the charm of music with the rapture of the seer'. Margot Asquith picked Cecil as 'the best young speaker in the House, bold and highly literary, with a first-rate manner and enormous passion in a cool brain'. But such triumphs of oratory took their toll on Linky's frail physique. 'Speechmaking,' he told Nelly, 'makes me ill.'

Hugh Cecil also caught the ear of the Commons by persistently opposing the repeal of the statute that forbade a man to marry his deceased wife's sister. The union, among those declared 'incestuous and unlawful' in 1604 by the canons of the Church, had by the late nineteenth century come to be considered socially oppressive. The Queen herself, hardly a radical reformer in other fields, wished to see such marriages legalized. A tragedy in her own family lent weight to her compassion. Her second daughter, Princess Alice, dying of diptheria in 1878 at the age of thirty-five, left a brood of children to be brought up by the widowed husband, the Grand Duke of Hesse. How satisfactory it would have been had the law permitted him to marry the Queen's youngest daughter, Princess Beatrice, and so provide the children with a loving step-mother. Abandoning any pretence of royal neutrality, the Prince of Wales presented several petitions to the House of Lords in favour of the necessary legislation and in 1896 annoyed the Cecils by helping to carry such a Bill by 142 votes to 104.

LORD HUGH CECIL (1869–1956)

The majority included nearly all the most disreputable peers [Bob wrote to Linky] and people are saying that it is the uprising of vice against virtue.... The result is owing to the violent canvass of H.R.H. The Prince of Wales (confound him) who brought both his brothers down to vote on the same side. Jem says gloomily that when the House of Lords is not frightened by the Commons it gives in to the Royal Family.*

In spite of that victory in the Upper House, the Bill lapsed when the Commons refused to consider it before the end of the session. Linky met each subsequent attempt to enact it with a combination of rhetoric and craft. In 1901 he appealed to the House to uphold a Christian law of marriage which had 'built a causeway across the morass of Eastern shame and lust'. A year later he claimed to be striving 'in an honourable cause to maintain the unstained purity of the most precious, the most ancient and the most essential of all the institutions of mankind'.

His subsequent conduct during that debate of 1902 was on a less elevated plane. Realizing that the second reading of the Bill seemed certain to be carried by a substantial majority of the House, he and a small band of like-minded conspirators resorted to a stratagem. They deliberately dragged their feet through the division lobby, prolonging the count of votes until the measure had exceeded its allotted time and could make no further progress that session. By the summer of 1907, however, a Bill permitting a man to marry his deceased wife's sister had been approved by both Lords and Commons and received the royal assent from its former patron, King Edward VII.

Lord Hugh Cecil refused to surrender. Statute law, he conceded, now permitted certain marriages that were still forbidden by canon law; but he urged that those who contracted such marriages should be allowed neither to wed in church nor to receive Holy Communion. Although he had lost his parliamentary seat in the general election of 1906, he pursued the controversy in the correspondence columns of *The Times*. The newly-sanctioned marital relationships, he wrote provocatively, were 'as immoral as concubinage or bigamy'. He continued: 'I find it hard to believe that any person of Christian feeling or even civilized instincts can wish to inflict the sort of insult that would be involved in using our churches and our services for carrying out what is in our conviction only an act of sexual vice.'

The letter did its author lasting harm. To many, Cecil's interpretation of Christian doctrine seemed almost to exclude the charity of Christ; and even those who shared his dour beliefs recoiled from the

* The Prince was in fact accompanied into the division lobby by one brother, the Duke of Connaught, and his only surviving son, the Duke of York, later King George V.

235

violence of his pen. Certainly he earned no laurels from his sister Gwendolen.

> I am getting a good deal worried about him [she told Maud] so much so that I have departed from my usually inviolable rule of not intruding advice on my brothers. I have just finished composing a letter to him on the use and abuse of language and the dangers of publication and the grave risk he is now running of being classified permanently as 'impossible'.

The most bizarre result of his intransigence was the forfeit unwillingly paid on his behalf by Bob and Nelly Cecil. Linky was among the earliest visitors to Gale, the small country house they built at the very end of the nineteenth century. But he proved a querulous guest. He complained that an excess of iron in the Sussex water gave him indigestion and that the forest was infested with poisonous snakes. ('Do not sit in your garden unless on a very high chair,' he later warned his hostess. 'I have been told that snakes are afraid of the human voice, so you must talk aloud all the time – reciting poetry, perhaps.') What upset him more than either of those hazards was the discovery that the occupant of a nearby estate had married his deceased wife's sister. Linky urged Bob and Nelly not to show them the least cordiality; and when the neighbour's carriage broke down one day on a road near Gale, he swept by in his own without stopping to offer help. The insulted man and wife took an unusual revenge. Along the edge of their property they planted a line of trees that increasingly obscured the Cecil's view of the South Downs. The screen remained for many years, until the estate was sold to another family, who willingly agreed to cut a gap. The name of the neighbouring house was Birch Grove and its new occupant the father of Mr Harold Macmillan.

There was always more than a touch of the schoolmaster about Hugh Cecil, and in Winston Churchill he found his most promising pupil. When they met for the first time at the end of 1898, Churchill felt himself at a disadvantage. The assurance he had acquired in Cuba, on the North-West Frontier of India and at Omdurman was no protection against the dialectic of Linky and his friends:

> They were all interested to see me, having heard of my activities, and also on account of my father's posthumous prestige. Naturally I was on my mettle, and not without envy in the presence of these young men only two or three years older than myself, all born with silver spoons in their mouths, all highly distinguished at Oxford or

Cambridge, and all ensconced in safe Tory constituencies. I felt indeed I was the earthen pot among the brass....

The conversation drifted to the issue of whether peoples have a right to *self* government or only to *good* government; what are the inherent rights of human beings and on what are they founded? From this we pushed on to Slavery as an institution. I was much surprised to find that my companions had not the slightest hesitation in championing the unpopular side on all these issues; but what surprised me still more, and even vexed me, was the difficulty I had in making plain my righteous and indeed obvious point of view against their fallacious but most ingenious arguments. They knew so much more about the controversy and its possibilities than I did, that my bold broad generalities about liberty, equality and fraternity got seriously knocked about. I entrenched myself around the slogan 'No slavery under the Union Jack'. Slavery they suggested might be right or wrong: the Union Jack was no doubt a respectable piece of bunting: but what was the moral connection between the two? I had the same difficulty in discovering a foundation for the assertions I so confidently made, as I have found in arguing with the people who counted that the sun is only a figment of our imagination. Indeed although I seemed to start with all the advantages, I soon felt like going out into St James's Street or Piccadilly and setting up without more ado a barricade and rousing a mob to defend freedom, justice and democracy.

Churchill's stimulating experience prompted him to inquire whether even in his twenty-fifth year he could not embark on a course of study at Oxford. But on being told that he must first pass examinations in both Latin and Greek, he abandoned the plan with regret. 'I could not contemplate toiling at Greek irregular verbs,' he wrote, 'after having commanded British regular troops.' By October 1900, however, he had been elected Member of Parliament for Oldham and at once enrolled in that small band of young, aristocratic, independent-minded Conservatives whose attachment to Cecil earned them the name of Hughligans. Here Bob describes one of their dinners in January 1901 at which he himself was a guest:

We all talked at times so loudly as to remind me of Puys in the old days. And we all argued, Winston more or less *contra mundum*. With much of what he said I agreed. But he has not properly speaking any opinions ... Winston is a journalist and he adopts a view because it would look well in print. Unless he can correct this it will ultimately be fatal to him in politics. On the other hand he is very young and may change greatly. He has none of Linkey's subtlety of mind or dexterity of expression. But he has considerable force and I think

237

courage. He is both original and receptive. His worst defect mentally is that he is a little shallow – satisfied with a phrase.

The alliance between a young Cecil and a young Churchill revived uneasy memories in the Conservative ranks. Neither family cared much for party loyalty. Linky's father had seemingly cut short his own early career by denouncing Disraeli's opportunism. Winston's father had in opposition mercilessly exposed the inadequacies of Conservative leadership and in office all but brought down the government in a moment of pique. Inspired by filial piety, what might the two sons not achieve together?

It was fortunate for the Conservative party that Hugh Cecil and Winston Churchill were at first united by no common theme other than a relish for parliamentary strife. Linky might have been speaking for them both when he wrote: 'The House of Commons that appeals to my imagination is the House of Commons of the eighteenth and nineteenth centuries, with its oratorical figures, its vehement and even violent debates, its impression of the grandeur of historic controversy.' Although Churchill agreed to thwart the passage of the Deceased Wife's Sister Bill by lingering in the lobby, he cared little for such doctrinal disputes. And Cecil lacked the concern for social reform which moved the Member for Oldham to sigh for a middle party, 'free at once from the sordid selfishness and callousness of Toryism on the one hand and the blind appetites of the Radical masses on the other'. Not until 1903 did the two friends embrace a shared political cause with equal fervour: the defence of Free Trade within a party increasingly committed to Tariff Reform. Yet such was the explosive passion of the controversy that it drove Churchill into the Liberal party and Cecil into the wilderness.

An account of the conflict between the two wings of the Unionist party and the fate of that dwindling minority of MPS who refused to compromise their Free Trade principles may be found in the earlier pages of this book.* A few Conservative Free Traders were fortunate enough to find constituencies willing to defy the Chamberlain caucus. Most, however, were obliged to choose between crossing the floor of the House and parliamentary extinction. For Linky, such a choice hardly existed. He was as dedicated a Free Trader as any Liberal; but that was his only affinity with a party whose every other tenet repelled him. 'It is Gladstonian in foreign, colonial and Irish questions,' he wrote; 'non-conformist in ecclesiastical and educational questions; radical in questions affecting labour and capital.' To remain a Conservative might be uncomfortable; to become a Liberal would betray his entire political faith.

* See pages 72–73 and 138–145.

Cecil seems to have felt confident that his intellectual ascendancy over Churchill would ensure the same choice of party allegiance. He was mistaken. In October 1903 Churchill wrote to warn him that before long he intended to join the Liberals:

> I understand your plan very clearly; and it is not mine. I do not want to be enrolled in a narrow sect of latter-day Peelites austerely unbending in economics, more Tory than the Tories in other things. I do not intend to be a 'loyal supporter' of the Unionist party or of this present administration, and I object to be so labelled. . . . You like this sort of thing. You derive a melancholy satisfaction from the idea of being driven out of politics nursing your wrongs. And when I think that no one will be more mercilessly outspoken than you I think you will have your martyrdom as you wish.
>
> But I do not share this view. I am an English Liberal. I hate the Tory party, their men, their words and their methods. . . . Free Trade is so essentially Liberal in its sympathies and tendencies that those who fight for it must become Liberals. The duty of those who mean to maintain it is not to remain a snarling band on the flank of a government who mean to betray it, but boldly and honestly to range themselves in the ranks of that great party without whose instrumentality it cannot be preserved. . . .

Having written that letter, Churchill decided not to send it. But Linky, spending the winter on the Nile for the sake of his health, had only to open an English newspaper to measure the gulf that now separated him from his friend. In December he wrote to Churchill from the British Agency, Cairo, where he was staying as Cromer's guest:

> Your silly letter and speech – especially the speech – make you impossible as a Unionist. . . .
>
> It is not only the folly of the proceeding that fills me with despair. It is your lamentable instability. We have gone into this question ten or twenty times. All the arguments have been considered; and you have assented – sometimes much more than assented – to the proposition that till Parliament met you not less than I ought to keep firm to the Unionist Party and fight the battle from inside. But now in one of your thousand foolish passing moods you wholly abandon this line and fling yourself into the arms of the Liberals. This instability makes you quite impossible to work with; and will unless you can cure it be a fatal danger to your career. . . .
>
> As you know, it is a fixed principle with me not to allow personal considerations to interfere with a political design. To this rule I must

keep and we must be separated. I have for some time foreseen that this would happen after the meeting of Parliament. You have only slightly accelerated what was inevitable. . . .

Winston, however, was too dear a friend to be abandoned at such a crisis in his political fortunes. Linky continued to advise him on parliamentary tactics; and when in March 1904 almost the entire Conservative party insultingly walked out of the Chamber of the Commons as Churchill rose to speak, Linky publicly protested at their unchivalrous conduct. It was no less characteristic that within a day or two of formally taking his place on the Liberal benches, Winston should write affectionately to Linky: 'You are the only person who has any real influence on my mind.'

Four years later Churchill invited his mentor to be best man at his wedding to Miss Clementine Hozier. Linky did not regard his duties as wholly social or administrative. He wrote to Winston:

I earnestly hope you will be both good and happy married; but remember that Christian marriage is for Christians and cannot be counted on to succeed save for those who are Christians. And the marriage vow must be kept altogether – you cannot merely abstain from adultery and leave loving, cherishing, etc. etc. to go by the board.

By then Churchill was President of the Board of Trade in Asquith's Cabinet and Cecil at the nadir of his political career. Throughout the Tariff Reform controversy the Member for Greenwich believed himself to be as much the victim of Balfour's indifference as of Chamberlain's enmity; for all his cousin and leader seemed to care, he might as well have followed Churchill into the Liberal party. Balfour replied to his aggrieved letters in a tone of cold reproof:

Let me say that while I am duly grateful to you for having substituted the epithet 'unfair' for the epithet 'dishonourable', it would really be desirable for you (as for all of us) to carry on party controversy as far as may be without attributing unworthy motives to those from whom at the moment we may happen to differ.

Soon after Churchill's defection Linky admitted that only by prodigious self-restraint could he continue to vote for a Conservative government so blindly wedded to Protection. In the summer of 1905, as the administration slid to its doom, he received an anguished appeal from the Prime Minister. 'I do beg you,' it began, 'even if I die, to remain in the party!!' Linky responded to his call. Yet at the general election of January 1906 Balfour did nothing to dissuade a Tariff Reformer from standing against him at Greenwich and so splitting the Conservative vote. The seat fell to a Liberal. Few letters of commiseration can have brought Linky more pleasure than this:

> I am greatly distressed at your defeat. I am afraid we must take it as a definite decision that high-minded honourable independence, however much recommended by ability, is anathema to our political system, and that Party unalloyed is to rule the roost. Great is the god Caucus, let us fall down and worship him.
>
> However your exclusion will not be for long. One main result of the annihilation of the Tory Party must be that they will drop and drown the cursed theory Protection; and so you will be restored to orthodoxy.

The writer was the discounted Lord Rosebery, who for the past five years had looked indulgently on the Hughligans, entertained them, found a vicarious pleasure in watching them disrupt the established complacencies of Westminster.

'Linky is here and rather low, I guess,' Nelly Cecil wrote from Hatfield a few days after the general election. 'There seems no prospect of his getting another seat at present – or in the visible future.' Nor did Maud Selborne share Rosebery's optimism about her brother's chances of returning to the Commons:

> His intimacy with Winston and his rather erratic voting, combined with his High Church views, cause a good many of the dunderheads to look at him with suspicion. They are not quite sure if he is going over to Rome, or to the Liberal party, and they are quite sure he is a d——d sight too clever to be safe.

Bob, one of the few Conservative Free Traders elected to the new Parliament, interceded with the party managers on his brother's behalf. Bonar Law replied that he would rather let twenty men into the Commons than so troublesome a Tory as Hugh Cecil.

Excluded from the only calling he knew, Linky found himself unemployed at the age of thirty-six. He thought of taking Holy Orders, decided against it; toyed with the proffered editorship of a new church weekly, rejected that too. 'What really distresses me about him', Gwendolen told her sister, 'is that as far as I can gather he is doing nothing. . . . He visits perpetually and eclectically, seeming to go wherever he is asked, living the life of the middle-aged young man of society – which is intolerable with his abilities.' Lady Gwendeline Bertie took a less austere view of Linky's belated plunge into the world of fashion. She wrote in the autumn of 1907 to her future brother-in-law, Winston Churchill:

I have been staying in the same house as him, and he is very delightful, I liked him very much – what is so nice about him is that he is all life and spirit, and he deals so delightfully in those rapid transitions by which one's attention and one's imagination is arrested and excited. He is very instructive, never tedious; his intellect is elevated to a great height, he is wonderfully familiar with all sorts of abstract subjects, but at the same time he conciliates the pretentions of inferior minds, like my own, by dropping down to this level, in to these pursuits and ideas with a naturalness and fervour, which delights his humble listeners, and which above all puts them at their ease, that is a great art, which only the great and clever can achieve, I am sure.

The breathless enchantment which Linky could evoke in the young was not always echoed by their parents, who found him an outspoken guest. When the chatelaine of Avon Tyrrell asked him one morning how he had slept, he replied: 'I was cold, but I remedied the paucity of bedclothes with the hearthrug.' Lady Cynthia Charteris forestalled such a snub at Stanway by offering him a hot-water bottle. 'No, no,' he told her, 'it would disturb the privacy of my couch.' Few other visitors would have thought it necessary to include in a letter of thanks: 'The conversation was surprisingly well sustained and the dishes various and sufficient.' Nor did he hesitate to commend another hostess for her 'charming if parsimonious hospitality'.

Foxhunting was a new-found pleasure of Linky's middle years. Not everybody is born to grace a horse, and the first time Margot Asquith saw his knobbly frame in pursuit of hounds she said: 'Strings of onions.' But in dialectic if not in equestrian skill he could well outpace the hard-riding Leicestershire crowd:

> I used to bump a good deal into the people in the gateways [he confided to Lord Halifax] and they were often rather rude to me. But I told them one day that I did not think they would be so rude if they weren't a little frightened, and that as we were all hunting for pleasure, if they weren't enjoying it, they might as well go home. They seemed better after that.

Sport brought an unexpectedly eighteenth-century flavour to his huge correspondence. Sandwiched between long letters from Balfour on Tariff Reform and even longer memoranda of his own on high ecclesiastical policy may be found a veterinary certificate of soundness for an eight-year-old bay gelding or a note from a groom at Hatfield to say that 'your Lordship's horse Sunrise has been sold for £110'.

With the end of the foxhunting season he could look forward to polo, particularly the tournament held by the Duke of Westminster each summer at Eaton. 'Having no scoffing relative near,' he wrote one year, 'I threw myself into horsey conversation with the utmost relish. It was quite a dissipation.' And he entertained Alice Salisbury with an account of how cunningly he had endeared himself to the Duchess:

I was particularly anxious to please, partly from the large toady element in my character which loves to court the rich and great, partly because I want to have the polo week next year again; but with all my efforts I had to do a great deal with a highly deferential manner and many glances of admiration to eke out the poverty of our joint conversational resources.

Between such exertions he would return to Hatfield, his only home for the first sixty-seven years of his life. On inheriting the house in 1903, his eldest brother willingly continued the arrangement by which Hugh occupied his own small set of rooms. Like all his generation of the family, Linky was aesthetically insensible to most of the fine arts. Neither architecture nor painting caught his imagination except for their historical associations. Music moved him to deplore 'the tyranny of the organist' and to ask a friend if he knew of 'a horrible man called Byrd'. And the furniture which he chose for his private rooms at Hatfield was of penitential design. On that hard horsehair sofa, however, he devoured whole libraries, browsing with the apolaustic ease of a man required neither to earn his living nor keep a family. Reading brought him a solace second only to prayer, although his knowledge of the world, to borrow Dr Johnson's phrase, perhaps suffered from being strained through books.*

Less indulgent hosts than Jim and Alice might have thought him inconsiderate. He was habitually unpunctual for meals, resentful of calls on his ample leisure and indifferent to the domestic routine necessary to run so large an establishment. A late riser, he hated to be disturbed by servants. 'Do you want me, woman?' he would bark at a maid anxiously waiting to make his bed in mid-morning. 'No, m'lord, just seeing if you're up.' 'Well, don't *pursue* me.' He liked a prolonged read in his bath, too, although convinced that there were curious female eyes at the keyhole.

One of Linky's nieces used to compare him with a tree in a protective iron cage; even those who loved him most sometimes hurt themselves

---

* He rarely published his reflections on what he had read unless they touched on current religious and political controversies. An exception was the article he wrote in 1927 on Anthony Trollope's *The Warden*. Beneath the narrative, he detected a veiled satire on leading Anglican prelates of the mid-Victorian Age. Archdeacon Grantley, he surmised, represented the Church of England; his three sons the Bishops of London, Exeter and Oxford; his two daughters the Archbishops of Canterbury and York.

in attempting to penetrate his defences. Alice's nervous request for his appearance on some social occasion would be brushed aside with an air of grievance. On the early death of Lord Percy, an original member of the Hughligans and intimate friend of all the Cecils, Gwendolen wrote to her sister: 'Poor Alice is crying whenever she can do so without being found out by Linky, who is characteristically fierce and snubbing of emotion.' And a telegram from Alice to wish him *bon voyage* as he set out on a cruise at sea evoked the scolding reply: 'Why waste money – now so lamentably scarce – on telegraphing to say good bye, as if I ever relished that gloomy ceremony. . . . You have long been an addict to the telephone and these evil habits are connected.' Yet he was devoted to Alice, and when she died he could not bear to speak of her or of the old days at Hatfield.

Only with children did he establish a perfect relationship. He delighted in educating young minds, but on an apparent footing of complete equality; he took immense pains to teach clarity of thought and precision of language, but so amusingly that it hardly seemed like a lesson at all. Lord David Cecil has recalled how at thirteen he once described somebody as 'good'. His uncle inquired what he meant.

David: 'Someone who makes other people happy.'
Linky: 'Any capable licensed victualler can do that.'

He caught the interest of his little nephews and nieces by a stimulating turn of phrase. Who else would have illuminated an account of an adventure in a bus with the phrase: 'By then I was at what I call the west door'? Or on being asked to admire a glorious sunset, would have replied: 'Yes, extremely tasteful'? Linky's poetry readings were also memorable. 'He must have known those people very well,' one of his listeners observed after a recital of Keats.

Christmas inspired him to display his full repertoire. From informal tutorials in theology and metaphysics he would pass to an annual and much applauded rendering of 'You should see me dance the polka'; then, still wearing a comic paper hat, to animated talk on the perils that beset Church and State.

Those locust years away from Westminster did nothing to moderate Cecil's beliefs. Both publicly and in private he continued to disparage Balfour's vacillating leadership, until even his own family were tempted to disown him. 'I must say Linky's attitude to Arthur enrages me,' Selborne wrote to his wife in June 1907. 'Can you wonder that Unionists don't jump at him as a candidate? What a contrast between your father's reserve and silence and Linky's hysterical rushing into print.'

Like his brother Bob, who sat uneasily for St Marylebone, Linky hoped that political salvation might lie in a new political party of the centre, composed of Conservative Free Traders and moderate Liberals. In March 1908 Bob told his brother that Balfour 'was very much distressed evidently at the idea of my joining Rosebery and said with great candour that it was open to you and me to destroy the Tory Party'. It is unlikely that Balfour could have taken the threat so seriously. Rosebery was by then lonely and discredited, growing ever more moody and irresolute. Dining with him a few years earlier, Bob himself had noted his exceptional vanity:

> I escaped to look at his pictures. He followed me. 'That (pointing to one of Pitt) Charlie Carrington would give me, and put that inscription on it. (Pitt to Carrington 1795, Carrington to Rosebery 1895.) I tried my best to stop him,' and so on. It was all rather entertaining. I think he is injured, among other things, thinking of himself as one of the great men of Pitt's time with a 'connection' which could make or unmake ministries.

Balfour was no less aware of Rosebery's failings, and a more plausible interpretation of his apparent concern is that he wished to spare his Cecil cousins a fruitless political journey.

The exaggerated weight which Linky attached to Rosebery's name led him into one of the oddest episodes of his career. Still without a seat in Parliament, he wrote in October 1909 to King Edward VII's private secretary, Lord Knollys, about the impending rejection of Lloyd George's Budget by the House of Lords:

> It may be that they are imprudent and that they would do better to pass it; but things are as they are. The crisis that will follow the rejection will be formidable; and it is plain that if we are to escape without the serious weakening, if not the destruction of the House of Lords, no means must be omitted to secure a Unionist majority or at worst a very great reduction of the present Liberal majority at the ensuing general election. No one can prophesy what the electors will do. But this seems to me certain: that Lord Rosebery is more likely to lead them against the Budget and in the defence of the Lords than any other man. I am not of course forgetful of Mr Balfour's great powers: but those powers are rather parliamentary than popular and he does not possess Lord Rosebery's gift of arresting the attention of the public. Nor I think has Mr Balfour to the same degree the confidence of moderate and central-minded men.
>
> If then – and it is here that I fear you will blame me as audacious and impertinent – it were possible that a Ministry headed by Lord Rosebery could come into being, the chances of success for the Lords

at the elections would be, as our ancestors said, on a broad bottom. It might comprise men of all shades of thought who are opposed to the Budget. It would be in all probability only of a temporary character: it would preside over the elections, and if the result was a Unionist majority of at all a decisive kind, it would naturally give place to a Government of the ordinary party type. I have already gone too far or it would be possible to say how all this might come to pass without breach of constitutional propriety.

The scheme was indeed 'audacious and impertinent': also perilously unconstitutional. The King certainly possessed the theoretical right to dismiss Asquith's administration and to invite Rosebery to form a new ministry such as Cecil envisaged. But not for 126 years had a sovereign dared to eject a prime minister whose party commanded a majority in the Commons.* And even if Edward vii could have been persuaded to act so rashly, Asquith would have fought the subsequent election not on the issue of the Budget alone but on the misuse of the royal prerogative. What remains curious is that the experienced and cautious Knollys should have given the least encouragement to the plot. No reply is to be found in Cecil's papers; yet Knollys must have discussed it with him, for a few days later he received a second letter from Cecil:

> In respect to your objection touching Lord Rosebery's want of nerve, frankness is best in matters of importance – so let me say that what I rely on in my own mind is that Lord Rosebery would probably include me in his Government and that I could make up for this single defect in his qualifications for the task.

That excursion into fantasy was as near to power as Hugh Cecil ever approached. For whatever Rosebery's 'want of nerve', his experience of high office, including sixteen months as Prime Minister, had taught him the realities of political change. On learning from Linky of the role intended for him, he replied:

> I thought I knew all your brilliant qualities, but did not credit you with so much imagination. . . . I remain where I have been ever since I resigned the leadership of the Liberal party in 1896; certainly where I have been since 1905; that is outside the party game. my feelings towards which I could not describe in terms fit to be perused by the eminent Churchman whom I am addressing. . . . I am not obliged to be a barrel organ like the party man. I have said my say, and have no more to say unless fresh circumstances arise.

* It has sometimes been alleged that William iv dismissed Melbourne's ministry in 1834. Later historians conclude that the King did no more than accept a contingent resignation.

Now as to your principal project, it implies:

1. The initiative of the King, than whom I know no one less likely to undertake it.
2. Ministers to serve, and a party to support them, of whom I cannot see a symptom.
3. An influence of mine in the country as to which I am wholly sceptical.

These are three serious obstacles, added to my own abhorrence of office! But I acknowledge that I have always thought that the right outcome of this crisis was a united anti-socialist temporary government, but I never could name its components....

That was the end of the matter. The Lords duly threw out the Budget, Asquith demanded a general election and the country returned him to power with a majority which, although reduced, sufficed to keep him in Downing Street for seven more years.

The increasingly radical programme of the Liberal ministry also helped to save both Linky and Bob from political isolation, perhaps extinction. In the abstract, the Cecils preferred Conservatism to Liberalism and Free Trade to Tariff Reform. In practice, they believed, there was little to choose between Liberalism allied to Free Trade and Conservatism compromised by Tariff Reform. But not even the allurement of Free Trade could persuade them to tolerate a government that favoured land taxes, an emasculated House of Lords and Home Rule for Ireland. Hence their ultimate willingness to return to the Conservative fold, even if that obliged them to swallow a small dose of Tariff Reform.

Linky was nevertheless fortunate to be adopted in 1909 as Conservative candidate for Oxford University;* an industrial constituency might have shown more reluctance in absolving him of his Free Trade heresy. It had long seemed to him a desirable seat. He was after all the son of a Chancellor of the University, and as a Fellow of Hertford College since 1891 had followed Oxford's perpetual controversies with relish. One of the two sitting Members, Sir William Anson, constitutional historian and Warden of All Souls, proposed to stand again at the next election. The other, the Right Hon. J. G. Talbot, first elected in 1878, intended to retire. A nephew of Lord William Cecil's predecessor as Rector of Hatfield, Talbot wrote gracefully to Linky as early as November 1907: 'In resolving, as I have done, to surrender the great Honour of my Life, it will be an immense satisfaction if I can feel that it will

---

* Since 1603 the Universities of Oxford and Cambridge had each elected two Members of Parliament, known as Burgesses. Similar representation was later extended to the graduates of other universities in the United Kingdom. All university seats were abolished by a Labour government in 1950 and not revived by subsequent Conservative administrations.

come to your hands, where it must receive so much greater distinction, though I think no greater affection.'

By May 1909 a committee had begun to collect pledges of support on Cecil's behalf. He could depend on the votes of many heads of house, although Macan, by now Master of University College, regretted that his old pupil was neither in favour of the Territorial Army nor against female suffrage. Non-resident graduates who declared themselves for Linky included the Archbishops of Canterbury, York and Armagh, nineteen other bishops, seven deans, eighteen archdeacons, 114 canons and a host of lesser clergy. They were joined by the Oxonian head-masters of all the great public schools except Joseph Wood of Harrow. Eton's Head Master, Edward Lyttelton, happened to be a Cambridge man. His predecessor, however, Edmond Warre, came forward. ('I have no politics', he used to say, 'but I vote Conservative because I think it is safer for the country.') Among professional politicians, hardly a single orthodox Conservative was yet prepared to support him; Cecil's accep-tance of qualified Tariff Reform had come too late to dispel years of accumulated resentment. The canvass that continued throughout the summer nevertheless showed a steady swell of opinion in his favour, and it seemed possible that he would be elected unopposed.

On 20 June, however, in the smoking-room of All Souls College, Professor C. H. Firth bet his fellow historian Charles Grant Robertson half a crown that Lord Hugh Cecil would not be returned as Burgess at the next election. Within a very few days Professor Firth had assumed the chairmanship of a committee to promote the candidature of Arthur Evans, the archaeologist. Its *eminence grise* was that experienced medd-ler L. R. Farnell, Fellow and afterwards Rector of Exeter College, whose invitation reached Evans as he was excavating Knossos:

> Hugh Cecil, whom no other constituency will look at, neither the Unionists because he is a Free Trader nor the Radicals because of his reactionary sacerdotal views, is being forced upon us by the High Church ecclesiastical party, who have duped a lot of others into supporting them on the ground that he is a very striking personality in the House. . . . He is in no sense, either by performance, occupa-tion or intellectual outlook, fit to be representative of a University that is trying to reform itself and to rise in the world.

Farnell went on to ask whether Evans would enter the impending contest as a Tariff Reformer and as an advocate of university reform. The acceptance of the role by Evans caused astonishment. His daughter Joan, also a distinguished archaeologist, later wrote: 'Of all men of any intelligence, he was the last who was fitted to represent a constituency. He had a profound contempt for forms and procedure; he was a halting, involved and inaudible speaker, and he had no respect whatever for mass opinion or the party system.' His already slender chances of defeating Cecil were further diminished by Macan. The conversion of Evans to Tariff Reform, he reminded the electors, must have been extremely recent, for at the general election of 1906 he had openly worked in Berkshire for the return of a Liberal Free Trader.

By mid-December 1909 the canvassers estimated that Cecil would attract more than 3,600 votes, compared with only 600 for his rival. Shortly afterwards Evans withdrew his candidature. In the following month the country went to the polls, Linky was returned unopposed as junior Burgess for Oxford University and the Regius Professor of Modern History lost half a crown.

'I'm a little distressed about Linky,' Bob Cecil wrote in December 1912, nearly three years after his brother had resumed an interrupted career in the Commons. 'His position in the House is no doubt not what it was, and I fear he feels it. Especially does he resent being left out of the Party Council, to which I am summoned.' Even those Conservatives who shared his dread of modernism in religion and egalitarianism in politics regarded him as an uncertain ally. One day he would hold the House entranced with the magic of his eloquence: the next invoke some shabby trick to obstruct a division or silence an opponent. Here is a passage from one of the speeches in which he defended the House of Lords against Liberal assault:

> I look upon our Constitution with something much more than the reverence with which a man of good taste would look upon an ancient building. I look upon it as a temple of the twin deities of Liberty and Order which Englishmen have so long worshipped to the glory of their country. Let us then go into the temple, con over its stones, and saturate ourselves with its atmosphere, and then, continuing its traditions, let us adorn and embellish it. So we too shall partake of something of its renown, our figures will, perhaps, be found in it, and our names be graven on its stones. In this way we shall attain to a measure of its immortality and nigh on the eminence of its glory our fame will stand secure, safe from the waters of oblivion, safe from the tide of time.

By contrast, here is how Violet Asquith described that reverent worshipper of the Constitution during a later stage of the Parliament Bill:

> The House was more densely crowded than I had ever seen it, and my father got a tremendous reception as he walked up the floor, members of our side waving hats and handkerchiefs. But through

the deafening cheers I began to hear shouts of 'Traitor', and when he rose to speak he was greeted by an organized uproar. For half an hour he stood at the box while insults and abuse were hurled at him by a group of Tory members led by Lord Hugh Cecil and Mr F. E. Smith. There was a background chorus of 'Divide, divide,' against which articulate shouts and yells rang out – 'Traitor!' – 'Redmond–!' – 'Who killed the King?' I could not take my eyes off Lord Hugh Cecil, who screamed, 'The King is in duress!' and in his frenzied writhings seemed like one possessed. His transformation, and that of many other personal friends, was terrifying. They behaved, and looked, like mad baboons.

Winston Churchill, who in a letter to the recently crowned King George v called it 'a squalid frigid organised attempt to insult the Prime Minister and to prevent debate', nevertheless tried to keep alive his old intimacy with Linky. He wrote from the Home Office at a moment of particular tension:

I was offended by your neglect to answer my letter, because I thought it was an act of disdainful rudeness arising out of your political feeling. I am very glad indeed to find that I had no right to draw such an inference: and I am grateful to you for a letter which clears the matter wholly from my mind. ...

It would need much more fierce antagonisms than those who now distract us to destroy the admiration and affection which I have felt for you: and while you are no doubt right in your present mood in wishing to suspend personal relations, I shall always hope we may continue to think of each other with kindness and charity.

Two weeks later, however, Churchill felt obliged to deliver a short lecture to the Member for Oxford University on the gravity of obstructing the popular will:

If you care about the ancient British Constitution, you have an easy way of preserving it. Make it equal and fair to both great parties. Place your House of Lords on the same broad basis of national acceptance that the Monarchy has come to occupy. After all it ought not to be beyond the reach of wit and goodwill to make a reasonable provision for resolving a deadlock between the two Houses. But war policies and peace policies cannot be mixed; and while I see no disposition even to recognise the intolerable ill-usage we have received in the last five years or to seek an honourable settlement on a fair basis, I am well content to ride that good war-horse Veto forward on the shortest and straightest path I can find. Be careful not to get in his way.

Both men professed to care about the British Constitution with equal fervour; but they did not mean the same thing. Churchill so revered parliamentary democracy that even as a heavily burdened Prime Minister with almost dictatorial wartime powers he would never neglect the Commons. Cecil relished the high drama of Westminster, but had little faith in its collective wisdom. 'The formidable fact,' he wrote, 'is that the highest authority of our immense and unequalled Empire lies alternately in the hands of one or two knots of vehement, uncompromising and unbalanced men.' Hence his alarm at the determination of Churchill and his Liberal colleagues to protect radical legislation from the veto of the Upper House. It was not that Cecil believed the Lords to be inherently wiser than the Commons: but they were irremovable until death and thus independent of popular pressures.

His innate suspicion of change led him to enrol in the Tory ranks not only the peers but also the crown:

Conservatism ought to take up the task of preparing public opinion for the idea that the Monarchy should openly take an active part in politics. Doubtless any such assumption of activity after the long interval of years in which the Crown has been screened from all criticism would be attended by many obvious perils; but though less obvious, the danger of Monarchy becoming discredited as an inoperative ornament and sinking slowly from being the centre of loyalty to be received, first with good-natured toleration and finally with impatient contempt, is perhaps now the more real menace. An active Monarchy would incur the enmity of many, but it would enjoy the respect which in the long run is only given to acknowledged power.

Again and again he returned to his reckless and literally irresponsible doctrine. In 1909 he tried to persuade Knollys that Edward VII should replace Asquith by Rosebery; in 1911 he wanted George V to reject Asquith's demand for a creation of Liberal peers large enough to ensure the passing of the Parliament Bill; in 1914 he would gladly have seen the King withhold the royal assent from the measure giving Home Rule to Ireland. He refused to recognize that such a revival of arbitrary power could well mark the end not of the Lloyd George Budget or of the Parliament Bill or of Irish Home Rule, but of the Monarchy itself. Nor was he prepared to consider the result of releasing from constitutional constraint a Sovereign who happened to be of radical disposition: such a King as might frustrate Conservative legislation, even dismiss a Conservative Prime Minister.

That plea for a more powerful Monarchy was one of Hugh Cecil's few political aberrations. On most other themes he embraced a staid nineteenth-century Toryism that owed much to the inspiration of Edmund Burke. He paid homage to his mentor in a little volume entitled *Conservatism*, published in 1912 and unhappily the only book he ever wrote:

> In the first place Burke insisted on the importance of religion and the value of its recognition by the State.
>
> Secondly, he hated and denounced with his whole heart injustice to individuals committed in the course of political or social reform.
>
> Thirdly, he attacked the revolutionary conception of equality, and maintained the reality and necessity of the distinctions of rank and station.
>
> Fourthly, he upheld private property as an institution sacred in itself and vital to the well-being of society.
>
> Fifthly, he regarded human society rather as an organism about which there is much that is mysterious.
>
> Sixthly, in close connection with this sense of the organic character of society, he urged the necessity of keeping continuity with the past and making changes as gradually and with as slight a dislocation as possible.

Those half-dozen sentences could well serve as Cecil's own political epitaph. And the skill with which he expanded them into a persuasive apologia delighted the two scholars who had commissioned the volume for the Home University Library. Gilbert Murray wrote to the author: 'It is a most brilliant and sympathetic book, and extraordinarily just and free from any partisanship or unfairness.' H. A. L. Fisher told him: 'Two points struck me as being particularly valuable, first your protest against injustice to the individual, and secondly your demonstration that competition can never really be eliminated.' Both editors were dedicated Liberals.

Linky sent a copy of *Conservatism* to Winston Churchill in April 1912, receiving in return a belated present of a silver pencil 'as a souvenir of my wedding and of our association in former days, which was of such great value and pleasure to me'. But the political gulf separating the two men was by now too wide to be bridged by friendship. For the next twenty years they hardly ever corresponded and rarely met except on public occasions.

The parliamentary battle for Irish Home Rule, particularly Asquith's refusal to exclude the Protestant loyalists of Ulster from its provisions, once more roused Cecil to impassioned ingenuity. He was warned by his brother not to try the gambit of howling down the Prime Minister. 'If there is to be a row,' Bob wrote, 'it must be done by the Ulster men.

I do not think English opinion would approve of F.E. or you taking an active part in disorder. But we ought to be ready at all times to say to the government, "See what comes of tyranny".'

Linky, however, still had an armoury of neater devices at his command, all of them depending on an impregnable Conservative majority in the Lords. 'I very earnestly hope,' he noted in May 1914 'that the utmost advantage will be taken of all the intricacies of procedure between the two Houses, which the Parliament Act has so greatly complicated, in order if possible to wreck the Bill.' Linky's first suggestion, contained in a memorandum to his fellow conspirators two months later, was indeed adroit:

It seems therefore that there is a flaw in the Parliament Act. For the rejection by the House of Lords for the third time, on which the presentation of a Bill for Royal Assent depends, may not, if the Lords choose merely to adjourn the Bill from day to day, take place until Parliament is prorogued. But when Parliament has been prorogued, it is too late to give the Royal Assent.

The decision of this question lies with the Speaker. He has to endorse on a Bill which is to be presented for Royal Assent under the Parliament Act, a certificate stating that the requirements of the Parliament Act have been fulfilled. If he refuses to certify that the Home Rule Bill has been rejected by the House of Lords for the third time, it cannot be presented for the Royal Assent. What he will decide no one knows.

There is serious doubt as to whether, if the House of Lords do not reject the Home Rule Bill but merely adjourn its consideration from day to day, the Bill can be presented to the King for Royal Assent under the Parliament Act.

The Parliament Act says that a Bill which has fulfilled the required conditions (two years consideration and three passings in the Commons) shall on its rejection for the third time by the House of Lords, be presented for the Royal Assent; and the Parliament Act also declares that a Bill shall be deemed to be rejected, if the House of Lords shall not have passed it. . . .

But within two weeks, Great Britain was at war, and the Tory peers did not press their plan. In any case, as Linky discovered several years later, Speaker Lowther was prepared to thwart such sophistry by certifying that the conditions of the Parliament Act had been met.*

* 'Speaker Lowther', Linky wrote in 1922, 'is of course a man of the most brilliant ability; but I believe that he quite mistook his vocation. He would have been a most valuable Minister of the Crown; but he was, I truly think (I speak of modern times), the worst Speaker that has occupied the Chair. . . . He was on the side of officialdom and officials against Members of Parliament and free criticism.'

Another Cecilian stratagem rested upon the belief that the House of Lords could physically prevent the Home Rule Bill from being presented for the royal assent by directing the Clerk not to relinquish the document for endorsement by the Speaker. After long discussion, Austen Chamberlain, Walter Long and Edward Carson were tempted to use the weapon and so extract a concession from the government on behalf of the Ulster Loyalists. But when neither Lansdowne nor Bonar Law would support the plot, it was abandoned. The Home Rule Bill received the royal assent in September 1914, although its operation was suspended for the duration of the war. 'Not for the first time, I am afraid,' Linky wrote of the Conservative leader in the Upper House, 'Lord Lansdowne's want of nerve at a crisis was a mischief.' Who but Linky would have dared give so distinctive a meaning to the word mischief?

Before 1914 was out, Linky had attached himself to the Royal Flying Corps: not in the senior administrative role to which his age and parliamentary service would have entitled him, but as a pilot under training. It was an astonishing choice. Except for occasional placid tours by bicycle he had never shown the least interest in mechanical objects. Balfour's early motor cars had positively frightened the life out of him. 'We expect to put on cousinly mourning before long through that infernal machine of Arthur's,' Nelly wrote in 1899. 'Linky trembles at the thought of it, and resolves to be confined to the house with a very bad cold the next time he stays at Whittingehame.' When he came to write his *Conservatism*, published only two years before the outbreak of war, he chose the aeroplane as a symbol of those unknown perils which the sensible man would do well to avoid:

> We read an account of an accident to a flying machine in which the aviator has been killed. It seems a foolhardy affair to us; how can men trust themselves so recklessly among such dangers? For our part we do not mean to go flying till there shall have been a great deal more experience of these machines. We do not understand how they work or what their strength or weakness is, and we have no leisure to learn. Plainly they are dangerous at present. We will let flying alone; a motor-omnibus is fast enough for us.

Yet here he was at the Royal Flying School, Netheravon, 'toying with the sensation of fear, which is not altogether unpleasurable'. He told Alice in the New Year of 1915: 'I have felt as in a dream – or as after death: and I should wish to go on with the experience as far as I could in spite of a sense of unreality.' To another sister-in-law he wrote:

'Simple flying does not seem difficult to learn – much easier than bicycling: but then a fall from a bicycle does not matter.'

By April he was at Shoreham, where the nearness of the badly sited aerodrome to the river caused the clumsy machines to bump, even to stall, as they flew alternately over land and water. To these hazards Linky brought his own. Once he extricated his sleeve from the controls only just in time to pull out of a steep and apparently fatal dive. Another day he repeatedly found it difficult to keep the wings of his plane horizontal as he came in to land. So he took to the sky again, circling round and round while he applied his fine logical mind to the matter. Eventually he concluded that one of his legs had more muscular power than the other and that he was inadvertently putting unequal pressure on the two sides of the steering-bar. Having solved the problem, he touched down like gossamer. On 11 April 1915 he wrote modestly to Alice Salisbury:

> Yesterday, after ten days waiting on the weather which blew in the most obstinate way, we got a calm afternoon and I took my 'ticket' successfully. I have been frightfully slow but in the end did it quite respectably with three good landings. So now I am an aviator though not a 'pilot': my instructors thinking that it would take an immoderately long time for me to pass the Central Flying School – if I could do it at all.

It is doubtful whether he ever again flew alone; his family affected to believe that he received his certificate only by promising never to make use of it. But his hours in the air were not wasted. To have tamed those primitive machines in middle age awoke some latent chord of chivalry in his bleakly rational mind, gave him a more romantic cause than politics. He was proud to think of himself as one of a band of brothers, and on leaving Shoreham presented a silver cigar-box to the officers' mess of No. 14 Squadron, Royal Flying Corps. Dean Inge helped him to compose its Latin inscription: *'Nuper sodalis semper amicus.'* ('Recently in comradeship, always in friendship.') Linky also asked the Royal Aero Club to confirm that he was the first Member of the House of Commons to possess an aviator's ticket.

Until the last months of the war the Burgess for Oxford University rose no higher than lieutenant, a rank which many officers half his age had already put behind them. Jim, by contrast, was in 1915 raising a division for Kitchener's armies, Bob blockading Germany from the Foreign Office, Nigs wielding exceptional powers in Cairo; even William would soon become a diocesan bishop. Yet the most nimble-minded Cecil of all felt neither resentment nor humiliation at his own unspectacular progress. Service in a *corps d'élite* was not to be measured in terms of ambition.

From the War Office, where he spent some weeks helping to select would-be aviators, he was posted to the headquarters of Hugh Trenchard, the near-legendary commander of the Royal Flying Corps on the Western Front. As a member of the general's small personal staff, he formed a lasting admiration for that able and visionary but difficult and taciturn man, always more at ease visiting his airmen in the field than entrenched behind a desk.

The atmosphere of the mess might sometimes have grown oppressive but for the lively mind and high spirits of Maurice Baring. A pre-war diplomatist of literary tastes, he served Trenchard as private secretary, French interpreter and irreplaceable confidant. His wit was touched by a glorious mad logic. He would inquire suspiciously while buying a sheet of stamps: 'Are they fresh? They are for an invalid.' And when asked to suggest a Latin motto for the newly formed Tank Corps, he replied: '*Nihil obstat.*' Within the Royal Flying Corps, Baring's foibles made him scarcely less of a hero than Trenchard. Visiting one of the Squadrons, he insisted on declaring open a new circular saw by cutting his uniform cap in half: and was only prevented from sacrificing his tunic by being carried away on the shoulders of cheering spectators. Meals in the GHQ mess could melt even Trenchard's reserve. There was a memorable evening when Hilaire Belloc dined after lecturing to the troops. Knowing his friend disliked mutton, Baring bought some crayfish and gave special orders that they were to be served to Belloc alone. But when the mutton was brought in, a mess waiter handed round the crayfish as a vegetable. Everybody took one, and only two were left for the extremely hungry lecturer. Belloc is unlikely to have gone entirely without entertainment that evening, for Baring could always be persuaded to perform his party piece: balancing a full glass of port on the flat top of his bald head.

Such farce may have been rather broad for Linky's fastidious taste; but he too had his following. A brother officer in the Royal Flying Corps later wrote in his memoirs:

> The superior intellect of Hugh Cecil dominated the whole place. It was one of the most outstanding things I remember in my life. I knew he was a distinguished speaker in the House and a big figure in British politics, but this didn't mean a thing to us in the mess. It was simply that he completely dominated us by virtue of his intellect, debating ability, charm and courtesy.

J. T. Moore-Brabazon, the author of that tribute, had in 1909 become the first Briton to fly a heavier-than-air machine under power;

Although his flight lasted hardly more than a minute and ended in a crash, it entitled him to Pilot's Certificate No. 1 of the Royal Aero Club. Part of the war he spent at Trenchard's headquarters as a pioneer of air photography. Linky liked his courage, his ingenuity and his independence. (To an officious major who reminded him that he must obey the order of a superior officer, Probationary Second-Lieutenant Moore-Brabazon replied: 'Superior officer? *Senior*, if you please, Sir.') And the younger man, like Winston Churchill before him, valued the stimulating course of adult education which Linky delighted to dispense. He wrote to his mentor, on leave in the summer of 1916: 'Send me some good books if you can think of any to stop that parrot-like cry you were so wont to use – "How ignorant you are." My literature at present is the scandal column of the *Daily Sketch* and *Motor Cycling*, so that I am not up in the very latest thought.*

Linky was always generous with his advice. Another member of Trenchard's staff had, while still a civilian, consulted him on the most critical decision of his career. Linky made a note of it on 4 August 1914, the day Great Britain and Germany went to war:

A singular episode occurred last night. While sitting in the House about 8 p.m. I got a note from the Attorney-General, Sir John Simon, asking me to come and speak to him. I went and he then said to me in strict confidence that he was in doubt about his duty; that he was very averse from war; that he thought Grey so saturated with his diplomatic friendship with France and antagonism to Germany that he did not quite trust him; that Winston was animated by 'something worse' – I suppose a desire to attack Germany and make an end of her fleet; that he did not think Grey's speech altogether convincing; that he understood my feeling was also against the war and that he would be glad to know my opinion.

I said that I hated war and jingo rhetoric made me sick; that I did not much like or approve the triple entente; that I thought Grey's speech extremely able and skilful tho' not in all points quite sound. But that . . . we were bound by treaty to support Belgium and defend her neutrality and that I advised him to remain in the Government and not weaken it at such a moment. . . .

We talked on these lines for about twenty minutes or longer. I talked too much, being tired and excited, which prevented him

* Persuaded by Linky to enter politics, he successfully stood for the Commons in 1918, becoming parliamentary private secretary to Winston Churchill in the following year. His career continued to flourish until in 1942, as Minister of Aircraft Production, he made an indiscreet speech about Russia at what he believed to be a private luncheon. Churchill felt obliged to relieve him of his office. In the same year he was created Lord Brabazon of Tara, taking for his armorial supporters two gulls which do not touch the ground.

saying as much as perhaps he might have said. . . . In the end he brought the interview to a close by saying that he thought he saw where his duty lay. Today he has not resigned.*

Simon, by now Home Secretary, had a second crisis of conscience in January 1916. He could not bring himself to support the Bill imposing military conscription. This time he resigned from the government, voluntarily abandoned a successful law practice to join the Royal Flying Corps and was posted to Trenchard's headquarters in France. He adapted himself less well than Linky to his new role. The ice-cold intellect that later carried him to the Foreign Office, the Treasury and the Woolsack mastered the problems of aviation with remarkable speed; but he did not easily rid himself of a juridical manner that irritated Trenchard profoundly. When the general handed him a telegram one day, telling him to deal with it urgently, the former Attorney-General replied primly: 'Perhaps, after studying the relevant facts, some form of future action may be advisable.' Soon, however, he acquired brisker habits and became a hardly less indispensable member of Trenchard's staff than Baring.

The value of Cecil and Simon to Trenchard lay as much in their continuing Membership of the Commons as in their military competence. For, like other senior commanders, Trenchard was obliged to fight two quite separate but often simultaneous campaigns: one against the enemy in battle, the other against political denigration at home. To retain a pair of loyal and experienced parliamentarians on his staff was no more than prudent. And in the spring of 1918 both played a part in one of the most convulsive episodes of Trenchard's career.

A few months earlier Cecil had been recalled to London to help General Smuts prepare a report for the War Cabinet on the future of British air power. It recommended that the Royal Flying Corps, a branch of the Army, should amalgamate with the Royal Naval Air Service to form an independent Royal Air Force under the control of a newly created Air Ministry. Trenchard, although reluctant to abandon his command in France, agreed to become the first Chief of Air Staff, with headquarters in the requisitioned Hotel Cecil. Whatever happy associations that name might evoke, he soon discovered that the Air Ministry lacked the harmony of Hatfield. The Secretary of State for Air was Lord Rothermere, the newspaper owner, a man of imperious temperament who repeatedly made decisions of high policy without

---

* In another note made on 4 August 1914, Linky wrote: 'It is regrettable that the advocates of peace almost always seem silly and the advocates of war almost always vulgar.' Simon dwelt on his dilemma in *Retrospect*, the volume of memoirs he published in 1952, but does not refer to any conversation with Hugh Cecil.

consulting his principal official adviser. Trenchard thought his conduct
not only personally offensive but also damaging to the Service. And on
receiving no satisfactory reply to his complaints, he struck back at
Rothermere by offering his resignation. After much anxious discussion,
the War Cabinet authorized the Secretary of State to accept it.

Linky at once sprang to the defence of his hero and master. In
a memorandum which, he admitted, was 'mainly derived from
what General Trenchard has told me in friendly conversations', he
wrote:

> It is of course true that he is a man of a high-strung, nervous
> temperament, conscious of great powers and of great achievements,
> and with the natural desire to have his own way which belongs to an
> able and successful man. Yet he is very far from being stubborn and
> obstinate; a man of tact and courtesy would not have had the
> slightest difficulty in working with him and in persuading him to
> adopt new ideas. But Lord Rothermere, without real knowledge and
> with a low standard both of manners and truthfulness, vexed him
> beyond endurance.

That memorandum, sent or shown to potential political allies, was
not Linky's only weapon. Between Trenchard's offering of his resignation in mid-March and its acceptance a month later, he entirely abandoned the reticence which military discipline normally imposes on any
serving officer. No more than a subaltern in rank, he lobbied members
of the War Cabinet, including Milner and Smuts, emphasizing the
damage to RAF morale that Trenchard's departure would cause
and pleading for the sacrifice of Rothermere in his place. Trenchard
himself did not quite hold aloof from these manoeuvres, offering Linky
copies of his official correspondence with the Secretary of State, 'to
try and show you that I acted properly'. He added: 'I would like to say
thank you – it is no use my saying more.' On the following day, however, Linky received a very different sort of letter, to which he replied
in kind.

15 April, 1918

Air Ministry, Strand
S.W.1.

Dear Lieut. Lord Hugh Cecil,

I am told that you personally approached a Member or Members
of the War Cabinet with the object of influencing him or them to
reject proposals in connection with organisation and command in
the Royal Air Force, which, in my capacity as Secretary of State, I
had submitted to the Prime Minister.

I cannot believe that, holding as you do a junior officer's

commission in the Royal Air Force and a staff appointment in this office, you would take such a step but in view of the report which has reached me I should be obliged if you would be good enough to place the matter beyond doubt.

> Yours very faithfully,
> Rothermere

15 April, 1918

> 20 Arlington Street,
> S.W.1.

Dear Lord Rothermere,

I have received your letter of today's date and have read it with some surprise. I am a Member of Parliament and am in that capacity accustomed to approach ministers and discuss with them all sorts of matters of public interest. I am also on terms of personal friendship with many of them. I am afraid that I cannot enter upon any discussion with you about what I may or may not do in relation to Ministers of the Crown in the course of my parliamentary duties or in private conversation with my personal friends.

> I am,
> Yours faithfully,
> Hugh Cecil

16 April, 1918

> Air Ministry, Strand
> W.C.2.

Dear Lieut. Lord Hugh Cecil,

I am not interested in the fact that you are a Member of Parliament. It is no concern of mine.

I am, however, concerned in the report which reaches me that you, a Lieutenant in the Royal Air Force holding a staff appointment in this office, have approached members of the War Cabinet urging them not to accept recommendations made by me as Secretary of State for the Royal Air Force in a secret memorandum which I sent to the Prime Minister.

In the interests of the discipline of the Royal Air Force, I must ask you to make a full and satisfactory explanation. The matter is most pressing. Neither myself nor anyone else can possibly hope to maintain any form of discipline here or in the Air Force generally if junior officers, although senior in age, continue to act in the manner which you, from your letter, tacitly admit you have done.

> Yours very faithfully,
> Rothermere

17 April, 1918

20 Arlington Street,
S.W.1.

Dear Lord Rothermere,

I received your letter of yesterday's date. But I fear I have nothing to add to my former reply.

My relations with Ministers of the Crown are of course parliamentary; they arise, that is, out of my functions and position as a Member of Parliament. It does not seem to me that it would be useful or desirable to enter into any discussion with you about what may or may not take place in the course of these parliamentary relations.

I am,
Yours faithfully,
Hugh Cecil

Rothermere sent no direct reply. Instead he gave orders that Lieutenant Cecil should instantly be relieved of his staff appointment at the Air Ministry. His victim thereupon hastened to take his revenge on Rothermere in the Commons; on 22 April, with the support of John Simon, he pressed the Leader of the House for an early debate on the Trenchard episode.

Within twenty-four hours Rothermere himself resigned as Secretary of State for Air, his health and spirit broken by overwork and the death in battle of his two elder sons. It is significant, however, that his original letter of resignation to the Prime Minister specifically mentioned his two tormentors by name. 'Why in the House of Commons', he demanded of Lloyd George, 'should they flout disciplinary codes where elsewhere similar conduct by any other Staff Officer would form the subject of enquiry by his superior officers?' Rothermere was persuaded by his friend Lord Beaverbrook to delete that passage, which could only inflame the controversy; and Austen Chamberlain, a member of the War Cabinet, similarly pleaded with Linky not to pursue his vendetta:

Will you forgive me for presuming on our friendship to make an appeal to you as to your own conduct? I understand that you and Simon were serving on Trenchard's staff, and I venture to press very earnestly upon you that under these circumstances it would be improper for you to use your position as a member of the House to take part in the controversy. I feel that if you can bring yourself to look at the matter from a detached point of view, you will recognise that you cannot, as Member of Parliament, properly criticise or attack the Minister at the head of your Service. The position of a Member of Parliament like yourself is a difficult one, but if he accepts service on the staff of the administration, he surely must forgo his full Parliamentary liberties.*

Neither on constitutional nor on personal grounds would Linky withdraw from the debate; and, although disclaiming any wish to be provocative, he entered into an ill-tempered squabble with Lloyd George that robbed his speech of grandeur. It was left to John Simon, who spoke only after much heartsearching, to make a cooler and so more effective eulogy of his old master. Trenchard was grateful to his pair of parliamentary liegemen, but not unhappy at returning to France a few weeks later with the command of a strategic-bombing force. In 1919 he resumed his former appointment as Chief of Air Staff, retaining it with distinction for the next ten years.

Hugh Cecil's demobilization with the rank of captain did not end his interest in the Royal Air Force. Soon after the war he accepted the chairmanship of a committee reporting on the education and training necessary for flying men, and sat on another committee inquiring into the law and rules of procedure for courts martial. At Trenchard's pressing invitation he also became chairman of the RAF Memorial Fund.

Not everybody shared his encouragement of peacetime flying. When in 1921 the government offered to sponsor a university air race between the undergraduates of Oxford and Cambridge, the Vice-Chancellor of Oxford proved querulous. With Linky's entire approval, the contest was therefore removed from his reach. It took place near London during the long vacation and under the patronage of the Duke of York, later King George VI. The senior Burgess for Oxford felt no remorse at having thwarted the embodiment of university authority. For the office of Vice-Chancellor was then held by Dr Farnell, the don who eleven years earlier had vainly plotted Linky's defeat at the polls.

In the New Year of 1918 Linky was appointed a member of the Privy Council. Two of his brothers, Jim and Bob, had already been similarly honoured by virtue of the ministerial offices they held. But it was rare for a back-bench parliamentarian to be admitted to the Privy Council and probably unique in military history for a serving lieutenant to add the prefix Right Honourable to his rank and name. Lloyd George, currently being urged by Lord Salisbury to curb the prodigality of political honours, must surely have found an elfin pleasure in bestowing his patronage on the House of Cecil. Yet none thought it undeserved. In just such a picturesque way as reflected Linky's love of the past, it

---

* Such a conflict of loyalties can occur only in time of war. In peace, no serving member of the Armed Forces may sit in the House of Commons.

21 Violet Maxse: a sketch by Sickert. The daughter of Admiral Frederick Maxse, a noted atheist and Radical, she was married to Lord Edward Cecil in 1894. Lord Salisbury was alarmed by her precociousness. 'Hatfield', he warned her, 'is Gaza, the capital of Philistia.' The Cecils sent her to be instructed in Christianity by the Bishop of London. 'I spent some hours with him,' Violet wrote, 'and I was not asked to go again.'

22 This sketch of Lord Edward Cecil by Leslie Ward reveals something of the inner melancholy that lay behind his high-spirited humour.

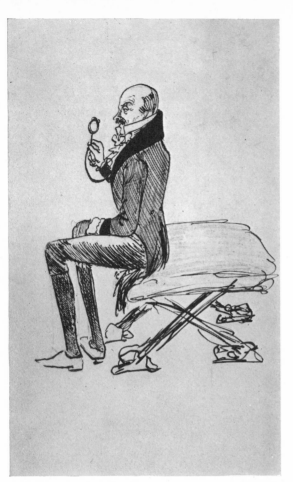

23, 24 Lord Hugh Cecil, sketched at
two fancy-dress balls by Lord Basil
Blackwood, the illustrator of
Hilaire Belloc's *Cautionary Tales*.
For a man immersed in grave
matters of Church and State he took
an unexpected delight in society.
But he could be a disconcertingly
outspoken guest and once
commended a hostess for her
'charming if parsimonious
hospitality'.

25 Four of the five Cecil brothers painted at Hatfield by F. H. S. Shepherd in 1928. The picture was commissioned by the Master of University College, Oxford, where all four brothers had been undergraduates. *Left to right:* Lord Hugh Cecil; Viscount Cecil of Chelwood; James, fourth Marquess of Salisbury; Lord William Cecil, Bishop of Exeter.

26 In 1936 Lord Hugh Cecil became Provost of Eton College, an appointment similar to that of Dean of a cathedral. He had long believed that controversy, particularly when acrimonious, was one of the privileges of a civilized life. Eton brought him many rewarding opportunities for the practice of his art and the exercise of a lifelong contempt for schoolmasters. This photograph was taken soon after he had been created Lord Quickswood on the recommendation of his old friend Winston Churchill.

27 Lady Gwendolen Cecil, photographed by Lewis Carroll. The girl who caught the fancy of the ageing Disraeli 'in the wild grace of extreme youth' never married. Instead she became a trusted private secretary to her father. Her knowledge of politics was prodigious, but an utter lack of method obliged her to take forty years in writing four volumes of the Prime Minister's life. She died aged eighty-five, her task uncompleted.

28 The Prime Minister's two daughters: Maud, Countess of Selborne and Lady Gwendolen Cecil. 'There are only men in that family', a French visitor observed of Hatfield. In strength of character Maud eclipsed even her own husband, a much respected Cabinet minister and British High Commissioner in South Africa.

recognized the courage and independence of his parliamentary life.

Nearly all his causes were in defence of liberty: the freedom to obey one's own will and conscience rather than the will and conscience of others. It was, he believed, the creed not of anarchy but of moral discipline. To allow a person to choose between right and wrong, between wisdom and foolishness, was for him the essential condition of human progress and, in its perfection, the consummation of that progress. He developed the point in a lecture at Edinburgh University in 1909:

> Virtue is attained in proportion as liberty is attained: for virtue does not consist in doing right, but in choosing to do right. This is the great distinction, surely, between the animal and man. The animal always does right; it cannot do wrong. But it has no virtue, for it lacks the indispensable power to choose between right and wrong. The animal, though it never does anything but right, remains without virtue; but a human being is capable of wrong as well as right; and because he is capable of wrong his virtue is real virtue and not the mere performance of righteous acts.

He conceded that it was sometimes the duty of the State to impose restrictions. But he likened all such curbs on the liberty of the individual to the bandages that support a strained limb: however necessary, they tended to weaken and to cramp, and were best removed at the earliest possible moment. Thus even an insistence by the State on compulsory education stunted the growth of parental responsibility and authority. As successive governments of all political shades increasingly claimed the right to erode personal liberty in the name of social and economic progress, Linky's voice would as regularly sound a note of reasoned dissent.

During his early years in the Commons he once dismissed a manoeuvre of Campbell-Bannerman with the scornful words: 'There is no more ungraceful figure than that of a humanitarian with an eye to the main chance.' No such ambiguity clouded Cecil's attitudes, which might have been expressly designed to affront public opinion. Even in peace they sometimes seemed perverse; in war they could be made to appear unpatriotic. Thus in 1915 he threatened to throw up his flying career in order to denounce a government plan imposing total prohibition on the nation. It was not that he doubted the widespread loss of industrial production caused by drunkenness – Lloyd George called it a deadlier foe than Germany – or wished to discourage temperance. But he resented intensely the intrusion of the State into what ought to remain a matter of personal decision. 'The prohibitionist', he wrote, 'destroys true temperance. Temperance consists not merely in abstaining from getting drunk, but in choosing to abstain from getting drunk. There is no temperance except where it is open to a man to get drunk and he deliberately refuses to do so.'

He displayed the same polemical agility in opposing military conscription. Two years before the war, when Lord Roberts asked him to support a policy of national service, Linky replied with a memorandum that from any other pen would have seemed decidedly cheeky. He told the veteran Field-Marshal that preparation for war was largely a waste of time, as the unknown factor of generalship practically decided the issue; that defeat was less serious than it seemed, for it never really destroyed a nation; that Great Britain had always flourished in spite of inadequate military preparations; and that national service would have a prejudicial effect on the character of the British people. Mounting casualties on the Western Front during the first eighteen months of the war failed to convince him that he was wrong. To the prejudices of an amateur Clausewitz he added the faith of a Christian. Cynthia Asquith, a daughter-in-law of the Prime Minister, overheard a furious exchange between Linky and Charles Whibley, the literary critic:

'There is nothing fine in killing, but there is something fine in being killed, and conscription takes that away.'
'Epicure! Do you want boys of eighteen slaughtered to satisfy your aesthetic greed?'

Once compulsory military service had been introduced, Conservative colleagues were no less exasperated by his tenderness towards conscientious objectors. 'We are Christians first and Englishmen afterwards,' he told the House of Commons in November 1917. 'Christianity can never compromise with any national claim.' He did draw a distinction between the man who sincerely believed that to bear arms was wicked and the man who evaded his duty either from sloth or fear; one he would allow the right to undertake some approved form of non-military service, the other he would imprison. But as Archbishop Davidson pointed out to him, there was a class of objector

absolutely refusing any kind of public service, direct or indirect, which would facilitate the carrying on of the war . . . e.g. making boots or digging potatoes . . . The conscience of the man seems to me in these cases to mean simply his abdication of the duties of a citizen to the corporate life of the communion to which he belongs and whose civilized order he enjoys.

The degree of conscience, Linky urged, should be determined by a non-military tribunal; and he wanted an end to those opinionated inquisitions which 'have entered into long casuistical discussions, and put hard cases in order to show the objector what a fool he is'. Members as patient and sympathetic as his eldest brother, chairman of the supreme appeal board, were not easy to find. But the administrative reforms proposed by Linky were both humane and practical. He asked that no objector be enlisted in the Army until his case had been either upheld or rejected by a civilian tribunal; thus the military authorities would be spared the degrading task of imprisoning men who might later be vindicated. He also spoke out against a proposal to deprive conscientious objectors of the vote. In the same courageous vein, he demanded the release of all those who remained in prison after the end of the war. 'I do so,' he wrote to *The Times*, 'not so much for the sake of the objectors as for the sake of the nation now involved in grave wrong-doing.'

Yet his efforts to preserve the liberty of the individual against the pressures of public opinion or of a coercive government sometimes led him on to dubious ground. In 1917 he protested at the prosecution by the National Society for the Prevention of Cruelty to Children of a father who had refused to allow an operation on his child's dangerously enlarged tonsils. And five years later he rejected Baden-Powell's request for help in introducing legislation that would protect the name and dress of the Boy Scouts. Linky maintained that everybody, even Communists, should be free to imitate that admirable movement.

Cecil's vagaries of belief and behaviour unsettled some of his Oxford constitutents. The Dean of Christ Church warned him in 1918 that his howling down of Asquith seven years before and his recent expressions of concern for conscientious objectors had evoked resentment. Nevertheless, Dr Strong added: 'The tradition here is against dislodging sitting members unless they have done acts of monstrous impiety – like Mr Gladstone.' Linky took no chances. To establish both his sobriety and his patriotism, he wrote a letter to *The Times* in his best amplifying style:

> The war must be fought till it end in the submission of Germany. . . . In familiar language we seek to 'abate their pride, assuage their malice, and confound their devices'; for their pride made them strive to dominate the world, their malice has defiled both land and sea with murder, and their devices, untiring if also unskilful, have been traced in every land, stirring up discord and violence and revolt.

That seems to have dispelled any lingering doubts of his soundness. It evoked the congratulations of George Curzon and a request from the Bishop of Carlisle for it to be read from every pulpit in the diocese.

At the general election of 1918 he was returned to the Commons with a comfortable majority. And although Lloyd George rejected Churchill's suggestion that Linky should join the post-war coalition as Under-Secretary for War, the Member for Oxford University was as busy as at any time in his life. A succession of memoranda offered ingenious solutions to the problems of the day. The congestion of parliamentary business was to be relieved by the establishment of provincial councils; the coal industry pacified by allowing the miners to acquire two-fifths of the capital of each company; Ireland united under an independent sovereign appointed from among the princes of the House of Windsor. His belief in the civilizing role of the British Empire also led him to inquire about the future welfare of the African population of Southern Rhodesia when in 1922 the territory seemed likely to be absorbed into the Union of South Africa. The Colonial Secretary, Winston Churchill, wrote soothingly:

> There is no occasion to apprehend that the natives will be ill-treated. The importance of the native problem is fully recognized by all responsible people in the Union. . . . You will no doubt agree that the suggestion that Imperial control over native affairs should be retained even if Southern Rhodesia enters the Union is hardly practicable.

He was less inclined to influence the domestic affairs of his constituency and resisted most demands for reform. Dean Inge, who sat with him on the governing body of Hertford College, described him as 'obstructive'. Linky himself used to say: 'A university is like a very old cheese. Whatever you do to it makes it worse.' But his arguments against schemes of supposed improvement were always cogent and never dull. Thus he opposed degrees for women not because he wished to deny them as sound an education as men but because he thought their presence in a university to be socially enervating:

> What I value in Oxford [he told Nelly] is principally what may be called nervous intensity. No doubt there are great drawbacks in this. It leads to nervous breakdown, and it leads to drunkenness and riotous evenings in the colleges. But the benefits far outweigh these disadvantages. It produces a certain sort of temperament which, as far as I know, is not to be obtained in any other way; and it makes the ancient universities the seed-beds of movements of great importance to the community. This function is already much interfered with by the presence of the wives of Fellows, who have relaxed the tension very considerably. . . . And if there were a great flood of female undergraduates, almost all that is valuable in the university

would be destroyed for men and would never come into existence for women.

He relished all those questions of ceremonial which clung to his ancient office. In 1922 he was annoyed to discover that neither he nor his fellow Burgess, Sir Charles Oman, had been invited to join a University delegation in presenting a formal address to the King. There was a stiff exchange of letters with his old enemy Farnell, the Vice-Chancellor, from whom he extracted a promise that the Burgesses would always be summoned in future.

Twelve years later he complained to another Vice-Chancellor that for the Proctors to have marched ahead of the Burgesses in the annual Encaenia procession was 'a violation of precedent and of the law and custom of the University'. He added ingratiatingly: 'The discourtesy was so gross that I do not doubt it was inadvertent.' Months of correspondence failed to resolve the issue, until the Vice-Chancellor, F. J. Lys, was unfortunate enough to plead that the Proctors had intended no slight to the Burgesses, but merely conformed to the custom of Cambridge.

> What in the world has Cambridge to do with us? [Linky demanded]. We claim to be the older and the greater University and do in fact by law take precedence of Cambridge. Why should we imitate its customs? Forgive me if I say that an appeal to the example of Cambridge seems very unworthy and ignominious on the lips of a Vice-Chancellor of Oxford.

His rebuke continued:

> I must now consider what step ought to be taken to vindicate those rights which you admit but the expression of which you violate. One rough but efficient way of bringing the matter to an issue would be that the Burgesses should attend at the next Encaenia, should insist on their right of precedence and take their accustomed place. If you remove them by force, they would of course have their right of action against you for assault and claim nominal damages and they might obtain a judicial decision. This remedy would have the disadvantage of causing a great deal of talk and fuss in the newspapers, which we probably would all dislike. It would also be expensive. But on the other hand I feel bound to bear in mind that I am the guardian of the rights of my office and must not suffer those rights to be invaded while they are in my keeping.

His old friend Lord Halifax, to whom he sent a copy of the correspondence, slyly egged him on: 'Unofficially, and not as Chancellor, I think your letter is quite perfect. I read and re-read it with great delight. Do keep me informed of developments.' Oxford, however, was spared a public brawl among her higher dignitaries. A few weeks later the Vice-Chancellor conceded defeat. He wrote to Linky in January 1935:

I propose during the brief remainder of my tenure of office, in order to avoid any dispute, to use the authority which I am thought to have to arrange that the Proctors, since you do not like their accompanying the Vice-Chancellor, shall not go before the Burgesses, and I hope that you will be satisfied with this.

Linky accepted his submission graciously; and when a new Vice-Chancellor took office, he prudently secured a renewal of the promise.

On another front, however, he suffered a setback. Sir Charles Oman, his fellow Burgess for the past sixteen years, decided to retire from the Commons at the general election of 1935. To run in harness with Linky for the two-seat constituency, the Conservative committee selected C. R. M. F. Cruttwell, Principal of Hertford College and like Oman a military historian. His success seemed assured. At every general election since 1910 Linky and his Conservative partner had topped the poll, with Gilbert Murray, the Liberal candidate, invariably in third place. In 1935 the prospects for the two Conservatives appeared particularly bright. Murray did not stand and the Labour candidate could depend on little support. Then an intruder appeared. A. P. Herbert,* one of the most versatile humorous writers of the day but a serious social reformer, put himself forward as an Independent. Nobody rated his chances high. When, however, the votes were counted and distributed under the system of proportional representation used in university constituencies, one seat went to Cecil and the other to Herbert. Poor Cruttwell, with less than one-eighth of the first preference votes, forfeited his deposit. Linky was mortified by the defeat of his Conservative partner but even more by the victory of a man who proclaimed his intention to press for the reform of the marriage laws.

Soon after the result had been announced, Herbert wrote politely to the senior Burgess: 'As your most unworthy junior, may I congratulate you on your return and great majority. I should be very grateful if you could tell me if there are any particular courtesies or formalities I ought immediately to observe.' Linky replied: 'Thank you for your very kind

* He and Linky had already met more than once. As part of a campaign to have the licensing laws made less restrictive, Herbert, not yet an MP, challenged the right of the Houses of Parliament to suspend such regulations within the Palace of Westminster. Linky agreed with him that a matter of constitutional importance was a stake and offered to provide evidence by buying him a whisky and soda in the House of Commons bar at 11.20 one morning. Herbert, however, could find no court prepared to test the issue to its end.

congratulations. I wish I could reciprocate them, but sincerity obliges me to say that I deeply and keenly regret, on public grounds, your election to the University seat.' He then added several pages of most useful advice.

At a meeting of Lloyd George's Cabinet in the last year of the war, an impassioned letter from Hugh Cecil was read out, protesting against a proposal to conscript priests in Ireland. 'He considers religion an essential occupation,' Bonar Law observed cynically. Linky would have accepted the sneer as a compliment. From childhood to old age, the faith of a Christian pervaded and sustained his life. He liked to borrow a metaphor from his flying days, declaring that a man who flouted moral laws would suffer just such a penalty as the aviator who scorned the laws of aerodynamics; retribution might not be as swift but it would ultimately be as sure. He reproved honest doubt hardly less sternly than apostasy. When a clergyman pleaded that there were some aspects of divine will which he could not possibly know, Linky replied sharply: 'Then you ought to try to find out. You always throw a cloak of assumed humility over your ignorance to excuse your persistent intellectual indolence.' He failed to see why the Bible and the teachings of the pious down the ages should not lead others to his own position of spiritual security within the Church of England.*

Theologically, he found no great gulf between his own High Anglicanism and the creed of the Roman Catholic Church; he accepted, for instance, the Real Presence in the Eucharist. But he could not subscribe to a religion which interposed other human beings between individual Christians and their God. He was further separated from the Roman Church by his view of the Reformation, that sixteenth-century convulsion which gave birth to the Church of England. He described it as 'a movement originally divine and emanating from the Holy Spirit, though, like many other movements – like indeed all His actions in the Church – perverted and corrupted by human error and not impossibly by diabolic intrusion'.

If the Devil continued to mislead Christian minds, it was through no lack of vigilance on Linky's part. 'What we want to revive,' he urged in 1921, 'is belief in a God, Sovereign, Law Giver, Judge, Avenger, and see His Will as an inexorable law of righteousness.' Although never known to have contemplated matrimony, he was obsessively concerned to preserve the Christian laws of marriage. Just as he described marriage

---

* He disliked the name Protestant Reformed Church, by which the Church of England was known in Statute Law, for aesthetic rather than historical reasons. 'It is a jejune description of your religious society', he told Halifax, 'to announce that you disagree with somebody else and were once worse than you are now.'

with a deceased wife's sister as 'an act of sexual vice', so he branded a man who divorced an erring wife as 'an accomplice in her adultery'. The provision of the Marriage Amendment Act of 1920 allowing divorce after three years' desertion evoked his particular scorn:

> What we have to do is to discover the mind of God. Can anyone seriously suppose that in the mind of God remarriage is lawful after three years' separation, but adulterous and unlawful after two years? ...
>
> If the State is of opinion that the Christian law of marriage is too hard for a world that has ceased to be Christian, it should allow licensed unions to which all the legal consequences of marriage would attach, though not recognized by the Church ... What is now sought is that all sorts of unions, which under the teachings of Christ are adulterous, should be recognized as marriages by Christian people and the Church.

His argument was logical but lacking in compassion; and when in 1937 he demanded legislation to prohibit the use of the marriage service for all divorced persons, he received almost no support in the Church Assembly.

In the course of a long correspondence about divorce, Nelly Cecil put a pertinent question to her brother-in-law:

> Why are you so severe only about the ethics of marriage? I don't find the married state singled out in the same way in the Gospels and Epistles. St John seems to make no moral distinction between the lust of the flesh and the lust of the eyes and the pride of life. ... We of Mayfair and the country houses worship money, comfort, food and physical beauty. Is that Christian?

Adultery, he replied, was a grave social mischief, in the same category as murder or theft; and his purpose in censuring it was not to pass moral judgement on his neighbour but to uphold the fabric of society.

In his relish for religious controversy, Linky was in fact more vulnerable to quite another charge: that he lacked perspective, and would as readily condemn an unconscious lapse of taste as a mortal sin. Thus in 1920 he discovered 'an anti-Christian bias' in the plans for cemeteries drawn up by the Imperial War Graves Commission.

> The only references to religion [he wrote] are in connection with the religious symbols which the relatives of the fallen are to be permitted to put upon the headstones, and these symbols are referred to as though they were of much the same importance, or perhaps of not quite so great importance, as the regimental badges.

No man was more a master of the offensive parenthesis than Linky. Again, in complaining of an official proposal to commemorate the war dead of India by erecting a Mohammedan mosque and a Hindu temple in France, he wrote of those religions in language that could not fail to give pain.

A few years later he sought to put an end to the use of the crypt chapel of the Houses of Parliament for the service of baptism. He did not let off the Speaker lightly:

> If you will read the title, opening rubrics and the later part of the service in the P.B., you must surely see how improper and unseemly it is to use the service in a deserted and secularized crypt, shared with schismatic baptisms, not from any religious or charitable motive but in order to gratify the vanity of M.P.s who are to have the exclusive right to these secluded and pandenominational baptisms, just as they have to tea on the terrace: tea and baptism being much the same sort of thing – something that may be the opportunity for adding an exclusive amenity to others enjoyed by M.P.s. Happy M.P. who may have his baby christened in the crypt and with a choice of rite (episcopal, presbyterian, etc.) and can then entertain the select christening party (representing *pro hac vice* the whole Catholic Church) to tea on the terrace – with a choice of teas (China or Indian).

'As regards your religious objections to the ceremony of Baptism being performed in the Crypt Chapel,' the Speaker replied, 'I do not share them, but still think it is a matter which may be left to the spiritual consciences of the parents of the child concerned.'

Nothing eluded Linky's liturgical eye. As an occasional worshipper at a church some dozen miles from Hatfield, he was distressed that at Holy Communion the vicar administered the consecrated wine in separate glasses. So he wrote to denounce the practice as 'unscriptural, unprimitive and uncatholic'; and of course he sent a copy of his admonition to the Bishop of London. The vicar replied with spirit, justifying the abandonment of the common cup on grounds both of health and of pleasant usage. 'Can unity or the sharing of the sufferings of Christ be in any sense dependent upon the use of any particular symbol?' he asked Linky. 'I cannot think that it is the Will of Christ that we should do in His Name what we would not dream of doing at any other time.'

Few clergy were prepared to stand up so sturdily to Linky's inquisition. 'I would rather see any bishop on the bench walk into church when I am preaching,' one of them wrote, 'than see Lord Hugh Cecil sitting in a pew.'

Throughout the post-war Coalition, Linky grew increasingly mistrustful of Lloyd George's leadership. The sale of honours, the spoliation (as he called it) of the Welsh Church, the use of irregular troops in Ireland, ministerial hostility to the League of Nations: all drove him to cross the floor of the Commons with his brother Bob and to sit uneasily on the opposition benches as an Independent Conservative.

Almost simultaneously, however, he acquired a new and absorbing interest. He became a founder member of the National Assembly of the Church of England. Established at the end of 1919, with wide powers of ecclesiastical legislation, the Assembly was composed of bishops, clergy and laity. Linky relished a second arena where Christian principles as he saw them could be defended by forensic logic and an artful grasp of procedure. His skill in those fields was already known, and an invitation to draft the standing orders of the Assembly ensured that he should play a permanent and commanding role in its business.

Long years in the Commons had taught him that any gathering of six hundred delegates, most of whom were used to exercising authority in their everyday lives, required self-restraint, particularly if the rights of those holding unpopular views were to be preserved; hence his insistence on the technicalities of procedure, some of which his critics thought burdensome or pedantic. He never forgot the true function of the Church Assembly. When in 1921 Bishop Winnington-Ingram complained that it did not touch the heart of the people, Cecil replied that he did not want it to touch the heart of the people. The Assembly, he continued, was not the voice of the Church of England and could not be so while it spoke for only fifteen days of the year. It ought to be thought of as a mechanism doing very important work, but not work which touched the heart of anybody. Its purpose was first, legislative, and secondly, financial.

In the half century that elapsed from the inaugural meeting of the Assembly in 1920 to its supersession by the General Synod of the Church of England in 1970, Parliament approved more than 150 of its measures and rejected only four. Yet without the discipline and brevity which Linky strove to impose, its legislative programme would again and again have foundered.

Randall Davidson, Archbishop of Canterbury and the first chairman of the Assembly, could be more obstructively fluent than most. Hensley Henson wrote of him: 'His Grace has an inveterate habit of adding qualifications to every apparently clear declaration, until the final impression left is entirely different from that originally made. I call it the habit of *prophylactic verbiage.*' Linky pressed an early copy of standing orders on the Archbishop, who replied: 'I am most grateful to you for the mighty volume with which you have endowed me for study and guidance. I have already plunged into its pages, though it would require a long life to read them all.' One of the tests by which Linky measured a prelate's worth was possession of 'that rather strange power, a natural sense of procedure which resembles an ear for music'. Neither Davidson nor his successor at Canterbury, Cosmo Lang, earned many marks; William Temple did better; and Geoffrey Fisher did best of all.

Lang once paid a teasing tribute to Hugh Cecil as 'both in place and in person the power behind the throne, ready to rebuke any lapses into irrelevant pleasantries or even into common sense'. The role of procedural commissar was unofficial, but accepted by the Assembly with no more than an occasional growl of resentment. Punctiliously polite to members who privately sought his advice, he could be down-right rude to the Assembly as a whole. This sort of exchange puntuates the official record:

> Cecil: 'The Assembly has been wasting its time deplorably this morning. Nothing that you have done or are doing this morning matters at all, except the instructions to the committee to enable them to bring forward something which does matter.'
> Lang: 'I entirely object . . .'

He once said of certain proposals: 'They are simple, but in the sense that the village idiot is simple, being ungoverned by any rational principle.' On another occasion he warned the Assembly against 'a notion that the moral witness of the Church consists in uttering, very loudly, platitudes that no one disagrees with'. He considered the bishops to be the worst offenders against clarity of thought, and epithets such as 'sloppy' and 'gaseous' easily escaped his lips.

Rarely did he speak of the episcopal bench without a disobliging qualification. 'Our bishops,' he declared, 'are men of great personal holiness, but they are terribly unprincipled.' Sometimes he castigated them with banter, as when he said: 'The House of Lords does much more harm to the bishops than the bishops do to the House of Lords.' But he could also be savage. During his last years in the Church Assembly he resisted a proposal that incumbents of benefices which had ceased to exist as a result of wartime or post-war reorganization should lose part of their income through no fault of their own. The sponsor of the measure happened to be Geoffrey Fisher, Bishop of London, whom Linky chastized with a line of Kipling:

> I cannot think that anybody who has a conscience or who believes in the Eighth Commandment can have much doubt about the propriety of the preamble. It was said of the late Lord Haldane that his

spiritual home was Germany. The spiritual home of the Bishop of London must be 'somewheres east of Suez, where there aren't no Ten Commandments'.

Fourteen years later, as Archbishop of Canterbury, Fisher took a Christian revenge. At the first meeting of the Assembly after Linky's death, he deliberately broke the rules of procedure in order to pay tribute to the memory of an old antagonist.

'You should be gazetted as a Brevet Archbishop,' an admiring peer wrote to Hugh Cecil. In his reproofs to the Assembly he was certainly as authoritarian as any prelate. He demanded not only an orderly agenda, clarity of thought and conciseness of speech, but also an abstention from those social, political and economic questions to which there were no specifically Christian solutions. Such self-indulgent debates, he urged, both wasted time and detracted from the prerogative of the Assembly in ecclesiastical matters. He believed for instance that unemployment could not be cured in a way wholly satisfactory to the Christian conscience; that it was impossible to escape from the evils of competition without encountering the evils of regulation; that it was therefore futile and wrong for so inexpert a body to flourish its supposed palliatives.

In the Church at large he disapproved no less of parochial instruction on the problems of modern life. The duty of the clergy, he claimed, was to teach their flock the Christian principles of love, goodwill and charity. But when they ventured on to the topical application of those principles, they were all too often betrayed by ignorance. Bishops, of course, he thought more culpable than most. 'They constantly try to be encyclopaedias, but become jacks of all trades and masters of none.'

The equation of Christianity with socialism was a perennial irritant. Linky conceded that the New Testament addressed emphatic warnings to the rich and pronounced blessings on the poor; what he denied was that a doctrine seeming to exalt the poor over the rich necessarily contained the elements of socialism. The socialist, he maintained, sought to improve life on earth by redistributing material wealth; the Christian, by contrast, concerned himself with riches only as a spiritual peril that could prevent his inheriting the kingdom of heaven. The socialist believed that it was better to be rich than poor, the Christian that it was better to be poor than rich.* That, as Linky wrote in his

---

* Linky used to say that of all his acquaintances he could recall only one who combined immense wealth with an amiable temperament: Sir Philip Sassoon (1888–1939), First Commissioner for Works in the Cabinet of Neville Chamberlain. He, however, was not a Christian, but a Jew.

book, *Conservatism*, did not absolve the Christian from abhorring the evils of competitive capitalism:

Christ was not a social reformer, but the Christian is driven to become one. For the Christian disciple, finding himself bound by the rule that he must love his neighbour as himself, warned with the utmost emphasis of the dangers of riches and of their selfish use, looks round upon the world and sees a condition of his fellow men intolerably reproachful to his conscience, terribly menacing to his peace of mind.

The antipathy of the Cecils to Tariff Reform was roused less by economic theory than by distaste for the grasping commercialism of its adherents. Linky similarly deplored capitalism not for its inequality of reward but for its inherent self-interest:

No change in machinery will meet this criticism, for what is amiss lies in the character of those who work the system; or rather the system is the expression of men's partly defective characters. It requires, therefore, a change in human character to satisfy the Christian objection to the competitive organization of trade and industry. Socialism does not pretend to change human nature. It claims only to substitute the action of a regulating State for the working of competition.

Believing that virtue consists not in doing right but in choosing to do right, Linky found no merit in socialist designs to mulct the rich for the benefit of the poor:

To relieve distress is the duty of all Christians: to abandon all wealth may be the duty of some: but these acts of self-denial lose the only thing that gives them their Christian character if they are done by compulsion. From the standpoint adopted in the Gospels, riches are in themselves nothing; but they may be the means of dragging down their owners into selfishness, or they may give an opportunity to their owners of practising love by self-sacrifice. The mere transference of material wealth from one pocket to another is a thing which Christianity ignores as indifferent if done by just means, and rebukes as dishonest if done by unjust....

Christian self-sacrifice is altogether wanting in such a transfer. The State sacrifices nothing; and the rich are merely victims of confiscation. They are impoverished but still selfish; for compulsion can be no remedy for selfishness. The very idea of unselfishness is voluntary. Like mercy, its quality is not strained. Compulsory unselfishness is an absurdity, a contradiction in terms.

275

Gwendolen Cecil was exasperated by her brother's 'more than French passion for logic and incapacity for looking on either side of the narrowest path'. She added in a letter to Maud: 'Our Lord said poverty was blessed – therefore it cannot be a Christian object to do away with it except in so far as almsgiving is healthy for the individual rich man's soul!' Maud, like her sister a dedicated philanthropist, also showed more concern for the poor man's pocket than for the rich man's soul. If the State were to tax the rich for the benefit of the poor, she wrote, it would have at least one good result: 'Several old screws who never subscribe to anything will have to stump up.'

Linky practised what he preached, overcoming a frugal nature to support a variety of charitable causes. All his life, it is true, he enjoyed what many would call affluence; he lived at Hatfield until the age of sixty-seven, did not have to provide for wife or children and left £40,000 at his death. But his benefactions touched many hearts. They included £5,000 for an Oxford college, £5 towards the tombstone of a poor Jewish refugee from Austria.

Throughout the 1920s the proceedings of the Church Assembly and latterly of Parliament were dominated by proposals to revise the Book of Common Prayer, in use since 1662. The demand for revision was provoked by the growing boldness of Anglo-Catholic clergy in adopting practices expressly abandoned at the Reformation and forbidden by law. The most controversial was the reservation of consecrated bread and wine that enabled the sick to receive Holy Communion in their homes, but which Evangelicals thought indistinguishable from the Roman Catholic practice of adoration. Only a minority of churchmen demanded the restoration of clerical discipline through severity. Most were prepared to stretch the limits of permissible ritual rather than embark on a liturgical civil war.

Lord William Cecil, Bishop of Exeter, belonged to the party of in-flexibility,* his youngest brother to that of compromise. It was not that Linky cared any more than Fish for elasticity of worship; but he saw the advantage of appeasing the Anglo-Catholics in return for a clearly defined and enforceable boundary between the permissible and the forbidden. Prayer Book revision, he told a correspondent, would at least end episcopal connivance at illegality, a custom as demoralizing as the traffic between the eighteenth-century parson and the smuggler who supplied him with cut-price contraband. But if the revised Prayer Book were rejected, 'every minister of the Church of England will do just what he thinks best – and the Church of England is rich in eccentricity'.

* See pages 123–124.

Linky was no less concerned when members of the Church Assembly began to tinker not only with the liturgy of the Prayer Book but also with its majestic seventeenth-century cadences. Was the Church justified, he asked, in damaging a literary classic that ranked with Milton's *Paradise Lost* for the sake of making it intelligible to the uneducated? He similarly deplored attempts to remove from the Prayer Book what was of historic interest, even though perhaps meaningless to some of the congregation: as if Westminster Abbey were to be stripped of its monuments because they were inconvenient or distracting in a place of worship. He continued:

> I regret striking out of the Calendar the name of Bishop Evurtius, which was only inserted in order to keep Queen Elizabeth's birthday; I regret dropping St Valentine, so deeply interwoven with English literature; I regret omitting 'the vulgar tongue' from the Baptismal Service, since the words remind the educated reader or worshipper of an important side of the Reformation movement. I value these things as I value the monuments in the Abbey; they are part of history. If it be said that unlettered people do not understand them, unlettered people will understand very little of the Prayer Book, and it is idle to hope that you will adapt it to their use by slight alterations. The better plan is to give a wide and unfettered power to individual ministers to make what changes they think edifying, and to preserve all the historical interest and all the artistic beauty of the text of the Prayer Book unspoilt by change.

Linky was equally repelled by a suggestion that the final verse should be omitted from Psalm 137: 'Blessed shall he be that taketh thy children: and throweth them against the stones.' He compared the would-be censors with 'those who hang flannel petticoats round Greek statues in the name of purity'. Always he preferred familiar usage to supposed intelligibility: 'It is impossible to make any progress in religious study without accepting the idea of symbolic language. . . . I was an exceptionally nervous child, but nobody is ever frightened by the use in respect of a divine person of the name Ghost.'

In July 1927 all three Houses of the Church Assembly approved the final draft of the revised Prayer Book: the Bishops by 34 votes to 4, the Clergy by 253 votes to 37, the Laity by 230 votes to 92. Supported, therefore, by a vote of 517 to 133, the measure was submitted to each House of Parliament in turn. On 14 December the Lords approved it by 241 votes to 88. But on the following day the Commons rejected it by 238 votes to 205. The labour of seven years was smashed in as many minutes.

For Linky, it was both a national tragedy and a personal humiliation:

> The Members of the House of Commons [he wrote] have neither corporately nor individually received any commission to exercise spiritual jurisdiction and are personally often irreligious and often immoral and, with very few exceptions, ignorant of the history and the theology on which liturgical questions depend.

Yet Parliament did undoubtedly possess a legal right to reject ecclesiastical legislation, even though a measure had received the overwhelming approval of churchmen. Short of disestablishment, there was no remedy. Parliament, moreover, had accurately reflected a widespread dislike of the Anglo-Catholic version of Anglicanism and of the seemingly weak concessions made to it by the rest of the Church. The derided Bishop of Exeter had been proved right after all. Another member of the episcopal bench wrote of the episode:

> The real causes of the vote on Thursday night (which might fairly be described as a vote of censure on the Bishops) were certainly not the defects of the Revised Book, nor the arguments advanced against it, but mainly the volume of exasperation against the excesses of the law-breaking clergy, which has been accumulating all over the country for many years and has at length found an opportunity of expression, and a Cabinet Minister to express it.

The Cabinet Minister was the Home Secretary, William Joynson-Hicks, who, like all other Members of Parliament that day, spoke in a personal capacity. Archbishop Lang, listening to the debate from the peers' gallery, described how the previously unconsidered orator skilfully 'reached and inflamed all the latent Protestant prejudices in the House. It was not a very scrupulous speech, but it was extremely effective.' The hopes of the Church party rested on Hugh Cecil, who was perhaps unwise not to devote more time to vigorous refutation. Instead he chose the uncharacteristic theme of unity, commending the Church of England as 'the peacemaker of Christendom' and the revised Prayer Book for its power to remove the slur of lawlessness from those who were otherwise good Christians. The speech reads well enough, glowing with an elevated eloquence that Mr Gladstone would not have scorned. But those who heard him noted that he seemed agitated and that the subtlety of his arguments irritated an assembly where he had always been ecclesiastically suspect. As he proceeded, the House of Commons began to thin; by the time he sat down, it was half-empty. 'His failure,' a fellow MP observed, 'was complete and lamentable.'

Linky retrieved his reputation as an orator when the Prayer Book measure was reintroduced in the following year, temptingly amended to disarm Evangelical fears. His speech in the Commons drew a chorus of congratulation from those he had disappointed in 1927. 'I was delighted to see that this time you held the attention of the House from first to last,' Lang wrote, not too tactfully. 'I felt that you were making a real impression and I almost wondered whether, if the vote had been taken then, it might not have been different.' As it was, the spectre of No-Popery continued to haunt the House, which confirmed its previous rejection of the measure by an increased majority.

That double defeat much upset Linky, and not even a protracted altercation with the Evangelical Sir Thomas Inskip, in which words like 'artifice' and 'manoeuvre' were freely exchanged, could raise his spirits. Perhaps the shock was sharper than he realized. Never in robust health, he began to suffer from indigestion and increasing numbness of the limbs. This time it was no trivial ailment. In the autumn of 1929 the doctors diagnosed pernicious anaemia, a disease of the red blood corpuscles, complicated by nervous exhaustion. The patient was ordered to bed, told to cancel a tour of India as the guest of the Viceroy, Edward Halifax, and prescribed a therapeutic diet of raw liver (which his scientifically-minded brother William suggested could be varied, perhaps improved upon, by a preparation of dessicated pig's stomach). On New Year's Day 1930 Gwendolen reported to her sister on his progress:

> Linky is getting rather a problem . . . the London consultant has told him that he can work now in moderation. But he still persists in living a quasi-invalid life, doesn't come down to dinner, takes a solitary measured constitutional, lies upon a sofa in his own room in the interval, sees practically no one but his family and, I believe, still has the nurse in attendance. And, of course, is full of his own symptoms past, present and to be feared.

> My hopes lie in the Church Assembly; he is keen to get back to that and he also has not made any effort to resign from the Electoral Reform Committee which begins its business meeting in the middle of this month. So I trust that the cords of work will drag him out of the danger of valetudinarianism. But there's no doubt that all men ought to be married – unless they're missionaries or explorers. By no means all women – that's why Providence has made the numbers unequal.

Gwendolen's fears were exaggerated. Even from his sick bed, Linky maintained an exhortatory correspondence with members of both the Church Assembly and the Commons; and soon after his return from a winter holiday in Madeira the newspapers were once more recording his undiminished zeal for controversy. There was a satisfactory skirmish against the Bishop and Dean of Liverpool for having allowed a Unitarian to preach in the cathedral; a less successful attempt to forbid the marriage service to all divorced persons; and a proposal to curb the alarming rise in unemployment by a 25 per cent cut in wages.

For Neville Chamberlain in those pre-war years he reserved a two-fold antipathy. He likened his appeasement of the dictators to 'scratching a crocodile's head in the hope of making it purr', and greeted the Munich settlement with the sardonic lines

> If at first you don't concede
> Fly, fly and fly again.

Linky thought it even more unseemly that a Unitarian Prime Minister should advise the crown on the appointment of Anglican bishops; and told the Church Assembly that if Chamberlain had lived in another age he would not be exercising authority in Downing Street but being burnt at Smithfield. In reply to a hardly less inflammatory suggestion from Linky that the appointment of bishops should become the personal responsibility of the King, the Prime Minister replied stiffly: 'This seems to me so much at variance with the theory of constitutional monarchy as to be out of the sphere of practical politics.' That was not the kind of answer that Linky ever found convincing.

'You have the most delectable of all academic appointments,' H. A. L. Fisher wrote to Linky in July 1936 on reading that Baldwin had nominated a new Provost of Eton. It was bold, perhaps a shade mischievous, of a Harrovian Prime Minister to offer Eton's crowning glory to so wayward an Etonian. The least robust of Lord Salisbury's sons had been withdrawn from the school after only two years: long enough, however, to leave him with a lifelong disrespect for schoolmasters that sometimes erupted into public controversy. He thought them as obtuse as bishops but far less holy, and had annoyed the Head Master by denouncing the Erastianism of their religious instruction. He openly mocked what he called the Bushido, or ancestor worship of Eton chapel, and 'those who when they recite the Apostles' Creed always substitute for *the Catholic Church; the Communion of Saints*, the words *Eton College; the Old Etonian Association*'. Asked to support a grandiose scheme for an Eton war memorial, he replied that he would rather see the tomb of the Unknown Etonian. But not all Old Etonians awaited his arrival with anxiety. 'To think of you as Provost,' one of them assured him, 'almost reconciles me to Eton, which I so hated.' The writer was Osbert Sitwell, whose entry in *Who's Who* proclaimed to the world: 'Educated: during the holidays from Eton.'

Linky embarked on his new career in no spirit of retribution. As if to make peace with the past, he invited his old Eton tutor, whom he had not seen for more than half a century, to the installation ceremony. Mr Marindin, a brisk nonagenarian, heard himself saluted in Latin by his distinguished pupil and later sat next to him at luncheon.*

The Provost of Eton, whose office continues to lie in the gift of the crown, bears a threefold responsibility. He has authority over the chapel and its services, although not required himself to be in Holy Orders. He admits and on ceremonial occasions presides over the seventy boys known as King's Scholars who constitute the original fifteenth-century foundation of King Henry VI and live in an ancient part of the school called College. He is resident chairman of the governors, or Fellows, who administer Eton's finances. Education and discipline, however, remain the prerogative of the Head Master.

The duties of a Provost are not burdensome; nor, unless he chooses, need he be drawn into the daily life of the school. Many Etonians are scarcely aware of his existence. Cecil's predecessor, the biblical scholar, palaeographer and antiquary Montague Rhodes James, fell into conversation with a small boy one afternoon while walking through the playing fields. After they had talked for some time, the boy said: 'You must pardon my curiosity, Sir, but are you a master?' And when James explained that he was 'a thing called the Provost', the boy replied: 'Oh, yes, I've often seen you about and I felt sure you were something of the kind.'

Linky may at first have been tempted to follow the same tranquil path as Montague James. 'I am afraid the prospect of influencing 1,100 boys, for good or even evil, seems rather visionary,' he wrote in reply to Nelly's congratulations. 'However, they will see me and my appearance will I hope do them good.'

Certainly they enjoyed his hospitality. The handsome rooms of the Provost's Lodge gave him the first home of his own in sixty-seven years, and he entered on his inheritance with delight. Usually rather careful about money, he insisted that his dinner parties should bear every mark of genial extravagance. His butler, Tucker, had orders never to leave a glass empty and would blithely pour wine over the fingers of any nervous young guest attempting to staunch the flow. A housemaster who later complained that one of his boys had returned from the Provost's not quite sober would be told very sharply to mind his own business. The teaching staff were invited to dine far less often

---

* George Eden Marindin, born in 1841, saw Dr Hawtrey installed as Provost of Eton in 1853, the year after obtaining leave from school to attend the funeral of the great Duke of Wellington. He became an assistant master in 1865, but felt obliged by ill-health to give up his boys' house in 1887. His remarkable recuperative powers, however, enabled him to survive until February 1939, when he died at the age of ninety-seven.

than their pupils. Summoned by a peremptory telephone call from Tucker, they were further put out by their host's apparent difficulty in distinguishing one guest from another; the social arbiter of such occasions, they concluded gloomily, was not the Provost but his butler.

Dr Hornby, Provost of Eton at the turn of the century, was once asked whether during his years as Head Master he knew all the boys. 'No,' he replied, 'but they all knew me.' Linky could match his boast. When Cabinet Ministers and ambassadors came down from London to address the school, the boys would find far more enlightenment in the asides of their chairman than in the platform platitudes of the visitors. 'Oh dear,' he would murmur to himself in a whisper too loud for any stage, 'I thought we were going to hear something interesting.' The leading architect of the day, who sought to ingratiate himself with the young audience by telling a mildly improper story, noticed that the Provost had begun to drum his fingers on the table. He paused and inquired with nervous truculence: 'I hope I am not boring you.' 'Not yet,' Linky replied with a smile.

The articles he occasionally contributed to the *Eton College Chronicle* also served to imprint his personality on the drab routine of public-school life. The most memorable, which chanced to appear at a particularly dark moment of the Second World War, was a plea for the abandonment of the black tail coats which, legend has it, Etonians have worn as their everyday dress since the death of King George III in 1820:

> To mourn for 120 years seems to go too far: it is to make bereavement artificial, a mere affectation. And it is depressing. When I come into School Yard before Chapel and see solid and swarthy troops of black-clad boys, I am haunted by the delusion that the Vice-Provost and the Head Master have organised a rehearsal of the Provost's funeral ('To save any distressing hitch on the day, you know') . . . Haunted and saddened, I cry out for colour . . . I should like boys to wear blue coats.

It is by the renewed vigour he brought to the services in College chapel that his span as Provost will best be remembered. 'The two dangers which beset the Church of England', he said, 'are good music and bad preaching.' He never reconciled himself to the austere offerings of Dr Henry Ley, the Precentor, which he thought dull to the untrained ear and distracting to the trained. But he took immense trouble in the selection of visiting preachers. With the help of a few senior boys, he kept a book in which each received a mark as in an examination: alpha, beta, gamma. No gamma was ever invited again;

a beta might be given a second chance, but not for a year or two; an alpha was pressed to return as often as he could. Only one preacher ever earned a higher mark than alpha minus: Archbishop Lang, unanimously judged alpha plus.

Hensley Henson, Bishop of Durham, might have achieved a full alpha had not he and the Provost grated on each other. In 1918 Linky was among those to challenge Henson's belief in the Virgin Birth and the Resurrection. Although the antagonists later made their peace, it remained a wary friendship. Linky, who with the years fell into the eighteenth-century habit of dropping an occasional aitch, confided to an Eton boy: 'Bishop 'ensley 'enson always seeks to please, but he can't 'elp annoying you with the first words he utters.' And Henson, after an evening of 'deep disagreement' at the Provost's Lodge in 1939, wrote in his journal: 'I was astonished at the obsoleteness of his opinions, the subtlety of his arguments and cast-iron rigidity of his mind. He is a mediaevalist in the methods of his reasoning, the strength of his prejudices, and the obscurantism of his outlook.'

For all that, Linky's own addresses in College chapel were heard with interest and sometimes awe. He would preface them with an invariable disclaimer, 'I speak as a layman to laymen, without the authority of the priesthood,' then go on to be very authoritative indeed. Convinced that most of his congregation were already good Christians, he allowed himself the luxury of speculative themes. Where is Hugh Cecil, is he in the pulpit or is he in the pit of his stomach? Need one believe in angels? Why does God allow the common cold?

Nor have the daily lessons from the Bible ever been read quite as he read them. The earnest, swaying figure surmounted by a green eye-shade; the old-fashioned diction; the incisive, perhaps provocative commentary on the text, often the excuse for a pitying side-swipe at episcopal learning: all were noted, recalled and imitated. So too was the occasion when he announced, almost choked by his own laughter: 'We shall now sing the *Narcissus* . . . I mean the *Nunc Dimittis*.'

The practical side to his mind showed itself in two innovations. He introduced microphones and amplifiers to penetrate the soaring spaces of the late fifteenth-century chapel. And so that the young worshippers should not lose their concentration or relapse into boredom, he cut the length of the Sunday service from one hour to thirty-five minutes. But his determination to make liturgical changes 'greatly shocked and disturbed' Edward Halifax, a Fellow of Eton as well as one of his closest friends. Linky was obdurate. 'You see,' he replied, 'I value immensely what you don't like, and that is the respectful treatment of the Protestant tradition . . . In short, Pharaoh's heart was butter compared with mine.' He displayed a similar intransigence in all matters touching his authority over College chapel; and when divorced persons of otherwise blameless life sought Holy Communion there, his stern interpretation of the Church's marriage laws seemed to lack Christian charity. In happier vein he replied to an Old Etonian who had asked permission to be married during Holy Week: 'Yes, provided the penitential character of the service is sufficiently emphasized.'

The Provost regarded the outbreak of war in 1939 as an affront to his orderly life. 'This is the end of capitalism,' he was heard to murmur, 'and the end of me.' He nevertheless continued to dine in knee breeches and silk stockings, and expected his guests to uphold the same courtly standards. Archbishop William Temple, invited to preach at Eton, wrote nervously to his host: 'I find that in most quarters evening dress has been tacitly dropped; and it is so great a convenience in these days to travel very light that I shall venture to come without that equipment unless you tell me you wish me to have it.'

Even while Hitler's bombers were obliterating Warsaw, Linky deprecated air-raid precautions as a sympton of war hysteria. It was wrong, he wrote to *The Times* in September 1939, that men and women should be encouraged to think too much of their own safety. 'Indeed,' he added, 'would it matter very much to the event of war if a theatre full of people were bombed?' The same week he mistook a group of Eton masters busily filling sandbags for 'an unusually rough lot of navvies'. The Head Master, Claude Elliott, took a less detached view of Eton's needs. As early as January 1939 he declared that the school had a moral responsibility for the lives of the boys, and demanded large sums of money to build shelters. The Provost disapproved. 'I cannot myself imagine anything more insane,' he wrote to Elliott, 'than we should bring ourselves to the verge of bankruptcy, if not beyond the verge, in order to safeguard ourselves from a danger which is in the highest degree unlikely.'

It was a plausible argument. In the early months of 1939 the prospect of a deliberate attack on an historic town of no military importance seemed remote; so there remained only the risk of a stray bomb intended for London, more than twenty miles away. The Provost also reminded Elliott that under the Eton statutes the Head Master was responsible for the studies and discipline of the school, duties which could not possibly be held to include the protection of the boys from bombs. Elliott replied by asking how he could be expected either to teach or to discipline the boys if they were dead. As the two men were by now scarcely on speaking terms, the schism was referred first to Lord Halifax and ultimately to the entire Governing Body. Their decision to build the shelters was unanimous; they preferred Elliott's excess of sentiment to Cecil's excess of logic.

In the event, the only serious damage suffered by the school took place fortuitously and without warning. On the night of 4 December 1940, a few hours before Eton would in peacetime have celebrated the five-hundredth anniversary of her foundation, a single German aircraft shed two bombs over the blacked-out Thames valley. One shattered the dining-room of Dr Ley, who providentially was late for dinner. The other ploughed through the Head Master's schoolroom, buried itself in the ground, but failed to explode. When in the early days of the war Linky was asked what he would do if a bomb fell on Eton, he replied: 'I should ring for Tucker.' But for once Tucker minutely misjudged the Provost's mood in that moment of crisis. As Linky set off to inspect the damage, the butler handed him a particularly shabby old hat that would not mind the dust. 'No, no, Tucker,' he exclaimed, 'my best 'at to see the ruins.' He was next observed prodding the hole made by the bomb with his umbrella. 'It's a dud, it's a dud,' he kept saying. Later that day, safely fenced off, it exploded.

There were other wartime adventures to be shared with Tucker. One evening Linky remembered some urgent business which he had to discuss with the Conduct, as the senior chaplain is called at Eton. So he emerged into the winter darkness and groped his way round to the Conduct's house, which lay in the same pleasing jumble of buildings as the Provost's Lodge. He pushed open the door and there, to his astonishment, stood Tucker in a green baize apron, cleaning silver. Linky, always suspicious of servants, was rather pleased with himself at having discovered his butler's double life. 'Tucker,' he demanded menacingly, 'what are you doing in the Conduct's house?' 'You have just walked in through you own back door, my Lord.'

Linky loved the tranquillity of Eton and the leisure it gave him for long hours of reading; a second waste-paper basket in his library was reserved for whole books. But having been obliged to give up both his seat in the Commons and regular attendance at the Church Assembly, he was often bored. There was only one effective remedy: the smoke of battle. Sometimes he found it at meetings of the Governing Body, where he could depend on antagonists like Maynard Keynes and Edward Halifax, men of the world as subtle and dextrous in argument as himself. It was at one such session that he endeared himself to his cousin Lord Rayleigh, the experimental physicist, with the dictum: 'Science is nothing but organized curiosity.'

The Head Master took less easily to the Provost's fretful temper. A precise and conscientious administrator, he was already harassed by wartime restrictions and shortages, and in no mood to appreciate the medieval schoolman's analysis to which Linky subjected even the most trivial problem. On various occasions the Provost told him that he was a coward (he wanted air-raid shelters for the boys); that he was greedy for power (he unwittingly infringed the Provost's prerogative by giving permission for a meeting to be held on College land); and that he would go to hell (he refused to dismiss an assistant master whose entirely respectable marriage did not conform to Linky's rigid canons of churchmanship).

Their most bizarre encounter was in the summer of 1940, as England awaited a German invasion by sea and air. At the formal meeting to elect the King's Scholars for that year, the Provost observed that Elliott and two other examiners had omitted to wear their academic gowns. They apologized for the lapse, yet he continued to scold them in outrageous terms. The Head Master kept his temper with difficulty. Later that day, however, he wrote to protest that the circumstances could not possibly justify such a want of civility; nor, he added in an aside designed to pierce Linky's legalistic armour, did the Eton statutes require gowns to be worn at that particular meeting. The Provost's reply was disarming, yet not without a touch of contempt:

My dear H.M.,

Very likely I was cross and unduly severe in manner. I was tired and when I am tired I am often cross. But how can you mind? What does it matter? If hard words break no bones still less does a cross manner. However, I am of course sorry if I hurt anybody's feelings. But it is silly to be hurt – a kind of mental haemophyllia (is that spelt right?).

As to the merits whether the meeting is mentioned or not, it is clearly a meeting to carry out a most important statutory duty: and therefore to be conducted with due ceremony. But I will not argue with you, my manners are too bad!!

Ever yours,
H.C.

In the last year of the war there was another angry skirmish between Provost and Head Master about air defence. The Germans had begun to launch pilotless aircraft against London; and when some of the missiles overflew their target, Eton found herself in the line of fire. It was agreed that these intermittent and generally unpredictable attacks must not be allowed to interrupt the school routine; but that if a warning of imminent danger happened to arrive during a chapel service, the congregation should instantly disperse to individual boys' houses. Linky, however, insisted that he and the choir, who were not members of the school, would remain behind to complete their devotions. He

286

explained his far from illogical decision in a letter to one of the Fellows:

> In 1940 the theory was that people went out to go to shelters and other places of security, and obviously if that were now the practice, the choir would have as good a right to go to security as anybody else. But it has long been found unworkable that everybody should go to shelter whenever the siren sounds, and a lower level of security has been accepted for all purposes. The principle that underlies the present practice is this: a bomb may fall anywhere: it is therefore wise that nowhere should there be a large assembly of people gathered together, because if a bomb fell on them, the casualties would be numerous. There is no reason to suppose that people in Chapel are in greater danger than people anywhere else. It is my own personal view that we are rather safer in Chapel than the boys are in their Houses because of the stronger walls of Chapel.

The Provost ended his apologia on a magisterial note that is both moving and compulsive:

> I am afraid you are prone to forget that the worship of God is an important thing, and that it really matters whether it is carried out with propriety on behalf of the College. On Sunday it is a positive moral obligation for Christians to worship, and though we cannot in these circumstances worship together, being dispersed, each little company can worship apart. . . . I am sure we all wish that Eton College should be a God-fearing College and a divinely-blessed College, and we must not, therefore, neglect the official worship of the College. For these reasons I feel sure it is right that the choir should stay, and they themselves quite concur in the opinion.

Elliott had no authority to challenge the Provost on such a matter. He nevertheless saw himself as the guardian of Eton's reputation; and when Linky wrote a letter for the *Eton College Chronicle* in defence of his decision, the Head Master ordered the boy editor not to print it. The outside world, he feared, would draw a damaging contrast between rich Etonians hurrying away to safety while poor choristers remained exposed to bombs by the whim of an unbalanced Provost. Elliott explained the decision to the victim of his censorship as tactfully as he could, but the Provost's anger led him to suppose that all remaining cordiality between them was at an end. He was mistaken. The very next morning Linky met him outside chapel, and with much agonized wringing of hands apologized for his wounding words. 'You must remember,' he told the Head Master, 'that I was one of a large family brought up to say exactly what we wanted to each other and not to mind what others said to us.'

Those obliged to endure the Provost's polemics were never quite certain whether he was striving to uphold some fundamental principle of human belief or merely savouring what Dr Alington called 'the national sport of Baiting the Schoolmaster'. Was he in search of truth or merely of a sparring partner? He did not often inspire love among those overworked and worried men; yet even the most ill-used retained an exasperated affection for their tormentor. One assistant master whom Linky had unpardonably rebuked in front of his pupils still treasures the Provost's graceful amende: 'Far as I have progressed along the road to canonization, I have not yet overcome a certain infirmity of temper.'

Since 1914 not a dozen letters had passed between Linky and Winston Churchill; their intimacy had perished in the fierce party conflicts of Parliament Bill and Irish Home Rule. But in December 1940 the Prime Minister remembered his old friend and mentor:

My dear Linky,

I hope you will give me the pleasure of submitting your name to the King for a Barony. It would be good to have you in the House of Lords, to repel the onset of the Adolf Hitler schools, to sustain the aristocratic morale, and to chide the Bishops when they err: and now that I read in the newspapers that the Eton flogging block is destroyed by enemy action, you may have more leisure and strength.* Anyhow I should like to see a brother Hughligan in the legislature and feel that your voice was not silenced in the land.

Yours ever,

Winston S. Churchill.

The announcement of the honour on New Year's Day 1941 brought him many congratulations. He told Nelly: 'What with people who are sorry that Eton was bombed and those who are glad I have been made a peer, my correspondence has greatly aggravated the paper shortage.' As head of the family, Jim offered his youngest brother a splendid roll of Cecil properties from which to choose a title. He could be Lord Crendall or Lord Aldersholt, Lord Gascoyne or Lord Childwall. Eventually he settled on Quickswood, the site of the long demolished house six miles from Hatfield where the sixth Earl had installed his mistress. 'Though the tradition is not entirely edifying,' Jim assured him, 'anything nearly 200 years old is immunized.' Linky revelled in the legal

* An erroneous sentiment. The Provost of Eton has no power to punish boys.

niceties of his peerage, but thriftily declined to pay £55 for the privilege of adding supporters to his heraldic arms.

One of the first to welcome him to the House of Lords was Archbishop Lang: 'Though I know you object to Bishops being there, and may find my presence a provocation, I hope you may be able to treat them with at least outward respect!' Linky, however, was feeling his seventy years and more. 'Public schools and Church may sometimes bring me there,' he wrote, 'but I am supernaturally old and best like anecdotes of the 19th century.'

He took his seat in February 1941* and delivered his maiden speech in the following month. As the first Provost of Eton to sit in the Lords since Francis Rous became a member of Oliver Cromwell's Second Chamber, he could hardly have found a more congenial theme: a Bill allowing public schools more latitude in the use to which they put their trust funds. He tempered his approval of the measure with a disobliging indictment of the government, on whose permission all such changes were to depend:

> I cannot say that I like what may be called the atmosphere of the Bill. It reeks of dictatorship. We live in an age which welcomes dictatorship and we must think with respect henceforth of the President of the Board of Education as *Der Führer*, of the President of the Council as *Il Duce*, and of the Secretary for Scotland as *El Caudillo*. In that way we may bring them into line with their own legislation and accustom our minds to an age which is obviously going to be, before all other things, authoritarian.

Quickswood did not speak again at Westminster until 1943. He then demanded that church bells, silenced by government order except as a warning of invasion, should again ring freely; that parents should retain the right to decide what education best suited their children; and that every pupil should be encouraged to acquire his own lifelong habit of reading. On those perennial notes of faith, liberty and learning, he closed his parliamentary career.

Again and again in the Church Assembly he had scolded the clergy, particularly the bishops, for their reluctance to retire before the onset of senility. 'It may be doubted,' he said in 1939, 'whether even misconduct does so much harm to the life of the Church as the growing

---

* By the end of the year, a cohort of Cecils thronged the red benches of the Upper House. There were the three surviving sons of the third Marquess, Salisbury, Cecil of Chelwood and Quickswood; a son-in-law, Selborne; two grandsons, Cranborne and Wolmer, each called up in a lesser peerage of his father's; a nephew, Balfour; and two great nephews, Rockley and Rayleigh. All but the last two were members of the Privy Council. Exeter and his cousin Amherst of Hackney represented the other branch of the House of Cecil.

incapacities of old age.' And he proposed (on a day, as it happened, when the Assembly was preparing to say farewell to the octogenarian Bishop of London) that every holder of a benefice should normally retire at seventy-five. As Provost of Eton, essentially an ecclesiastical appointment, he resolved to share the same discipline. His seventy-fifth birthday fell on 14 October 1944. A few days later he addressed the school from the steps of College chapel. No transcript of the speech is known to exist, but a few sentences long remained in the memory of his audience:

> I dare say that at fifteen the prospect of having nothing whatever to do is alluring. I can assure you that at seventy-five it is irresistible. . . . In these last weeks people whom I have met have addressed me in sympathetic tones, as though a death were imminent. But I have not been sure whether I was cast for the part of the corpse or the chief mourner – the corpse, I hope, for its position is more reposeful. And so I go to Bournemouth in lieu of Paradise.

During the remaining twelve years of his life he returned to Eton only once: for the funeral of his successor Sir Henry Marten, under whom the office of Provost subsided into its former quiescence. As Linky emerged from College chapel he said: 'Such a mistake to have that lesson. There is nothing Marten would less like to see than "a new heaven and a new earth".'

Lord Quickswood did not find it at all incongruous to exchange the architectural glories of Hatfield and Eton for No. 16, Beechwood Avenue, Bournemouth: a small and unlovely villa in a coastal resort much favoured by retired tradespeople and professional men. 'I like the sea,' he would reply to anxious inquiries, 'it never changes.' He sharpened his wits on a new friend and fellow disputant, the Rev. W. Yorke Batley, who later wrote of their theological duels: 'Though he kept the button on his foils, he never allowed the buttons to be so large that they prevented all discomfort from the recipient when his lunges reached their mark.' Linky's genial touch extended to Mrs Yorke Batley. 'Here comes the destroyer of intellectual conversation,' he would exclaim as she entered the room. And with a Socratic compliment her husband did not relish, he always referred to her as Xantippe.

He continued to find the world and its problems of intense interest. Even when he could no longer read with ease or write legibly, he dictated letters and memoranda by the dozen. He wrote to the Archbishop of Canterbury about the procedure of the Church Assembly; to the Lord Chief Justice about the need for a new Court of Punishment to correct gross inequalities of sentence; to the BBC on the surfeit of music that marred the Christian content of religious broadcasts; to the Provost of Eton on baptism and confirmation ('I enclose a feast of reason which, unlike carnal meals, you must return to me'). The very last letter of all, dictated only a few days before his death, was in support of a local member of parliament whose views he did not always share but whose freedom of conscience he felt to be threatened by the constituency association.

Another pleasure of old age was the revival of friendship with Winston Churchill, who sent him a present of his war memoirs. 'It is a most interesting performance,' Linky replied, 'only matched by Julius Caesar.' In 1954 the celebration of the Prime Minister's eightieth birthday in Westminster Hall prompted Linky to offer a second sparse but well-meant bouquet: 'It really is a very interesting thing that you should have had so much literary talent mixed up with more obvious historical values.' At eighty-five he felt too infirm to attend the ceremony, but young enough in spirit to deplore the continuing absence of colour in public life. He wrote to Winston:

I wish English people – who really love pageantry – would realise that you must dress up in fine clothes for the purpose. But you can hardly get them to put on peers' robes unless for the Opening of Parliament or for a Coronation: and the House of Commons dressing in Court dress or uniform would shudder at itself. Even the Duke of Edinburgh, who ought to be a most splendidly dressed person, takes refuge in the sombre bagginess of an Admiral of the Fleet, although there are plenty of pictures of Nelson dying in an extremely picturesque dress 150 years ago. But then that would not be 'gentleman-like', and English people are torn between the desire for splendour and pageantry and the desire to have the reticence of aristocratic gentility. I fancy this reticence only began towards the end of the 18th century. It was in 1772, I think, that Hickey, back from India, went to the opera magnificently dressed in red and gold, and was greeted by a scoffing friend with 'We all thought you were the Lord Mayor's trumpeter'! These words expressed the beginning of a feeling that spoils so much pageantry today.

There were few opportunities for peacock feathers in Linky's own career. But during the year or two he had spent as a young private secretary to his father he delighted in the uniform of a Civil Servant, fifth class, with knee breeches, cocked hat and sword; half a century later he asked Buckingham Palace, in vain, whether he might not receive King George v's silver jubilee medal. Of all the Cecils, he alone not only minded what he wore but also demanded the most exacting standards in others. Soon after his nephew Lord David Cecil had been appointed Goldsmiths' Professor of English Literature at Oxford, Linky wrote to Alice Salisbury from Bournemouth: 'I saw David the other day, who seemed to be better in health, though lamentably untidy in appearance. I think a Professor should have more seemliness of decorum in his clothing.' Lord Lambton, by contrast, earned full marks for 'a really decorative shooting suit, purple in colour and elegant in form'.

Old age, he used to say, was the out-patient's department of purgatory. But as a lifelong valetudinarian he bore its afflictions with resignation, almost with pride. On one of Linky's last visits to London, the present writer happened to hear his distinctive voice floating down the staircase at a wedding reception. 'I am sorry I could not come to the Abbey,' he was explaining, 'I am unable to genuflect owing to my pernicious anaemia.' In Bournemouth, however, he was driven each Sunday to the church door, then struggled on crutches as far as a specially placed armchair. The pious congregation, he told Nelly, found it most edifying.

Even under the shadow of increasing blindness he remained philosophical. One page of a book, he explained, gave him quite enough to think about for the rest of the day. He found solace in listening to the wireless and to recordings of whole volumes, such as *Adam Bede*; but he missed browsing in the newspapers and the daily inspiration of a passage from the Gospels. His niece Lady Manners, to whom he bequeathed his Bible, found a sheet of paper folded inside. On it Linky had scrawled: 'I finished the parable of the Prodigal Son and this is probably the last thing I shall ever read.' He had to leave some record of that personal disaster, but nobody must know of it until he was dead.

'My dear, are you eighty-six?' Violet Milner wrote. 'You still have the freshness of mind of twenty-five, when I first knew you.' It was sixty years since Linky had failed to convert her to Christianity and still they sparred affectionately. 'I always hope I shall soon die,' Violet told him. 'I have lived much longer than I wanted to into an uncomfortable age when the things I most cared for – good music, good pictures, good company and *Paris* – are impossible to achieve.' Linky rose serenely above such tribulations:

> I have lost the power of reading and my body is so infirm that I have very little satisfaction in moving about. My external circumstances are such as would not afford personal happiness, but . . . I am still able to look forward and enjoy the interesting prospect of what will happen after death.

In his last years he would compare himself to a traveller sitting in the hall waiting for the fly; and like all good Victorians he did not remain idle. On All Souls Day 1954 he composed a sparkling memorandum on his funeral arrangements:

Theologically, it should always be remembered that the body has been the temple of the Holy Spirit, and is on that ground entitled to be treated with reverence. It has also been, of course, alike the expression and the instrument of the personality of the deceased, but that does not amount to much. We do not treat a telephone with reverence because through it the deceased was always accustomed to call us up – often to our annoyance . . .

The governing consideration of Christians ought always to be that they must not identify the body with the dead person, and they must always think of the dead person living a new life, and one which must necessarily engage the interest of their surviving personality. No doubt the grave must be kept in proper order – if there is a grave – but this should be thought of rather as belonging to horticulture than to necrology.

It was just like Linky to go out on a joke.

9

Lady Maud Cecil
Countess of Selborne
1858–1950

Maud, eldest child of third Marquess of Salisbury. Born 11 April 1858. Married 27 October 1883 William Palmer, only son of first Earl of Selborne, Lord Chancellor 1872–4 and 1880–5. From 1882 to 1895, when he succeeded his father as second Earl of Selborne, Palmer bore the courtesy title of Viscount Wolmer.

Palmer was born 17 October 1859 and educated at Winchester and University College, Oxford. Elected Liberal MP for Petersfield 1885. Re-elected in 1886 as Liberal Unionist and retained the seat until succeeding to his father's title in 1895. Under-Secretary of State for the Colonies 1895–1900. First Lord of the Admiralty 1900–5. High Commissioners, South Africa, and Governor of the Transvaal and the Orange River Colony 1905–10. President of the Board of Agriculture and Fisheries 1915–6. Privy Counsellor 1900. Knight of the Garter 1909. Chairman of House of Laity, Church Assembly, 1924–42. Died 26 February 1942.

Their eldest son, Roundell Cecil Palmer (1887–1971), known to family and friends as Top, bore the courtesy title of Viscount Wolmer from 1895 until 1942, when he succeeded his father as third Earl of Selborne (having in 1941 been summoned to the House of Lords as Baron Selborne, one of his father's lesser titles). He was Conservative MP 1910–40 and held office in several governments. Companion of Honour 1945. An assiduous churchman.

Lord and Lady Selborne had two other sons. Robert, known as Bobby, was killed in the First World War and Lewis, known as Luly, became a noted horticulturist. Their only daughter, Mabel, was married to Lord Howick, who later succeeded his father as fifth Earl Grey.

Lady Selborne died 27 April 1950.

The Liberal journalist Wilson Harris once astonished Lord Robert Cecil by absent-mindedly taking off his hat to him as he drove past in a car. 'I am so sorry,' Wilson later explained, 'I thought you were Lady Selborne.' It was an understandable blunder. The strong features and assertive personalities of Maud and Gwendolen Cecil inspired a French visitor to write of Hatfield: *'Il n'y a que des hommes dans cette famille-là.'* Others referred less delicately to the two sisters as the Salisbury Plains.

If such unkind whispers reached the ears of Lord Salisbury's elder daughter, they failed to disturb her self-confidence. Even as a débutante she was an early champion of women's rights. 'What can't I do that you can?' she asked a young man arguing the case for male superiority. 'You can't knock me down,' he replied. 'Can't I?' she said, and did.

She nevertheless married, and married well. Her husband was William Palmer, Viscount Wolmer, only son of the first Earl of Selborne. On 29 October 1883 a ponderous leading article in *The Times* saluted the marriage of the eldest child of the Conservative leader in the House of Lords to the eldest child of the Liberal Lord Chancellor. The *Daily Telegraph* similarly blessed the union with a daring reference to the Montagues and the Capulets. The ceremony was performed by Canon Henry Liddon, of St Paul's Cathedral, the noted preacher who as a life-long friend of the Cecils had supervised the bride's education.

'It's rather a bore getting into a new family,' Maud wrote a few weeks later from Lord Selborne's house in Hampshire, 'worse than new stays on the whole. In fact nothing could be more friendly than they all are and I feel I shall soon shake down with them.' But the girl who alone of her brothers and sister had never acquired a childhood nickname insisted on maintaining her independence. She asked to be called not Viscountess Wolmer but Lady Maud Wolmer, an unusual style that owed more to filial pride than to wifely devotion. And when in 1885 her husband successfully stood for the House of Commons as a Liberal, she declined to play any part in his election campaign. Gladstone, however, unwittingly eased that marital strain in the following year by proclaiming a policy of Home Rule for Ireland. Wolmer felt unable to follow his leader, and at the general election of 1886 defended his seat as a Liberal Unionist. For the rest of his life he remained, in all but name, as devoted a Conservative as any Cecil.

Selborne, as he became on the death of his father in 1895,* brought

* For an account of his attempts to relinquish his peerage nearly seventy years before

solid qualities to every political post he occupied: industry, ability, balanced judgement and a calm temperament. He was successively Under-Secretary for the Colonies (1895–1900), First Lord of the Admiralty (1900–5), High Commissioner for South Africa (1905–10) and President of the Board of Agriculture (1915–16). Three times, too, the Viceroyalty of India seemed almost within his grasp. On the first two occasions, changing circumstances robbed him of the prize; on the third, his own refusal to accept any favour from the hand of Lloyd George.

The widow of General Smuts recalled in her old age that Selborne had been thought something of a martinet in South Africa. Arriving in a strange town one Sunday morning, the High Commissioner had apparently knocked at the first house he came to and inquired the way to the nearest church. The door was opened by a boy in tennis clothes, who said he did not know. 'You young people always know where the tennis court is,' Selborne admonished him, 'but never the church.'

In the home, however, it was his wife who ruled the roost. She brought up their children on Hatfield principles, drawing a sharp distinction between breaches of the moral law and those of mere custom. To lie, to steal, to act selfishly or unkindly: they were the real vices. Any neglect of social obligations – unpunctuality and untidiness, an antipathy to soap or to silence – was by contrast accepted with the utmost parental indulgence. The tradition of nicknames, itself a mark of family cohesion, flourished as happily among the Palmers as it had among the previous generation of Cecils. The eldest son Roundell was known as Top, Robert as Bobby, Lewis as Luly.

All grew up with lively minds, and the anecdotes of their childhood are less mawkish than most. At the age of six Bobby announced that he was going to be 'a lawyer who shoots on Saturday'; and when playing the game of Twenty Questions at Hatfield one Christmas he quite turned his illustrious Uncle Linky inside out. Luly, rebuked for bathing in an African river where crocodiles were said to lurk, replied: 'It was perfectly safe. I made the servants stand in a ring round me.' A visitor who found Mabel with her feet on the dining-room table and inquired whether her mother did not discourage the practice, received the majestic dismissal: 'Mama would not presume to interfere.'

Maud shared her own parents' mistrust of the English boarding-school. She wrote to her sister from Johannesburg:

the ultimately successful campaign of the second Viscount Stansgate (Anthony Wedgwood Benn), see pages 142–145 of the author's *Superior Person: a Portrait of Curzon and his Circle in late Victorian England* (London: Weidenfeld and Nicolson, 1969).

Of all the wicked customs that have grown up in this world of sin, next to the binding of Chinese girls' feet I think the worst is that of sending a poor little boy of nine away from all his natural relations into a moral atmosphere of which you can know absolutely nothing, except that it is bound to favour deceit and probably cruelty.

Selborne accepted his wife's demand that their children should be educated at home until the age of thirteen or fourteen. Then, he insisted, the boys should leave for Winchester College, founded by William of Wykeham in 1382. The connection between the Palmer family and the school was no more than a generation old but already a tradition. From her five centuries of history, Winchester had chosen Lord Chancellor Selborne to be one of the only four Wykehamists commemorated by a marble bust on the outer wall of the school museum;* his daughter Laura was married to the headmaster, George Ridding; and Willy himself, having spent several pleasant, mildly distinguished years at Winchester as a schoolboy, later became Warden or chairman of the governing body.

Unable to resist such sentimental pressures, Maud said goodbye to each of her three sons in turn. The most generous compliment she would pay the school was to compare it to a cold bath: 'Quite a good experience if you get it over quickly.' She saw to it that Top and Luly spent only three years at Winchester (although Bobby survived five), warned them against too much cricket and kept up their spirits with subtly subversive letters. 'I have been reading the life of Lecky the historian,' she wrote to Luly, 'and he makes the remark that what he disliked about being at a public school was that he never could get away from the other boys. I expect there are a lot of people who feel the same.'

Nor did she hide her contempt for schoolmasters and their prim ways. When Luly was spending the holidays with his parents in South Africa one summer, Maud noticed that the most convenient ship home would not reach England until just after the beginning of the Winchester half, or term. So she wrote asking whether her son might arrive three days late. Luly's housemaster replied that all boys had to be back at school by the stated date unless they could produce a doctor's certificate. Maud at once sent him a telegram: 'Your letter received. Which disease would you prefer?'

'It is rather a nuisance, but here I find myself on the side of everything radical,' Maud wrote to her brother Bob within a few weeks of arriving

---

* The other three are William Grocyn (1446–1519), the Greek scholar; Thomas Ken (1637–1711), Bishop of Bath and Wells and hymnologist; and Field-Marshal Lord Seaton (1778–1863), a hero of Waterloo.

at Government House, Johannesburg. 'I am rapidly getting a downright revolutionist, only I don't say so except to trusted friends like you, as it might be awkward for poor Willy.' For twenty years Selborne's conventional parliamentary career had brought her no more exacting a role than that of political hostess. But his acceptance in 1905 of the post of High Commissioner for South Africa, together with the governorships of the two recently-annexed colonies of the Transvaal and Orange River, plunged her into a tense new world of conflicting values.

She was particularly disturbed by the cases of cruelty and injustice that came to her notice:

> Two Dutch farmers named Vermack flogged a native to death [she told Bob]. The Government very properly prosecuted them for murder. The jury found that the boy died of kidney disease, and acquitted them altogether. In Rhodesia an equally bad case of an English farmer named Laidlaw happened a few weeks ago. The jury brought him in guilty of an assault, and the judge gave him six months' hard labour, which was probably all he could. I am glad to say those two cases have shocked even the South African conscience, which is pretty tough in these matters. . . .
>
> In both, the Governments did their duty, it was the juries who behaved scandalously . . . Trial by jury ought to be abolished here.

The colour bar was equally abhorrent to her Christian principles. She wrote to Luly about the consecration of a new cathedral in Pretoria:

> We also had eight black clergy seated in the chancel right among the whites, which was a bold step to take in Pretoria. I wonder whether the papers will be besieged with correspondence on the subject of whether South African feeling is really undergoing a change.

Whatever her private sympathies, she was reluctant to give a lead in challenging local custom. She noted that aboard the Royal Mail Steamer *Briton* her fellow passengers included 'a black bishop, travelling first class. Poor man, he is put at a table quite by himself, which I think is unkind. I wish him good morning when we meet on deck, but I have not got further than that at present.' And a note of disapproval, almost of fear, pervades this letter to Bob:

> I don't see very much prospect of this becoming a white man's country in spite of all the tub thumpers who go round and say it shall be. Already there is a large number of distressed whites, both Dutch and English, while the blacks are getting fatter and fatter and more uppish every day. They come in deputations to Willy and ask him why

they shouldn't be allowed to travel in first class carriages, and become lawyers and doctors. They are beginning to grumble at the pass law, and various other laws which were designed to keep them in their proper place.

The full weight of Maud's censure, however, fell not on black aspirations but on white cupidity. 'I have no sympathy with mine magnates,' she wrote, 'as they are so unblushingly interested in nothing but their dividends, and they don't consider anything under 20 per cent a decent dividend, which really is greedy.' She returned to the theme in the following year:

> These capitalist companies take all the rights of a landlord and none of his duties, and it seems to me a day will come when they want to clear the Kaffirs off their land, and then a good deal of hardship will ensure. It is really just the way the Irish difficulties must have begun.

A whole generation of Cecils shared her sentiments. Bob and Linky endangered their parliamentary careers by rejecting Tariff Reform, a policy which they believed to be tainted by commercial greed. Fish flirted with trade unionism. Nigs strove to save the Egyptian fellahin from economic exploitation. Maud, too, made strange alliances. She wrote of one British visitor to South Africa:

> I really do like Keir Hardie. He was met at every station by infuriated whites, mostly armed with rotten eggs, and at Standerton he told them that there was an insolence of tone in the Colonies which you didn't meet with in England. It is rather good for the Colonials to meet someone ruder than they are themselves.

The leader of the Parliamentary Labour Party at Westminster never again received so warm a tribute from a Cecil.

During their five years in what Gwendolen Cecil called 'an imitation Windsor', neither of the Selbornes showed much regard for protocol or precedence. Visiting South Africa in 1908, the historian H. A. L. Fisher noted that the High Commissioner's knowledge of farming and ability to smoke strong Dutch tobacco inspired more confidence among the republican Boers than any amount of viceregal state. And when the King crossly inquired why Government House did not insist on traditional courtesies being paid to his representatives, Maud replied by asking whether the Sovereign had ever witnessed the daunting sight of a Boer lady attempting to curtsy. 'You have nothing like as much affection for the institution of monarchy as I have,' her husband sighed.

It was as well that neither attempted to impose the rigid etiquette of the Edwardian court on their South African guests; for even the simplest entertainments at Pretoria or Johannesburg were strewn with pitfalls unknown to Buckingham Palace.

> I am going through a rather trying social ordeal tonight [Maud confided to Nelly in 1909]. A little time ago ———— married a Gaiety actress. I asked them to dinner this evening with carefully chosen guests of robust moral sensibility. The Archbishop of Cape Town has proposed himself for this evening, with his wife. He is a dear old saint who probably never heard any of the gossip that has been flying about with reference to the lady.

The birth of a child to the wife of another much respected citizen after only three months of marriage also exercised Maud's judgement:

> He now says he has been married quite a long time but never thought it worth while to mention it before. It's not a thing I care much about myself; I rather hold with the poor people, who think that as long as the marriage gets in front of the baby, all is as it should be. But there is an ultra virtuous section of Johannesburg society who will be very much shocked....
>
> Personally, I think his own account is very likely to be true, but it would have saved a lot of trouble if he had just put an announcement of the real date of his marriage in the paper.

Among Maud's few failings as a hostess was a tendency to doze off during a party. (Her father suffered from the same torpor whenever ambassadors called on him at the Foreign Office and would try to keep sleep at bay by repeatedly digging himself in the thigh with a sharp wooden paper-knife.) When in her drawing-room a visiting hero was prevailed upon to describe how he had won the Victoria Cross in battle, Maud awoke only in time to hear her guest's peroration. 'Goodness,' she exclaimed with simulated interest, 'what a nasty accident!' Here her daughter Mabel describes another moment of somnolence:

> We were visited by the British Association ten days ago. . . . We had to attend Professor Darwin's presidential address on Evolution and the Origin of the Universe. Mama slept peacefully for two hours on end, and was woken by the applause when he finished. I laughed awfully at Lady Lawley [wife of the Lieutenant-Governor of the Transvaal] who was sitting next to Mama bolt upright and very wide awake with an air of 'I at least am behaving as a Governess should!' She and Sir Arthur are awfully nice – but distinctly inclined to a sense of their Position – and I see a suppressed shudder pass over

them occasionally in my parents' presence. Not that Papa won't be *awfully* pompous if he had his own way, but Luly and his mother are a very good antidote.

Members of the High Commissioner's staff were sometimes embarrassed by their employers' freedom from social inhibitions. At a grand ball for the officers of Volunteer Regiments, the pretty girl chosen by Selborne as his partner in the state lancers turned out to be the wife of the hottest bookmaker in town. Lord Howick, the aide-de-camp, was asked why he had not interfered. 'He stuck his nose in the air', Mabel reported, 'and said he had no idea who the lady was. In Lord Milner's time they had *never* met such people!'

Young Lord Howick, however, had a generous nature. By the following year he had so far forgiven the Selbornes their gaucherie as to make Mabel his wife.

'Of course the best class of English don't come out to the Colonies,' Maud observed, 'and those that do are apt to be frightful bounders.' From one group of them, however, she drew perpetual refreshment during her years of exile. Even after Milner had returned to England in 1905, that band of clever young British administrators known as the Kindergarten remained to serve his successor, Selborne, and to help him guide South Africa towards ultimate union.

> I seek their society as a most welcome relief from the Johannesburg mining magnate or the Dutch farmer or lawyer [she told Bob]. They are a little infected with what you call Imperiolatry, but severely exclude all jingoism as being both immoral and in bad taste. They often make me laugh, they are so tremendously in earnest, but I enjoy it.

Three of them in particular won her affectionate friendship:

> There is Patrick Duncan, the Colonial Secretary, who never goes out without a Greek book in his pocket, and always knows what Plato recommended.
>
> Then there is W. L. Hichens, the Treasurer. He is not quite so cultured as he would like to be. He tries his best, but has a lamentable tendency to philistinism, which he contracted I think by rowing in his college eight, and has never entirely shaken off.
>
> Then there is Lionel Curtis. . . . He is not only cultured himself, but is very anxious that his fellow creatures should also live lives of beauty and simplicity. I am afraid that he has cast his pearls before a good many swine, who spend a good deal of time in rending him. I cannot truly say that he tempers the wind to the shorn lamb. I heard

Duncan say of him the other day, 'If Curtis cannot get his way, he throws the world at you.'

It was Curtis who stimulated her most. 'He is quite mad,' she wrote, 'and might be a very dangerous politician. He has the same kind of mind as the late W.E.G. and could persuade himself that anything was right if he wanted to do it.' Having spurned handsome offers of employment from the mine-owners, he became a leading apostle of Commonwealth unity, an authority on the constitutional affairs of India and a colleague of Lord Robert Cecil at the Paris Peace Conference. Hichens also refused the offer of a substantial salary from a Rand mining concern, began a new career in British industry and became chairman of Cammell Laird, the shipbuilding engineers. Alone of the three, Patrick Duncan continued to dedicate himself to South African affairs. Thirty years later he was appointed Governor-General.

Selborne returned to England in 1910, leaving as his legacy the newly fashioned Union of South Africa. Maud's farewell present from the Kindergarten was a chest of African teak bound with British brass.

They were glad to be home. Selborne, appointed to South Africa during the last year of the Balfour Government, had been obliged to spend the next four under the restraint of a Liberal administration. Returning to Westminster in 1910 he relished a resumption of open party warfare, and in opposing Asquith's Parliament Bill played as vigorous a part as his brother-in-law Salisbury. Maud was hardly less active as a non-violent supporter of votes for women. During a luncheon for Knights of the Garter at Windsor Castle, King George v spoke sternly to Selborne about her. He urged that she should publicly pledge herself to abandon the suffragette cause unless its militants ceased their campaign of damage and intimidation. Selborne gently replied that he could not commit himself on his wife's behalf; privately he wondered whether she herself would have given so diplomatic an answer.

What Maud had most resented in South Africa were long periods of separation from her children. Now she was able to make a home for them once more at Blackmoor, the huge sombre house built by Lord Chancellor Selborne in Hampshire. Mabel lived with her husband in remote Northumberland. But Luly was still at Winchester, less than twenty miles away; Bobby was about to take a First Class in his final schools at Oxford (Maud studied all his classical texts in translation so that she could discuss them with him); and Top, having failed to be elected to the Commons at his first attempt in January 1910, succeeded eleven months later at the age of twenty-three.

Although the outbreak of war in 1914 shattered their reunion, each member of the family cheerfully assumed a patriotic role. Maud turned Blackmoor into a military hospital, treating the medical staff with the same brisk contempt she had formerly reserved for schoolmasters. She wrote to Luly in 1915:

> I found a letter from the Surgeon-General asking me to put up a notice warning the men that they were to salute officers when they met them out walking, and if unable to salute they should turn their head and eyes towards the officer and stand at attention. . . . I really do believe men grow rather silly when they haven't got any women to criticise them. Monks and soldiers do think of quite extraordinarily foolish things.

Deciding that her wounded nephew Victor Cecil was not receiving the proper treatment in a Royal Army Medical Corps hospital, she simply broke every known regulation by whisking him away to a nursing home run by the royal surgeon, Sir Alfred Fripp. 'You should have seen me tackling generals and colonels,' she wrote. 'The final obstacle was the Home Office. But I got in there. Victor has now a great respect for me. I hope to convert him to women's suffrage before he gets well.'

Selborne was recalled to office in Asquith's Coalition of 1915 and served as President of the Board of Agriculture until provoked to resign in the following year by the Prime Minister's renewed enthusiasm for Irish Home Rule. Maud could find little merit in the Liberal elements of the Coalition. She thought Asquith dilatory, Lloyd George devious, Churchill reckless. As for Harcourt, First Commissioner of Works, 'I don't think a Secretary of State in the middle of a European War ought to curl his moustaches, he does with a hot iron, I am sure'. Not even Sir Edward Grey seemed to realize the desperate plight of the country. Breakfast at Blackmoor one morning was interrupted by Selborne's private secretary who had set off from London at dawn with a Foreign Office despatch-box marked secret. Inside was an envelope, also marked secret, addressed in the Foreign Secretary's own handwriting. It contained six shillings, Grey's debt to Selborne after an evening of bridge.

Maud saw that it was not easy to preserve Christian ideals in a world at war. 'I can't feel warlike,' she wrote. 'I can't square it up with Christianity any way, and it shocks me every day to find what unchristian feelings it breeds in all my friends and fellow countrymen – and in my own self, as I can't help rejoicing when I hear of Germans being killed.' She nevertheless avoided some of the worst excesses of patriotism, and wrote sharply of a memorial service she attended in 1917:

There was a rather awful parson who preached what I call a Prussian sermon and had 'Land of Hope and Glory', a song which I don't think at all suitable for singing in Church. I dislike imitating the Kaiser with his 'Good German God' by setting up an English divinity.

Nor, like Linky, did she hesitate to embrace unpopular causes, such as the Lansdowne letter published later in the same year.

It seems to me very good sense, but one of the rules of the game is that no one may talk sense when there is a war on. . . . As you will observe, Lord Lansdowne does not advise us to make peace, but merely to state the conditions on which we should be prepared to negotiate. He certainly does not speak for the Conservative party, nor for London society, but I think his words will express the feelings of a good many people who, though determined not to grant a 'German peace', do not wish the war to go on any longer than is necessary.

By then she had suffered the cruellest blow of her life. Bobby was killed in Mesopotamia while serving as a captain in the Hampshire Regiment. During his brief years at the Bar he had shown much promise. 'Very soon I came to regard Palmer as a man who would rank with the foremost lawyers of his generation,' the future Lord Chief Justice Goddard wrote of him. 'His grasp of legal principles can only be described as intuitive; all he needed to learn was the everyday practice.' Like Nigs and Fish, Maud bore the loss of a favourite son with outward stoicism: 'It is easy to think of him with God, and in time these wounds heal. It is a poor use to put his great gifts to, but he is only one among many others who would have been much more useful living for his country than dying for her.'

Those closest to her, however, believed that from the moment of Bobby's death her life was never quite free from sadness.

Between the wars, Maud became as matriarchal as her own mother. She insisted that her two surviving sons and their families should spend nearly all their holidays at Blackmoor; and in her London house she reserved bedrooms for Top and Luly just too small to accommodate their wives as well as themselves. The family circle, however, lacked both comfort and tranquillity. Maud chose her domestic servants less for their willingness and efficiency than for independence of character. A visitor might find a dustpan in his bed instead of a hot-water bottle; and Gwendolen, the least exacting of guests, was moved to complain that the head parlour-maid Charlotte had completed a piece of her embroidery left overnight in the drawing-room.

Even Selborne could expect scant consideration in his own home. 'Maud,' he would say earnestly, 'Charlotte has not done what I asked her to do yesterday. Will you please speak to her?' Perhaps Maud would do so, perhaps not. He suffered acutely from draughts and begged his wife not to leave the windows open in cold weather. Her answer was to keep the windows shut, having first removed an entire pane of glass from each in the belief that her husband would never notice. She also neglected his repeated requests for a larger size of writing-paper: to the end of his days he was obliged to use mean little sheets ill-suited to his bold hand. Selborne's orderly mind, as respected in the City boardroom as in the House of Lords or the Church Assembly, must have been outraged by such deficiencies in the home. Yet in nearly sixty years of married life he was never heard to address his wife except in terms of courtly affection.

Only in the education of her sons at a public school had Maud been unable to prevail over the conventional views of her Wykehamist husband. But the physical health and spiritual welfare of their children and grandchildren bore every mark of her own strong personality. Like her father, she mistrusted experts, and of all experts she found none more dogmatic than doctors. The advice she pressed upon the young might have been expressly designed to thwart orthodox medical opinion. She wrote to one small son at Winchester: 'In the cold weather you should eat plenty of sweets, as sugar is a heat giver. As you have unlimited credit at the tuck shop you need have no hesitation in following this prescription.'

When that eccentric diet caused boils, indigestion and toothache, she had her remedies for those, too. An infuriated school doctor eventually refused to give the boy further treatment until his mother ceased to interfere across six thousand miles of ocean. As each of her sons married, Maud presented the new daughter-in-law with the bridegroom's medical history, an alarming chronicle of past suffering and future peril: Luly must never be allowed to touch a potato, Top would be afflicted with a stiff neck if he took so much as a single bite of ham sandwich. The regime she prescribed for her grandchildren was indulgently sybaritic. When the gardener at Blackmoor complained in despair that the peaches and grapes he was about to cut for the dining-room had been stolen by small hands, she replied: 'That is why I grow them.' She also determined to forestall any tendency to alcoholism by introducing her grandchildren to light wine quite early in life. A guest aged ten was one day heard to inquire whether he had been given luncheon claret or dinner claret. On being told it was luncheon claret, he replied: 'No thank you. I don't care for Granny's ink.'

In such a household, doctors were never welcomed and rarely

appreciated. Selborne once had the misfortune to be bitten in the leg by an adder while inspecting his fine collection of fir trees. The local doctor, proud of the speed with which he had neutralized the venom and reduced the swelling, later remarked to Maud how lucky it was that her husband's leg had been partially protected by his trousers. 'He would hardly have been out in the garden without them,' she replied frostily.

Nor did her devout Christianity exclude a persistent anti-clericalism.

> Don't let any fool of a clergyman have anything to do with her [she wrote to her eldest son about a granddaughter who had reached the age of confirmation]. She is a rebel by nature and might easily be driven into unbelief. Either prepare her yourself or let Grace [Top's wife] do it or just make Eyres [the vicar] give her her ticket or choose a really clever parson who can hold his own against her.*

It delighted Maud to discover that the car she intended giving to the local vicar required the petrol and the oil to be poured through the same hole: an operation sufficiently simple, she affected to believe, for even a cleric to understand. And among her helpful rules of life most quoted in the family was this injunction: 'Never take a reference from a clergyman. They always want to give someone a second chance.'

Maud's sharpness of tongue brought a discordant note into the Cecil family circle. Linky in particular resented being reproved in middle age as if he were still the youngest of her brothers in mind as in years. Jim and Alice Salisbury, too, shrank from her provoking dogmatism. Only with her sister did she retain an almost conspiratorial intimacy; their shared interests ranged from political strategy to district nursing, from Anglican attitudes to the care of gardens.† Gwendolen was always a welcome guest at Blackmoor, even if she did burn holes in the bed-linen with her cigarettes, then naïvely trim the charred edges so that the housekeeper might put it down to wear and tear.

Among her brothers, Maud cared most for Bob, who would often use her London house when his wife was in the country. 'Just left Maud,' he wrote to Nelly, 'whose nose I had bitten off because she would propose plans for dealing with unemployment at 8.15 breakfast.' And again: 'Maud was rather perverse denouncing League of Nations' mandates, of which she was sublimely ignorant, till I had to tell her

---

* The task of preparing Anne Palmer for confirmation was entrusted to just such a man: the Rev. George Bell (1883–1958), chaplain to the Archbishop of Canterbury and from 1929 Bishop of Chichester.

† Her youngest son, Lewis Palmer, became a horticulturist of distinction. Although a most observant botanist, he found it difficult to recognize people by their faces. 'If only they all looked as different as snowdrops,' he would complain.

she was a diehard and we should never agree. We parted in complete amity, but she is provoking.'

More than one of their sparring bouts concerned the most controversial politician of the age. Maud wrote to her brother in 1927: 'If you are thinking of having a secret society for the murder of Winston Churchill in a strictly pacific manner, I shall be prepared to join it.' Bob replied: 'Why do you hate Winston? He is, believe me, your best leader: anti-Bolshevik, a big navyman, a friend of capitalists, a hater of trades unions. What more can you want?'

At heart they shared a passionate common cause. The death of Bobby in 1916 had inspired in Maud the same horror of war that led her brother to devote his life to the League of Nations. They differed only in the means by which peace could be secured:

> I don't value disarmament very much myself [she told her daughter Mabel in 1933]. If people want to fight they will fight, arms or no arms. When they cease to want to fight they will disarm naturally without any conventions. But Bob can't see this, and thinks he can make them peaceful by taking away tanks and aeroplanes, bless his heart!

She was justified in mistrusting the effectiveness of negotiated disarmament as a deterrent to aggression, wrong to reject the only other honourable safeguard of peace: resistance to dictatorial pretensions, backed by vigorous rearmament. Alone of her family, she felt neither anger nor shame at the betrayal and dismemberment of Czechoslovakia in 1938. While Wolmer, in common with his Cecil uncles and cousins, was refusing to support the Munich agreement, his mother wrote to Luly:

> I think a lot of nonsense is being talked and written on the Czechoslovak question. We have managed to put our case extraordinarily badly, but really there was nothing to go to war for, except a very natural desire to teach Hitler manners.
>
> His demand that the Sudeten Germans should be detached from the Czechs and joined to the Germans was not unreasonable. If he had made it politely, no one could have objected, except the Czechs, who probably like Pharaoh would have declined to let the people go. It is fair to say that the detachment by Hitler's methods is a good deal quicker than under the old diplomacy....
>
> I can't see Winston's point at all. Another world war would be no more likely to give a final quietus to Germany than the last one did – even if we won it, which is very doubtful. A long good peace which would enable the quarrelsome disposition of the Germans to exert itself in internal politics is the best cure for the Nazi regime.

In a long life of self-assurance and many good works, it was among the worst of Maud's misjudgements.

Lady Selborne was eighty in the year of Munich. She lived on for more than a decade, enduring war, widowhood and Winston Churchill with spirited defiance. Even in his finest hour, the Prime Minister failed to win her esteem. 'The military genius of the great Duke of Marlborough has not descended to him,' she wrote to Gwendolen in 1942, 'although I am afraid he thinks it has.' To the very end, too, she retained her prejudice against surplice and scalpel, clattering out of church if the sermon displeased her and jovially addressing the doctor who had more than once saved her life as 'my enemy'.

She slew her last enemy of all on 27 April 1950, in her ninety-third year.

Lady Gwendolen Cecil
1860—1945

Gwendolen, second child of third Marquess of Salisbury. Known to the family as Tim or T.T. or Titi.

Born 2 July 1860. Author of the four-volume, uncompleted biography of her father.

Lady Gwendolen died, unmarried, 28 September 1945.

Lord Salisbury did not believe in higher education for women. In 1883, the very year in which his younger daughter might have been experiencing the intellectual excitements of Somerville or Girton, he wrote: 'I dare say these Colleges are useful as furnishing a diploma to ladies who wish to be Governesses: but for any other purpose I should do my utmost to dissuade any female relation over whom I had influence from going there.' So Gwendolen remained at home in the dual role of confidential private secretary to her father and lady-in-waiting to her mother.

The first of those experiences was itself an education: an insight into practical politics enjoyed by no other girl in England except perhaps the daughters of Queen Victoria. But it lacked both the breadth and discipline of a university course. Her vigorous and inquiring mind was not subjected to sustained effort under criticism or made to acquire the habit of prolonged concentration. From observing her father's nightly toil behind the double doors of his study, she came to realize the inadequacy of her own training; and when her brothers were being particularly fractious one day, she wrote them this majestic reproof:

I would advise you to retire to your apartments for an hour or two daily, between breakfast and luncheon, and there study some of our best authors, committing to memory such passages as strike you as peculiarly elegant or felicitous; further, I would counsel you to seek anxiously for information upon various subjects of intellectual interest; by the writing of themes and essays practise yourselves in arranging the same in a methodical and orderly manner in your minds; take an intelligent interest in all that surrounds you, and by opposing cause to effect, and effect to cause, accustom yourselves to logical exercises. By these, and other means, you will in time succeed in cultivating your minds to that elementary point, as not to so unutterably bore each other as at the present moment you so evidently do.

Yet Gwendolen herself was denied just such hours of reading, writing and meditation: or rather the certainty that they would be available on any given day. After her elder sister's marriage to Lord Wolmer in 1883, Lady Salisbury increasingly required her to share the duties of the Hatfield household and estate. This attendance on her mother was not in itself a burden; but it was distracting and often prolonged by Lady Salisbury's love of gossip and disdain for punctuality. Salisbury used to say that while waiting for his wife to come down to dinner he had read right through the Church Fathers. Lacking his strength of purpose, Gwendolen fell into more desultory ways; between such mentally undemanding tasks as parish visiting and rehearsing a choir of footmen and housemaids, she dawdled away most of the day and half the night with newspapers and cigarettes and talk.

What should have been the most creative period of her literary life produced no more than a ghost story or two. For one of them, entitled 'The Closed Cabinet', the proprietor of Blackwood's Magazine paid her the considerable fee of 50 guineas: it would have been more, he wrote reproachfully, had she not insisted on its being published anonymously. Eventually, on the verge of middle age, she undertook to write the official biography of her father. It is a magnificent monument both to the memory of the Prime Minister and to her own insight and industry. But the locust years had taken their toll. The work caused her immense worry, progressed at a snail's pace and remained unfinished at her death more than a generation later.

The girl who caught Disraeli's fancy 'in the wild grace of extreme youth' never married. One by one the Cecil children broke away from Lady Salisbury's possessive affection to lead lives of their own. Gwendolen, however, remained her parents' constant and indispensable companion. They had no need to dissuade her from matrimony; her own unselfish love for them kept her tied to Hatfield as effectively as any ball and chain. Nor, in spite of being a Prime Minister's daughter, was she considered a bargain in the marriage market. Her features were expressive rather than beautiful; her appearance owed nothing to artifice ('Lady Gwendolen rather more grubby than usual', one of Queen Victoria's ladies-in-waiting noted during a visit to La Bastide); her shyness and short sight turned every social occasion into a penance. 'The nervous strain of continuous small talk here is terrific,' she wrote while staying with Maud in Johannesburg. 'It's appalling to think that if I had married my life might have been *always* in such conditions. What dreadful fates a merciful Heaven saves one from.' Returning to England by sea, she made friends with the Bishop of Pretoria so that she could 'refuse all such flippancies as sports and dances'.

On only one suitor was she suspected of smiling without indifference: the Duke of Norfolk, a widower thirteen years her senior and brother of her closest friend, Lady Margaret Howard. Salisbury thought highly enough of the Duke to make him Postmaster-General in the administration of 1895–1900, but would hardly have welcomed his daughter's betrothal to the lay leader of England's Roman Catholics. The proposed match, if such it was, remained no more than a whispered family legend.

Gwendolen made her last concession to the demands of a London season when she attended the Devonshire House ball that marked Queen Victoria's diamond jubilee. Half a century later Nelly recalled her sister-in-law's striking appearance as Portia, in deep red cap and lawyer's gown: 'She looked splendid. It gave one an idea of what a little more attention might have done: she had beautiful hair, a warm brown with gold lights in it and an attractive wave.' But within a year or two, Lady Salisbury was dead; from then until Lord Salisbury too died in 1903, Gwendolen hardly had a life of her own. 'She became everything to her father,' Violet wrote, 'and all the world to the rest of us.'

Soon after succeeding to the family honours, Jim installed his sister in a small house on the Hatfield estate; and with her deliverance from domestic thraldom came both rejuvenation and a fulfilment of intellectual promise. She was consulted, revered, loved. Nephews and nieces demanded her company while their parents were abroad. Those little Cecils and Palmers found her as exciting a friend as any, and sixty years later still delight in recalling her innocent eccentricities: the fervour with which she played the piano or read aloud, unruly pince-nez tinkling against a battery of brooches; the familiar posture of kneeling before the fire, close enough on one alarming occasion for the combs on her hair to start smouldering; her disregard for school-room routine or the approaching shadow of bedtime; the eloquent intensity she brought to themes as various as the causes of European unrest or the best way to wash a dog.

'She imputed to all her dogs,' a niece has written, 'every degree of human sensibility.' To avoid hurting their feelings when she could not take them with her, she would smuggle her hat and coat to the kitchen, then creep out of the back door. As a canine psychologist, however, she had her disappointments. A collie called Rally developed the nasty habit of jumping at horses' heads. Knowing that the dog was gun-shy, she devised an ingenious way of curing it. As soon as Rally barked at the horse's head, she would fire a revolver and the dog would stop. What in fact happened was that the horse bolted and the dog barked more furiously than ever.

Even after acquiring a place of her own, Gwendolen often had her meals at the big house. The domestic staff had long grown accustomed to her erratic hours, moving her breakfast to a little side table as they laid places for lunch. One day she told the butler: 'I forgot to come for lunch today. So I have brought a bag of buns and will eat them in the summer drawing room.' 'But it is only eleven o'clock.' 'Oh, good. Then I will stay for lunch.' There were dyspeptic occasions, too. Here is Bob describing one moody encounter with this sister:

> Tim* said this evening that she thought as a matter of reason it would be better if she never talked. No one took any interest in the things that at the moment interested her and she did not care for what then interested them. Curiously sensitive we all are! But I'm afraid this particular crank of Tim's is partly my fault. I've behaved very badly to her this summer owing to my illimitable self-conceit and vanity.

The angel of unselfishness could turn into a tornado of vehemence. Red in the face, her chin thrust out, she was a match even for Linky. The rest of the family much enjoyed their gladiatorial contests, perhaps on the moral implications of saving the life of a fly that had fallen into one's bath, or on the aesthetics of removing a clump of rhododendrons. 'If you really care for those scrofulous growths,' was her *coup de grâce*, 'I pity you.' But the antagonists were united in deep affection, personal piety and a scorn for most ecclesiastics. 'I remember a garden party at Fulham which filled me with depression,' she told Maud. 'The clergy did look such poops.'

Once released from the restraints of a Prime Minister's establishment, Gwendolen found no less freedom of expression in her clothes:

> She either thought a lot about them or not at all [wrote her niece, Lady Manners]. When she thought – and we were kept up in the

* Gwendolen was known in the family as Tim or T.T. or Titi.

progress of the scheme – it was not only to invent an Admirable Crichton sort of garment, whose top could be worn by day or in the evening, but it should be made by a distressed dressmaker. The skirt would be a remnant her secretary had bought for her. This would gratify the secretary and the conjunction of aiding, pleasing and being useful was delightful. If only the blouse could have been used as a sponge as well it certainly would have been adopted. But on the whole she did not think about clothes, so she would wear black stockings with brown shoes and brown stockings with black shoes. The stockings wrinkled and the shoes untied. Two or three really good diamond brooches would be pinned on anyhow. If she had a good tweed, the hat would be her wedding hat. Her hats were of the same type. Anyway after a short time they were battered into the same type, though some reached such fame as to be nicknamed by the family – Bersaglieri was one. Bersaglieri blew off into the sea, was retrieved sodden, and clapped on again, Aunt T.T. remarking 'not much the worse'.

Gwendolen remained defiant of Edwardian fashion even when the arbiter himself came to Hatfield:

> The King and Queen have proposed themselves here for Sunday week. I am going to shirk as much as I can and am feeling very republican. I have just come to the conclusion that if I avoid them Saturday, one new skirt to match a blouse I've got will meet the occasion, and feel soothed.

She was prepared to make fewer concessions to foreign sovereigns. 'With one morning and one high evening gown, both old and rusty,' she wrote from Egypt, 'I have attended royal and official banquets in the height of the Cairo season.' Kitchener himself could not have put the Khedive more firmly in his place.

In the summer of 1906 Gwendolen undertook to write her father's life. She told Bob: 'Though I could never make such a fine work of it as Linky would do, I frankly believe I understand him better.' It was a formidable task. The man who had been Prime Minister for fourteen years and Foreign Secretary for almost as long left an immense bulk of papers:

> I am getting a good few of my father's letters in [Gwendolen noted], and now Eric Barrington* has offered the whole of his F.O. private correspondence, saying significantly that it can be sent by carrier's

---

* Sir Eric Barrington was Principal Private Secretary to Lord Salisbury throughout his entire tenure of the Foreign Office.

cart from London. When once I have plunged into the work I feel I shall be lost to human sight for years to come.

Hardly any of the archives had been sorted or docketed, and some even arrived in 'filthy packing-cases, with all the elastic bands broken and the piles mixed'. Then there was the background reading of blue books and diplomatic despatches, files of newspapers and articles from the *Quarterly Review*; forty volumes of Hansard brought Gwendolen only up to 1885, with the entire premiership still to be covered. The most severe handicap of all, she confessed, was her 'utter want of method and discipline . . . and at my age it seems almost an insane optimism to think I can change'.

Thus it was not until after the publication of her first two volumes in 1921 that she began to put her father's papers in order.

I never did it before [she explained to Nelly], only searched through them to pick out what I wanted for the earlier history, and the mass that's got to be looked through and classified and dated is appalling. But it's not a waste of time. It will prevent the repeated rewriting which my unmethodic procedure forced on me before by the constant discovery of overlooked material.

She added unnecessarily to her labour by haphazardly filling notebooks with whatever came to hand from the archives, so that whole days were later wasted in rummaging for the particular extract she needed.

Gwendolen was all too easily distracted from her work, as when she discovered 'bars of yellow soap and tins of blacking and tea in a box which the cook had just assured me with dramatic emphasis was filled with sweetheart letters from her husband. There was also a fish napkin which she said she had bought herself and had apparently marked with a coronetted S.' Exhausted by domestic deceit, the biographer fled to a Kent farmhouse with her books and her bicycle.

Indifferent health was another obstacle to progress. Here is one of the many dramatic medical bulletins which punctuated her correspondence.

I've had a queer feverish attack which might be flu or mosquitos or undetermined Mediterranean fever. I felt deplorable and my temperature went up to $100\frac{1}{2}$. I promptly took 8 grains of quinine and slew the beastly thing in 24 hours. Now I'm quite well again except for a cough.

Neither her ailments nor her accidents were quite like those of other people. 'Today,' Nelly wrote of Gwendolen, her guest in Sussex, 'she is rather sick and seedy – which she attributes either to some cheap

Turkish cigarettes she got near Victoria Station or to having forgotten to put on her fur coat when waiting at Three Bridges!' A deficient sense of time obliged Gwendolen to spend many hours waiting on station platforms. Twice in the course of a single railway journey she had been known to pass her destination: once because she was immersed in a book, and again because she had boarded the wrong train.

Twice, too, she was run over in remarkable circumstances. Driving an early model of motor car, she stopped on a hill to open a gate, but forgot to put on the brake. As the machine slowly bore down on her, she attempted to stop it with her own weight and was knocked to the ground with broken ribs. Some years later, on foot this time, she was hit by a London taxi-cab. She had a theory that one should cross the road diagonally, but got it just wrong and set off with her back to the traffic. 'Tim says she has a right to cross the road when she likes,' Nigs wrote. 'The principles of my family are very inconvenient, not to say dangerous.'

Perhaps it was while recovering from such an experience that she made a valuable discovery. 'I work better in bed than out of it,' she told Maud. 'So I only get up for a few hours daily, mainly to take Nigger for a run. If I hadn't a dog I believe I should easily become bedridden.' An alternative whim was to work throughout the night, free from interruption. Once she lingered so long at her writing table that the housemaids were already up and about; she only just managed to jump between the sheets (with her shoes on) in time to be called. But it was not her father's biography alone that consumed those silent hours. A nephew in whose house she was staying taxed her with not going to bed until 6.30 one morning. She admitted that she had read all night: 'Such a rotten novel, too.'

Gwendolen wrote the opening lines of her *magnum opus* in 1910 while staying at La Bastide. The house near Monte Carlo bequeathed to her by her father was, she believed, 'peculiarly haunted by him'. Nearly a decade later she was still not satisfied with the manuscript of her first two volumes, carrying Salisbury's life only down to 1880. As she toiled away year after year, rewriting and tearing up each chapter as many as eight times, her family came to believe that it would never be published. 'I wish she would print some of her stuff at once,' Nelly wrote to Bob in 1919. 'I have urged her to get proofs of the manuscript for purposes of correction – perhaps if she saw them she would take the plunge. I believe she dreads it.' By the autumn of 1920, however, Gwendolen had reluctantly surrendered her text to the publishers Hodder and Stoughton in return for a handsome advance of no less than £5,000. Volumes I and II of *Life of Robert, Marquis of Salisbury* appeared in the bookshops a year later.

'I have certainly had a wonderful press,' Gwendolen wrote in November 1921:

> I was surprised to see, repeated in one notice after another, how much of what the critics read was a revelation to them. A kind of myth had grown up of the haughty and rather inhuman and cold aristocrat....
>
> One is pleased naturally at having one's work praised – but it is a far deeper and more enduring cause for thankfulness that one has been the instrument of making him and the lesson of his life known to others. It is a mystery of mercy that it should be so.

Lord Birkenhead's review alone displeased her. 'F.E., I think, read the first chapter, glanced through the second and third and read a couple of pages in the sixth – otherwise I am convinced he didn't even cut it.'

In style, the biography owes something to the volumes of Macaulay which Linky pressed on his sister, although its elegance and vigour are sometimes overlaid by a fatiguing weight of interpretation. Virginia Woolf, however, could find no fault. 'Lady G.', she told Nelly Cecil, 'writes like twenty able men crushed into one, as hard as a paving stone.'

For those who seek to understand Salisbury either as man or states-man, his daughter's first volume remains indispensable. She broke with biographical tradition by making his character her prologue rather than her epilogue: a portrait rich in humour and affection yet framed in those religious and political principles that governed his entire career. Her second volume is more laborious, dominated by an elaborate analy-sis of the Eastern Question between 1876 and 1878. It evoked respect; but it also cast a shadow. Gwendolen was sixty-one and had taken fifteen years to carry the story of her father's life no further than 1880. Who dared forecast its completion?

The biographer herself was undaunted. Having belatedly put her archives in order, she went to work on the labyrinthine politics of the 1880s. They were years she too had spent at the very heart of affairs, so that again and again she was able to enliven documentary evidence with the snapshots of memory. Yet her second pair of volumes failed to pro-gress any faster than her first; for every completed year of her father's life she sacrificed one of her own. Not until 1932 did she publish the next instalment. Covering the period 1881–1892, it recorded Salisbury's first two ministries but fell short of his last and longest.*

---

* The eleven-year interval between publication of the two pairs of volumes diminished the commercial success of the work. Volume I sold 5,263 copies, volume II, 5,265; volume III, 1,655; volume IV, 1,304. The four volumes together earned only £3,000 of her publisher's advance payment of £5,000.

And there, unhappily, it stuck. Now in her seventies, Gwendolen found the effort of further composition increasingly burdensome. A single passage would trouble her for months. 'I have cut it about,' she told Maud in 1935, 'transposed it, rewritten it till I was sick of it, and put it away as hopeless.' At her death ten years later she left no more than a few chapters in draft.

Gwendolen's quest for literary perfection was not the only cause of her taking almost forty years to write four volumes. The lure of politics also distracted her from her task. She was the daughter of one Prime Minister and the cousin of another, the sister of four parliamentarians, the aunt of enough ministers to make or mar an administration. Born a generation later, she herself might have sat at Westminster, even in Cabinet. As it was, she could never be more than an absorbed spectator.

As early as 1885 she conspired with Jim to send a professional lecturer round the country, charged with exposing the vacillations of Mr Gladstone's policy and the needless sacrifice of General Gordon in Khartoum. Yet she herself was as persuasive a partisan as any: sometimes in vehement argument, more often in sheet upon sheet of her tiny myopic hand. Only the telephone she rejected as a medium of serious political discussion. It was not until 1925, when her nephew Wolmer was Assistant Postmaster General, that she could be persuaded to become a subscriber; even then, she ordered the instrument to be installed in the servants' sitting-room.

'I have a passion for interfering in other people's business,' Gwendolen admitted. 'Left to my own impulses, whenever I see anything going wrong – or going as I don't think it ought – I want to rush in and take action, whether it's my affair or not.' All five of her brothers received unsolicited advice over the years; from so saintly and sympathetic a counsellor, it was not resented. She chided Linky for intemperate language, Nigs for idleness, Bob for an unwise flirtation with the Liberals, Fish for opposing the new Prayer Book, Jim for allowing himself to be tyrannized by his doctors. Neither blood nor friendship, much less a professed Conservatism, spared public men her censure. Cousin Arthur Balfour failed her over Tariff Reform, Curzon over House of Lords reform, Halifax over appeasement. 'All yesterday', she wrote on 30 August 1939, 'I must confess that I was more afraid of the Government turning tail than of the actual war.'

In common with most of her family, Gwendolen was disturbed by the slow pace of British rearmament throughout the 1930s. But her own attitude towards the dictators had not always been robust. Travelling in Italy with the Bishop of Winchester and his wife, Edward and Lavinia Talbot, she wrote from Capri in November 1923:

We must begin to look out for a Mussolini. The Bishop has got a French history of the Fascisti movement which is rapidly converting him into an enthusiastic disciple of Il Duce. . . . It appears to be thrilling. Though he undoubtedly stands for intense nationalism he is not, I understand, a Jingo in any way.

Scarcely ten weeks had passed since Mussolini's occupation of the Greek island of Corfu and defiance of the League of Nations: a humiliating episode for the rest of Europe, and in particular for Bob Cecil. Five years later, Gwendolen's admiration for the Italian dictator was near to ecstasy:

Thank you very much for the Mussolini [she wrote to Maud]. It makes one's mouth water to read of his accomplishing all the things we would give our eyes for, rising budgets – leaping trade – strikes ended – industrial co-operation in full working order – religious schools – unemployment at a minimum – 30 per cent of the Civil Service got rid of. It's like a dream! He *can't* be such a fool as to let it all be upset by war.

I'm beginning to have serious doubts about liberty, except under an oligarchy. It must be under *some control or else it becomes anarchy* – and an oligarchy is the only controlling body which sympathises with it. If you don't have that you are driven to bureaucracy or dictatorship because democracy is only a name – it can't govern. We have got bureaucracy, and I'm inclined to think dictatorship's better and about the same as far as liberty goes. Socialism is simply bureaucracy in excelsis.

But by 1935 she had begun to recognize both the arbitrary restraints and the military menace of dictatorship, even its malign hold on the climate:

The East wind always seems to have an effect quite distinct from its temperature; but this year it was positively poisonous. Perhaps one of these days when they have worked out the connection between mind and matter more thoroughly, it won't seem wholly fantastic to think that layers of air coming straight from Ludendorff's neo-paganism and Stalin's reign of terror can have a poisonous influence.

The author of so capricious a theory could also display an acute judgement of character. On the birth of the future Queen Elizabeth II in 1926, Gwendolen wrote of the young Prince of Wales: 'I don't suppose that he'll ever marry now, and I should never be surprised to hear that he was going to make a formal abdication. He's rather a tragic figure, weighted down by an inheritance that he loathes – and I'm afraid likely to go to the bad in consequence.'

Ten years and a few months later, as King Edward VIII, he abdicated.

More than one visitor to Hatfield was startled by an untidy apparition in the park: Lady Gwendolen bicycling by on an errand of charity, clad perhaps in an old evening dress that still had useful wear in it. From an early age she had been encouraged to help her mother in parish visiting and other neighbourly duties. Lady Salisbury's brusque bounty included the distribution of a much appreciated restorative to elderly cottagers. She made it by collecting all the family's medicines that were not actually marked poison, pouring them into a jug, adding an equal quantity of the Prime Minister's best port and rebottling. In her own philanthropic sorties, Gwendolen more resembled Fish, entering into the lives of the poor without a trace of either self-consciousness or condescension. During the last hard winter of the war she told her sister how miserably they were enduring a diet of vegetable sausages, potato and onion stew, purée of swedes, macaroni and chopped carrots.

> Sunday dinner without meat is an almost incredible catastrophe for the working man – worse than death or wounds, bereavement or raids. . . . Jem has been having all the pheasants and rabbits killed he can – but for the sacred purpose of a Sunday dinner, game is only accepted grudgingly as a quite unsatisfactory substitute for beef or mutton.

The soaring price of milk led nearly every cottage to keep goats. 'But no husband was to be found for them at Hatfield,' Maud wrote to Luly, 'so Tim gallantly threw herself into the breach and bought one. . . . It is a fine spirit but I am afraid she lacks experience in goat-keeping, and I expect he will add to her cares.'

Gwendolen also inherited her father's concern in housing the poor, the old and the infirm. She was an able architect whose beautifully drawn plans and precise calculations contrasted sharply with the disorder of her daily life. When in 1925 she read that the average cost of maintaining each inmate of a poor-house was more than twenty-five shillings a week, she reacted with a practical plan of her own:

> If I wasn't writing a book [she told Maud] I'd like to start a company. . . . I would guarantee, even at present prices, to build single bed-sitting room almshouses, with central heating supplied, which would *pay* at a rent of 10s. a week per head. Old people can feed themselves with a comfortable margin on 10s. – so that they could really have a peaceful comfortable old age pottering about in their own rooms at a saving of some £15 a year per head for the ratepayers.

The plight of the mentally disturbed was another cause close to her heart. In advance of her time, she believed that a cheerful room could have a considerable effect on a patient's recovery; she pressed relentlessly for the rebuilding of asylums and later financed a home for decertified lunatics at Aylesbury. She brought the same imaginative touch to the design of sanatoria for consumptives, each ward reassuringly small in itself but with large windows and an airy balcony. Yet another of her campaigns was to prevent the children of bargees from being compulsorily educated apart from their parents.

Yet Gwendolen was not one of those brisk and businesslike ladies who form the backbone of charitable enterprises. In spite of a comfortable private income and substantial literary earnings, her personal finances were often confused. La Bastide, the Mediterranean villa which her father had bequeathed to her, she sold for a fraction of its value; and her trusting nature delivered her, uncomplaining, into the hands of every professional beggar and confidence trickster in the home counties. Her sole luxuries were fifty cigarettes a day and a small romantic garden, but in 1931 she confessed that she could not afford the cost of a railway ticket to visit her niece in Northumberland.

Compassion and unworldliness were but two facets of a lifelong Christian belief. Those who saw her at prayer never forgot the trembling fervour of her self-abasement, the utter submission to an unseen power. The faith of the Cecils, however, was not without an ultimate serenity. When Edward Talbot died in his ninetieth year, Gwendolen wrote of her friend: 'He had always had rather a distressing and, as it seemed to me, incongruous dread of death: and he just dropped asleep, talking at tea time, in his chair, and never really woke again. It was a great tenderness of God's.'

Epilogue

When asked what place Arthur Balfour would have in history, Lloyd George replied: 'He will be just like the scent on a pocket handkerchief.' His Cecil cousins cannot justly claim a more resounding epitaph. Their failure to leave an imprint on the course of events was partly a matter of temperament. They spurned all those political artifices which lie easily on the consciences of practical men, all those half-truths essential to the exercise of parliamentary democracy. They preferred to denounce rather than to persuade, to resign rather than to compromise.

They were not only rigid in their attitudes but isolated in their beliefs. The creeds they embraced were already unfashionable, sometimes obsolete: religious education, free trade, a strong House of Lords. In Egypt and in India, too, the Cecils strove to preserve a benevolent paternalism against insistent demands for self-government.

When not affronting egalitarian sentiment, they were embarrassing their fellow Tories with a quite separate set of heresies. It included votes for women, sympathy for conscientious objectors, contempt for commercialism, the subordination of British foreign policy to the demands of the League of Nations. Hatfield, more than once the seat of power, had become the home of lost causes.

The failure of their designs provoked in them neither dejection nor resentment. Although vehement in discussion and hot-tempered over trifles, the Cecils met tragedy or ill-fortune with an impregnable serenity. It was a question of values. They were not indifferent to the results of the next general election: but they cared more about the immortality of the soul. Ultimately this unfitted them for the shifts and manoeuvres of political life. The nightingale, an Oxford scholar declared, wins no prizes at the poultry show.

Family names and nicknames

Alice	Wife of James, fourth Marquess of Salisbury.
Arthur or A.J.B.	Arthur James Balfour, Prime Minister 1902–5.
Bob	Lord Robert Cecil, later Viscount Cecil of Chelwood.
Bobbety	Robert Cecil, Viscount Cranborne, elder son of fourth Marquess of Salisbury.
Bobby	Robert Palmer, second son of second Earl of Selborne.
Cranborne	Courtesy title of James, fourth Marquess of Salisbury until 1903. Thereafter the courtesy title of Robert, later fifth Marquess of Salisbury.
David	Lord David Cecil, younger son of fourth Marquess of Salisbury.
Edward	Lord Edward Cecil.
Eleanor	Lady Robert Cecil, later Viscountess Cecil of Chelwood.
Fish	Lord William Cecil.
Florence or Fluffy	Wife of Lord William Cecil.
George	Only son of Lord Edward Cecil.
Georgina	Wife of Robert, third Marquess of Salisbury.
Gwendolen	Lady Gwendolen Cecil, younger daughter of third Marquess of Salisbury.
Helen	Only daughter of Lord Edward Cecil.
Hugh	Lord Hugh Cecil.
Jim or Jem	James, fourth Marquess of Salisbury.
Linky or Linkey	Lord Hugh Cecil, later Lord Quickswood.
Luly	Lewis Palmer, youngest son of second Earl of Selborne.

322

Mabel	Only daughter of second Earl of Selborne.
Maud	Lady Maud Cecil, elder daughter of third Marquess of Salisbury and wife of second Earl of Selborne.
Nelly	Lady Robert Cecil, later Viscountess Cecil of Chelwood.
Nigs	Lord Edward Cecil.
Robert	Lord Robert Cecil, later Viscount Cecil of Chelwood.
Salisbury	Third Marquess of Salisbury from 1868 to 1903. Thereafter, James, fourth Marquess of Salisbury.
Tim or T.T. or Titi	Lady Gwendolen Cecil.
Top	Roundell Palmer, Viscount Wolmer, eldest son of second Earl of Selborne.
Violet	Wife of Lord Edward Cecil.
William	Lord William Cecil.
Willy	William, second Earl of Selborne.

Sources

It may be helpful to some readers if I summarize the principal manuscript and printed sources which I have used in writing about the third Marquess of Salisbury and his children. I must add, however, that some of the archives in which I have been privileged to work are not yet freely available to all students of the period.

ROBERT, THIRD MARQUESS OF SALISBURY (1830–1903)

His papers in the library of Christ Church, Oxford (but to be removed to Hatfield during 1975), although largely political, contain letters from his children that illustrate an affectionate relationship. The same theme emerges from the letters of Lord and Lady Salisbury which are to be found in the papers of their children.

The Prime Minister's daughter-in-law, Alice, wife of the fourth Marquess of Salisbury, wrote a long and delightful essay entitled *Hatfield Memories, 1887–1903*. Many members of the Cecil family possess typescript copies, but it has never been published.

The four volumes of Lady Gwendolen Cecil's uncompleted biography of her father, *Life of Robert, Marquis of Salisbury* (volumes I and II, 1921, and volumes III and IV, 1932) are essential to any understanding of that complex character. Three years after Lady Gwendolen's death in 1945 her nephew, the fifth Marquess of Salisbury, had printed for private circulation a volume of her essays entitled *Biographical Studies of the Life and Political Character of Robert, third Marquis of Salisbury*. It adds little of substance to her previous four volumes.

In addition to the more obvious printed sources in my bibliography, I must mention an article from an unidentified French magazine unearthed for me by the fifth Marquess. Entitled *Lord Salisbury dans sa Famille*, it contains some amusing reminiscences by Dr Coppini, the boys' French tutor.

JAMES, FOURTH MARQUESS OF SALISBURY (1861–1947)

There is a huge collection of his papers at Hatfield, sorted into categories and in process of being indexed.

Like his brothers Edward and Hugh, Lord Salisbury often dictated letters to a shorthand-typist. Thus I have usually had the advantage of finding both sides of a particular correspondence at Hatfield: the letters which Salisbury received together with carbon copies of his own.

The papers of his old friend and political colleague Lord Curzon contain valuable material. Curzon's political papers are in the India Office Library; his letters to his second wife, on which I have also drawn, are in the possession of his nephew, Viscount Scarsdale, at Kedleston.

Lady Salisbury's papers, rich in family letters, are at Hatfield. They contain her two long unpublished essays, *Childhood Recollections, 1867–1880* and *Hatfield Memories, 1887–1903*. She also wrote a moving monograph on her husband, privately printed after his death in 1947. It is called *A Memory, 1887–1947*.

There are sensitive biographical portraits of both Lord and Lady Salisbury in the final chapter of *The Cecils of Hatfield House* (1973) by their younger son, Lord David Cecil.

Lord Salisbury's only published work is a pamphlet entitled *Post-War Conservative Policy* that appeared in 1942.

LORD WILLIAM CECIL (1863–1936)

He was not methodical in his habits, and few of his papers seem to have survived. One or two interesting letters, however, are in the possession of his elder daughter, Mrs Richard Benyon. Her twin sister, the Dowager Lady Manners, is the author of an exceptionally perceptive and privately printed memoir of her father, *Some Recollections of W. G. C. Written for his Grandchildren* (1937).

Lord William himself wrote two little volumes about his pastoral mission, *Difficulties and Duties* (undated) and *The Possibilities of Doing Good in a Country Parish* (1937), as well as a weightier, less illuminating work entitled *Changing China* (1910).

LORD ROBERT CECIL, LATER VISCOUNT CECIL OF CHELWOOD (1864–1958)

In 1954 he gave the bulk of his papers, comprising 134 volumes, to the British Museum. They include important correspondence with Balfour, Asquith, Grey, Churchill, Curzon and Baldwin, as well as a mass of material about the League of Nations.

The residue of his papers are at Hatfield and include the entire correspondence that passed between Lord Robert and his wife, beginning with their first meeting in 1888 and ending with his death seventy years later. Lady Robert's letters to her husband are a perpetual delight. The archive is also rich in letters from other members of the Cecil family. All have been expertly catalogued. Another important document at Hatfield is Lord Robert's private diary of the Paris Peace Conference of 1919.

Lord Curzon's papers in the India Office Library contain some brisk exchanges with Cecil about foreign policy.

In old age Lord Robert wrote two eviscerated volumes of autobiography, *A Great Experiment* (1941) and *All the Way* (1949). His candid friend Gilbert Murray, whose own papers in the Bodleian Library contain many letters from Robert and Eleanor Cecil, told him that he lacked both the egotism and the malice needed to write successful memoirs.

Lady Robert's papers are also at Hatfield and include letters from Virginia Woolf and Gilbert Murray. She was much in demand as a correspondent.

LORD EDWARD CECIL (1867–1918)

There are two boxes of his papers at Hatfield. The first includes his remarkable account of dining with Bismarck in 1886, as well as papers of lesser interest about his military career. The second box contains the letters which he wrote to or received from other members of the family, particularly his brother and sister-in-law, Lord and Lady Salisbury.

At the time I was writing my chapter on Lord Edward Cecil, the rest of his private papers were in the possession of his only daughter, the Dowager Lady Hardinge of Penshurst. She has now deposited them, together with some papers of Lady Edward Cecil, in the Kent Archives Office at Maidstone.

Three years after her husband's death in 1918 Lady Edward, by now married to Viscount Milner, arranged for the publication of *The Leisure of an Egyptian Official*, a collection of light-hearted sketches which Lord Edward had written over the years to amuse his family. In 1951 she brought out *My Picture Gallery, 1886–1901*, an entertaining volume of reminiscences.

LORD HUGH CECIL, LATER LORD QUICKSWOOD (1869–1956)

His papers, a voluminous collection, are at Hatfield, skilfully arranged and catalogued.

Many of his letters to Sir Winston Churchill can be found in Companion Volume II (1901–14) of Randolph S. Churchill's *Winston S. Churchill*.

Lord Hugh published only two works: *Liberty and Authority* (1909), an extended version of a lecture at Edinburgh University, and *Conservatism* (1912).

The Rev W. Yorke Batley, a neighbour in Bournemouth, had printed for private circulation in 1956 a pamphlet entitled *Personal Memories of Lord Quickswood*. And the anonymous obituary notice in the *Eton College Chronicle* of 7 February 1957 could scarcely be bettered; the author is in fact Mr Richard Martineau.

MAUD, COUNTESS OF SELBORNE (1858–1950)

Lady Selborne is believed to have destroyed many of her own papers, including the letters she wrote to her husband. But those which he wrote to her are in his papers in the Bodleian Library.

Many of the letters she wrote to her children are in the Hampshire County Archives at Winchester. Others are in the possession of her daughter-in-law, the Hon Mrs Lewis Palmer.

LADY GWENDOLEN CECIL (1860–1945)

There are four boxes of her papers at Hatfield, including both sides of a life-long correspondence with her sister, Lady Selborne. Her niece, the Dowager Lady Manners, has written a privately printed memoir of Lady Gwendolen, a masterpiece of humour and understanding.

Acknowledgments

CECIL FAMILY PAPERS

I owe an enduring debt of gratitude to Robert, fifth Marquess of Salisbury, who in 1970 gave me permission to use the several large collections of hitherto unseen papers at Hatfield that had belonged to his parents and to other members of the Cecil family. Without his help, trust and encouragement, this book could not have been written.

Since his father's death in 1972 Robert, sixth and present Marquess of Salisbury, has been no less generous in allowing me to consult and to quote from the Hatfield archives, as well as from other letters and papers of which he owns the copyright. I am also grateful to him for permission to reproduce pictures and photographs in his possession.

Lord David Cecil, younger brother of the late Lord Salisbury and author of that graceful and imaginative volume, *The Cecils of Hatfield House*, was kind enough to read my book in typescript. His guidance has been invaluable.

The Dowager Lady Hardinge of Penshurst put at my disposal the papers of her parents, Lord and Lady Edward Cecil, buttressed by her own perceptive and illuminating recollections.

Professor A. K. S. Lambton has allowed me to quote from the letters and other manuscripts of her uncle and aunt, Lord and Lady Robert Cecil, of which she owns the copyright.

I am similarly obliged to the Earl of Selborne for permission to quote from the letters of his great-grandmother, Maud Countess of Selborne. Many of these were kindly lent to me by her daughter-in-law, the Hon Mrs Lewis Palmer, who also searched her memory on my behalf. Lady Anne Brewis, Lady Laura Eastaugh, Lady Mary Howick and the Hon Robert Palmer, all grandchildren of Lady Selborne, gave me their recollections of her. I must record with much sadness that another grandchild of Lady Selborne, the Hon Edward Palmer, died in August 1974. His labours on my behalf were prolonged and unsparing.

Mr Victor Cecil, Mrs Richard Benyon and the Dowager Lady Manners, the three surviving children of Lord and Lady William Cecil, have patiently answered my many questions and lent me letters, photographs and privately printed or unpublished family memoirs.

The Dowager Lady Harlech and the Dowager Duchess of Devonshire, daughters of the fourth Marquess of Salisbury, talked with charm and humour of their early years. And two of Lord Salisbury's grandchildren, Lord Harlech and the Hon Mrs Maurice Macmillan, recalled life at Hatfield through eyes of a later generation.

My own researches at Hatfield were wonderfully eased by the knowledge and kindness of Miss Clare Talbot (now Mrs Peter Grant), the devoted librarian and archivist of what remains perhaps the most important collection of English historical papers in private hands. I must also thank her successor at Hatfield, Mr Robin Harcourt Williams, and the librarian of Christ Church, Oxford, Dr J. F. M. Mason, for their invariable helpfulness and courtesy.

OTHER MANUSCRIPT SOURCES

I am deeply grateful to all those who have given me permission to reproduce letters and other manuscripts of which they hold the copyright or who have allowed me access to papers in their possession or care.

Her Majesty the Queen, for a letter written by the Duke of York, later King George v; and for letters written by his private secretary, Lord Stamfordham.

The Warden and Fellows of All Souls College, Oxford, for information about the third Marquess of Salisbury's emoluments as a Fellow. This was kindly extracted for me from the college 'Song Books' by the Librarian, Mr J. S. G. Simmons.

The Earl of Antrim, for letters written by Sir Schomberg McDonnell.

The Earl Baldwin of Bewdley, for letters written by his father, the first Earl.

The Earl of Balfour, for letters written by his uncle, the first Earl.

The Beaconsfield Trustees, for letters written by Benjamin Disraeli, Earl of Beaconsfield.

Professor Quentin Bell, for letters written by his aunt, Virginia Woolf.

Mrs John Bennett, for letters written by her father, H. A. L. Fisher.

The Curators of the Bodleian Library, Oxford, for access to its collections of manuscripts.

The Hon Mark Bonham Carter, for letters written by the first Earl and Countess of Oxford and Asquith.

Lord Brabazon of Tara, for a letter written by his father, the first Baron.

The Trustees of the British Museum, for access to its collection of manuscripts.

C. & T. Publications, Ltd, for unpublished letters written by Sir Winston Churchill.

The Viscount Cobham, for an extract from the manuscript diary of his great-aunt, Lavinia Talbot.

ACKNOWLEDGEMENTS

Mr C. S. A. Dobson, Librarian of the House of Lords, for an extract from the manuscript diary of Sir Edmund Gosse.

The late Sir Claude Elliott, for his correspondence with Lord Quickswood.

Mr I. J. C. Foster, Keeper of Oriental Books at Durham University, for access to the papers of General Sir Reginald Wingate.

The Hampshire Record Office, for access to the papers of Maud Countess of Selborne and of Lady Laura Ridding.

Mr John Herbert, for a letter written by his father, the late Sir Alan Herbert.

The Librarian of the India Office Library for Crown Copyright letters written by Lord Curzon of Kedleston and Lord George Hamilton.

Lord Lambton, for a letter written by the third Earl of Durham.

Mrs Stephen Lloyd, for a letter written by her father, Neville Chamberlain.

Sir John Masterman, for his correspondence with Lord Quickswood.

Mr Reginald Maudling for a letter of his own.

Colonel Terence Maxwell, for a letter written by Austen Chamberlain.

Mr Stephen Murray, for letters written by his father, Gilbert Murray.

The Warden and Fellows of New College, Oxford, for a letter written by Viscount Milner.

The Earl of Rosebery, for letters written by his grandfather, the fifth Earl.

The Viscount Rothermere, for letters written by his father, the first Viscount.

The Viscount Scarsdale and the Kedleston Trustees for letters written by the Marquess Curzon of Kedleston.

Mr T. G. Talbot, for a letter written by his grandfather, J. G. Talbot.

Mr A. J. P. Taylor, for access to the Lloyd George papers in the Beaverbrook Library and for help in tracing elusive documents.

HELP AND ADVICE

I should like to thank all those who have given me their personal recollections of the Cecil family or who have generously helped in other ways:

HRH Princess Alice, Countess of Athlone; Miss Betty Askwith (the Hon Mrs Keith Miller Jones); Miss Eva Bestley; the Lord Blake; Mr Andrew Boyle; the Lord Boyle of Handsworth; the Viscount Brentford; Professor Asa Briggs; Sir Ernest Bullock; Canon Howard Dobson; Lady Douglas-Home; Dr H. C. Ferens; Mr John Gere; Mr Martin Gilbert; Mr Sam Goodenough; Mr John Grigg; Canon E. F. Hall; Mr Walter Hamilton; Sir Archibald James; Mr T. A. R. Levett; the staff of the London Library; Mr Harold Macmillan; Mr Eric Major; Mr John B. Marriott; Mr Richard Martineau; the late Very Rev W. R. Matthews; Mr J. G. Milner; Mr E. P. Poole; Mr D. S. Porter and other members of the staff of the Bodleian Library; Mrs M. A. Rawlinson; Dr A. L. Rowse; the Hon Giles St Aubyn; Sir John Guillam Scott; Major J. P. Smiley, Grenadier Guards; Miss Marion Strachan; Mr A. B. Twist; Mr J. H. Tunnell; Mr Oliver Van Oss; Miss Joan Watson; Mr Peter Winckworth.

I am particularly in the debt of Mr Norman Knight who, with the assistance of Mrs Valerie Chandler, has compiled an exceptionally valuable index.

Finally I must express my gratitude to Mr Simon Dally and his colleagues at Weidenfeld and Nicolson for the energy, skill and cheerful enthusiasm which they have brought to the production of the present volume.

Bibliography

I am grateful to the authors, publishers and copyright owners of the under-mentioned books for permission, where necessary, to quote from them. Each individual mention is acknowledged in 'Source References'. This bibliography includes only a very few of the unpublished or privately printed memoirs which I have used; most of them are to be found under 'Sources'.

ALDERSON, CHARLES, *Selections from the Charges and Other Detached Papers of Baron Alderson*, John W. Parker & Son, West Strand, 1858.

AMERY, L. S., *My Political Life*, Vol III, 1929–40, Hutchinson, 1955.

ARBUTHNOT, MRS, *Journal, 1820–1832*, 2 vols, Macmillan, 1950.

ARTHUR, SIR GEORGE (Ed), *The Letters of Lord and Lady Wolseley*, Heinemann, 2nd edition, 1923.

ASQUITH, LADY CYNTHIA, *Remember and Be Glad*, Barrie, 1952.

ASQUITH, MARGOT, *Autobiography*, Thornton Butterworth, Vol. II, 1922.

ATTLEE, C. R., *As It Happened*, Heinemann, 1954.

AUERBACH, ERNA, and ADAMS, C. KINGSLEY, *Paintings & Sculpture at Hatfield House*, Constable, 1971.

BALFOUR, LADY FRANCES, *Ne Obliviscaris*, 2 vols, Hodder & Stoughton, 1930.

BARING, MAURICE, *R.F.C. H.Q., 1914–1918*, Bell, 1920.

BATEMAN, JOHN, *The Great Landowners of Great Britain and Ireland*, Harrison, 4th edition, 1883.

BEAVERBROOK, LORD, *Men and Power, 1917–18*, Hutchinson, 1956.

BELL, RT REV G. K. A., *Randall Davidson, Archbishop of Canterbury*, OUP, 2nd edition, 1938.

BEVERIDGE, LORD, *Power and Influence*, Hodder & Stoughton, 1953.

BIRKENHEAD, 1st EARL OF, *Contemporary Personalities*, Cassell, 1924.

BIRKENHEAD, 2nd EARL OF, *Halifax: the Life of Lord Halifax*, Hamish Hamilton, 1965.

BLAKE, ROBERT, *The Unknown Prime Minister: the Life and Times of Andrew Bonar Law*, Eyre & Spottiswoode, 1955.

BLAKE, ROBERT, Disraeli, Eyre & Spottiswoode, 1966.

BLAKE, ROBERT (Ed), *The Private Papers of Douglas Haig, 1914–19*, Eyre & Spottiswoode, 1952.

BLUNT, W. S., *My Diaries, 1888–1914*, Martin Secker, 1932 Edition.

BONHAM CARTER, VIOLET, *Winston Churchill as I Knew Him*, Eyre & Spottiswoode & Collins, 1965.

BOWRA, MAURICE, *Memories*, Weidenfeld & Nicolson, 1966.

BOYLE, ANDREW, *Montagu Norman*, Cassell, 1967.

BOYLE, ANDREW, *Trenchard*, Collins, 1962.

BOYLE, CLARA, *Boyle of Cairo*, Titus Wilson, Kendal, 1965.

BRABAZON OF TARA, LORD, *The Brabazon Story*, Heinemann, 1956.

BRETT, M. V. (Ed), *Journals and Letters of Reginald, Viscount Esher*, Nicholson and Watson, 4 vols, 1934 and 1938.

BUCKLE, G. E. (Ed), *Letters of Queen Victoria, 1886–1901*, Third Series, 3 vols, Murray, 1932.

BUCKLER, B., *Stemmata Chicheleana*, OUP, 1765.

CARROLL, LEWIS, *Complete Works*, Nonesuch Press, 1939.

CARROLL, LEWIS, *Diaries*, Ed Roger Lancelyn Green, Cassell, 1953.

CARTER, J. C. [Anon], *William Johnson Cory*, Rampant Lions Press, Cambridge, 1959.

CECIL, ALGERNON, *A Life of Robert Cecil first Earl of Salisbury*, Murray, 1915.

CECIL, ALGERNON, *Queen Victoria and her Prime Ministers*, Eyre & Spottiswoode, 1953.

CECIL, LORD DAVID, *The Cecils of Hatfield House*, Constable, 1973.

CECIL, LORD EDWARD, *The Leisure of an Egyptian Official*, Hodder & Stoughton, 1935 Edition.

CECIL, LADY GWENDOLEN, *Life of Robert, Marquis of Salisbury*, Hodder & Stoughton, Vols I & II, 1921; Vols III & IV, 1932.

CECIL, LORD HUGH, *Conservatism*, Home University Library, 1912.

CECIL, LORD HUGH, *Liberty and Authority*, Arnold, 1910.

CECIL, LORD WILLIAM [Assisted by Lady Florence Cecil], *Changing China*, Nisbet, 1910.

CECIL, LORD WILLIAM, *Difficulties and Duties*, Nisbet, ND.

CECIL, LORD WILLIAM, *The Possibilities of Doing Good in a Country Parish*, SPCK, 1937.

CECIL OF CHELWOOD, VISCOUNT, *A Great Experiment*, Cape, 1941.

CECIL OF CHELWOOD, VISCOUNT, *All the Way*, Hodder & Stoughton, 1949.

CHADWICK, OWEN, *The Victorian Church*, Pt II, Black, 1970.

CHURCHILL, RANDOLPH S., *Winston S. Churchill*, Companion Volumes, 1901–14, 3 vols, Heinemann, 1969.

CHURCHILL, WINSTON S., *Lord Randolph Churchill*, Odhams, New Edition, 1951.

CHURCHILL, WINSTON S., *My Early Life*, Odhams, 1930.

CHURCHILL, WINSTON S., *Thoughts and Adventures*, Odhams, 1932.

CLARENDON, EARL OF, *History of the Rebellion and Civil Wars*, OUP, 1826 edition.

COLE, G. D. H. [and Raymond Postgate], *The Common People, 1746–1938*, Methuen, 1938.

COLERIDGE, ARTHUR DUKE, *Eton in the Forties*, Richard Bentley, 2nd Edition, 1898.

Complete Peerage, St Catherine Press, 1910–59, 13 vols.

COOPER, DUFF, *Old Men Forget*, Hart-Davis, 1953.

CURZON OF KEDLESTON, EARL, *Modern Parliamentary Eloquence*, Macmillan, 1914.

CURZON OF KEDLESTON, MARCHIONESS, *Reminiscences*, Hutchinson, 1955.

DALTON, HUGH, *Call Back Yesterday*, Muller, 1953.

DENNIS, G. RAVENSCROFT, *The House of Cecil*, Constable, 1914.

DICKENS, CHARLES, *The Adventures of Oliver Twist*, Chapman & Hall, 1913.

Dictionary of National Biography, suppplementary volumes, 1901–60, OUP.

DILKS, DAVID, *Curzon in India*, Hart-Davis, Vol I, 1969, Vol II, 1970.

DINO, DUCHESSE DE, *Memoirs, 1831–1835*, Princess Radziwill (Ed), Heinemann, 1909.

DONALDSON, FRANCES, *The Marconi Scandal*, Hart-Davis, 1962.

DRIBERG, TOM, *The Mystery of Moral Re-Armament*, Secker & Warburg, 1964.

DUGDALE, BLANCHE E. C., *Arthur James Balfour*, Hutchinson, 2 vols, 1936.

DUGDALE, BLANCHE E. C., *Family Homespun*, Murray, 1940.

EDWARDS, DAVID L., *Leaders of the Church of England, 1828–1944*, OUP, 1971.

EVANS, JOAN, *Time and Change*, Longmans, Green & Co, 1943.

FISHER, H. A. L., *An Unfinished Autobiography*, OUP, 1940.

FITZROY, SIR ALMERIC, *Memoirs*, Hutchinson, 2 vols, ND.

FLETCHER, C. R. L., *Edmond Warre*, Murray, 1922.

FLOWER, NEWMAN (Ed), *Journals of Arnold Bennett*, Vol II, 1911–21, Cassell, 1932.

FOOT, M. R. D. (Ed), *The Gladstone Diaries* Vol I 1825–32, OUP, 1968.

FOX, ADAM, *Dean Inge*, Murray, 1960.

GARDINER, S. R., *History of England*, Longmans, Green, 1884.

GLEICHEN, COUNT, *With the Mission to Menelik*, Arnold, 1898.

GORE, JOHN (Ed), *Creevey's Life and Times*, Murray, 1934.

GRINNELL-MILNE, DUNCAN, *Baden-Powell at Mafeking*, Bodley Head, 1957.

GUEDALLA, PHILIP, *A Gallery*, Hodder & Stoughton, N.D.

GWYNN, STEPHEN (Ed), *Letters & Friendships of Sir Cecil Spring Rice*, 2 vols, Constable, 1929.

HALIFAX, EARL OF, *Fulness of Days*, Collins, 1957.

HARDINGE OF PENSHURST, LORD, *Old Diplomacy*, Murray, 1947.

HARE, AUGUSTUS, *In My Solitary Life*, Allen & Unwin, abridged edition, 1953.

HARRIS, WILSON, *Life So Far*, Cape, 1954.

HAZLEHURST, CAMERON, *Politicians at War: July 1914 to May 1915*, Cape, 1971.

HENSON, HERBERT HENSLEY, *Retrospect of an Un*important Life, 2 vols in 1, OUP, 1943.

HENSON, HERBERT HENSLEY, *Letters*, SPCK, 1950.

HERBERT, A. P., *Independent Member*, Methuen, 1950.

HEUSTON, R. F. V., *Lives of the Lord Chancellors, 1885–1940*, OUP, 1946.

JENKINS, ROY, *Mr Balfour's Poodle*, Heinemann, 1954.

JENKINS, ROY, *Asquith*, Collins, 1964.

JENNINGS, SIR IVOR, *Cabinet Government*, Cambridge, 2nd edition, 1951.

JOHNSTON, J. O., *Life and Letters of Henry Parry Liddon*, Longmans, Green, 1904.

JONES, THOMAS, *Lloyd George*, OUP, 1951.

JONES, THOMAS, *A Diary with Letters, 1931–1950*, OUP, 1954.

JONES, THOMAS, *Whitehall Diary*, Vol I, 1916–25, OUP, 1969.

KENNEDY, A. L., *Salisbury 1830–1903: Portrait of a Statesman*, Murray, 1953.

LEVESON GOWER, SIR GEORGE, *Mixed Grill*, Muller, 1947.

LOCKHART, J. G., *Cosmo Gordon Lang*, Hodder & Stoughton, 1949.

LUBBOCK, S. G., *Montague Rhodes James*, OUP, 1939.

LUCY, HENRY W., *A Diary of the Salisbury Parliament 1886–1892*, Cassell, 1892.

LUTYENS, MARY (Ed), *Lady Lytton's Court Diary 1895–1899*, Hart-Davis, 1961.

LYALL, SIR ALFRED, *Life of Dufferin*, 2 vols, Murray, 1905.

MACAULAY, T. B., *History of England*, 3 vols, J. M. Dent, 1934 edition.

MACMILLAN, HAROLD, *Winds of Change*, Macmillan, 1966.

MACMILLAN, HAROLD, *The Blast of War*, Macmillan, 1967.

McCALLUM, R. B., *Public Opinion and the Last Peace*, OUP, 1944.

McCONNELL, J. D. R., *Eton Repointed*, Faber, 1970.

McKENZIE, R. T., *British Political Parties*, Heinemann, 1955.

MAGNUS, SIR PHILIP, *Kitchener*, Murray, 1958.

MALLET, VICTOR, *Life with Queen Victoria: Marie Mallet's Letters from Court, 1887–1901*, Murray, 1968.

MARLOWE, JOHN, *Cromer in Egypt*, Elek, 1970.

MARSH, EDWARD, *A Number of People*, Heinemann, 1939.

MARSH, EDWARD & HASSALL, CHRISTOPHER, *Ambrosia and Small Beer*. Longmans, 1964.

MATTHEWS, VERY REV, W. R., *Memories & Meanings*, Hodder & Stoughton, 1969.

MAXWELL, SIR HERBERT (Ed), *The Creevey Papers*, Murray, 1912.

MAXWELL LYTE, H. C., *A History of Eton College*, Macmillan, 3rd edition, 1899.

MERSEY, VISCOUNT, *A Picture of Life, 1872–1940*, Murray, 1941.

MERSEY, VISCOUNT, *Journal and Memories*, Murray, 1952.

MIDDLEMAS, KEITH & BARNES, JOHN, *Baldwin*, Weidenfeld & Nicolson, 1969.

MILNER, VISCOUNTESS, *My Picture Gallery, 1886–1901*, Murray, 1951.

MONYPENNY, W. F., and BUCKLE, G. E., *The Life of Benjamin Disraeli, Earl of Beaconsfield*, 6 vols, Murray, 1910–20.

MOSLEY, SIR OSWALD, *My Life*, Nelson, 1968.

NAPIER, PRISCILLA, *A Late Beginner*, Michael Joseph, 1966.

NICOLSON, HAROLD, *Curzon: the Last Phase*, Constable, 1937 edition.

OMAN, CAROLA, *The Gascoyne Heiress: the Life and Diaries of Frances Mary Gascoyne-Cecil, 1802–1839*, Hodder & Stoughton, 1968.

OMAN, CHARLES, *Memories of Victorian Oxford*, Methuen, 1941.

OMAN, CHARLES, *The Text of the Old Betting Book of All Souls College, 1815–1873*, privately printed, Oxford, 1912.

OMAN, CHARLES, *The Text of the Second Betting Book of All Souls College, 1873–1919*, privately printed, Oxford, 1938.

OXFORD AND ASQUITH, EARL OF, *Fifty Years of Parliament*, 2 vols, Cassell, 1926.

PEPYS, SAMUEL, *Diary, deciphered by the Rev. J. Smith*, 2 vols, Dent, 1927.

PINTO-DUSCHINSKY, MICHAEL, *The Political Thought of Lord Salisbury, 1854–1868*, Constable, 1967.

PONSONBY OF SHULBREDE, LORD, *Henry Ponsonby*, Macmillan, 1942.

PORTLAND, DUKE OF, *Men, Women and Things*, Faber, 1937.

PURCELL, WILLIAM, *Fisher of Lambeth: a Portrait from Life*, Hodder & Stoughton, 1969.

QUENNELL, PETER (Ed), *The Private Letters of Princess Lieven to Prince Metternich, 1820–1826*, Murray, 1937.

REMPEL, RICHARD A., *Unionists Divided*, David & Charles, 1972.

RHODES JAMES, ROBERT, *Memoirs of a Conservative: J. C. C. Davidson*, Weidenfeld and Nicolson, 1969.

RIDDING, LADY LAURA, *The Life of Robert Palmer, 1888–1916*, Hodder & Stoughton, 1921.

ROBBINS, KEITH, *Sir Edward Grey*, Cassell, 1971.

RODD, SIR JAMES RENNELL, *Social & Diplomatic Memories*, Second Series, 1894–1901, Arnold, 1923.

ROSKILL, STEPHEN, *Hankey: Man of Secrets*, Vol I 1877–1918, Vol II 1919–31, Collins, 1970 and 1972.

ROWSE, A. L., *The England of Elizabeth*, Macmillan, 1951.

SALISBURY, JAMES, FOURTH MARQUESS OF, *Post-War Conservative Policy*, Murray, 1942.

SIMON, VISCOUNT, *Retrospect*, Hutchinson, 1952.

SMITH, PAUL (Ed), *Lord Salisbury on Politics: a Selection of his Articles in the Quarterly Review 1860–1883*, CUP, 1972.

SPEAIGHT, ROBERT, *The Property Basket*, Collins, 1970.

STEINER, ZARA S., *The Foreign Office and Foreign Policy, 1898–1914*, CUP, 1969.

STEINHART, HAROLD (Ed), *The History of the Oxford Canning Club*, privately printed, Oxford, 1911.

STERN, SIR ALBERT, *Tanks 1914–1918*, Hodder & Stoughton, 1919.

STONE, LAWRENCE, *Family and Fortune: Studies in Aristocratic Finance*, OUP, 1973.

STRACHEY, LYTTON AND FULFORD, ROGER (Ed), *The Greville Memoirs, 1814–1860*, Macmillan, 8 vols, 1938.

TOYNBEE, ARNOLD J., *Acquaintances*, OUP, 1967.

ULLSWATER, VISCOUNT, *A Speaker's Commentaries*, Arnold, 2 vols, 1925..

WALPOLE, HORACE, *Visits to Country Seats*, Vol XVI, Walpole Society, OUP, 1928.

WEBB, BEATRICE, *Diaries, 1912–1924*, Longmans, Green, 1952.

337

WHEELER-BENNETT, SIR JOHN (Ed), *Action This Day*, Essay by John Colville, Macmillan, 1968.

WILLIAMS, NEVILLE, *The Royal Residences of Great Britain*, Barrie & Rockliff, 1960.

WILSON, JOHN, *C.B.: A Life of Sir Henry Campbell-Bannerman*, Constable, 1973.

WILSON, LADY SARAH, *South African Memories*, Arnold, 1909.

WINGATE, RONALD, *Wingate of the Sudan*, Murray, 1955.

WINTERTON, EARL, *Order of the Day*, Cassell, 1953.

YOUNG, KENNETH, *Balfour*, Bell, 1963.

I am also grateful to the editors of *The Times*, the *Daily Telegraph*, *Parliamentary Debates: Official Report (Hansard)*, *Proceedings of the Church Assembly*, the *Eton College Chronicle* and other publications from which I have quoted. Each individual mention is acknowledged in 'Source References'.

Source References

To avoid distracting the general reader, I have adopted a system of references that does not deface the text with innumerable figures or letters of the alphabet, yet allows each quotation or allusion in the book to be traced swiftly to its source. All references have been grouped together here, each being prefaced by the number of the page, the number of the line and a catch-phrase for easy recognition. The line number is that of the *last* line of the quotation or other statement in the main text.

BOOKS AND PERIODICALS

Each reference to a quotation or allusion consists of a catch-phrase to identify the topic, the surname of the author, the title of the book or article (sometimes abbreviated for convenience) and the volume number (where necessary) and page. The full name of the author, the title of the book, the publisher and the date of publication can be found listed alphabetically under the author's surname in 'Bibliography'.

LETTERS

Each reference consists of a catch-phrase to identify the topic, the name of the writer of the letter, the name of the recipient, the date, the archive where the letter is to be found and, where possible, its serial number.

The Marquess of Salisbury of the day is referred to simply as Salisbury, and his eldest son by the courtesy title of Cranborne. Other members of the Cecil family are referred to by their Christian names. There is a list of all such names on pages 322–3.

The following abbreviations have been used to indicate the manuscript collection in which each quoted letter is to be found:
A   Alice, fourth Marchioness of Salisbury. Hatfield.
B   Lord Robert Cecil. British Museum.

C   Lord and Lady Robert Cecil. Hatfield.
D   Robert, third Marquess of Salisbury. Christ Church, Oxford, but to be
      removed to Hatfield.
E   Lord Edward Cecil. Hatfield.
F   Second Earl of Selborne. Bodleian Library, Oxford.
G   Lady Gwendolen Cecil. Hatfield.
H   Lord Edward Cecil. Papers of the Dowager Lady Hardinge of Penshurst,
      most of which are now in the Kent Archives Office, Maidstone.
J   Fourth Marquess of Salisbury, Hatfield.
K   Maud, Countess of Selborne. Hampshire County Archives, Winchester.
L   Maud, Countess of Selborne. Papers of the Hon Mrs Lewis Palmer.
M   Professor Gilbert and Lady Mary Murray. Bodleian Library, Oxford.
N   Marquess Curzon of Kedleston. Kedleston.
P   Marquess Curzon of Kedleston. India Office Library.
Q   Lord Hugh Cecil, later Baron Quickswood. Hatfield.

PERSONAL REMINISCENCES

These, whether given to me in conversation or by letter, are acknowledged
in the form : Lord Harlech to author. 7 December 1971.

CHAPTER ONE: FAMILY HISTORY

p. 3. l.5   Original name. Robert Cecil. Diary. 24 May 1919. C 75.
      l.17 Mafeking ode. *The Times.* 21 May 1900.
      l.19 Austin's solecism. Eleanor to Violet. 26 May 1900. H.
p. 4. l.1   Sir Spirit. Rowse. *England of Elizabeth.* 280.
      l.26 Elizabethan economics. *Ibid.* 156.
p. 5. l.9   Prudent friendship. Algernon Cecil. *Robert Cecil.* 11.
      l.18 Ship into harbour. Dennis. *House of Cecil.* 176.
      l.28 Honesty and fortune. Algernon Cecil. *Robert Cecil.* 197.
      l.38 £25,000 a year. Stone. *Family and Fortune.* 27.
      l.40 Equivalent value. *Ibid.* 57.
p. 6. l.7   Building programme. *Ibid.* 32.
      l.12 Theobalds. Williams. *Royal Residences.* 166.
      l.21 Cost of entertainment. Algernon Cecil. *Robert Cecil.* 197.
p. 7. l.10 Design of Hatfield. *Ibid.* 327.
      l.35 Family intelligence. Gwendolen Cecil. *Salisbury.* I. 2.
      l.38 Shades of Proust. Harold Macmillan to author. 6 August 1970.
      l.42 No words. Clarendon. *History.* III. 559.
      l.42 Simple. Pepys. *Diary.* I. 526. 16 October 1664.
p. 8. l.3   Incompetent. Gardiner. History. VIII. 70.
      l.11 Page of Honour. *Complete Peerage.* XI. 407.
      l.13 Intact fortune. Stone. *Family and Fortune.* 145 *et seq.*
      l.15 Friend of Wotton. Auerbach. *Paintings and Sculpture.* 26.
      l.19 Pepys. *Diary.* I. 178. 22 July 1661.

l.29 Cold welcome. Dennis. *House of Cecil.* 228.

l.36 Family allowances. Stone. *Family and Fortune.* 152–5.

l.40 Portraits. Auerbach. *Paintings and Sculpture.* 163.

l.43 Gambling. David Cecil. *The Cecils.* 177.

p. 9. l.1 Extravagance. Stone. *Family and Fortune.* 157–8.

l.2 Salisbury House. David Cecil. *The Cecils.* 180.

l.10 Miscalculation. Abraham de la Pryme's Diary. Quo. *Complete Peerage.* XI. 408.

l.15 Sluggish mind. Macaulay. *History of England.* I. 656.

l.33 Disrepair. Walpole. *Country Seats.* XVI. 35. 7 June 1761.

l.36 Cecilian phoenix. Dennis. *House of Cecil.* 234.

p. 10. l.12 Forty years on. Maxwell. *Creevey.* 379.

l.16 Poor relief. G. Cecil. *Salisbury.* I. 3.

l.20 Jumping fences. Dennis. *House of Cecil.* 238.

l.21 Fourth of June. Gore. *Creevey,* 265.

l.23 Whist. *Ibid.* 229.

l.24 Horseplay. *Ibid.* 236.

l.30 Shabby fellow. Dino. *Memoirs.* I. 35.

l.33 Swollen leg. Arbuthnot. *Journal.* II. 73.

l.36 Invitations. Carola Oman. *Gascoyne Heiress.* 187.

p. 11. l.5 Fire at Hatfield. Dickens. *Oliver Twist.* 307–8.

l.9 Jewels in pawn. Gore. *Creevey.* 415.

l.10 Blue ribbon. Arbuthnot. *Journal.* I. 240.

l.24 No employment. Carola Oman. *Gascoyne Heiress.* 46.

l.33 Brains and beards. Strachey and Fulford. *Greville.* IV. 2.

l.40 Citizen class. G. Cecil. *Salisbury.* I. 2.

p. 12. l.2 Married for money. Arbuthnot. *Journal.* I. 68.

l.19 Without charm. Quennell. *Princess Lieven.* 335. 14 October 1824.

l.29 Royal dukes. Carola Oman. *Gascoyne Heiress.* 127.

l.32 Godparent. *Ibid.* 71.

CHAPTER TWO: THE PRIME MINISTER

p. 15. l.18 Devils. G. Cecil. *Salisbury.* I. 9.

l.25 Scientific research. *Ibid.* I. 10.

l.30 Evidence of physique. Coleridge. *Eton in the 'Forties.* 3.

l.37 Unhappy return. G. Cecil. *Salisbury.* I. 16.

fn. Rising sun. Fletcher. *Warre.* 14.

p. 16. l.6 Clever essays. Lyall. *Dufferin.* II. 320.

l.27 Mortified pride. Foot. *Gladstone Diaries.* I. 290. 24 March 1830.

l.30 Bullies routed. G. Cecil. *Salisbury.* I. 23.

l.39 Honorary degree. *Ibid.* I. 20.

p. 17. l.1 Few openings. *Ibid.* I. 37.

l.11 Detestable career. *Ibid.* I. 50.

l.27 Annual income. *Ibid.* I. 59–60.

l.35 Founder's kin. Charles Oman. *Victorian Oxford.* 121.

l.37 Sixteen candidates. G. Cecil. *Salisbury.* I. 38.

fn. 2 Boardroom peers. *Complete Peerage.* V. 780
fn. 3 Chichele blood. Buckler. *Stemmata Chicheleana. passim.*
p. *18.* l.8 Fellowship stipend. All Souls 'Song Books', 1854–8.
    l.31 Death penalty. Alderson. *Baron Alderson.* 64.
    l.34 Forms of murder. *Ibid.* 78.
    l.39 Minute observance. *Ibid.* 50.
p. *19.* l.2 Betting men. *Ibid.* 117.
    l.17 Letter to a schoolboy. *Ibid.* 6–7.
    l.28 Never bored. G. Cecil. *Salisbury.* I. 56.
    l.39 Descent from Burghley. F. A. Alderson to Gwendolen.
        12 Jan. 1905. G.
p 20. l.15 Cutting retort. G. Cecil. *Salisbury.* I. 59.
    l.21 Absent father. Salisbury to Robert. 23 June 1857. D.
    l.25 Disapproving brother. Cranborne to Robert. 23 June 1857. D.
    l.31 Intolerably complacent. Gwendolen to Maud. 3 Aug. 1906. G.
    l.36 Oxford Street. G. Cecil. *Salisbury.* I. 63.
    l.38 Georgina's income. *Ibid.* I. 65.
p. *21.* l.17 Unsatisfactory jobs. *Ibid.* I. 65–9.
    l.28 Newspapers. *Ibid.* I. 37.
    l.38 Early journalism. Smith. *Salisbury on Politics.* 3–4.
    l.39 Hateful occupation. G. Cecil. *Salisbury.* I. 70.
p. *22.* l.11 Labourers and Rothschild. Q.R. CXVI. 266 (1864). quo. Smith.
        Salisbury on Politics. 45.
    l.19 Electioneering. *Bentley's Quarterly Review.* I. 355 (1859).
    l.31 Damaged goods. *Ibid.* I. 5–6 (1859).
    l.36 No escape. *Ibid.* I. 360 (1859).
p. *23.* l.3 Writing to sell. G. Cecil. *Salisbury.* I. 86. 25 July 1859.
    l.9 Railway chairman. *Complete Peerage.* XI. 413.
    l.12 Banking failure. Smith. *Salisbury on Politics.* 4.
    l.22 Agitated mind. *Ibid.* 9.
    l.25 Depression and lassitude. G. Cecil. *Salisbury.* I. 49.
    l.31 Misanthropus. Quo. Dennis. *House of Cecil.* 168.
    l.35 Ishmaelite. G. Cecil. *Salisbury.* I. 123.
p. *24.* l.1 Maligned attorneys. *Ibid.* I. 134.
    l.4 Tamerlane. Q.R. CXVII (1865). 269. Quo. Smith. *Salisbury on Politics.* 9.
    l.6 Flouts and jeers. *Hansard.* 5 Aug. 1874.
    l.15 Early education. Pinto-Duschinsky. *Political Thought.* 24.
    l.25 Graduated terms. Carter. *Cory.* 1.
    l.35 French tutor. Coppini. *Lord Salisbury.*
p. *25.* l.3 No connection. G. Cecil. *Salisbury.* I. 126.
    l.15 Sincere Jew. *Ibid.*

CHAPTER THREE: CHILDHOOD AT HATFIELD

p. 26. l.27 Fur rug. Lord Esher. *National Review.* April 1923.
p. 27. l.2 Gallery race. Robert to Eleanor. 14 March 1897. C 2/197.

l.14 Age of twelve. Robert Cecil. *All the Way*. 15.

l.22 Anglican church. Kennedy. *Salisbury*. 125.

l.26 Weekly Communion. Alice Salisbury. *Hatfield Memories*.

l.28 Dogmatic theology. Alderson. *Baron Alderson*. 137.

l.29 Refreshment. Georgina to Robert. 9 April [   ]. C 51/47–8.

p. 28. l.1 Explaining God. G. Cecil. *Salisbury*. I. 113.

l.12 No paternal counsel. *Ibid*. III. 15.

l.18 Stopped argument. Robert to Eleanor. 2 Sept. 1888. C 1/54.

l.27 Humble and silent. Georgina to Eleanor. 25 Jan. [   ].
C 51/30–1.

p. 29. l.6 Relations with children. G. Cecil. *Salisbury*. III. 11–13.

l.26 Metaphysical argument. Gwendolen to Frances Balfour.
11 Dec. [1886]. C 58/119.

l.41 Regretful departure. Alice Salisbury. *Hatfield Memories*.

p. 30. l.4 Talking till dawn. Balfour. *Ne Obliviscaris*. I. 341.

l.11 Fire-fighting. *Ibid*. I. 310–11.

l.17 Cause of explosion. G. Cecil. *Salisbury*. I. 176.

l.21 Early telephone. *Ibid*. III. 8.

l.31 Gracious reception. Carroll. *Diaries*. 288. 25 June 1870.

l.37 Perfectly at ease. *Ibid*. 301. 2 July 1871.

p. 31. l.3 Suggestions. Dodgson to Salisbury. 30 Aug. 1895, 3 Sept. 1895,
7 June 1897. D.

l.8 Breaking the rule. Carroll. *Diaries*. 348. 31 Dec. 1875.

l.18 Revolutionary dimensions. Carroll. *Complete Works*. 277.

l.22 Unruly spirits. Carroll. *Diaries*. 471. 10 June 1889.

l.26 Princess Alice to author. 10 November 1971.

l.36 Jaw-bone of an ass. G. Cecil. *Salisbury*. I. 128.

l.40 Unfortunate love. Alice Salisbury. *Hatfield Memories*.

p. 32. l.3 Spartan rooms. Fifth Marquess of Salisbury to author.
20 Dec. 1970.

l.7 Cradle for charades. Lord Harlech to author. 7 Dec. 1971.

l.10 Ellen Terry. Dodgson to Salisbury. 9 May 1875. D.

l.11 Royal Academy. Carroll. *Diaries*. 300–1. 27 June and 5 July 1871.

l.22 Public opinion. Q.R. CXXIII (1867). Quo. Smith. 42.

l.26 Eight beggars. *Ibid*. 214 (1860). Quo. Smith. 137.

l.35 Superior fitness. G. Cecil. *Salisbury*. I. 160.

p. 33. l.5 Greasy pole. Blake. *Disraeli*. 487.

l.11 Congratulations. Edward to Salisbury. 28 Jan. 1886. D.

l.16 Deaf to the mob. Eleanor to Robert. 6 Apr. 1923. C 18/116.

l.38 Supposed default. Alice Salisbury. *Hatfield Memories*.

p. 34. l.1 High Toryism. Gwendolen to Robert. [3 Dec. 1884]. C 53/32.

l.9 Welsh Bishops. Johnston. *Liddon*. 378–79. 2 May 1890.

l.14 Gladstone's nose. Diary of Lavinia Talbot. 17 Dec. 1870.

l.23 Prime Minister. Georgina to Robert. 28 May [1886]. C 51/54.

l.28 Dislike of Disraeli. Mersey. *Journal and Memories*. 47.

l.34 Knock at the door. Humphrey Paul to Robert. 12 June 1950.
C 93/328.

p. 35. l.2 Perfect bore. Edward to Robert [   ]. C 55/4–5.
l.3 Old lunatic. Georgina to Edward. 19 April 1886. H.
l.10 Entirely inhuman. Georgina to Frances Balfour. 1 Jan. 1895.
C 58/45–50.
l.25 Returned letter. Winston S. Churchill. *Lord Randolph Churchill.* 804.
l.31 Randolph's health. Georgina to Frances Balfour. 19 Jan. 1895.
C 58/51–2.
l.39 Throstle. Georgina to Robert. 13 Sept. [1894]. C 51/15.
p. 36. l.9 The Hamlets. Georgina to Frances Balfour. 10 Feb. 1894.
C 58/43.
l.20 Glancing deer. Blake. *Disraeli.* 418. 3 Aug. 1855.
l.27 Unwelcome embrace. G. Cecil. *Salisbury.* I. 97.
l.35 Honour unsafe. *Ibid.* I. 291.
l.38 Nightmare. *Ibid.* II. 46.
p. 37. l.8 Extreme youth. Beaconsfield to Queen Victoria. 24 April 1878.
Quo. Lord Stamfordham to Gwendolen. 2 Aug. 1923. G.
l.13 Order of the Bee. Monypenny and Buckle. *Disraeli.* II. 1512.
l.18 Distraction. *Ibid.* II. 1261. 4 Nov. 1878.
p. 38. l.9 Beaconsfield to Gwendolen. 27 Aug. 1879. G.
p. 39. l.13 *Ibid.* 20 Sept. 1879. G.
l.20 Assassination. Robert Cecil. *All the Way.* 22.
l.23 Courage. Gwendolen to Eleanor. 26 Oct. 1935. C 53/172–5.
l.32 Exquisite flavour. Blake. *Disraeli.* 710–11.
l.36 End of mine. Robert Cecil. *All the Way.* 20.
fn. Mr Waddington. Monypenny and Buckle. *Disraeli.* VI. 327.
23 June 1878.
p. 40. l.1 With a phrase. Robert to Eleanor. 3 Feb. 1899. C 3/61.
l.12 Infant murderers. Georgina to Edward. 25 Sept. [   ]. H.
l.18 Interminable argument. Eleanor to Robert. 15 Feb. 1897.
C 15/35.
l.22 Bad listeners. *Ibid.* 24 Feb. 1899. C 15/170.
l.26 Waste of tissue. Robert to Edward. 7 Aug. 1896. H.
l.32 Up at 4 a.m. Dennis. *House of Cecil.* 16.
l.33 Laying for lunch. Alice Salisbury. *Hatfield Memories.*
l.38 Early start. Georgina to Salisbury. 15 Sept. 1886. D.
p. 41. l.9 Woke up tired. Eleanor to Lady Manners. 14 Jan. 1946.
Manners Papers.
l.11 Dawdling. Robert Cecil. *All the Way.* 20.
l.17 Temperatures. Eleanor to Gilbert Murray. 23 Oct. 1946. M.
l.23 Chemists' shops. Georgina to Frances Balfour. 15 Feb. 1897.
C 58/67.
l.25 Cracked china. Alice Salisbury. *Hatfield Memories.*
l.34 Glacial Balmoral. Buckle. *Letters of Queen Victoria.* III. 75.
15 Sept. 1896.
l.42 Bloodless Linky. Robert to Eleanor. 15 April 1902. C 3/140.
p. 42. l.9 Household bills. Alice to Eleanor. 16 July 1944. C 52/82–3.

l.12 Lost £50. Hugh to Salisbury. 4 Aug. 1886. D.

l.16 Collecting seaweeds. G. Cecil. *Salisbury*. III. 3.

l.20 Freethinkers. Georgina to Frances Balfour. 13 July 1886.
C 58/39.

l.23 Wading through filth. *Ibid*. 20 March 1899. C 58/80–1.

l.33 Bathing with Auguste. Robert Cecil. *All the Way*. 19.

l.38 Nasty smell. Hugh Cecil. 'Notes on the Chalet Cecil'. [1884?].
Q. Box 20.

l.41 Very odious. Florence to Violet. 23 Sept. 1895. H.

p. 43. l.2 Point of tears. Alice to Eleanor. 27 Jan. 1944. C 52/80–1.

l.13 Great woman. *Ibid*. [1951]. C 52/102–7.

l.25 Fourteen to dine. Lady Hardinge to author. 6 Sept. 1971.

l.30 Empty chair. Eleanor to Violet. 16 March 1900. H.

l.31 Mighty wind. Alice Salisbury. *Hatfield Memories*.

l.38 St John's Wood. Georgina to Edward. 29 July 1885. H.

p. 44. l.2 Patriotism. Salisbury to Edward. 15 May 1892. H.

l.14 Castle in order. Buckle. *Letters of Queen Victoria*. II. 563.
3 Sept. 1895.

l.21 Uncomfortable. Georgina to Frances Balfour. 15 Dec. 1895.
C 58/58–9.

l.24 Mephitic drains. *Ibid*. 17 Aug. 1895. C 58/55.

l.27 Ancient microbes. Gwendolen to Frances Balfour. 29 May 1901.
C 58/93.

fn. Charnel house. Curzon to Ampthill. 31 Oct. 1904. P.

p. 45. l.10 Unquenchable. Hugh to Robert. 30 Jan. 1885. C 92/245.

l.13 Four-day limit. Alice Salisbury. *Hatfield Memories*.

l.17 Feverish attack. Gwendolen to Eleanor. 22 Nov. 1923.
C 53/86.

l.19 Six-grain men. Hugh to Eleanor. 11 Jan. 1897. C 54/7–8.

l.20 Hospital. Maud to Frances Balfour. 21 May 1883. C 58/29.

l.23 Dr Dobell. Balfour to Eleanor. 29 March 1904. C 92/61.

l.31 Jem's illness. Robert to Eleanor. 12 March 1897. C 2/195.

l.34 Feeling well. Eleanor to Mary Murray. 29 Jan. 1937. M.

p. 46. l.3 Relative cleanliness. Bonham Carter. *Churchill*. 411.

l.11 Rabbit hole. Frances Balfour. *Ne Obliviscaris*. I. 336.

l.14 Twelve bathrooms. Dowager Lady Harlech to author.
13 Jan. 1971.

l.20 Soap and water. Alice Salisbury. *Hatfield Memories*.

l.23 Straw bonnet. Hare. *Solitary Life*. 147. 19 July 1879.

l.29 Royal haberdasher. Alice Salisbury. *Hatfield Memories*.

l.31 Sloppetty. George Hamilton to Curzon. 15 Sept. 1903. P.

l.33 Missing hat. G. Cecil. *Salisbury*. I. 10.

l.35 Monte Carlo. *Ibid*. III. 296.

l.38 Glove on head. Mabel Palmer to Violet. 9 Dec. 1900. H.

l.42 Deathly mixture. Georgina to Frances Balfour. 4 March 1897.
C 58/68.

p. 47. l.2 Less importance. Leveson Gower. *Mixed Grill*. 96.

l.8 Pervading shabbiness. Gwendolen to Maud. [1910]. G.

l.14 Egyptian fashion. Mersey. *Picture of Life.* 242.

l.18 Vrai ouvrier. Bonham Carter. *Churchill.* 143.

l.20 Grains of earth. *The Times.* 29 June 1936.

l.24 No bedroom sofa. Alice Salisbury. *Hatfield Memories.*

l.31 Roast meat. Robert to Eleanor. 28 Jan. 1897. C 2/150.

l.34 Strange fish. Lord Harlech to author. 7 Dec. 1971.

l.37 Gwendolen's food. Eleanor to Guendolen Osborne. 2 March 1919.
　　C 57/127.

l.43 No prohibition. Steinhart. *Canning Club.* 222. 29 April 1884.

p. 48. l.8 Train window. Gwendolen to Maud. 1 Dec. 1905. G.

l.10 Own dressmaker. Eleanor to Robert. 23 Jan. 1897. C 15/11.

l.13 Annual charity. *Ibid.* 20 Jan. 1897. C 15/8.

l.15 Buying bicycles. Household accounts. 1895–6. C 14/130.

l.18 Insane. Georgina to Violet. 19 April 1896. H.

l.22 Packing. Edward to Salisbury. 13 Dec. 1882. D.

l.24 Rector of Hatfield. Mrs Benyon to author. 24 May 1971.

l.27 Wages bill. Household accounts. 1895–6. C 14/130.

l.31 Modesty. Maud to Louise Alderson. 24 Dec. 1876. G.

l.33 Incestuous gardener. Hugh to Eleanor. 13 June 1956.
　　C 54/55.

l.42 Household quarrel. Gwendolen to Maud. 21 Feb. 1908. G.

p. 49. l.26 Living spirit. Alice Salisbury. *Hatfield Memories.*

l.36 Tennants' dinner. *Ibid.*

p. 50. l.6 Coming of age. Curzon to R. R. Farrer. 2 Dec. 1882. N.

l.20 Cranborne ball. Maud to Frances Balfour. 1 Nov. 1882.
　　C 58/27.

l.27 Facial signature. Eleanor to Violet. 16 March 1900. H.

l.31 Wideawake hat. G. Cecil. *Salisbury.* III. 115.

l.34 Third-class. *Ibid.* III. 135.

l.38 Hatfield station. Robert to Eleanor. 20 July 1893. C 2/76.

p. 51. l.3 Fifty years. *Ibid.* 19 Jan. 1912. C 5/79.

l.6 Impersonal courtesy. G. Cecil. *Salisbury.* III. 29.

l.12 Tory toes. Humphrey Paul to Robert. 8 Sept. 1951.
　　C 93/346–8.

l.16 Dukes and ministers. Robert Cecil. *All the Way.* 39.

l.29 Patriarchal blessing. *National Review.* November 1931.

l.35 Rain and Royalties. Salisbury to Cranborne. 13 July 1879. J.

l.41 Heir apparent. G. Cecil. *Salisbury.* IV. 369. 20 July 1891.

p. 52. l.3 Sixty to dine. Alice Salisbury. *Hatfield Memories.*

l.5 British admiral. G. Cecil. *Salisbury.* IV. 368.

l.11 Sovereign's door. *Ibid.* IV. 142.

l.23 *Quelle horreur.* Hare. *Solitary Life.* 229. 18 July 1889.

l.30 Royalties and mosquitoes. Salisbury to Hugh. 5 April 1897.
　　Q 1/10–11.

l.35 Elderly butler. Georgina to Eleanor. 3 April [1896?]. Q 51/45.

l.41 Duchess of Teck. Cranborne to Louise Alderson. 24 Aug. 1887. J.

p. 53. l.7 Burghley's advice. Rowse. *England of Elizabeth.* 271.

l.17 Unforgettable sight. Milner. *My Picture Gallery.* 229–31. 4 April 1895.

l.23 Patriot's boots. Robert to Eleanor. 8 March 1900. C 3/108.

l.33 Unwelcome prince. Eleanor to Robert. 7 April 1896. C 14/125.

l.39 Royal conundrum. Robert to Eleanor. 10 March 1897. C 2/193.

p. 54. l.6 Inexperienced youth. Salisbury to Selborne. 24 April 1905. F.5.

l.20 H. S. Salt. *Seventy Years among Savages.* (1921).

l.30 Unrebuked children. Dugdale. *Family Homespun.* 107.

l.35 Bishop Claughton. Alice Salisbury. *A Memoir.* 4.

p. 55. l.10 Horse and cow. Alice Salisbury. *Hatfield Memories.*

l.14 Admiring the door. Ponsonby. *Henry Ponsonby.* 273.

l.20 Bulgaria. Frances Balfour. *Ne Obliviscaris.* I. 90.

l.21 Dog Pharaoh. Hare. *Solitary Life.* 274. 17 May 1896.

l.23 To the Derby. Mallet. *Queen Victoria.* 81. 6 June 1896.

l.26 Fast quadrupeds. *National Review.* Nov. 1931.

l.35 No flogging. Robert Cecil. Draft for a broadcast. March 1955. C 72/312.

p. 56. l.2 Classics for pleasure. Robert Cecil. *All the Way.* 17.

l.7 How to cram. Edward to Violet. 8 Sept. 1912. H.

l.15 Unwholesome tea. Robert to Eleanor. [1911?]. C 5/31.

l.18 Winchester College. Robert to Edward. 25 Aug. 1907. C 55/118.

l.21 Schoolmaster. Robert to Eleanor. 29 July 1934. C 9/248.

l.24 Narrowing influence. Gwendolen to Eleanor. 25 Jan. 1906. C 53/34.

l.29 Salvation. Maud to Gwendolen. 25 April 1909. G.

l.34 School worship. Hugh Cecil. *The Times.* 29 April 1929.

l.37 Futile religion. Alington to Hugh. 2 May 1929. Q 37/230.

p. 57. l.11 Venerating Henry VI. Lang to Hugh. 29 Oct. 1940. Q 55/133.

CHAPTER FOUR: JAMES, FOURTH MARQUESS OF SALISBURY

p. 59. l.13 A policy in itself. Guedalla. *A Gallery.* 167.

l.37 Not to be read. Hugh to Alice. [1935]. A.3.

p. 60. l.3 Moral weapons. Salisbury to Selborne. 3 Oct. 1907. F.5.

l.15 Wonderful man. Robert to Eleanor. 11 March 1897. C 2/196.

l.22 Making a noise. Edward to Helen. 6 Oct. 1918. H.

l.26 Benign eyes. Marsh. *Ambrosia and Small Beer.* 149.

l.29 Rheumatism. Cranborne to Salisbury. 1 March 1877. D.

l.34 Prompt payment. Lord David Cecil to author. 27 March 1972.

l.39 Shannon's picture. Alice Salisbury. *A Memoir.* 5.

p. 61. l.2 Christmas in bed. Gwendolen to Maud. 6 Jan. 1927. G.

l.6 Fresh air. Eleanor to Robert. 17 Jan. 1897. C 15/4.

l.11 Unconscious. Dowager Duchess of Devonshire to author. 13 Jan. 1971.

l.14 Jenner. Georgina to Edward. 20 April [1883]. G.

l.16 Gibraltar. Gwendolen to Robert. 27 Feb. 1885. C 53/7–8.

l.21 Nearly killed. Gwendolen to Maud. 16 April 1921. G.

l.25 Born a Roman. *Ibid.* [1923]. G.

l.31 Passing time. Salisbury to Robert. 17 Aug. 1910. C 52/45.

p. 62. l.3 French and failure. G. Cecil. *Salisbury.* II. 91.

l.10 Stamboul. Georgina to Louise Alderson. 5 Jan. 1877. G.

l.12 Order of Chastity. Kennedy. *Salisbury.* 371.

l.15 Hair-oil. Cranborne to Louise Alderson. 18 Dec. 1876. G.

p. 63. l.2 Salisbury and Cranborne to Robert. 25 Dec. 1876. C 51/1–2.

l.10 B's compliments. G. Cecil. *Salisbury.* II. 280. 14 June 1878.

l.13 One fine street. Cranborne to Curzon. 28 May 1883. N.

l.30 No reappointment. Chadwick. *Victorian Church.* II. 447.

fn. Four brothers. Salisbury to Robert. 6 Feb. 1928. Robert to Salisbury. 7 Feb. 1928. B 51086.

p. 64. l.14 Lancashire. Salisbury to Cranborne. 22 Feb. 1881. J.

l.26 Cotton workers. Alice Salisbury. *A Memoir.* 20.

l.32 Conquering hero. Gwendolen to Robert. 3 Dec. 1885. C 53/11.

l.36 Disappointing. Quo. Hugh to Robert. 3 Dec. 1885. C 92/249.

p. 65. l.4 Darwen. Salisbury to Cranborne. 18 Aug. 1893. J.

l.20 Tragic tones. Lucy *Salisbury Parliament.* 395.

l.23 Aloof from Commons. G. Cecil. *Salisbury.* I. 295.

l.27 Seat for Goschen. Cranborne to Salisbury. 2 Dec. 1886. D.

l.41 Estate income. Bateman. *Great Landowners.* 394.

p. 66. l.6 Intention. G. Cecil. *Salisbury.* IV. 204. 1 April 1888.

l.9 Reconstruction. *Ibid.* II. 3–4.

l.21 Sticks for the poor. Cranborne to Salisbury. 18 April 1883. D.

l.38 Aloft to roost. Alice Salisbury. *A Memoir.* 14.

p. 67. l.17 First visit. Alice Salisbury. *Hatfield Memories.*

l.40 Justice of the Peace. Lord David Cecil to author. 27 March 1972.

p. 68. l.8 Hieroglyphics. Eleanor to Hugh. 30 June 1949. Q 59/141.

l.11 Triple damn. Dugdale. *Balfour.* I. 438.

l.14 Sharing. Milner. *My Picture Gallery.* 84.

l.23 Charles I and II. Alice to Eleanor. 27 Nov. 1930. C 52/70–1. And *The Times.* 7 Feb. 1955.

l.26 Kitchener. Dilks. *Curzon in India. passim.*

l.29 Mosley. Curzon to Grace Curzon. 21 March 1920. N.

l.40 Christian Science. Alice to Eleanor. 23 Feb. [1915]. C 52/124.

p. 69. l.2 Human nature. Alice to Hugh. 25 July 1940. Q 64/43.

l.11 Silk petticoat. *Ibid.* 20 May 1942. Q 64/62.

l.12 Auks' eggs. *Ibid.* 26 July 1945. Q 64/96.

l.19 Duchess of Sutherland. Alice to Eleanor. 12 Jan. 1944. C 52/78.

l.24 London garden. Alice to Hugh. 24 May 1949. Q 64/164.

l.29 Security. Alice to Eleanor. 27 Jan. 1944. C 52/80–1.

p. 70. l.9 Arranged defeat. Cranborne to Salisbury. 25 Aug. 1898. D.

l.15 Made my will. *Ibid.* 25 Feb. 1900. D.

l.23 Boer skirmish. Cranborne to Violet. 5 Sept. 1900. H.

l.29 Montagu Norman. Boyle. *Montagu Norman.* 48.

l.38 Stipendiary echo. *The Times.* 15 Dec. 1905.

p. 71. l.10 Administrative genius. *Hansard.* 6 Dec. 1900.

l.12 Hotel Cecil. *Ibid.* 10 Dec. 1900.

l.19 Queen's opinion. Buckle. *Letters of Queen Victoria.* l. 656. 26 Nov. 1890.

l.28 Supplementary questions. *Hansard.* 18 Feb. 1901.

l.39 Palmerston. *Ibid.* 3 July 1902.

p. 72. l.2 Picking up. Salisbury to Curzon. 23 Sept. 1901. P.

l.6 Told to conceal. Hamilton to Curzon. 21 Feb. 1901. P.

l.8 Halting obscurities. Curzon to Hamilton. 13 Feb. 1902. P.

l.12 Not much longer. McDonnell to Curzon. 3 Sept. 1902. P.

l.18 Jump with surprise. Curzon to St John Brodrick. 14 Oct. 1903. P.

l.19 Jealousy. FitzRoy. *Memoirs.* I. 236.

l.26 Lords and gentlemen. Beveridge. *Power and Influence.* 132.

l.37 Licensing Bill. Gosse. Diary. 11 March 1904. House of Lords.

l.25 Public life. Salisbury to Selborne. 18 March 1929. F.7.

p. 73. l.33 New Chancellor. Jenkins. *Asquith.* 154–8.

l.41 Thin and acrid. Birkenhead. *Contemporary Personalities.* 179.

p. 74. l.11 Voting strengths. Jenkins. *Mr. Balfour's Poodle.* 6–10.

l.31 Destinies of Empire. *The Times.* 16 Jan. 1906.

p. 75. l.15 A little giddy. Bowra. *Memories.* 134.

l.19 Bedrooms. Oxford and Asquith. *Fifty Years in Parliament.* II. 59.

l.32 Budget details. Jones. *Lloyd George.* 37.

l.36 Rents and rates. *Newcastle Daily Leader.* 6 April 1903.

fn. Plethora of pubs. Speaight. *Property Basket.* 22.

p. 76. l.5 Salisbury's taxes. Gwendolen to Maud. 7 May 1909. G.

l.19 Single-chamber rule. *Hansard.* 24 Nov. 1909.

l.31 No absolute veto. *Ibid.*

l.41 Wait and see. *Ibid.* 3 March 1910.

p. 77. l.12 Irresponsible demagogue. *Quo.* Margot Asquith. Autobiography II. 131.

l.27 Royal preoccupations. Gwendolen to Maud. 22 April 1910. G.

p. 78. l.3 Referendum. *Hansard.* 24 May 1911.

l.12 Act not promise. Young. *Balfour.* 305.

l.15 New Prime Minister. Salisbury to Balfour. 14 Dec. 1910. Quo. *Young.* 308–9.

l.19 Essentially theatrical. *Young.* Balfour. 310.

l.39 Neutrality of King. Salisbury to Selborne. 5 Aug. 1911. F.6.

fn. Aeroplane. Jenkins. *Mr. Balfour's Poodle.* 145.

p. 79. l.2 Bishops. Bell. *Davidson.* 628.

l.13 Consequences. *Hansard.* 9 Aug. 1911.

l.15 Hugh's prediction. FitzRoy. *Memoirs.* II. 459. 10 Aug. 1911.

l.22 Beastly politics. Salisbury to Edward. 12 Sept. 1911. E.1.

l.29 No immunity. Ullswater. *A Speaker's Commentaries.* II. 103.

p. 80. l.4 Quiet life. Salisbury to Selborne. 7 Sept. 1905. F.5.

l.30 Like judges. *Hansard.* 15 March 1910.

l.31 Life peers. Kennedy. *Salisbury.* 200–2.

p. 81. l.7 Reform of the Lords. *Daily Telegraph.* 11 Nov. 1932.

l.13 No facilities. *Hansard.* 8 May 1934.

l.32 Adequate defence. Gwendolen to Maud. 14 Aug. 1911. G.

p. 82. l.2 Vituperation. Curzon. Memorandum on Parliament Bill of 1911. P.

l.8 King's gratitude. Stamfordham to Curzon. 11 Aug. 1911. P.

l.19 Uneducated class. Steinhart. *Oxford Canning Club.* 136–8.

p. 83. l.7 Maggots and carbolic. Curzon to Salisbury. 22 Aug. 1904. J.

l.15 Revengeful manner. 29 Aug. 1904. J.

l.18 Entente Cordiale. Salisbury to Curzon. 5 Sept. 1904. J.

l.22 Embittered holiday. Curzon to Salisbury. 6 Sept. 1904. J.

l.39 The Cabinet. Dilks. *Curzon in India. passim.*

p. 84. l.7 Long apologia. Kitchener to Hugh. 24 Dec. 1905. Q 4/160–5.

l.13 Walmer furniture. Gwendolen to Maud. 11 Aug. 1905. G.

l.17 Great unwashed. Maud to Robert. 14 Oct. [1905]. C 56/72–5.

l.19 Brilliant men. Salisbury to Selborne. 1 Sept. 1905. F.5.

l.23 Military power. Cranborne to Curzon. 28 May 1883. N.

l.30 Anglo-German relations. Cranborne to Lansdowne. 18 Nov. 1901. Quo. Steiner. *Foreign Office and Foreign Policy.* 58

p. 85. l.10 Hatfield camp. Brett. *Esher.* II. 320. 5 June 1908.

l.14 Staff officer. Salisbury to Edward. 29 Sept. 1910. E.1.

l.26 Friendship. *Ibid.* Easter Day 1915. E.1.

l.32 Review by Kitchener. Alice to Edward. 2 Nov. 1915. E.2.

l.36 Two functions. *Ibid.* 13 Dec. 1915. E.2.

p. 86. l.5 Artistic method. Stern. *Tanks.* 56.

l.8 Privacy of grounds. Churchill to Salisbury. 2 April 1919. J.

l.21 Hoping for Derby. Salisbury to Curzon. 7 Jan. 1916. P.

l.30 New Prime Minister. Salisbury to Edward. 24 Dec. 1916. H.

l.34 Not consulted. *Ibid.*

l.41 Reconstruction. Jones. *Whitehall Diary.* I. 23–4. 17 Feb. 1917.

l.39 Prison cell. Alice Salisbury. *A Memoir.* 16.

p. 87. l.2 Praying aloud. Flower. *Journals of Arnold Bennett.* II. 194.

l.4 Talks incessantly. Webb. *Diaries, 1912–24.* 85.

p. 88. l.2 Sale of honours. Salisbury to Lloyd George. 25 March 1917. J.

l.12 Second request. *Ibid.* 7 June 1917. J.

l.21 Nothing indecorous. Salisbury: 'Notes on a Conversation with the Prime Minister, 20 June 1917.' J.

l.32 Benefit of the country. *Hansard.* 7 August 1917.

l.35 Resumed campaign. *The Times.* 29 Aug. 1918.

p. 89. l.4 Grand Crosses. *Ibid.* 31 Aug. 1918.

l.10 Rake's progress. *Hansard.* 17 July 1922.

l.24 No confidence. *Morning Post.* 20 June 1921.

l.29 Lonely. Salisbury to Gwendolin. 23 June 1921. G.

l.35 Political principles. *Ibid.* 28 Aug. 1921. G.

p. 90. l.2 Conservative feeling. McKenzie. *British Political Parties.* 94.

l.21 Second class. Blake. *Unknown Prime Minister.* 465.

l.36 Very often wrong. Salisbury to Milner. 11 Dec. 1916. Milner Papers. Private Letters, 1914–18.

p. 91. l.10 American public. Curzon to Reading. 13 June 1919. P.

l.17 Astonished. Salisbury to Curzon. 27 June 1919. P.

l.28 Page after page. Curzon to Salisbury. 19 Feb. 1923. J.

l.29 General or colonel. Salisbury to Curzon. 20 Feb. 1923. J.

p. 92. l.4 Tall hat. Rhodes James. *Memoirs of a Conservative.* 157.

l.8 Curzon's claims. Alice Salisbury. Memorandum written for the author. 15 June 1951.

l.12 Should be sent for. Quo. Middlemas and Barnes. *Baldwin.* 165.

l.21 Derby and Co. Curzon to Grace Curzon. 18 Nov. 1923. N.

l.43 Hankey's regard. Roskill. *Hankey.* II. 349–50.

p. 93. l.8 Baldwin's inexperience. Salisbury to Gwendolen. 24 Dec. 1923. G.

l.12 No consultation. Roskill. *Hankey.* II. 352.

l.13 Profound mistake. Salisbury to Baldwin. 19 Oct. 1923. Quo. Middlemas and Barnes. 223.

l.22 Disintegration. *Quo.* Middlemas and Barnes. 175.

l.24 Fatted calf. Salisbury to Robert. 28 Jan. 1924. B 51085.

l.32 Brothers in Cabinet. Salisbury to Eleanor. 25 July 1923. C 52/62.

l.39 Appeal to the King. Stamfordham to Salisbury. 22 Nov. 1923. J.

p. 94. l.12 Cold Sunday supper. Jones. *Diary with Letters.* 496.

l.16 State intervention. Jones. *Whitehall Diary.* I. 325–6. 5 Aug. 1925.

l.21 Schools of Conservatism. *Quo.* Middlemas and Barnes. 612.

l.31 First readings. *Hansard.* 6 June 1935.

p. 95. l.4 Constitutional enterprise. Halifax. *Fulness of Days.* 125.

fn. Declined invitation. A. E. C. Thornhill to Hugh. 4 and 18 May 1933. Q 45/133 and Q 45/162–3.

p. 96. l.12 Himmler. Salisbury: 'Notes on some of the impressions received at the house party in Lady Margaret Hall, Oxford, 26–29 July 1935.' J.

l.22 Hitler. *New York World Telegram.* 26 Aug. 1936. Quo. Driberg. *The Mystery of Moral Re-Armament.* 68.

l.28 Multiplying numbers. Salisbury to Bardsley. 9 Sept. 1936. J.

p. 97. l.14 Social degeneration. Salisbury: 'Notes on conference at Hatfield, 10–11 Oct. 1936'. J.

l.17 New vividness. Robert to Eleanor. 11 Oct. 1936. C 10/115–7.

l.25 Croix de Feu. *Ibid.* 12 Oct. 1936. C 10/118–9.

l.39 Perilous reaction. Salisbury. Memorandum. 27 July 1937. J.

p. 98. l.3 Hallmark for plate. Salisbury to Cranborne. 11 April [1890?]. J.

l.14 Birmingham speech. *The Times.* 30 March 1937.

l.37 Disassociation from Group. John Roots to Salisbury. 13 Feb. 1939. J.

p. 99. l.17 Abdication. Salisbury to A. P. Charles. 9 Dec. 1936. J.

l.21 Coronation. Salisbury to Lang. 19 March 1937. J.

l.24 Broadcast tribute. Athlone to Salisbury. 4 Dec. 1939. J.

l.30 King's refusal. Alexander Hardinge to Salisbury. 29 Nov. 1939. J.

l.39 Board of Trade. Salisbury to Oliver Stanley. 27 April 1939. J.

l.41 Well-wishers. Lang to Salisbury. 6 Feb. 1937. J.

p. 100. l.11 Greek royal family. Salisbury to Buchman. 19 March 1937. J.

l.18 Guidance. Buchman to Salisbury. 16 Jan. 1939. J.

l.24 Best bedroom. Baldwin to Salisbury. 16 Jan. 1939. J.

l.41 Eastbourne. John Roots to Salisbury. 27 Jan. 1939. J.

p. 101. l.3 Meekness. Salisbury to Roots. 29 Jan. 1939. J.

l.13 Christian position. Lang to Salisbury. 26 Jan. 1940. J.

l.21 In Papua. Salisbury : 'Memorandum on Oxford Group meeting in Bournemouth, Jan. 1940.' J.

l.31 M R A officers. Brig.-Gen. C. R. P. Winser to Salisbury. 21 Jan. 1940. Salisbury to Winser. 25 Jan. 1940. J.

p. 102. l.4 Parliamentary debate. *Hansard.* 8 Oct. 1941.

p. 103. l.2 Estate reorganisation. Gwendolen to Maud. 15 Jan. 1937. G.

l.25 Morals and politics. *The Times.* 11 May 1936.

l.38 Chamberlain's policy. Cranborne to Violet. 5 July 1938. H.

p. 104. l.3 Bourgeois timidity. Robert to Eleanor. 29 May 1936. C 10/60.

l.6 Middle-class monster. *Ibid.* 17 April 1939. C 11/7.

p. 105. l.6 List of members. Minute Books of Watching Committee. J.

l.10 Friendly footing. Salisbury: 'Record of Conversation with Neville Chamberlain, 10 April 1940.' J.

l.22 No power. Winston S. Churchill. *Second World War.* I. 463.

fn. Private property. Amery. *My Political Life.* III. 330.

p. 106. l.4 Birmingham politics. Salisbury : 'Record of Conversation with Neville Chamberlain, 10 April 1940.' J.

l.15 Not his fault. Cranborne to Salisbury. 15 April 1940. J.

l.23 Not satisfied. Minutes of Watching Committee. 29 April 1940. J.

l.36 Advice disregarded. Joseph Nall to Salisbury. 9 May 1940. J.

l.40 Visit to Halifax. Salisbury : 'Memorandum on Change of Government, 9 May 1940'. J.

p. 107. l.9 Cranborne in office. Gwendolen to Eleanor. 20 May 1940. C 53/203–5.

l.15 £1,500 a year. Robert to Eleanor. [   ]. C 10/42.

l.19 Sugar tongs. McDonnell to Curzon. 30 Sept. 1899. P.

l.23 Retainers. Salisbury to Churchill. 17 Nov. 1904. Quo. R. S. Churchill. *Winston S. Churchill.* Companion Volume II. 1. 373.

l.26 Demeanour. Salisbury to Churchill. 20 Nov. 1904. *Ibid.* II. 1. 376.

p. 108. l.2 Arms from USA. Salisbury to Churchill. 7 & 13 June 1940. J.

l.2 Complacent reply. Churchill to Salisbury. 25 June 1940. J.

l.13 Peace-time technique. Salisbury to Bracken. 27 June 1940. J.

l.19 Indignantly digested. Bracken to Salisbury. 27 June 1940. J.

l.27 Not effective. Salisbury to Morrison. 10 Feb. 1941. J.

l.33 Revolutionized. Salisbury to Churchill. 3 July 1940. J.

l.35 Dangerous time. Churchill to Salisbury. 4 July 1940. J.
p. 109. l.20 Appeasement. Salisbury to Churchill. 2 Oct. 1940. J.
fn. Maudling to Salisbury. 21 Sept. 1942. J.

CHAPTER FIVE: LORD WILLIAM CECIL

p. 111. l.15 Rheumatism. Cranborne to Salisbury. 1 March 1877. D.
l.21 Fish. Manners. *Some Recollections.* 13.
l.25 Broken rules. A. Dendy to William. [   ]. Benyon Papers.
p. 112. l.3 Rejoicings. *Ibid.* [   ]. Benyon Papers.
l.6 Dog in college. F. C. Conybeare to William. [   ]. Benyon Papers.
l.9 Hampstead Heath. Metropolitan Water Board to William. 15 March 1881. D.
l.27 Pitiless. *Bentley's Quarterly Review.* I. (1859).
l.30 Peel. Coppini. *Lord Salisbury.*
l.36 Salt-pork. Manners. *Some Recollections.* 4.
l.40 Saint-Sulpice. Coppini. *Lord Salisbury.*
p. 113. l.5 Ordination. *Church Assembly Proceedings.* II. 2. 46. 12 July 1921.
l.22 £2,000 a year. William to Salisbury. 17 July 1890. D.
p. 114. l.8 Worldly goods. *Difficulties and Duties.* 2.
l.16 Services and visiting. *Possibilities of Doing Good.*
l.25 Useful advice. Rev F. C. Alderson to William. 1 Aug. [   ]. Benyon Papers.
l.29 Awkward book. Eleanor to Mary Murray. 1 July 1939. M.
l.34 Knife-boy and squire. *Possibilities of Doing Good.*
p. 115. l.13 Homilies. William to Eleanor. 25 Sept. [   ]. C 54/60.
l.16 A crime. *Possibilities of Doing Good.*
l.18 Nightmare. Manners. *Some Recollections.* 5.
l.24 Spiritual doctor. *Difficulties and Duties.* 26.
l.28 Indifference. *Ibid.* 32.
p. 116. l.6 Unjust dealings. *Possibilities of Doing Good.*
l.16 Wiping his feet. Manners. *Some Recollections.* 17.
l.24 Twenty-four years. William to Alice. 23 Sept. 1912. A.3.
l.32 Lawlessness. Eleanor to Robert. 31 March [   ]. C 21/15.
l.35 Paralysis. Edward to Eleanor. 24 Nov. 1909. C 55/67.
p. 117. l.2 Declined to move. Edward Talbot to William. 14 Nov. 1908. Benyon Papers.
l.8 Personal sacrifice. Gwendolen to Maud. 2 Feb. 1932. G.
l.22 Round tour. Gwendolen to Maud. 7 July 1905. G.
l.31 Foreigners. *Changing China.* 102.
l.33 French literature. *Ibid.* 218.
l.37 Scottish philosophy. *Ibid.* 257.
p. 118. l.3 Across Siberia. Gwendolen to Maud. 2 Aug. 1907. G.
l.31 Foreign travel. Manners. *Some Recollections.* 25–6.
l.38 Nunc dimittis. Lady Manners to author. 21 June 1971.

p. 119. l.10 Sensibility. Eleanor to Robert. 15 Jan. 1899. C 15/121–2.

l.22 Suffering. William to Alice. 7 Dec. [1934]. A.3.

l.27 Omdurman. Cranborne to Salisbury. 12 Sept. 1898. D.

l.33 Jingoism. Gwendolen to Maud. 2 Feb. 1932. G.

p. 120. l.2 Enjoying himself. *Ibid.* 8 Nov. 1915. G.

l.6 In the garden. *Ibid.* 6 Sept. 1916. G.

l.9 Remorse. Manners. *Some Recollections.* 7.

l.12 Restless. Florence to Salisbury. 14 Jan. 1916. J.

l.21 Buttoned gaiters. Eleanor to Robert. 10 Oct. 1916. C 17/167.

l.41 Historic position. Henson. *Retrospect.* II. 67.

p. 121. l.24 Under a bushel. Eleanor to Edward. 5 May 1918. H.

l.37 La belle asperge. Manners. *Some Recollections.* 17.

p. 122. l.5 Heating system. David Cecil. *The Cecils.* 293.

l.13 Copper sulphate. Matthews. *Memories and Meanings.* 171.

l.19 Healthiest diet. *Ibid.* 174.

l.23 Hands and feet. William to 'the Family'. [   ]. Benyon Papers.

l.29 Following hounds. Lady Manners to author. 21 June 1971.

l.40 Half-digested ideas. Henson. *Letters.* 28. 26 Nov. 1923.

p. 123. l.5 Bodily sins. Robert to Eleanor. 28 Feb. 1897. C 2/183.

l.11 Vice in the old. *The Times.* 29 Dec. 1904.

l.21 Working man. William to Robert. 14 June 1912. B 51160.

l.35 Mission of cheer. Canon E. F. Hall to author. 12 Oct. 1970.

p. 124. l.16 Not much use. Gwendolen to Maud. 1 April 1927. G.

l.22 Shadow of Rome. Manners. *Some Recollections.* 9.

l.27 Obey or starve. Fox. *Dean Inge.* 218.

l.34 Clear boundary. Hugh to W. G. Pennyman. 28 Feb. 1928. Q 35/50–5.

p. 125. l.13 Difficult to forgive. Henson. *Retrospect.* I. 252.

l.15 Not very placable. *Ibid.* I. 258.

l.32 Organs. Sir Ernest Bullock to author. 25 March 1971.

l.38 Archdeacons. *Difficulties and Duties.* 7–8.

p. 126. l.8 Parish links. Gwendolen to Maud. 2 March 1921. G.

l.12 Welcoming back. *Ibid.* 3 July 1936. G.

CHAPTER SIX: LORD ROBERT CECIL

p. 127. l.17 Two grievances. Robert Cecil. *All the Way.* 13.

l.21 Oxford Union. *Ibid.* 72.

p. 128. l.5 Study of the law. A. V. Dicey to Robert. 17 July 1886. D.

l.19 Ample brains. Lang to Robert. 5 Nov. 1886. C 93/137.

l.22 Little to do. Robert Cecil. *All the Way.* 39.

l.25 My Lord. Robert to Hugh. [1885?]. G.

l.27 Randolph Churchill. Robert Cecil. *All the Way.* 34.

l.28 Snuff. *Ibid.* 32.

l.32 Walton. Robert to Salisbury. 31 July 1888. D.

l.34 Law books. Hugh to Robert. 10 Nov. 1887. C 92/252–3.

p. 129. l.4 Politics v. religion. Lockhart. *Lang.* 63–4.

l.9 Law and politics. Lang to Robert. 24 Jan. 1942. C 93/207.

l.18 Primrose League. Robert to Eleanor. 12 Oct. 1888. C 1/80.

l.23 First brief. *Ibid.* 22 Oct. 1888. C 1/110–11.

p. 130. l.8 Verse. Robert Cecil. 'Suggested by a Conversation with N.L. at Lady W's. 9 May 1888.' C 29/3.

l.23 The Lambtons. Robert to Edward. 27 May 1896. H.

l.29 Emperor of Japan. Robert Cecil. *Great Experiment.* 28.

l.32 How to dress. Eleanor to Robert. 24 March 1928. C 19/83.

p. 131. l.5 Financial warning. Durham to Eleanor. 21 July 1888. C 22/1–2.

l.19 Smart women. Eleanor to Mary Murray. 26 Feb. 1947. M.

l.22 Disturbed. Robert to Eleanor. 29 July 1888. C 1/11–12.

l.26 Wrong cards. Dowager Lady Manners to author. 21 June 1971.

l.29 £1,000 a year. Salisbury to Edward. 17 March 1894. H.

p. 132. l.8 Self-doubt. Robert to Eleanor. 11 Dec. 1888. C 1/209–10.

l.11 Sick schoolgirl. Eleanor to Robert. 1 Sept. 1888. C 13/39.

l.14 Deep wound. Robert to Eleanor. 16 Oct. 1888. C 1/89–90.

l.15 Carrion-crow. Eleanor to Robert. 30 July 1888. C 13/9.

l.24 Declaration. 22 Nov. 1888. C 1/127–8.

l.32 Compliment. Eleanor to Gilbert Murray. 13 Jan. 1949. M.

p. 133. l.12 Manslaughter. Robert to Eleanor. 18 Dec. 1889. C 2/45–6.

l.16 Murder and outrage. Robert Cecil. *All the Way.* 51.

l.18 Free beer. *Ibid.* 70.

l.21 Tiny circle. Robert to Eleanor. 26 July 1888. C 1/5.

l.30 Straining justice. *Ibid.* 27 July 1889. C 2/31–2.

l.34 Grantham. Heuston. *Lord Chancellors.* 42 and 257.

l.39 Sudden civility. Robert to Eleanor. 12 Nov. 1895. C 2/117.

p. 134. l.8 Bucknill. *Ibid.* 10 Jan. 1899. C 3/33.

l.14 Halsbury. *Ibid.* 24 Jan. 1899. C 3/52.

l.32 Gun cotton. Georgina to Robert. 16 Feb. [1894]. C 51/38.

l.35 Parliamentary Bar. Robert to Eleanor. 10 Feb. 1897. C 2/164.

p. 135. l.10 Beastly slow. *Ibid.* 11 Feb. 1897. C 2/158.

l.16 Shrewsbury. Eleanor to Guendolen Osborne. 25 Jan. 1903. C 57/3–4.

l.19 Young pupil. Attlee. *As it Happened.* 17.

l.22 £5,000 fee. Robert Cecil. *All the Way.* 92.

l.28 Bar Council. Robert to Eleanor. 16 Jan. 1899. C 3/40.

l.41 Circuit dinner. *Ibid.* [   ]. C 1/13.

p. 136. l.13 The Union. Robert to Edward. 1 Nov. 1883. H.

l.20 Furniture. Robert to Eleanor. 17 July 1893. C 2/73–4.

l.25 Public consciences. *Ibid.* [   ]. C 8/105. His host was Lord Harrowby at Sandon.

l.28 Treated like dogs. Eleanor to Robert. 2 Oct. 1914. C 17/161.

l.36 Balfour's car. *Ibid.* 1 Oct. 1907. C 17/15.

l.41 Gale. Robert Cecil. *All the Way.* 81.

p. 137. l.2 Carpentry. Eleanor to Guendolen Osborne. 10 Aug. 1925. C 57/147–8.

l.8 Meredith. *Ibid.* 17 Feb. 1907. C 57/58.

l.10 Carlyle. Catherine Maclean to Eleanor. 1 June 1955.
C 36/39.

l.16 Growing old. *National Review.* Nov. 1907.

l.27 Hunting women. Robert to Eleanor. 14 July 1895. C 2/118.

l.39 In the Highlands. Robert to Edward. 30 Aug. 1910. C 55/125.

p. 138. l.6 Chilly holiday. Eleanor to Edward. 29 Aug. 1909. C 17/52.

l.13 In reverse. Balfour. *Ne Obliviscaris.* 375–6. And Dugdale.
Family Homespun. 111.

l.14 Vulgar pastime. Robert Cecil. *All the Way.* 84.

l.21 Nonconformists. Robert to Edward. 25 Aug. 1907.
C 55/118–9.

p. 139. l.32 Gwendolen to Eleanor. 30 Oct. [1903]. C 53/96.

l.42 Economic enigma. Jones. *Whitehall Diaries.* II. 244.

p. 140. l.1 No settled convictions. *Hansard.* 10 June 1903.

l.13 Visit to Balfour. Gwendolen to Eleanor. 30 Oct. [1903].
C 53/96.

l.18 No reply. Eleanor to Robert. 14 July 1939. C 20/254.

l.19 Cocaine. Edward to Robert. 5 April 1906. C 55/36.

l.23 Pecksniffian. Balfour to Hugh. 2 March 1905. Q 3/46–7.

l.35 Alcohol. Eleanor to Robert. 15 May [   ]. C 17/7.

l.40 Peel and Dizzy. Robert to Eleanor. 15 July 1904. C 4/22.

p. 141. l.2 Shopkeepers. Eleanor to Gilbert Murray. 5 May 1928. M.

l.7 Short notice. Robert to Balfour. 10 Jan. 1906. Quo.
Rempel. *Unionists Divided.* 159.

l.32 Joe as leader. Robert to Hugh. 21 Jan. 1906. Q 5/26.

l.35 Arthur preferred. Robert to Balfour. 25 Jan. 1906. B 51071.

p. 142. l.1 Foolery. *Hansard.* 13 March 1906.

l.4 Vote against party. Robert Cecil. *All the Way.* 111.

l.8 Burke. Eleanor to Guendolen Osborne. 29 March 1906. C 57/5.

l.22 Radical in disguise. Maud to Robert. 18 May [   ].
C 56/33–4.

l.28 Benevolent hawk. Winterton. *Orders of the Day.* 64.

l.35 Profound distrust. Eleanor to Guendolen Osborne. 11 April 1907.
C 57/59.

p. 143. l.27 Wretched question. Robert to Hugh. 10 March 1908. Q 9/60.

l.34 Liberal withdrawal. Robert to Asquith. 21 Jan. 1909.
C 93/309–11.

p. 144. l.3 Particular circumstances. Asquith to Robert. 27 Jan. 1909.
C 93/313.

l.5 Any other solution. Robert to Hugh. 22 Aug. 1909.
Q 12/53–6.

l.13 Cursed politics. *Ibid.* 3 Aug. 1909. Q 12/42.

l.15 Moderate dose. *Ibid.* 26 Aug. 1909. Q 12/60–1.

l.24 Vernacular. Salisbury to Robert. 11 Dec. 1909. C 5/12.

l.26 F. E. Smith. Robert Cecil. *All the Way.* 103.

l.33 Meeting Balfour. Robert to Eleanor. 12 July 1910. C 5/23.

l.36 Mental dishonesty. Eleanor to Robert. 3 Sept. 1911. C 17/97–8.
p. 145. l.5 Fiscal measures. Robert Cecil. *All the Way.* 119.
l.23 Not disregarded. Alice to Edward. 16 Dec. 1911. E.2.
p. 146. l.16 Information: 'Select Committee on Marconi's Wireless Telegraph Co. Ltd. (Agreement) 1912. Special Report proposed by Lord Robert Cecil and agreed by the Unionist members of the Select Committee.' C 71/19.
l.22 Isaacs' shares. Donaldson. *Marconi Scandal.* 36.
l.36 In spite of Marconi. Robert to Edward. 19 Oct. 1914. C 55/148.
p. 147. l.9 Whitaker Wright. Balfour to Robert. 7 Oct. 1913. B 51071.
l.18 Cures and kills. Eleanor to Robert. 18 Feb. 1899 (misdated 1898). C 15/89.
l.24 Polite circles. Eleanor to Guendolen Osborne. 14 Dec. 1906. C 57/6.
l.30 Religious Easter. Eleanor to Edward. 30 March 1918. H.
l.36 Mad about Greek. Eleanor to Guendolen Osborne. 29 March 1906. C 57/5.
fn. Financial incompetence. Young. *Balfour.* 321.
p. 148. l.3 Separating the two. Virginia Woolf to Eleanor. [1905]. C 37/17.
l.12 Pearls and diamonds. *Ibid.* [   ]. C 37/90.
l.17 Zeppelin raid. *Ibid.* 29 Sept. [1915]. C 37–67.
l.22 Literary society. Eleanor to Guendolen Osborne. 11 April 1908. C 57/15–8.
l.32 Dorothy Nevill. *Ibid.*
l.38 Duncan Grant. Virginia Woolf to Eleanor. [1917]. C 37/80.
l.40 Scent of poetry. Eleanor to Robert. 30 May 1929. C 19/104.
p. 149. l.2 Galsworthy. Eleanor to Gilbert Murray. 20 Nov. 1944. M.
l.3 A. C. Benson. Eleanor to Robert. 15 May 1930. C 19/137.
l.15 Mark Rutherford. C 34/1–89 *passim.*
l.19 Saturated roads. Eleanor to Robert. [1931]. C 19/227.
l.35 Field-Marshal French. Robert to Salisbury. 1 Dec. 1914. C 52/50–5.
p. 150. l.2 Distinction. Edward to Eleanor. 10 Feb. 1918. C 55/89–90.
l.10 Society of gentlemen. Quo. Hazlehurst. *Politicians at War.* 140.
l.25 Larger enterprises. Robert to Edward. 1 April 1915. C 55/150–3.
l.32 No alcohol. *Ibid.*
l.42 Change of office. Robert Cecil. *All the Way.* 129.
p. 151. l.12 Secretary of State. Hardinge. *Old Diplomacy.* 197.
l.14 Warehouse clerk. Eleanor to Guendolen Osborne. 12 April 1918. C 57/99.
l.30 Anglo-American relations. Spring-Rice to Lord Newton. Quo. Gwynn. *Spring-Rice.* II. 321.
l.38 Asquith in Cabinet. Robert to Eleanor. 27 April 1916. C 5/149.
l.41 Philandering. *Ibid.* [Oct. 1916]. C 5/153.
p. 152. l.2 All circumstances. Robert Cecil. *Great Experiment.* 43
l.14 Prime Minister. Crowe to Robert. 20 July 1918. C 92/495.

l.28 Versailles. Robert to Edward. 12 Oct. 1918. H.
l.30 Level-headed. Blake. *Haig.* 256.
p. 153. l.14 No disarmament. Robert Cecil. *Great Experiment.* 61.
l.24 Pacifist. Robert to Eleanor. 14 Aug. 1918. C 6/4.
l.35 Self-determination. Roskill. Hankey. I. 479.
p. 154. l.6 Austria's shape. Toynbee. *Acquaintances.* 65–6.
l.19 Habitual resigner. Robert to Edward. 8 April 1918. H.
l.23 Exchange of prisoners. Robert Cecil. *All the Way.* 136.
l.24 Siberia. Robert to Edward. 16 June 1918. H.
l.34 Asks for appointment. Robert Cecil. *All the Way.* 146.
p. 155. l.11 Women eligible. Robert to Eleanor. 28 March 1919. C 6/35.
l.17 Aseptic Geneva. Robert Cecil. *Great Experiment.* 71.
l.23 Moral prestige. Robert Cecil to Lloyd George. 27 May 1919.
     C 75/219–21.
l.30 Admitting Germany. Robert Cecil. Diary. 9 June 1919. C 75.
l.34 Greedy nations. Robert to Eleanor. 9 March 1919. C 6/30.
l.38 No idealist. Robert Cecil. Diary. 6 Feb. 1919. C 75.
l.40 Scoring. Robert to Eleanor. 26 March 1919. C 6/34.
p. 156. l.14 Obligation of honour. Robert to Balfour. 5 April 1919.
     C 75/143.
l.22 Irregular situation. Robert to Eleanor. 2 June 1919. C 6/40.
l.27 Washington. Robert Cecil. Diary. 18 Feb. 1919. C 75.
l.34 No white beard. *Ibid.* 15 Jan. 1919. C 75.
l.38 Padding. Salisbury to Eleanor. 5 April 1919. C 52/59.
l.39 Wilson. Robert to Eleanor. [   ]. C 6/47.
l.41 Balfour. Robert Cecil. Diary. 27 March 1919. C 75.
l.43 Dancing. *Ibid.* 2 April 1919. C 75.
p. 157. l.11 Wrong man's beard. *Ibid.* 14 May 1919. C 75.
l.15 Powdered nose. Robert to Eleanor. 19 March 1919. C 6/32.
l.20 Without regret. G. Cecil. *Salisbury.* III. 301.
l.35 New men. McCallum. *Public Opinion.* 39–42.
p. 158. l.5 Exceedingly militarist. Robert Cecil. Diary. 19 May 1919. C 75.
l.8 Rid of him. Robert to Eleanor. 23 July 1920. C 6/53.
l.12 Joining Labour. Robert to Hugh. 1 Nov. 1919. Q 26/96–8.
l.31 Office under Grey. Robert to Asquith. 9 Oct. 1922. B 51073.
l.43 Consternation. Asquith to Robert. 19 Oct. 1922. B 51073.
p. 159. l.7 Bisexual. Brett. *Esher.* IV. 280–1. 25 April 1922.
l.10 Unbalanced mind. Hugh to Robert. 12 Jan. 1921. B. 51157.
l.32 Thought and action. Mosley. *My Life.* 147–8.
p. 160. l.2 Gladstone. Robert to Eleanor. 12 June 1921. C 6/105.
l.9 Rejected delegate. Robert Cecil to author. 7 May 1951.
l.11 Role of Smuts. Robert to Eleanor. 21 Oct. 1920. C 6/69.
l.33 Actively sick. Robert Cecil. United States Diary. 21 March to
     28 April 1923. C 76/1–38.
l.37 No concessions. *Ibid.*
l.38 Heart-breaking. Robert Cecil. *All the Way.* 179.
p. 161. l.13 Balfour's snub. Eleanor to Gwendolen. 18 May 1923. G.

l.18 Resigns from L.N.U. *Ibid.* 15 May 1923. G.

l.28 Tragic failure. *Ibid.* 18 May 1923. G.

l.40 Foreign Secretary. Robert Cecil. *All the Way.* 178.

p. *162.* l.18 Last three years. Robert to Curzon. 31 May 1923. P.

l.23 No delegation. Curzon to Robert. 2 June 1923. P.

l.37 Askance. Robert to Curzon. 16 June 1923. P.

p. *163.* l.10 Sphere of the League. Curzon to Robert. 18 June 1923. P.

l.13 Foreign affairs. Curzon to Grace Curzon. 18 Nov. 1923. N.

l.22 To be relieved. Curzon to Baldwin. 8 Aug. 1923. P.

l.33 Full steam ahead. Nicolson. *Curzon.* 370.

p. *164.* l.7 Out of his way. Mosley. *My Life.* 141.

l.16 Letter not sent. Robert to Baldwin. 14 Nov. 1923. B 51080.

l.25 Political deathbed. Salisbury to Robert. 11 Dec. 1923. C 52/63–4.

l.42 Ambition. Robert to Eleanor. 14 Jan. 1919. C 6/8.

p. *165.* l.9 Home policy. Gwendolen to Maud. 24 April 1922. G.

l.14 Bloody traitor. Robert Cecil. *All the Way.* 58.

l.36 Party office. *Ibid.* 180.

p. *166.* l.9 Hope he will decline. Curzon to Grace Curzon. 7 Nov. 1924. N.

l.25 Medieval king. Cooper. *Old Men Forget.* 137–8.

l.29 Opium den. Baldwin to Curzon. 21 Jan. 1925. P.

l.36 No reply. Robert Cecil. *Great Experiment.* 167.

fn. University robes. *Ibid.* 62.

p. *167.* l.13 Bismarck. Robert to Baldwin. 31 March 1926. C 92/48.

l.22 Rid of me. Robert to Salisbury. 2 Sept. 1927. B 51086.

l.23 No regret. Robert to Eleanor. 23 Jan. 1928. C 8/8–9.

l.29 Minute salary. *Ibid.* 20 July 1929. C 8/71.

l.33 Temperament. Gwendolen to Alice. 27 Aug. 1927. A.3.

l.40 Seven-inch guns. Jones. *Whitehall Diary.* II. 110.

p. *168.* l.1 Repute of politicians. Churchill to Robert. 14 Sept. 1927. B 51073.

l.18 Para pacem. Robert to Churchill. 27 July 1927. B 51073.

l.22 L. of N. Eleanor to Robert. 22 March 1924. C 18/145.

l.27 Landscape. Eleanor to Gilbert Murray. 11 Nov. 1948. M.

l.30 Bolingboke. Robert to Eleanor. 10 May 1934. C 9/91.

l.36 Great mistake. Robert to Gilbert Murray. 16 Dec. 1954. C 85/92.

p. *169.* l.1 Rearmament. Spoke 19 March 1936 and voted 24 March 1936. *Hansard.*

l.4 Allies and enemies. McCallum. *Public Opinion.* 10.

l.9 Resignation. Robert to Maud. 19 April 1926. B 51157.

l.17 Smashed up. Churchill to Robert. 9 April 1936. B 51073.

l.22 Protest. Robert to Neville Chamberlain. 18 Feb. 1938. B 51087.

l.25 Serenity. Gwendolen to Eleanor. 6 Jan. 1937. C 53/178–80.

p. *170.* l.20 Why I believe. Robert to Lord Daryngton. 5 July 1947. C 93/8–10.

l.23 Lenten services. Robert to Eleanor. Ash Wednesday. 1897. C 2/186.

l.26 Truth of Christianity. *Ibid.* 19 Feb. 1899. C 3/77.

l.34 Petition. Eleanor to Gwendolen. 19 Feb. 1933. C 20/2.

l.39 Cenotaph. Robert to Eleanor. 12 Nov. 1926. C 7/201.

p 171. l.4 St Michael's. *Ibid.* 14 Dec. 1930. C 8/114.

l.22 Prefer them educated. Robert to Eleanor. 10 Nov. 1927. C 7/236.

l.27 Middle-class Archbishop. *Ibid.* 27 March 1928. C 8/18.

l.32 Golfing Jews. Eleanor to Robert. Ash Wednesday 1919. C 18/27.

l.35 Butter and cream. *Ibid.* 12 Jan. 1919. C 18/3.

l.40 Nazi persecution. Robert to Eleanor. 25 April 1933. C 9/61. Also *The Times.* 7 June 1933.

p. 172. l.3 My relations. Eleanor to Hugh. 28 Oct. 1938. Q 66/24–5.

l.4 £28,000. *The Times.* 29 April 1959. £28,997 gross, £28,252 net.

l.22 P. G. Wodehouse. Eleanor to Gilbert Murray. 14 Jan. 1938. M.

l.26 Waste of time. Robert to Eleanor. 30 July 1929. C 8/82.

l.29 Anti-litter. *Ibid.* 25 June 1934. C 9/226.

l.32 Ill or resigning. Wheeler-Bennett. *Action this Day.* Essay by John Colville. 136.

l.40 Got the flue. Robert to Eleanor. 31 Dec. 1893. C 2/103.

p. 173. l.8 Cold better. *Ibid.* 26 March 1924. C 7/59.

l.15 Justice. Eleanor to Robert. 22 Jan. 1903. C 16/87.

l.20 Talk so much. *Ibid.* 20 Jan. 1897. C 15/8.

l.29 As I wished. Robert to Eleanor. [1943]. C 11/183.

l.33 Million votes. Jones. *Whitehall Diary.* II. 162. The M.P. was Sir John Power (1870–1950).

l.36 Birkenhead. Robert to Eleanor. 27 June 1928. C 8/26–7.

p. 174. l.12 Finding a room. Dalton. *Call Back Yesterday.* 222.

l.16 Medieval conference. Robert to Eleanor. 23 July 1929. C 8/74.

l.24 Lloyd George. Robert Cecil. *All the Way.* 197.

l.28 Nine months. Robert to Eleanor. 17 Dec. 1930. C 8/117.

l.34 Party vote. Gwendolen to Eleanor. 26 Oct. 1930. C 53/134–5.

p. 175. l.7 Formidable total. Robert to Eleanor. 19 Oct. 1931. C 8/193–4.

l.11 No instructions. *Ibid.* [Jan. 1932]. C 8/123. And 4 Feb. 1932. C 9/11–12.

l.18 Pigs. *Ibid.* 3 Dec. 1931. C 8/237.

l.20 Feeble acts. *Ibid.* 29 Jan. 1932. C 9/6.

p. 176. l.19 Last resort. Article on Robert Cecil by Philip Noel-Baker in *Dictionary of National Biography.* Also Macmillan. *Winds of Change.* 413–14.

l.27 Her obligations. Middlemas and Barnes. *Baldwin.* 856.

l.35 Conservative victory. Robert Cecil. *Great Experiment.* 269.

p. 177. l.15 Military sanctions. Gilbert Murray to Robert. 9 Dec. 1954. C 85/90.

l.18 Sometimes does. Robert to Eleanor. 6 July 1939. C 11/47.

l.24 Essential. Salisbury to Robert. 5 May 1941. B 51086.

l.34 Rearmament proposals. Robert to Salisbury. 8 May 1941. B 51086.

l.40 Essential opinion. Salisbury to Robert. 10 May 1941. B 51086.

p. 178. l.7 Awfully stupid. Eleanor to Robert. 31 Jan. 1933. C 20/21.

l.13 Stamp on Poland. Robert to Eleanor. 17 May 1935. C 9/69.

l.17 Tremendous news. *Ibid.* 7 March 1936. C 10/17.

l.27 Collective security. *Ibid.* 12 March 1936. C 10/25–6.

l.37 Common sense. Robert Cecil. *All the Way.* 215.

p. 179. l.3 Responsibility. G. Cecil. *Salisbury.* II. 286.

l.12 Central Office. Eleanor to Mary Murray. 22 Nov. 1936. M.

l.16 German visitors. Eleanor Cecil. MS. note. 1939. C 46/23.

l.22 Join Labour. Robert to Eleanor. 21 Dec. 1937. C 10/170.

l.33 Haile Selassie. 29 Nov. 1937. C 26/32–3.

p. 180. l.2 Well snubbed. Robert to Eleanor. 14 Feb. 1940. C 11/79.

l.8 Telephone. W. S. Morrison to Robert. 1 Nov. 1940. C 93/283.

l.9 Herrings. Robert to Lord Woolton. 26 Nov. 1942. C 93/413.

l.11 Coke. Robert to Gwilym Lloyd George. 18 June 1942. C 93/218.

l.16 Jet and spray. Eleanor to Robert. 18–19 June 1940. C 20/277–9.

l.28 Bolshevik panic. Eleanor to Gilbert Murray. 13 Jan. 1944. M.

l.32 Voting Labour. *Ibid.* 3 Aug. 1945. M.

p. 181. l.4 Industrial efforts. Robert to Salisbury. 30 June 1941. B 51086.

l.11 Capitalists. Robert to Eleanor. 31 Oct. 1945. C 11/191.

l.16 Labour whip. Robert to fifth Marquess of Salisbury. 3 March
1950. C 92/378. Not sent.

l.20 Attlee. Eleanor to Gilbert Murray. 8 Aug. 1948. M.

l.24 Greek in schools. Gilbert Murray to Eleanor. 14 March 1946.
C 42/76.

l.28 Vote in 1950. Robert to fifth Marquess of Salisbury. 3 March
1950. C 92/378. Not sent.

l.33 Doctrinaires. Robert to Eleanor. 26 Sept. 1950. C 11/236.

p. 182. l.2 Election of 1951. Robert to Lord Woolton. 20 Sept. 1951.
C 93/415. (Private secretary to private secretary.)

l.10 Political Pickwick. Eleanor to Gilbert Murray. 8 April 1948. M.

l.13 Refused meeting. Robert to C. W. Judd, 29 Sept. 1949. C 86/25.

l.16 Communists. Robert to Kathleen Courtney. 1 Aug. 1951.
C 87/223.

l.20 Honorary. Robert to C. W. Judd. 29 Jan. 1955. C 86/55. And
C. W. Judd to Robert. 3 March 1955. C 86/59.

l.24 UNESCO. Robert to Bishop of Chichester. 24 Jan. 1947.
C 29/112.

l.27 Paddington. Gilbert Murray to Robert. 1 April 1955. C 85/117.

l.36 Loyalty. Robert to fifth Marquess of Salisbury. 4 June 1955.
C 92/457.

p. 183. l.7 Lessons in church. Robert to Bishop of Chichester. 13 Aug. 1947.
C 92/116–17.

l.12 Polite rejection. Geoffrey Cumberlege to Robert. 26 Feb. 1948.
C 83/186.

l.16 Candid friend. Gilbert Murray to Eleanor. 8 March 1949.
C 42/89.

l.21 Curious man. Churchill to Robert and MS note. 8 Nov. 1952. C 92/489.

l.22 Tribute. *Church Quarterly Review*. Vol. 153. Oct.–Dec. 1952.

l.27 Memorandum. Eleanor to Gilbert Murray. 20 Oct. 1955. M.

l.29 Companion of Honour. Queen Elizabeth II to Robert. 22 Feb. 1956. C 105/4.

l.37 Leaving a record. Memorandum. [   ]. C 11/240.

p. 184. l.1 Approaching end. Robert to Eleanor. [   ]. C 11/243.

l.6 Bless you. Eleanor to Robert. 22 Jan. 1958. C 20/297.

l.9 Aged together. Robert to Eleanor. 18 July 1888. C 2/21–2.

CHAPTER SEVEN: LORD EDWARD CECIL

p. 185. l.19 Money. Edward to Salisbury. 3 Nov. 1883. D.

p. 186. l.2 Treadmill. G. Cecil. *Salisbury*. I. 50.

l.8 Army List. Robert to Edward. [   ]. H.

l.29 Grenadier Guards. Duke of Cambridge to Salisbury. 18 Oct. 1886. H.

l.33 Tweedledee. Edward to Robert. [   ]. C 55/1.

l.36 Decomposition. Edward to Salisbury. 2 Dec. 1885. E.1.

p. 187. fn. Herbert Bismarck. Hare. *Solitary Life*. 240–1.

p. 188. l.2 Extraordinary dinner. Edward to Salisbury. 16 Feb. 1886. E.1.

l.6 Compulsory lounging. Gwendolen to Violet. [   ]. H.

l.15 Special favour. Duke of Cambridge to Wolseley. 19 Sept. 1890.

l.28 Awful smells. Edward to Salisbury. [   ]. Sept. 1890. D.

l.32 Like a dog. *Ibid.* 10 Nov. 1890. D.

p. 189. l.6 Any stated time. Edward to Robert. 28 Nov. 1890. C 55/6–9.

l.14 Very amusing. Gwendolen to 'My dear Brothers'. 20 July 1885. C 53/10.

l.31 His character. Edward to Robert. 28 Nov. 1890. C 55/6–9.

p. 190. l.11 Wolseley's feelings. Childers to Edward. 14 July 1895. D.

l.32 Military expenditure. *Ibid.* 28 July 1895. D.

p. 191. l.4 Not P. M. Edward to Salisbury. 29 July 1895. D.

l.23 Marriage settlements. Salisbury to Edward. 17 March 1894. H.

l.28 Theodore Hook. Salisbury to Robert. 1 March 1885. C 51/5.

l.30 Stuff. Robert to Eleanor. 27 Jan. 1897. C 2/149.

l.33 Fine necklace. Alice Salisbury. *Hatfield Memories*.

p. 192. l.8 Extremest danger. Salisbury to Edward. 19 April 1891. H.

l.12 Large sums. *Ibid.* 25 May 1891. H.

l.14 While you live. Georgina to Edward. 20 April 1891. H.

l.29 Viceroy. Milner. *My Picture Gallery*. 52 .

l.31 Will be lasting. *Ibid.* 53.

l.36 Going to marry. *Ibid.* 56.

p. 193. l.2 Horrid row. Edward to Robert. [13 March 1894]. C 55/10.

l.5 Without injury. Robert to Edward. 14 March 1894. H.

l.21 Menacing geniality. Milner. *My Picture Gallery*. *passim*.

l.26 Lover-like rhetoric. Balfour to Edward. 17 March 1894. H.

l.39 Holy Week. Georgina to Eleanor. 22 March [1894]. C 51/20–1.

p. 194. l.1 Tone her down. Georgina to Frances Balfour. 23 March 1894. C 58/45.

l.12 Financial advice. Salisbury to Edward. 17 March 1894. H.

l.14 £400 a year. *Ibid.* 21 March 1894 and 26 March 1894. H.

l.17 More debts. Cranborne to Edward. 20 July 1894. H.

l.26 Like a herring. Blunt. *My Diaries.* 144.

l.35 Soured for life. Edward to Eleanor. 17 March 1918. C 55/94–6.

l.37 Park Lane ideas. Eleanor to Robert. 23 Jan. 1897. C 15/11.

p. 195. l.5 Maternal rebuke. Georgina to Violet. 12 Aug. [1894]). H.

l.10 Vindictive. Salisbury to Violet. 17 May 1896. H.

l.13 Generalities. Robert to Eleanor. 12 Feb. 1899. C 3/81.

l.21 Bad taste. *Ibid.* 9 March 1897. C 2/192.

l.27 Lending Liddon. Hugh to Violet. 1 June 1895. H.

l.30 Want to help. Gwendolen to Violet. 5 Jan. 1900. H.

l.35 Not asked again. Milner. *My Picture Gallery.* 82.

l.40 Effort at study. Salisbury to Edward. 21 March 1894. H.

p. 196. l.7 Mathematics. Gwendolen to Edward. 13 Nov. [1894]. H.

l.24 Kitchener. Edward Cecil. *Leisure of an Egyptian Official.* 175–6.

l.37 £1 a head. Magnus. *Kitchener.* 136.

l.39 Uncouth. Edward Cecil. *Leisure of an Egyptian Official.* 177.

p. 197. l.1 Twisted ankle. Arthur. *Wolseley Letters.* 277.

l.8 Better not talk. Edward to Robert. 18 June 1896. C 55/12.

l.23 Slept. Edward to Violet. 8 June 1896. H.

l.31 Inconsiderate. Edward to Robert. 12 Sept. 1896. C 55/13.

l.41 Guidance refused. Edward Cecil. *Leisure of an Egyptian Official.* 182–3.

p. 198. l.2 Sit on War Office. Edward to Salisbury. 25 May 1896. D.

p. 199. l.12 Abyssinian mission. Rodd. *Social and Diplomatic Memoirs.* And Gleichen. *With the Mission to Menelik. passim.*

l.21 Kind to the poor. Edward Cecil. *Leisure of an Egyptian Official.* 183.

l.26 Four hours. Gwendolen to Alice Balfour. 8 Oct. 1898. G.

l.32 Most popular. Georgina to Edward. 6 Oct. 1885. H.

l.34 Mahaffy. Edward Cecil. *Leisure of an Egyptian Official.* iii.

l.42 Jester. Edward Cecil. Diary of the Abyssinian Expedition. H.

p. 200. l.14 Motor drive. Violet Milner. *My Picture Gallery.* 123.

l.16 Trifle dangerous. Edward to Georgina. 11 July 1899. G.

l.24 Pro-Boer general. Violet to Gwendolen. 2 Aug. 1899. G.

l.27 Stocking Mafeking. Milner. *My Picture Gallery.* 129. And Violet to Gwendolen. 16 Jan. 1900. G.

l.34 Flag of truce. Salisbury to Gwendolen. 28 Feb. 1900. G.

l.38 Used to those. Edward to Violet. 19 Dec. 1899. H.

l.39 Practically invincible. *Ibid.* 25 Dec. 1899. H.

l.40 Fight this morning. *Ibid.* 26 Dec. 1899. H.

p. 201. l.5 That is behind me. *Ibid.* [   ]. H.

l.15 Boy Scouts. Grinnell-Milne. *Baden-Powell at Mafeking.* 120.

l.18 Food rationing. *Ibid.* 175.

l.19 Curried locusts. Sarah Wilson. *South African Memories.* 202.

l.28 Government office. Robert to Eleanor. 18 Jan. 1897. C 2/140.

l.29 Soap box. Mabel Palmer to Violet. 27 March 1900. H.

l.30 Grocer's shop. Gwendolen to Violet. 23 Feb. 1900. H.

p. 202. l.3 Military hospitals. Violet to Gwendolen. 2 May 1900. G.

l.12 Medical results. Violet to Salisbury. 30 May 1900. D.

l.15 Ordered back. Gleichen to Violet. 7 April 1900. H.

l.17 Duty or business. Violet Cecil. *My Picture Gallery.* 184–5.

l.20 The Queen's inquiry. Gwendolen to Violet. 4 May 1900. H.

l.24 Plays of Shakespeare. Cranborne to Violet. 8 April 1900. H.

l.26 Black and white. Edward Stanley to Violet. 16 April 1900 and 17 June 1900. H.

l.33 Set of liars. Edward to Gwendolen. 16 June 1900. G.

l.36 Bonfire. Gwendolen to Violet. 25 May 1900. H.

p. 203. l.6 Mafeking stamps. Duke of York to Edward. 20 Dec. 1900. H.

l.10 Repaying £1,000. Salisbury to Edward. 10 Aug. 1900. H.

l.27 Recording Angel. Edward to Robert. 9 Feb. 1903. E.4.

p. 204. l.14 Kitchener in Assuan. Edward to Alice. 8 Nov. 1902. E. 3.

l.21 Wandering Arabs. Edward to Gwendolen. 21 Nov. 1903. G.

l.26 To his opinion. Edward to Robert. 20 May 1904. C 55/24–6.

l.36 Order postponed. Gwendolen to Eleanor. 28–29 Dec. 1903. C 53/29–31.

p. 205. l.2 The Lord. Edward to Robert. 14 Aug. 1904. C 55/23.

l.31 Responsibility. Quo. Clara Boyle. *Boyle of Cairo.* 48.

l.41 Christian morality. Quo. Marlowe. *Cromer.* 280.

p. 206. l.10 Administration. Quo. Clara Boyle. *Boyle of Cairo.* 49.

l.16 Not as a master. *Ibid.* 51.

l.30 Dinner or lunch. Gwendolen to Eleanor. 28–29 Dec. 1903. C 53/29–31.

l.34 Thinks of it. Edward to Eleanor. 19 Feb. 1906. C 55/35.

l.38 Advisers. Edward to Violet. 27 June 1907. H.

fn. Edward VII. Storrs. *Orientations.* 46.

p. 207. l.7 All he is worth. Edward to Robert. 25 Nov. 1906. C 55/37.

l.14 Enthusiasm. *Ibid.* 10 Feb. 1907. C 55/51–2.

l.19 Recommended Gorst. Salisbury to Edward. 13 Aug. 1910. E.1.

l.29 Share of government. *Reports on Egypt and the Sudan, 1910.* Cmd. 5633. May 1911.

l.37 First boat. Clara Boyle. *Boyle of Cairo.* 155.

p. 208. l.13 Not reasonable. Edward to Violet. 27 June 1907. H.

l.27 Church mouse. *Ibid.* [   ]. H.

l.36 Cannot be certain. Hugh to Edward. 1 March 1908. E. 5.

p. 209. l.4 Future date. Churchill to Edward. 28 Feb. 1908. H.

l.11 Knowing little. Gwendolen to Maud. 11 Dec. 1907. G.

l.13 Prima donna. Edward to Violet. 18 Jan. 1912. H.

l.16 Sir Paul Harvey. *Dictionary of National Biography.*

l.20 Penal servitude. Edward to Violet. 27 June 1907. H.

l.23 Overpower. Georgina to Frances Balfour. 27 March 1894.
C 58/46.

l.42 Two grievances. Edward to Salisbury. 20 Aug. 1905. J.

p. *210.* l.6 Such a tangle. Edward to Robert. 9 Feb. 1903. E.3.

l.7 Yearly richer. Gwendolen to Maud. 27 April 1906. G.

l.14 Hope she won't. Edward to Robert. 25 Nov. 1906. C 55/37.

l.21 Poor luck. Edward to Violet. 27 June 1907. H.

l.25 Retrieved much. Gwendolen to Maud. 15 Nov. 1907. G.

l.31 Wifely support. Jones. *Diary with Letters.* 538.

p. *211.* l.12 From the rocks. Napier. *A Late Beginner.* 50.

l.19 Wigsell garden. Lady Hardinge to author. 30 April 1971.

l.37 Filing system. Edward to Helen. 9 April 1918. H.

p. *212.* l.3 Dreary old age. Edward to Violet. [c.1912]. H.

l.7 Board of Trade. Edward to Eleanor. 24 Sept. 1909. C 55/60–1.

l.16 Abandoned years ago. *Ibid.*

l.20 Plush and gilt. Edward Cecil. *Leisure of an Egyptian Official.* 23.

l.35 Single crop .*Ibid.* 56–7.

l.41 Plan cancelled. Napier. *A Late Beginner.* 67–8.

p. *213.* l.13 Stole largely. Edward Cecil. *Leisure of an Egyptian Official.* 206.

l.24 Ever forgive him. Napier. *A Late Beginner.* 68.

l.32 Bad headaches. Edward to Helen. 22 Feb. 1915. H.

l.7 Concealment of riches. Edward Cecil. *Leisure of an Egyptian Official.* 104.

l.13 Elementary kind. *Ibid.* 103.

l.17 Expectorations. Edward to Alice. 22 Sept. 1909. E.3.

l.27 Shall be exposed. Edward to Eleanor. 11 Nov. 1909. C 55/64–6.

l.36 Explaining. Edward Cecil. *Leisure of an Egyptian Official.* 207.

p. *215.* l.3 Opera bouffe. *Ibid.* 227.

l.19 Foreigner or native. *Ibid.* 90–1.

l.21 Jealousies. *Ibid.* 274.

l.24 See your face. *Ibid.* 137.

l.37 Not steady. Edward to Alice. 22 Sept. 1909. E.3.

p. *216.* l.15 Street wiper. Edward Cecil. *Leisure of an Egyptian Official.* 162.

l.17 Wash of life. *Ibid.* 124.

l.20 Unpleasantnesses. *Ibid.* 270.

l.21 Antiquated fallacies. *Ibid.* 231.

l.25 Laid by a mummy. *Ibid.* 21.

l.27 Lying in port. *Ibid.* 261.

l.31 British minds. *Ibid.* 225.

l.34 Medical reason. *Ibid.* 30.

p. *217.* l.3 Horseback. *Ibid.* 233.

l.12 Way to the door. *Ibid.* 140.

l.24 Obsequious smile. *Ibid.* 80–1.

p. *218.* l.4 Changed identities. Edward to Eleanor. [1911]. C 55/71.

l.8 Pray and beg. Ibid. 3 Dec. 1911. C 55/70.

l.12 Casket letters. Eleanor to Edward. [19 Dec.] 1911. C 55/158.

p. *219.* l.30 Kuchnir. Storrs. *Orientations.* 126–7.

l.33 Finances of Siam. Cromer to Edward. 11 Oct. 1911. H.

l.39 Brighter prospects. Edward to Cromer. 23 Oct. 1911. H.

p. 220. l.4 Windsor. Edward to Violet. 25 May 1913. H.

l.10 Defrauded. Salisbury to Edward. 7 Nov. 1913. H.

l.12 Budget of £20 million. 1913. Wingate Papers. 107/11.

l.15 In good training. Edward to Alice. 5 Oct. 1911. E.3.

l.18 Hunted rabbits. Ibid. [   ]. E.3.

l.23 Death warrant. Ibid. 1 Oct. 1911. E.3.

l.33 Missing antiques. Ibid.

l.42 Asking for balls. Edward to Violet. 22 March 1914. H.

p. 221. l.4 Required for the Khedive. Edward to Alice. [   ]. E.3.

l.31 Sense of humour. Ibid. 15 Feb. 1915. E.3.

l.41 Coal deal. Sir Arthur Webb to Edward. 8 May 1918. H.

l.42 Brother's promotion. Edward to Alice. 15 Feb. 1915. E.3.

p. 222. l.3 Expeditionary forces. Major F. T. Smith to Edward. 27 Oct. 1917. H.

l.5 Keeping one's head. Edward to Helen. 26 July 1916. H.

l.11 Reduced salaries. Edward to Advisers. 6 Oct. 1914. H.

l.30 Ministry of Finance. Advisers to Edward. 14 Oct. 1914. H.

l.38 Remonstrance. Edward to Advisers. 17 Oct. 1914. H.

p. 223. l.6 Helped to see. Edward to Alice. 6 Dec. 1914. E.3.

l.15 Assembled boys. The Wykehamist. December 1915.

l.27 Difficult to hold. Edward to Alice. 15 Feb. 1915. E.3.

l.31 Compromise. Ibid. 3 Sept. 1911. E.3.

fn. Crucifixion. Auerbach. Paintings and Sculpture. 98.

p.224. l.4 Directing policy. Graham to Wingate. 1 Oct. 1916. Wingate Papers. 236/5.

l.7 The Sultan. McMahon to Edward. 13 Sept. 1915. E.4.

l.10 Affection and confidence. Hayter to Violet. 26 Dec. 1918. H.

l.23 Responsible Minister. Robert to Edward. 30 Nov. 1916. H.

l.38 Subordinate role. Wingate. Wingate of the Sudan. 208.

p. 225. l.15 Had Kitchener lived. Edward to Salisbury. 28 July 1917. J.

l.17 Munitions adviser. Edward to Violet. 6 Aug. 1917. H.

l.27 Inferior intellect. Ibid. 5 Nov. 1917. H.

p. 226. l.17 Own interests. Hardinge to Wingate. 7 Sept. 1917. Wingate Papers. 236/7.

l.37 Quietus. Milner to Edward. 31 Dec. 1917. H.

p. 227. l.4 Despaired of. Edward to Alice. 13 Dec. 1917. E.3.

l.5 Pray for me. Edward to Helen. 6 Dec. 1917. H.

l.19 A little flat. Edward to Eleanor. 24 Jan. 1918. C 55/82–3.

l.27 Frozen hen. Ibid. 16 Feb. 1918. C 55/92–3.

l.30 Incendiarism. Ibid. 24 Jan. 1918. C 55/82–3.

l.32 Vulgar and stupid. Edward to Helen. 15 March 1918. H.

p. 228. l.8 Nothing to eat. Ibid. 16 April 1918. H.

l.23 Shirking discussion. Edward to Alice. 31 Oct. 1918. E.3.

l.30 Baked visitors. Edward to Eleanor. 24 Jan. 1918. C 55/82–3.

l.34 In writing. Edward to Alice. 25 Sept. 1918. E.3.

p. 229. l.4   Service of others. Gwendolen to Lavinia Talbot. 22 Dec. 1918. C 50/8–11.

        l.5   Gross estate. *The Times.* 27 March 1919.

        l.8   Pensions. A. J. Lloyd to Violet. 14 June 1919. H.

CHAPTER EIGHT: LORD HUGH CECIL

p. 230. l.14 Not quite orthodox. Alice Salisbury. *Hatfield Memories.*

        l.21 Gladstone at bay. Algernon Cecil. *Queen Victoria and her Prime Ministers.* 315.

p. 231. l.2   Cured my cold. Hugh to Gwendolen. [Dec. 1877]. G.

        l.6   Seven stone. Hugh to Robert. 10 Nov. 1887. C 92/252–3.

        l.15 Civilized life. Bowra. *Memories.* 117.

        l.28 Procedure. Hugh to Robert. 21 May 1888. C 92/254–6.

        l.34 Cause of misery. Steinhart. *Oxford Canning Club.* 329. 29 Oct. 1890.

        l.36 Labourer's wage. Cole and Postgate. *The Common People.* 430.

        l.38 £800 a year. J. C. Wedgwood to Hugh. 9 Feb. 1937. Q 53/28.

p. 232. l.3   Sexual vice. *The Times.* 22 Aug. 1907.

        l.8   Churchill. David Cecil. *The Cecils.* 303.

        l.10 At their heads. Dowager Lady Harlech to author. 13 Jan. 1971.

        l.25 Terrible theology. Georgina to Edward. 15 Feb. 1894. H.

        l.33 Ever narrower. Georgina to Eleanor. 11 Jan. [1899]. C 51/27–8.

p. 233. l.5   Conversation. Robert to Eleanor. 19 Jan. 1897. C 2/141.

        l.11 My affection. Balfour to Hugh. 20 Jan. 1897. G.

        l.18 Zeal and cruelty. *C.A.P.* XIII. 1. 37. 2 Feb. 1932.

        l.28 Unseen King. *Ibid.* XXV. 1. 145. 9 Feb. 1945.

        l.31 English children. Edwards. *Leaders of the Church of England.* 26.

        l.42 Chosen denomination. Hugh Cecil. *Conservatism.* 115–16.

p. 234. l.18 Empty room. *Hansard.* 16 May 1902.

        l.20 Curzon's congratulations. 1 June 1902. Q 1/68.

        l.22 Rapture of the seer. Curzon. *Modern Parliamentary Eloquence.* 48.

        l.24 Cool brain. Margot Asquith to Curzon. 12 Aug. 1902. P.

        l.26 Makes me ill. Hugh to Eleanor. 22 Oct. 1909. C 54/14.

        l.32 Marriages legalized. Queen Victoria. Journal. 7 May 1879. Quo. Lutyens. *Lady Lytton.* 48.

        l.42 Lords vote. *Hansard.* 10 July 1896.

p. 235. l.7   Royal family. Robert to Hugh. 12 July [1896]. G.

        l.13 Shame and lust. *Hansard.* 24 April 1901.

        l.15 Institutions of mankind. *Ibid.* 5 Feb. 1902.

        l.22 No progress. *Ibid.* Also Winston S. Churchill. *Thoughts and Adventures.* 35–8.

        l.37 Sexual vice. *The Times.* 22 Aug. 1907.

p. 236. l.8   Impossible. Gwendolen to Maud, 30 Aug. 1907. G.

        l.14 Poisonous snakes. Hugh to Eleanor. 13 June 1956. C. 54/55.

        l.17 Reciting poetry. *Ibid.* 6 July 1949. C 54/37.

l.28 Birch Grove. Mrs Maurice Macmillan to author. 28 April 1969.

p. 237. l.23 Justice and Democracy. Winston S. Churchill. *My Early Life.*
197–200.

l.29 Regular troops. *Ibid.*

p. 238. l.2 With a phrase. Robert to Eleanor. 14 Jan. 1901. C 3/128.

l.17 Historic controversy. Hugh Cecil. Memoir of Lady Astor.
Dec. 1951. Q 60/31.

l.23 Radical masses. Churchill to Rosebery. 10 Oct. 1902. R. S.
Churchill. Companion Volume II. 1. 168.

l.39 Labour and capital. Hugh Cecil. Memorandum. Jan. 1904.
Q 2/5–11.

p. 239. l.21 Preserved. Churchill to Hugh. 24 Oct. 1903. (Not sent.) And
R. S. Churchill. Companion Volume. II. 1. 242–3.

p. 240. l.3 Inevitable. Hugh to Churchill. [   ]. Dec. 1903. *Ibid.* II. 1. 268.

l.12 On my mind. Churchill to Hugh. 2 June [1904]. *Ibid.* II. 1. 346.

l.20 By the board. Hugh to Churchill. 5 Sept. 1908. *Ibid.* II. 2. 816.

l.32 Happen to differ. Balfour to Hugh. 16 July 1903. Q 1/108–12.

l.35 Wedded to Protection. Robert to Eleanor. 1 July 1904. C 4/6.

l.38 Remain in the party. Balfour to Hugh. 19 July 1905. Q 4/12–14.

p. 241. l.11 Orthodoxy. Rosebery to Hugh. 16 Jan. 1906. Q 5/16.

l.18 Visible future. Eleanor to Robert. 19 Jan. 1906. C. 17/2.

l.25 Too clever. Maud to Eleanor. 9 March [   ]. C 56/50–1.

l.29 Troublesome Tory. Robert Cecil. 'Notes on Conversation with
Bonar Law.' 16 July 1907. C 71/1–3.

l.32 Holy Orders. C. Wigan to Hugh. 15 June 1904. Q 2/51–2. And
Gwendolen to Maud. 17 Jan. 1906. G.

l.33 Church weekly. G. C. Curnock to Hugh. 19 Dec. 1906. Q 6/153.

l.37 Abilities. Gwendolen to Maud. 30 Aug. 1907. G.

p. 242. l.12 Great and clever. Gwendeline Bertie to Churchill. 7 Sept. 1907.
R. S. Churchill. Companion Volume. II. 1. 675.

l.17 Hearthrug. Lady Manners to author. 21 June 1971.

l.19 Privacy. Cynthia Asquith. *Remember and Be Glad.* 50.

l.22 Sufficient. Hugh to Eleanor. 15 Nov. [   ]. C 54/1.

l.23 Parsimonious. Lady Manners to author. 21 June 1971.

l.34 Foxhunting. Halifax. *Fulness of Days.* 169.

p. 243. l.4 Dissipation. Hugh to Alice. 13 Aug. 1905. A. 3.

l.11 Conversational resources. *Ibid.* 10 Aug. 1906. A.3.

l.19 Tyrannical organist. *C.A.P.* VIII. 3. 382–3. 16 Nov. 1927.

l.20 Byrd. Marsh. *Ambrosia and Small Beer.* 138.

fn. Trollope. Q 33/132.

p. 244. l.1 Penetrated defences. Lady Manners to author. 21 June 1971.

l.7 Emotion. Gwendolen to Maud. 31 Dec. 1909. G.

l.11 Evil habits. Hugh to Alice. 15 March 1932. A.3.

l.21 Licensed victualler. David Cecil. *The Cecils.* 280.

l.26 Tasteful. Cynthia Asquith. *Remember and Be Glad.* 50.

l.30 Metaphysics. Gwendolen to Maud. 6 Jan. 1927. G.

l.41 Rushing into print. Selborne to Maud. 9 June 1907. F.100.

p. 245. l.2 Moderate Liberals. Memorandum. January. [1908]. Q 9/43.

l.5 Destroy Tory Party. Robert to Hugh. 10 March 1908. Q 9/60.

l.16 Visit to Rosebery. Robert to Eleanor. 21 July 1904. C 4/28.

p. 246. l.8 Propriety. Hugh to Knollys. 11 Oct. 1909.

l.25 Qualifications for the task. *Ibid.* 15 Oct. 1909.

fn. William IV. Jennings. *Cabinet Government.* 376.

p. 247. l.11 Components. Rosebery to Hugh. 9 Oct. 1909. Q 12/101–2.

p. 248. l.2 Greater affection. Talbot to Hugh. 11 Nov. 1907. Q 8/54.

l.7 Female suffrage. Macan to Hugh. 10 June 1909. Q 11/114.

l.20 Political supporters. G. R. Y. Radcliffe to Hugh. Q 12 *passim.*
Also *Oxford University Gazette.* 22 June 1909.

l.24 Half a crown. Charles Oman. *Second Betting Book of All Souls
College.* 153.

l.36 Rise in the world. Quo. Evans. *Time and Change.* 357–8.

p. 249. l.6 Liberal Free Trader. *Ibid.* 358–61.

l.8 Comparative votes. G. R. Y. Radcliffe to Hugh. 14 Dec. 1909.
Q 12/164.

l.17 Party Council. Robert to Eleanor. 7 Dec. 1912. C 5/98.

l.35 Tide of time. *Hansard.* 30 March 1910.

p. 250. l.11 Mad baboons. Bonham Carter. *Churchill.* 207. 24 July 1911.

l.14 To prevent debate. Churchill to King George V. 26 July 1911.
R. S. Churchill. Companion Volume II. 2. 1103.

l.26 Kindness and charity. Churchill to Hugh. 7 May 1910.
Q 63/54.

l.41 Get in his way. *Ibid.* 22 May 1910. Q 63/55.

p. 251. l.9 Unbalanced men. Hugh Cecil. *Conservatism.* 238.

l.28 Acknowledged power. *Ibid.* 226.

l.33 Liberal peers. Lansdowne to Hugh. 26 July 1911. Q 14/129.

p. 252. l.20 Slight dislocation. Hugh Cecil. *Conservatism.* 48.

l.26 Unfairness. Murray to Hugh. 8 Feb. 1912. Q 15/6.

l.29 Never eliminated. Fisher to Hugh. 12 Feb. 1912. Q 15/7.

l.34 Value and pleasure. Churchill to Hugh. 1 May 1912. Q 63/58.

p. 253. l.3 Tyranny. Robert to Hugh. [1912?]. Q 15/206–7.

l.9 Wreck the Bill. Hugh Cecil. Memorandum on Home Rule.
9 May 1914. Q 17/80–3.

l.34 Passed it. Hugh Cecil. Memorandum on Possible Rejection of
Home Rule Bill. 22 July 1914. Q 18/24–9.

l.38 Conditions met. Hugh Cecil. Not. 1 June 1920. Q 27/99.

fn. Speaker Lowther. Hugh to Speaker Whitley. 19 July 1922.
Q 30/167–75.

p.254. l.13 Hugh Cecil. Memorandum on Home Rule Bill. [   ].
Q 18/191–4.

l.24 Whittingehame. Eleanor to Frances Balfour. 9 Sept. 1899.
C 58/91.

l.36 Fast enough. Hugh Cecil. *Conservatism.* 11.

l.38 Sensation of fear. Dowager Lady Harlech to author. 13 Jan. 1971.

l.41 Unreality. Hugh to Alice. 2 Jan. 1915. A.3.

p. 255. l.2 Bicycling. Hugh to Eleanor. [   ]. C 54/5.

l.5 Land and water. Mosley. *My Life.* 62–3.

l.14 Like gossamer. Lady Manners to author. 21 June 1971.

l.22 Taking his ticket. Hugh to Alice. 11 April 1915. A.3.

l.25 Grounded. Alice to Edward. 19 June 1915. E.2.

l.32 Latin motto. Inge to Hugh. [   ]. Q 19/48.

l.34 Assistant Secretary, Royal Aero Club, to Hugh. 29 April 1915. Q 19/37.

p. 256. l.15 For an invalid. Marsh. *A Number of People.* 69.

l.17 Nihil obstat. Baring. *R.F.C. HQ.* 225.

l.28 Crayfish. *Ibid.* 95.

l.31 Bald head. Simon. *Retrospect.* 114.

l.40 Charm and courtesy. Brabazon. *The Brabazon Story.* 98.

p. 257. l.7 Superior officer. *Ibid.*

l.14 Latest thought. Moore-Brabazon to Hugh. 11 June 1916. Q 20/11.

p. 258. l.3 Not resigned. Hugh Cecil. Memorandum. 4 Aug. 1914. Q 18/44.

l.12 Remarkable speed. Baring. *R.F.C. H.Q.* 259.

l.16 May be advisable. Boyle. *Trenchard.* 259.

fn. Always vulgar. Hugh Cecil. Memorandum. 4 Aug. 1914. Q 18/40–2.

p. 259. l.5 Resignation accepted. Beaverbrook. *Men and Power.* 217 *et. seq.*

l.18 Beyond endurance. Hugh Cecil. Notes on Sir Hugh Trenchard's Resignation. 22 April 1918. Q 23/223–8.

l.26 In his place. Milner to Hugh. 13 April 1918. Q 23/189–90. Also Boyle. *Trenchard.* 276.

l.30 Saying more. Trenchard to Hugh. 14 April 1918. Q 23/193.

p. 260. l.6 Beyond doubt. Rothermere to Hugh. 15 April 1918. Q 23/198.

l.21 Personal friends. Hugh to Rothermere. 15 April 1918. Q 23/201.

l.41 Tacitly admit. Rothermere to Hugh. 16 April 1918. Q 23/211.

p. 261. l.14 Parliamentary relations. Hugh to Rothermere. 17 April 1918. Q 23/215.

l.17 Air Ministry. Godfrey Paine to Hugh. 17 April 1918. Q 23/218.

l.28 Superior officers. Rothermere to Lloyd George. 23 April 1918. Quo. Beaverbrook. *Men and Power.* 381.

p. 262 l.2 Parliamentary liberties. Chamberlain to Hugh. 26 April 1918. Q 23/238.

l.6 His speech. *Hansard.* 29 April 1918.

l.7 Simon's heartsearching. Simon. *Retrospect.* 117.

l.8 Grateful. Trenchard to Hugh. 1 May 1918. Q 23/243.

l.26 George vi. *The Times.* 18 July 1921. Also Sefton Brancker to Hugh. 22 July 1921. Q 29/206.

p. 263. l.18 Righteous acts. Hugh Cecil. *Liberty and Authority.* 17–18.

l.25 Parental authority. *Ibid.* 40.

l.32 Main chance. *The Times*. 24 June 1901.

l.37 Prohibition. Hugh to Alice. 11 April 1915. A.3.

l.39 Deadlier foe. Jones. *Lloyd George*. 68.

p. 264. l.3 Refuses to do so. Hugh Cecil. *Liberty and Authority*. 21.

l.13 Conscription. Roberts to Hugh. 30 July 1912. Q 15/143.

l.23 Aesthetic greed. Cynthia Asquith. *Remember and be Glad*. 98.

l.28 National claim. *Hansard*. 21 Nov. 1917.

l.32 Imprison. Hugh Cecil. Memorandum on Conscientious Objectors.
    [   ]. Q 20/159–63.

l.39 Civilized order. Davidson to Hugh. 1 Dec. 1916. Q 20/157.

p. 265. l.2 What a fool. *Hansard*. 15 May 1916.

l.10 Retaining the vote. *Ibid*. 21 Nov. 1917.

l.14 Grave wrong-doing. *The Times*. 6 March 1919.

l.20 Enlarged tonsils. S. N. Harris (Home Office) to Hugh.
    4 May 1917. Q 21/36.

l.23 Scouts and Communists. Baden-Powell to Hugh. 19 July 1922.
    Q 30/163.

l.30 Mr Gladstone. T. B. Strong to Hugh. 31 July 1918. Q 24/36–7.

l.38 Violence and revolt. *The Times*. 26 Aug. 1918.

l.40 Congratulations. Curzon to Hugh. 27 Aug. 1918. Q 24/53.

l.41 Every pulpit. J. W. Diggle to Hugh. 30 Aug. 1918. Q 24/56.

p. 266. l.4 Under-Secretary for War. Churchill to Lloyd George. 14 July
    1919. Lloyd George Papers. F/9/1/5.

l.7 Provincial councils. Hugh Cecil. Memorandum. 28 Dec. 1918.
    Q 24/153.

l.9 Coal industry. *Ibid*. 24 July 1919. Q 26/37–9.

l.10 House of Windsor. *Ibid*. Nov. 1920. Q 28/70–81.

l.21 Imperial control. Churchill to Hugh. 26 April 1922. Q 63/70.

l.25 Obstructive. Fox. *Dean Inge*. 47.

p. 267. l.2 Degrees for women. Hugh to Eleanor. 4 April 1918. C 54/17.

l.9 Summoned in future. Hugh to Farnell. 22 March 1922. Q 30/55.

l.14 Inadvertent. Hugh to F. J. Lys. 25 June 1934. Q 47/157–60.

l.18 Cambridge custom. F. J. Lys to Hugh. 20 Nov. 1934. Q 47/264–5.

l.38 In my keeping. Hugh to F. J. Lys. 21 Nov. 1934. Q 47/266–70.

p. 268. l.2 Developments. Halifax to Hugh. 26 Nov. 1934. Q 47/286.

l.9 Satisfied. F. J. Lys to Hugh. 31 Jan. 1935. Q 48/33.

l.11 Renewed promise. A. D. Lindsay to Hugh. 28 March 1936.
    Q 50/195.

l.36 Formalities to observe. Herbert to Hugh. 18 Nov. 1935.
    Q 49/87.

fn. Licensing laws. Herbert. *Independent Member*. 9.

p. 269. l.4 Useful advice. *Ibid*. 20.

l.8 Essential occupation. Jones. *Whitehall Diary*. I. 58. 12 April 1918.

l.14 Retribution. Hugh to Lewis Palmer. 11 Oct. 1919. Q 26/77–80.

l.19 Indolence. W. Yorke Batley. *Personal Memories*.

l.32 Diabolic intrusion. Hugh Cecil. 'Notes on my Religious Position.'
    10 Dec. 1919. Q 26/138–72.

l.36 Righteousness. Hugh to Eleanor. 27 July 1921. C 54/23–4.

fn. Halifax. *Fulness of Days*. 169.

p. 270. l.2 Adultery. Hugh to Eleanor. 23 June 1921. C 54/22.

l.15 Marriage laws. *C.A.P.* II. 1. 141. 4 Feb. 1921.

l.19 Church Assembly. *The Times*. 20 Nov. 1937.

l.27 Is that Christian? Eleanor to Hugh. 28 June 1921. Q 29/199.

l.30 Fabric of society. Hugh to Eleanor. 4 July 1921. C 54/18–24.

p. 271. l.5 Giving pain. Hugh to Sidney Herbert. 21 Jan. 1920. Q 27/33–40.

l.22 China or Indian. Hugh to J. H. Whitley. 4 June 1927. Q 34/24.

l.26 Consciences. J. H. Whitley to Hugh. 13 June 1927. Q 34/28.

l.31 Uncatholic. Hugh to Rev B. C. Hopson. 15 July 1929.
Q 38/54–6.

l.37 Will of Christ. Rev B. C. Hopson to Hugh. 24 July 1929.
Q 38/73–5.

l.41 Sitting in a pew. W. Yorke Batley. *Personal Memories*.

p. 272. l.29 Financial. *C.A.P.* II. 3. 91. 24 Nov. 1921.

l.33 Rejected four. *C.A.P.* 9 July 1970.

l.41 Verbiage. Henson. *Retrospect*. II. 203.

p. 273. l.2 Read them all. Davidson to Hugh. 29 Nov. 1920. Q 28/44.

l.4 Ear for music. Hugh Cecil. 'Archbishop Lang as a Speaker.'
Q Box 22/29.

l.7 Best of all. Purcell. *Fisher of Lambeth*. 202.

l.10 Common sense. *C.A.P.* XV. 202–6. 6 Feb. 1934.

l.20 Entirely object. *C.A.P.* III. 2. 131. 30 June 1922.

l.23 Rational principle. *C.A.P.* XIII. 1. 38. 2 Feb. 1932.

l.25 Platitudes. *C.A.P.* IV. 2. 279. 13 July 1923.

l.27 Gaseous. Lang to Hugh. 4 March 1933. Q 45/70.

l.30 Unprincipled. W. Yorke Batley. *Personal Memories*.

l.32 House of Lords. *C.A.P.* XIX. 1. 29. 7 Feb. 1938.

p. 274. l.3 Ten Commandments. *C.A.P.* XXIII. 2. 189. 22 June 1943.

l.7 Old antagonist. *C.A.P.* XXXVII. 1. 90–2. 21 Feb. 1957.

l.9 Brevet Archbishop. Lord Midleton to Hugh. 5 June 1931.
Q 41/175.

l.15 Wasted time. *C.A.P.* VI. 2. 347. 10 July 1925.

l.20 Palliatives. *C.A.P.* XVII. 3. 583. 20 Nov. 1936.

l.25 Ignorance. *C.A.P.* VII. 3. 456–7. 19 Nov. 1926.

l.27 Masters of none. *Daily Telegraph*. 8 Feb. 1935.

fn. Sassoon. *Eton College Chronicle*. 15 June 1939.

p. 275. l.9 Peace of mind. Hugh Cecil. *Conservatism*. 86.

l.21 Competition. *Ibid*. 91–2.

l.40 Contradiction in terms. *Ibid*. 96–8.

p. 276. l.6 Rich man's soul. Gwendolen to Maud. 3 March 1925. G.

l.10 Stump up. Maud to Robert. 18 Nov. [   ]. C 56/71.

l.15 £40,000. *The Times*. 31 Jan. 1957.

l.16 Oxford college. Joan Watson, Hereford College, Oxford, to
author. 2 Dec. 1970.

l.17 Tombstone. Paul Gibson to Hugh. 27 Oct. 1942. Q 57/47.

l.38 Contraband. Hugh to W. G. Pennyman. 28 Feb. 1928. Q 35/50–5.

l.41 Eccentricity. *C.A.P.* IX. 2. 82. 27 April 1928.

p. 277. l.24 Unspoilt by change. Hugh Cecil. Memorandum on Revising the Prayer Book. [1924?]. Q 32/47–51.

l.29 Name of purity. *C.A.P.* I. 1. 118. 19 Nov. 1920.

l.33 Ghost. *C.A.P.* XXI. 1. 56. 12 June 1939.

p. 278. l.6 Depend. Hugh to George Nickson. 6 July 1928. Q 36/7–11.

l.21 Express it. Henson. *Retrospect.* II. 166–7.

l.28 Effective. Lockhart. *Lang.* 305.

l.33 Good Christians. *Hansard.* 15 Dec. 1927.

l.40 Lamentable. Quo. Henson. *Retrospect.* II. 175.

p. 279. l.7 Different. Lang to Hugh. 18 June 1928. Q 35/184.

l.13 Raise his spirits. Inskip to Hugh. 2 Aug. 1928. Q 38/76–80.

l.15 Numb limbs. Gwendolen to Maud. 7 Oct. 1929. G.

l.22 Pig's stomach. Florence to Hugh. 9 Aug. 1931. Q 42/51.

l.38 Numbers unequal. Gwendolen to Maud. 1 Jan. 1930. G.

p. 280. l.5 Cut in wages. *The Times.* 16 Feb. 1935.

l.8 Making it purr. *Daily Telegraph.* 10 Oct. 1938.

l.11 Fly again. Hugh to Eleanor. 26 Oct. 1938. C 54/33.

l.16 Smithfield. Church Assembly. 8 Feb. 1938.

l.20 Practical politics. Chamberlain to Hugh. 20 June 1938. Q 54/62–3.

l.24 Delectable appointment. Fisher to Hugh. 8 July 1936. Q 52/43.

l.31 Erastianism. Alington to Hugh. 30 April 1929. Q 37/210.

l.35 Bushido. *Eton College Chronicle.* 6 Dec. 1940.

l.39 So hated. Sitwell to Hugh. 9 July 1936. Q 52/97.

p. 281. l.24 Something of the kind. Lubbock. *M. R. James.* 45.

l.29 Do them good. Hugh to Eleanor. 13 July 1936. C 54/32.

p. 282. l.13 Something interesting. Oliver Van Oss to author. 3 Oct. 1971.

l.33 Blue coats. *Eton College Chronicle.* 6 Dec. 1940.

l.37 Bad preaching. Oliver Van Oss to author. 3 Oct. 1971.

p. 283. l.4 Alpha plus. Hugh Cecil. 'Archbishop Lang as a Speaker.' Q Box 22/29.

l.8 Resurrection. Copy of unpublished letter to *The Times.* 14 Jan. 1918. Q 23/27–32.

l.12 Words he utters. Lord Boyle to author. 13 June 1971.

l.17 Obscurantism. Henson. *Retrospect.* III. 67.

l.22 Authoritative. *Eton College Chronicle.* 7 Feb. 1957.

l.33 Narcissus. *Ibid.*

p. 284. l.1 Compared with mine. Hugh to Halifax. 29 Dec. 1936. Q 52/111–14.

l.7 Penitential character. *Eton College Chronicle.* 7 Feb. 1957.

l.10 End of me. Sir Claude Elliott to author. 12 Dec. 1970.

l.16 Evening dress. Temple to Hugh. 10 Nov. 1940. Q 55/139.

l.22 Would it matter? *The Times.* 12 Sept. 1939.

l.24 Navvies. *Eton College Chronicle.* 7 Feb. 1957.

l.31 Unlikely. Hugh to Elliott. 30 Jan. 1939. Elliott Papers.

l.40 If they were dead. Elliott to author. 12 Dec. 1970.

p. 285. l.2 Excess of logic. Halifax. *Fulness of Days.* 171–3.

l.10 Failed to explode. McConnell. *Eton Repointed.* 15.

p. 286. l.8 Churchmanship. Elliott to author. 12 Dec. 1970.

l.32 My manners. Hugh to Elliott. [June 1940]. Elliott Papers.

p. 287. l.27 In my opinion. Hugh to Jasper Ridley. 3 July 1944. Masterman Papers.

p. 288. l.2 Not to mind. Elliott to author. 12 Dec. 1970.

l.6 Baiting. Alington to Hugh. 22 Oct. 1932. Q 44/96.

l.13 Temper. Walter Hamilton to author. 29 Nov. 1970.

l.28 Barony. Churchill to Hugh. 21 Dec. 1940. Q 63/77.

l.32 Paper shortage. Hugh to Eleanor. 11 Jan. 1941. C 54/30.

l.39 Immunized. Salisbury to Hugh. 8 Jan. 1941. Q 56/72–3.

p. 289. l.2 Supporters. Sir Gerald Wollaston to Hugh. 27 March 1941. Q 56/139.

l.6 Outward respect. Lang to Hugh. 3 Jan. 1941. Q 56/57.

l.9 19th century. Hugh to Eleanor. 11 Jan. 1941. C 54/30.

l.25 Authoritarian. *Hansard.* 11 March 1941.

l.28 Church bells. *Ibid.* 31 March 1943.

l.29 Children. *Ibid.* 4 Aug. 1943.

l.31 Reading. *Ibid.* 6 June 1944.

p. 290. l.1 Old age. *C.A.P.* XX. 1. 39. 6 Feb. 1939.

l.16 Paradise. *Eton College Chronicle.* 7 Feb. 1957.

l.22 New earth. Walter Hamilton to author. 29 Nov. 1970.

l.35 Xantippe. W. Yorke Batley. *Personal Memories.*

l.39 Church Assembly. Hugh to Fisher. 17 Feb. 1949. Q 59/87.

l.41 Punishment. Hugh to Goddard. 14 July 1952. Q 60/111.

p. 291. l.1 Broadcasts. Hugh to Bishop of Bristol. 22 April 1952. Q 60/69–70.

l.3 Carnal meals. Hugh to Marten. 6 Jan. 1947. Q 58/122.

l.7 Conscience. Hugh to W. Yorke Batley. 3 Dec. 1956. Q 62/90.

l.11 Caesar. Hugh to Churchill. 29 April 1954. Q 63/96–7.

l.34 Pageantry today. *Ibid.* 1 Dec. 1954. Q 63/99–100.

l.40 Jubilee medal. Sir Frederick Ponsonby to Hugh. 20 May 1935. Q 48/174.

p. 292. l.5 Clothing. Hugh to Alice. 25 Jan. 1949. A.3.

l.6 Lambton. Hugh to Eleanor. 10 Feb. 1954. C 54/46.

l.7 Purgatory. *Ibid.* 30 May 1956. C 54/52–4.

l.15 Edifying. *Ibid.*

l.18 Rest of the day. Alice to Eleanor. Oct. 1950. C 52/92–4.

l.25 Prodigal son. Lady Manners to author. 21 June 1971.

l.27 First knew you. Violet to Hugh. 15 Oct. 1955. Q 65/99–100.

l.32 Paris. *Ibid.* 21 Nov. 1953. Q 65/29–30.

l.38 After death. *Ibid.* 27 April 1955. Q 65/80–2.

p. 293. l.40 'Notes as to my funeral.' 2 Nov. 1954. Q.

CHAPTER NINE: MAUD, COUNTESS OF SELBORNE

p. 295. l.7   Mistaken identity. Eleanor to Gilbert Murray. 22 May 1943. M.
l.10   Only men. Eleanor to Gwendolen. 19 Feb. 1933. C 20/2.
l.16   Knock me down. David Cecil. *The Cecils.* 259.
l.29   Soon shake down. Maud to Frances Balfour. 6 Dec. 1883.
C 58/30.
p. 296. l.9   Viceroyalty of India. *Dictionary of National Biography.*
l.17   Never the church. K. 9M. 68. 1052.
p. 297. l.5   Probably cruelty. Maud to Gwendolen. 7 March 1909. G.
l.27   Feel the same. Maud to Lewis. [   ]. K. 9M. 68. 103.
l.36   Which disease? Edward Palmer to author. 28 Dec. 1973.
p. 298. l.3   Awkward for Willy. Maud to Robert. 11 Sept. [1905].
C 56/41–2.
l.22   Abolished here. *Ibid.* 21 June [1908]. C 56/10–11.
l.27   A change. Maud to Lewis. 12 April 1909. K. 9M. 68. 181.
l.33   Black bishop. *Ibid.* [   ]. K. 9M. 68. 99.
p. 299. l.4   Proper place. Maud to Robert. 20 Aug. [1905]. C 56/43–5.
l.9   Greedy. *Ibid.* 11 Sept. [1905]. C 56/41–2.
l.15   Must have begun. Maud to Mabel. 24 July 1906. K. 9M. 68. 128.
l.26   Someone ruder. *Ibid.* 16 Feb. 1908. K. 9M. 68. 160.
l.30   Imitation Windsor. Gwendolen to Eleanor. 1 March 1907.
C 53/47.
l.34   Viceregal state. Fisher. *Unfinished Autobiography.* 151.
l.38   Attempted curtsy. Dorothy Palmer to author. 22 April 1974.
l.39   Monarchy. Selborne to Maud. 14 June 1914. F.102.
p. 300. l.11   The lady. Maud to Eleanor. 16 March 1909. C 56/48–9.
l.22   In the paper. Maud to Robert. 3 Nov. [1907]. C 56/48–9.
p. 301. l.3   Good antidote. Mabel to Robert. 12 Sept. 1905. C 56/14–17.
l.11   Such people. Mabel to Hugh. 12 Aug. 1905. Q 4/19–22.
l.16   Bounders. Maud to Robert. 23 April [1908]. C 56/2–4.
l.27   I enjoy it. *Ibid.* [   ]. C 56/31–2.
p. 302. l.2   Kindergarten. Maud to Eleanor. 30 Dec. [   ]. C 56/54–5.
l.6   Wanted to do it. Maud to Robert. 12 Aug. 1907. C 56/69–70.
l.7   Mine-owners. Maud to Mabel. 14 Dec. 1906. K. 9M. 68. 134.
l.10   Substantial salary. *Ibid.*
l.17   British brass. *Ibid.* 19 April 1910. K. 9M. 68. 204.
l.30   Diplomatic answer. Selborne to Maud. 14 June 1914. F. 102.
p. 303. l.11   Foolish things. Maud to Lewis. 18 Oct. [1915]. L.
l.19   Women's suffrage. *Ibid.* 26 Oct. [   ]. L.
l.25   Churchill. *Ibid.* 2 Nov. [1915]. L.
l.27   Hot iron. *Ibid.* 12 May [1915]. L.
l.34   Evening of bridge. *Ibid.* 1 Sept. [1915]. L.
l.40   Being killed. Maud to Laura Ridding. 25 Nov. [1917]. L.
p. 304. l.5   English divinity. Maud to Lewis. 25 Nov. [1917]. L.
l.15   Than is necessary. *Ibid.* 1 Dec. [1917]. L.

l.22 Everyday practice. Quo. Ridding. *Robert Palmer.* 109.

l.27 Dying for her. Maud to Gwendolen. 4 Feb. 1916. G.

p. 305. l.25 This prescription. Maud to Lewis. [   ]. K. 9M. 68. 112.

l.32 Future peril. Dorothy Palmer to author. 22 April 1974.

l.42 Fruit and wine. Edward Palmer to author. 28 Dec. 1973.

p. 306. l.7 Trousers. *Ibid.* 2 Jan. 1974.

l.14 Clever parson. Maud to Wolmer. 22 Sept. [1922]. Lady Laura Eastaugh Papers.

l.20 Second chance. Edward Palmer to author. 2 Jan. 1974.

l.34 Breakfast. Robert to Eleanor. 28 May 1921. C 6/98.

p. 307. l.2 Provoking. *Ibid.* 11 July 1939. C 11/53.

l.6 Churchill. Maud to Robert. 31 Aug. [1927]. B 51157.

l.9 What more? Robert to Maud. 2 Sept. 1927. B 51157.

l.19 Disarmament. Maud to Mabel. 22 Nov. 1933. K. 9M. 68. 704.

l.42 Nazi regime. Maud to Lewis. 10 Oct. 1938. K. 9M. 68. 1012.

p. 308. l.8 Miliitary genius. Maud to Gwendolen. 2 Feb. 1942. G.

l.11 My enemy. Edward Palmer to author. 2 Jan. 1974.

CHAPTER TEN: LADY GWENDOLEN CECIL

p. 309. l.12 Female relation. Salisbury to Lady John Manners. 7 Oct. 1883. Quo. Smith. *Lord Salisbury on Politics.* 18.

p. 310. l.11 Sisterly advice. Gwendolen to 'My dear brothers.' 20 July 1885. C 53/9.

l.22 Choir of footmen. Dugdale. *Family Homespun.* 112.

l.23 Dawdling. Eleanor to Lady Manners. 14 Jan. 1946. Manners Papers.

l.28 Anonymously. William Blackwood to Gwendolen. 25 June 1894. G.

l.36 Extreme youth. Disraeli to Queen Victoria. 24 April 1878. Quo. Stamfordham to Gwendolen. 2 Aug. 1923. G.

p. 311. l.5 La Bastide. Mallet. *Life with Queen Victoria.* 160. 23 March 1899.

l.10 Dreadful fates. Gwendolen to Eleanor. 28 Jan. 1906. C 53/25.

l.12 Sports and dances. *Ibid.* 9–10 Oct. 1906. C 53/36.

l.27 Attractive wave. Eleanor to Lady Manners. 14 Jan. 1946. Manners Papers.

l.31 All the world. Milner. *My Picture Gallery.* 80.

p. 312. l.2 Wash a dog. *The Times.* 2 Oct. 1945.

l.12 Barked furiously. Manners. *Gwendolen Cecil.* 6.

l.19 Stay for lunch. J. H. Tunnell to author. 11 May 1970.

l.27 Vanity. Robert to Eleanor. 2 Oct. 1894. C 2/110.

l.28 Vehemence. Milner. *My Picture Gallery.* 79.

l.37 Such poops. Gwendolen to Maud. 19 June 1908. G.

p. 313. l.17 Bersaglieri. Manners. *Gwendolen Cecil.* 5.

l.24 Feel soothed. Gwendolen to Maud. 4 June 1909. G.

l.28 Cairo season. Gwendolen to Eleanor. 28–9 Dec. 1903. C 53/29-31.

l.32 Understand him. Gwendolen to Robert. 11 July 1907. C 53/49.

p. *314.* l.2 Years to come. Gwendolen to Maud. 3 Aug. 1906. G.

l.5 Piles mixed. *Ibid.* 24 Aug. 1906. G.

l.8 Forty volumes. *Ibid.* 11 April 1921. G.

l.11 Insane optimism. Gwendolen to Robert. 11 July 1907. C 53/49.

l.19 Material. Gwendolen to Eleanor. 16 Feb. 1922. C 53/73–6.

l.22 Rummagiing. Manners. *Gwendolen Cecil.* 12.

l.28 Coronetted. Gwendolen to Maud. 15 May 1908. G.

l.37 A cough. Gwendolen to Eleanor. 22 Nov. 1923. C 53/86.

p. *315.* l.2 Three Bridges. Eleanor to Robert. 28 Feb. 1919. C 18/26.

l.6 Wrong train. Manners. *Gwendolen Cecil.* 15.

l.14 Taxi-cab. *Ibid.* 17.

l.16 Dangerous. Edward to Helen. [   ]. H.

l.20 Bedridden. Gwendolen to Maud. 9 March 1921. G.

l.28 Rotten novel. Manners. *Gwendolen Cecil.* 13.

l.31 Haunted by him. Gwendolen to Frances Balfour. 2 Dec. 1910. G.

l.35 Eight times. Robert to Eleanor. 2 July 1939. C 11/42.

l.39 Dreads it. Eleanor to Guendolen Osborne. 23 March 1919. C 57/129.

l.42 Advance of £5,000. Gwendolen to Maud. 15 Oct. 1920. G.

p. *316.* l.10 Mystery of mercy. Gwendolen to Laura Ridding. 23 Nov. 1921. G.

l.13 Birkenhead. Gwendolen to Maud. 18 Nov. 1921. G.

l.15 Macaulay. Gwendolen to Hugh. 2 Dec. 1909. Q 12/150–1.

l.19 Paving stone. Virginia Woolf to Eleanor. [   ]. C 37/123.

p. *317.* l.5 Hopeless Gwendolen to Maud. 18 Aug. 1935. G.

fn. Sales. Eric Major to author. 25 June 1974.

l.17 Khartoum. Alice Salisbury. *A Memoir.* 10.

l.23 Telephone. Gwendolen to Maud. 27 June 1925. G.

l.27 Take action. Gwendolen to Alice. [   ]. A.3.

l.37 Actual war. Gwendolen to Eleanor. 30 Aug. 1939. C 53/201–2.

p. *318.* l.5 Not a Jingo. Gwendolen to Maud. 22 Nov. 1923. G.

l.25 In excelsis. *Ibid.* 15 Feb. 1928. G.

l.34 Poisonous influence. *Ibid.* 15 April 1935. G.

p. *319.* l.1 In consequence. *Ibid.* 21 April 1926. G.

l.11 Rebottling. Violet Milner. *My Picture Gallery.* 84.

l.22 Beef or mutton. Gwendolen to Maud. 5 Feb. 1918. G.

l.27 Her cares. Maud to Lewis. 3 Sept. [   ]. L.

l.41 Ratepayers. Gwendolen to Maud. 19 May 1925. G.

p. *320.* l.3 Patient's recovery. *Ibid.* 14 July 1924. G.

l.19 Northumberland. *Ibid.* 16 Oct. 1931. G.

l.22 Self-abasement. Manners. *Gwendolen Cecil.* 19.

l.28 Tenderness. Gwendolen to Laura Ridding. 12 Feb. 1934. G.

Index

Compiled by Norman Knight MA, *President of the Society of Indexers, assisted by Valerie Chandler* BA, ALAA

Apart from their own entries, the chief characters are referred to by their nicknames, e.g. 'Top', 'Nelly', etc., as in the text. *bis* after a reference number denotes that the item is alluded to twice quite separately on the same page. *q.* stands for quoted; *bet.* (relating to illustrations) stands for between. Reference numbers in *italics* denote illustrations.

379